LITERACY, LANGUAGE,
AND LEARNING

LITERACY, LANGUAGE, AND LEARNING

THE NATURE AND CONSEQUENCES OF READING AND WRITING

Edited by
David R. Olson, Nancy Torrance,
and Angela Hildyard
Ontario Institute for Studies in Education

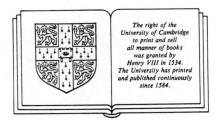

The right of the
University of Cambridge
to print and sell
all manner of books
was granted by
Henry VIII in 1534.
The University has printed
and published continuously
since 1584.

CAMBRIDGE UNIVERSITY PRESS

CAMBRIDGE

LONDON   NEW YORK   NEW ROCHELLE

MELBOURNE   SYDNEY

Published by the Press Syndicate of the University of Cambridge
The Pitt Building, Trumpington Street, Cambridge CB2 1RP
32 East 57th Street, New York, NY 10022, USA
10 Stamford Road, Oakleigh, Melbourne 3166, Australia

First published 1985

Printed in the United States of America

Library of Congress Cataloging in Publication Data
Main entry under title:
Literacy, language, and learning.
Bibliography: p.
1. Literacy – Addresses, essays, lectures.
2. Language and languages – Social aspects –
Addresses, essays, lectures. I. Olson, David R.
II. Torrance, Nancy. III. Hildyard, Angela.
LC149.L4995 1985 400 84–14299
ISBN 0 521 26488 x hard covers
ISBN 0 521 31912 9 paperback

Contents

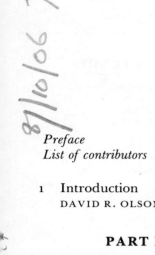

Preface   *page* vii
List of contributors   ix

1   Introduction   1
    DAVID R. OLSON

PART I   LITERACY AND SOCIETY

2   On the printing press as an agent of change   19
    ELIZABETH L. EISENSTEIN
3   Atlantans, Centaurians, and the litron bomb: some
    personal and social implications of literacy   34
    IAN WINCHESTER
4   The concept of literacy in print and film   50
    MICHAEL COLE AND HELEN KEYSSAR
5   Cognitive consequences of communication mode:
    a social psychological perspective   73
    ROCCO FONDACARO AND E. TORY HIGGINS

PART II   LITERACY AND LANGUAGE

6   Linguistic differences produced by differences
    between speaking and writing   105
    WALLACE L. CHAFE
7   Relative focus on involvement in oral and written
    discourse   124
    DEBORAH TANNEN
8   Are there really no primitive languages?   148
    IVAN KALMÁR
9   The story schema: universal and culture-specific
    properties   167
    WILLIAM F. BREWER

v

10   A metaphor for literacy: creating worlds or shunting
     information?   195
     FRANK SMITH

         PART III   LITERACY AND COMPETENCE

11   Literacy development: a psychogenetic perspective   217
     EMILIA FERREIRO
12   Preschool literacy-related activities and success in
     school   229
     GORDON WELLS
13   Oral and literate competencies in the early school
     years   256
     NANCY TORRANCE AND DAVID R. OLSON
14   Oral–written differences in the production and recall
     of narratives   285
     ANGELA HILDYARD AND SUZANNE HIDI
15   Development of dialectical processes in composition   307
     MARLENE SCARDAMALIA AND CARL BEREITER

         PART IV   LITERACY AND READING

16   Effects of printed language acquisition on speech   333
     LINNEA C. EHRI
17   Interactions between spelling and sound in literacy   368
     RODERICK W. BARRON
18   Effects of phonology on beginning spelling: some
     cross-linguistic evidence   389
     CHARLES READ
19   Phonology in reading   404
     PAUL A. KOLERS
20   Language, literacy, and learning: an annotated
     bibliography   412
     RON SCOLLON

     Subject index   427
     Author index   433

Preface

It was either Jerome Bruner, Patricia Greenfield, or Sylvia Scribner who first mentioned to us the possibility of "speaking a written language." The idea has a host of implications: Does writing affect language? Do reading and writing alter one's orientation to language and to the world – creating a world on paper, as Galileo put it? Do reading and writing require the development of those special competencies that we associate with schooling? These and a variety of related questions not only puzzled us but led us to initiate a research program on them and to organize a gathering of the distinguished scholars whose writings on these problems make up this volume. Support for both our research efforts and this gathering was provided by a generous grant from the Spencer Foundation, Thomas James, President. Although the Spencer Foundation does not ordinarily support conferences, in this case the meeting was construed as an important part of the general research grant "Oral Language Competence and the Acquisition of Literacy" that the foundation awarded the editors. We wish to express our gratitude to that foundation for their support. We are also deeply indebted to our mentors and our colleagues for the support that permitted us to produce this volume and to Susan Milmoe and Penny Carter of Cambridge University Press, as well as Janis Bolster and Bill Green, and our secretary Glenna Tufts for their help in seeing it through to completion.

D.O.
N.T.
A.H.

Contributors

RODERICK W. BARRON
Department of Psychology
University of Guelph

CARL BEREITER
Centre for Applied Cognitive
* Science*
Ontario Institute for Studies in
* Education*

WILLIAM F. BREWER
Department of Psychology
University of Illinois

WALLACE L. CHAFE
Department of Linguistics
University of California, Berkeley

MICHAEL COLE
Department of Communications
University of California, San
* Diego*

LINNEA C. EHRI
Department of Linguistics
University of California, Davis

ELIZABETH L. EISENSTEIN
Department of History
University of Michigan

EMILIA FERREIRO
Departamento de Investigaciones
* Educativas*
Centro de Investigacion y de
* Estudios Avanzados del*
* Instituto Politécnico Nacional,*
* Mexico City*

ROCCO FONDACARO
Department of Psychology
University of Western Ontario

SUZANNE HIDI
Centre for Applied Cognitive
* Science*
Ontario Institute for Studies in
* Education*

E. TORY HIGGINS
Department of Psychology
University of Western Ontario

ANGELA HILDYARD
Field Services and Research
Ontario Institute for Studies in
* Education*

IVAN KALMÁR
Department of Anthropology
University of Toronto

HELEN KEYSSAR
Department of Communications
University of California, San
* Diego*

PAUL A. KOLERS
Department of Psychology
University of Toronto

DAVID R. OLSON
Centre for Applied Cognitive
* Science*
Ontario Institute for Studies in
* Education*

*and McLuhan Centre for Culture
    and Technology*
University of Toronto

CHARLES READ
*Wisconsin Center for Education
    Research*
University of Wisconsin-Madison

MARLENE SCARDAMALIA
Department of Psychology
York University, Toronto

RON SCOLLON
Department of Linguistics
University of Alaska

FRANK SMITH
Faculty of Education
University of Victoria

DEBORAH TANNEN
Department of Linguistics
Georgetown University

NANCY TORRANCE
*Centre for Applied Cognitive
    Science*
*Ontario Institute for Studies in
    Education*

GORDON WELLS
*School of Education Research
    Unit*
University of Bristol

IAN WINCHESTER
Higher Education Group
*Ontario Institute for Studies in
    Education*

1

Introduction

DAVID R. OLSON

A detailed consideration of the nature and consequences of literacy is important and timely. It is important because it promises not only to help us understand some properties of our selves and our world but also to yield some improved understanding of how children acquire – or fail to acquire – literate competencies. It is timely in that literacy continues to be an important social problem: Literacy is a central concern of the schools, language development is one of the more lively areas of current research, and standards of literacy continue to stimulate a great deal of public interest.

The fact that literacy is accorded such attention suggests that there is more to literacy than meets the eye. Literacy is not merely the ability to read and write. The *Oxford English Dictionary* defines *literate* as that quality pertaining to a person who is able to read and write *or* to one who has some acquaintance with literature. In fact, in the popular imagination the concept of literacy goes considerably beyond the dictionary to endow both individuals and societies with a significance that more serious analysis shows to be difficult to justify. Illiteracy is often listed along with malnutrition, disease, poverty, and unemployment as a serious social ill. Hence, any threat to standards of literacy or any putative drop in literate competence is taken as the forerunner of a return to primitivism, ignorance, and savagery. In fact, the place of literacy in the modern world is under no great threat, but even if it were, no serious arguments have been advanced to indicate that civilization is tied to literacy. Indeed, Eric Havelock (1976) has shown that the remarkable culture that among other things generated the Homeric epics was a nonliterate culture.

But even if literacy does not necessarily make us civilized and even if a decline in the reading practices in our own society does not necessarily mark a return to barbarism, literacy remains a central

1

concern not only of laymen but also of educators who devote a
majority of their efforts to improving the literate competencies of
children, and of scholars who are interested in understanding the
role of literacy in personal and social change. These scholars come
from a wide range of disciplines including cognitive psychology,
linguistics, anthropology, sociology, education, history, and philosophy of language. That all of these disciplines are concerned with
language and communication scarcely needs mention; that they are
all coming to see the central role of written language is interesting
and in fact provides the basis for the explorations in this volume.

Ours is not the first generation of intellectuals to reflect on the
central role of writing in the social and intellectual activities that
characterize modernity. Francis Bacon in the *Novum Organum*
(1620/1965) observed that there were three inventions conspicuous
in his age that were unknown to the ancient world: printing,
gunpowder, and the compass: "These three have changed the
appearance and state of the whole world" (aphorism 129).

In more recent times, scholars have made attempts to trace the
roles of different forms of communication in social organization, the
most celebrated being the theory advanced by Canadian economic
historian Harold Innis, who analyzed the role of forms of communication in large-scale social and political organizations. In *Empire
and Communication* (1950) he argued:

In the organization of large areas, communication occupies a vital place, and
it is significant that Bryce's periods [three major historical epochs] correspond
roughly first to that dominated by clay and papyrus, second to that dominated
by parchment, and third to that dominated by paper. The effective government of large areas depends to a very important extent on the efficiency of
communication. (1950, p. 7)

Marshall McLuhan summarized this view with the quip to the effect
that "the Roman road was a paper route in every sense of the word"
(1964, p. 90).

Though we shall have some interest in, for example, the social
functions of literacy in the formation of a reading public, our primary
concern is with the intellectual consequences of literacy. In his chapter
in this volume, Ian Winchester quotes Alfred North Whitehead
(1933) as saying that the intellectual resources of humankind have
not changed since neolithic times but that the environment in which
we exercise that intelligence has changed dramatically:

Within that period it would be difficult to demonstrate that mankind has
improved upon its inborn mental capacity. Yet there can be no doubt that

there has been an immense expansion of the outfit which the environment provides for the service of thought. (p. 55)

Chief among these additions to the environment that Whitehead listed are "modes of communication, physical and mental, writing, . . . modes of literature, and mathematical symbolism" (p. 55).

This is a theme that has been elaborated greatly by writers as diverse as Sir Karl Popper and McLuhan. Popper (1972) adopts Samuel Butler's notion of the parallel between the evolution of organs and the evolution of tools or machines. Animal evolution, Butler had argued, proceeds primarily by endosomatic evolution – the biological modification of organs. Human evolution proceeds primarily by exosomatic evolution – the development of new organs outside our bodies. Popper adds:

But man instead of growing better eyes and ears, grows spectacles, microscopes, telescopes, telephones, and hearing aids. And instead of growing better memories and brains, we grow paper, pens, pencils, typewriters, dictaphones, the printing press and libraries. (1972, pp. 238–239)

But it is one thing to announce the importance of a technology such as writing or printing and quite another to explain just what such a technology may do to mind. McLuhan's *Gutenberg Galaxy* (1962), subtitled *The Making of Typographic Man*, was the first attempt to rethink problems of language, communication, and rationality from the perspective of altered media of communication. That McLuhan's hypotheses remain at best controversial testifies to the state of the art. It is widely agreed that literacy has had important effects on language and rationality, and yet those effects are not clearly formulated nor well understood nor empirically examined. Our concerns in this volume are to begin to advance the more painstaking, step-by-step analysis of the nature of literacy, the relationship between literacy and language structure, the relations between oral competence and literate competence, and the processes involved in comprehending and reading written texts.

Discussions of literacy in terms of consequences are easily misinterpreted. To forestall this misinterpretation, it is necessary to make some distinctions. *Consequences* as they are construed in this volume are not to be confused with what is sometimes referred to as *technological determinism*, the view that changes in the stimulus environment in and of themselves explain behavioral changes. At best, changes in the structure of the environment may influence behavior via alterations in the beliefs, abilities, and intentions of the people acting in that environment. Hence, when we discuss the consequences of literacy, we are not suggesting that environmental changes cause behavior; rather we are examining the ways in which human actions, intentions, goals, beliefs, and skills are executed and altered in an environment in which people have access to written language. To repeat, writing does not simply cause social or cognitive changes. Rather, a world with literacy is different from one without literacy, and people's beliefs and actions and intentions are formulated in that altered world. Only in this indirect way does the invention of a technology alter thought and action. To be more specific, a concern with the consequences of literacy is a concern with what humans do and how they do it in a literate as opposed to a nonliterate world: How do they use language? How do they store beliefs? Where do they appeal for authority? How do they relate the language to their prior knowledge? What beliefs do they hold about language? And finally, What special competencies are required by literacy and what special competencies are dependent upon literacy? These are the kinds of issues examined in this volume.

The chapters in this volume were written by a group of scholars from a variety of disciplines all of whom are both convinced of the significance of literacy in understanding the central issues of language and thought and are interested in examining the role of literacy from the perspective of their own disciplines. These disciplines help to determine, for example, if literacy has an effect on the structure of language, which is primarily a linguistic problem, whether it has an effect on patterns of speaking and comprehending, primarily a psychological problem, whether it has had an influence on social organization, a historical and anthropological problem, and so on. As a consequence, the problem of literacy is unalterably an interdisciplinary one.

For these reasons, these distinguished scholars were invited to a small country inn near Toronto for three days of presentation, discussion, and argument on October 2–4, 1981.

The primary questions for the conference were the following:

1. Is literacy, including the invention of writing systems and the development of printing, a decisive factor in historical and cultural change?
2. Does literacy alter the mental and social lives of individuals? And if so, how?
3. What is there, specifically, about literacy that is decisive in producing these social and personal changes? Is it the technology of writing? Is it the growth of an archival form? Is it the mastery

of the information stored in that archival form? Is it the growth of a "reading public"? Is it the degree of literacy that is significant?

4. Is there a homology between literacy and historical cultural change, on the one hand, and literacy skills and cognitive change in children growing up in a literate society, on the other hand? Does learning to read and write change children's speech, thought, or orientation to language?

5. What, specifically, is a child or an adult learning when they acquire literate skills? Are they learning grapheme–phoneme correspondences? Morpheme–word correspondences? Utterance–sentence correspondences? Meaning–intention correspondences?

6. Are there differences linguistically, psychologically, and functionally between speaking and writing?

7. Finally, are there important differences between oral and written language?

All these questions are attempts at specifying more clearly the nature of written language and its role in social and intellectual life. Their answers evolve in the sequence of chapters making up this volume. The chapters are organized in terms of a series of themes or topics of decreasing scope and, perhaps, increasing precision. The chapters comprising Part I address questions of literacy and social–cultural change; those in Part II examine the relations between language and literacy; the chapters in Part III examine the relations between literacy and such competencies as thinking, comprehending, and writing; and those in Part IV deal with more specific competencies involved in reading an alphabetic orthography. Below I introduce the papers individually and then conclude with a summary of some of the major themes, conclusions, and problems for future research and theory. These contributions mark the end of the simple notions that writing is merely speech written down and that reading consists simply of mastering an orthography. Literacy involves a set of structures ranging from the visual representation of sound, to the distinctive organization of mind, to the distinctive organization of society.

Part I: Literacy and society. The chapters in this part are concerned both with the cultural–historical transformations of mental and social life brought about by writing and printing and with the uses and effects of literacy within a literate society.

Elizabeth Eisenstein, a distinguished historian at the University of Michigan, summarizes the major themes of her recent two-volume work *The Printing Press as an Agent of Change* (1979). Her detailed historical examination of the role of printing in mental and social life is in some ways an extension of McLuhan's pioneering essay *The Gutenberg Galaxy*. Eisenstein examines in detail the role that print technology played in two of the major historical–cultural transformations of the early modern era, the Protestant Reformation and the rise of modern science. She concludes that print influenced the growth and distribution of knowledge by permitting the revision, updating, and augmenting of standard encyclopedic works on geography, astronomy, and plant and animal life and through reproducible pictures and texts. Print, in her view, is a major and relatively underestimated factor in the creation of our modern world.

Ian Winchester, a philosopher at the Ontario Institute for Studies in Education, discusses the role of literacy in contemporary society. Although literacy does seem to be tied to certain high levels of social organization, Winchester debunks the naïve assumptions that illiteracy is necessarily related to poverty, malnutrition, and ignorance and that literacy is the key to the solution of these problems in Third World countries. Winchester differentiates elementary literacy, that required for reading and writing, from the high-level literacy that is required for sustained theoretical enterprises, including literature, philosophy, and science. He examines his conjectures both by means of thought experiments and by means of his own historical research on the effects of literacy on the patterns of migration in eighteenth-century Sweden. Even people with elementary levels of literacy, it seems, had a somewhat different picture of the world and its possibilities than their nonliterate neighbors.

Whereas Eisenstein and Winchester consider the social and historical implications of literate technology, Michael Cole and Helen Keyssar of the University of California, San Diego, provide a detailed analysis of the nature of literate competence. They address the problem of generalizing a theory of print literacy to a more general theory of symbolically mediated activity. They then examine some of the principles of that theory in the context of the properties, uses, and effects of two media, print and film. They discuss in some detail the potentials of both these media for creating shared meaning and the sociocultural circumstances that make certain orders of meaning valuable. While in Western societies print literacy has been vital as a social and economic instrument, film literacy has been primarily important for its entertainment functions. Yet both provide distinctive ways of structuring symbolic material for particular communicative purposes.

Rocco Fondacaro and E. Tory Higgins, social psychologists at the University of Western Ontario, examine the social and cognitive consequences of speaking and writing for literate communicators. They argue that when a speaker or writer biases his account to suit the requirements of the listener or reader, that speaker or writer tends to recall not the original facts but the slant given them in the telling. Further, the authors argue and provide preliminary evidence that given the deliberateness, permanance, and authority of the written word, this effect is more pronounced in writing than in speaking. This research suggests that writing has a distinctive effect, not only on others' beliefs, a communicative function, but also on one's own beliefs, a cognitive function. Finally, it suggests that the effects of literacy should not be considered simply as the difference between being literate and not being literate, but as the difference between choosing to write and choosing to speak.

Part II: Literacy and language. These chapters are concerned with the structural differences between oral and written language and those between speaking and writing.

Wallace Chafe, a linguist at the University of California at Berkeley, examines differences in structure between conversational speech and written texts. The differences are organized in terms of two major dimensions, integration and involvement, the former characterizing writing, the latter, speech. In writing, people use many devices, such as nominalization, subordination, and modification, to pack many idea units within a single sentence. In speaking, people use fewer of these devices and more conversational devices for maintaining involvement with the listener, for pacing their discourse, and for hedging their verbal choices. Understanding these grammatical and lexical differences is important to our understanding of the differences between speaking and writing.

Deborah Tannen, a linguist at Georgetown University, examines some of the relations between oral and written language, pointing out some of the ways in which this dichotomy is misleading. In place of this distinction, she proposes to differentiate two modes of discourse, one focusing on involvement to produce a form of discourse that is context-bound, that requires listener/reader participation, and that involves the use of paralinguistic cues, and the other focusing on information to produce a form of discourse that is less dependent upon immediate context, that is more explicit, and that achieves coherence through lexicalization. While these forms of discourse tend to be correlated with oral and written forms, each can and does exist in either modality. Analyzing several samples of discourse, she shows that the differences between them can be accounted for in terms of their relative focus on either involvement or information.

In his chapter, Ivan Kalmár, an anthropologist at the University of Toronto, questions the received wisdom that there are no primitive languages. He provides arguments and evidence for the possibility of evolution of syntactic structures for integrating clauses or idea units into complex syntactic constructions. His arguments are based on the development of relativization in the newly evolving written form of Inuktitut, the language of the Inuit. Just as Chafe shows that writing is characterized by an increase in structural integration through nominalization, relativization, and subordination, Kalmár shows that when a language develops a written form, as Inuktitut is doing, it begins to develop at least some of these devices, including relative clauses marked by a newly invented relative pronoun derived from the demonstrative *this*. Kalmár suggests that linguistic structures may indeed evolve if such structures serve a relevant social function and if there is some means for constructing permanent texts.

It is interesting to note that the primary semantic problem that relativization is developed to cope with is indirect speech, involving the speech act and mental-state verbs that require complement constructions in English (e.g., "He said that . . . ," "He thought that . . . "). Hence the metalinguistic or speech-act verbs implicated in the developmental studies of Torrance and Olson (see Chapter 13) may be related to the syntactic devices studied by Kalmár.

William Brewer, a psychologist at the Center for the Study of Reading at the University of Illinois, examines linguistic structures larger than a single sentence, particularly those involved in story comprehension. He discusses the ways in which the elements of a story structure may be arranged to produce such affective states as surprise, suspense, and curiosity. In a series of experiments, Brewer and his colleagues confirmed their hypotheses regarding the relation between event structure, discourse structure, and affective states. He goes on to discuss the universality of these structures and the ways that writing may lead to the development of more specialized genres discussed by Eisenstein, Tannen, and Smith. It is interesting to note, for example, that the rise of the novel depended not only upon the evolution of planned discourse that writing permits but also upon the development of a sizable reading public (Watt, 1957).

Frank Smith, Lansdowne Professor of Education at the University of Victoria, argues that the acquisition of literacy and the uses of literacy can be understood only by abandoning the predominant assumption that language is for communication and replacing it with the assumption that language, particularly written language, is for creating and manipulating imaginative worlds. He notes the provisional nature of written language – it may be read and revised, pursued or abandoned – and concludes that it is an ideal medium for exploring possible worlds. We see here an important complement to the arguments of Eisenstein: Writing was crucial not only to the development of modern science but also to the evolution of modern literature. Smith points out that while children appear to begin writing with a sense of these possibilities, it is too often discouraged by schools' efforts at the teaching of writing that emphasize, Smith says, information exchange, that is, writing for the reader rather than writing for the writer. The effect is to produce a generation of secretaries rather than of writers.

Part III: Literacy and competence. The chapters here examine the particular changes in strategies of comprehending, thinking, and writing that are involved in using written language and the relations between these competencies and those involved in the comprehension and use of oral language.

Emilia Ferreiro, a developmental psychologist at the Departamento de Investigaciones Educativas, Centro de Investigacion y de Estudios Avanzados del Instituto Politécnico Nacional, Mexico City, describes a series of remarkable experiments on young children's hypotheses about reading and writing. Ferreiro shows that children's hypotheses are not identical to what parents and teachers usually assume and teach but rather reflect their progressive attempts to make sense of the world of print in a manner analogous to their attempts to make sense of the world of objects. Among the more interesting of these problems is that of coming to see a word as simultaneously reflecting a meaning and a sound pattern, a problem they solve only after trying out a number of limited-range hypotheses.

Gordon Wells, director of the Language and Literacy Project at the University of Bristol and currently a professor at the Ontario Institute for Studies in Education, pursues further his studies of the relation between children's oral competence and the process of their learning to read. His earlier studies showed that whereas children's out-of-school oral competence was not related to their parents' literacy levels, their oral and written competence in school was so related. In his chapter in this volume he shows that the parental activity mediating this relation was the more highly literate parents' practice of reading stories to their children and discussing the stories with them. This practice was highly related both to their children's concepts about literacy and to their subsequent reading achievement. What children learn from these activities, Wells suggests, is to handle decontextualized linguistic meanings. The major obstacle to becoming literate, he suggests, consists not so much of matters of word and letter recognition but of the construction of meanings on the basis of decontextualized texts. This is the form of mental activity that story reading calls upon.

Nancy Torrance and I, in a manner similar to that of Wells, have been examining the relations between various aspects of children's oral competence and their ability to cope with written texts in the early school years. Our chapter differentiates two sides of oral competence, one more linguistic, involving lexical and syntactic aspects of language, and the other more conversational, involving procedures for keeping conversations going. The former is quite closely related to progress in learning to read, the latter is not. The good conversationalists were more successful in complying with the speech-act requirements of their interlocutor, what Chafe called involvement; the good readers were more successful in constructing more complex utterances, what Chafe called integration. In addition, the good readers tended to use a wider range of metalinguistic verbs – verbs of saying – and of metacognitive verbs – verbs of thinking. Part of the syntactic complexity of the good reader's language may have been a by-product of these more complex verbs. These findings help specify what is involved in the transition from utterance to text.

Angela Hildyard and Suzanne Hidi, research associates at the Ontario Institute for Studies in Education, discuss their research on the relation between the processes involved in speaking as opposed to writing. Writing, unlike speaking, tends to help the producer remember not merely the gist of what has been said, but the very words. Writing, in brief, leads to an emphasis upon the surface structure of language, whereas speech tends to leave that surface structure transparent to the underlying meaning. This bias toward form may account for some of the distinctive properties of writing – literality, careful speech, and metalinguistic awareness as discussed by Barron and Ehri.

Marlene Scardamalia and Carl Bereiter, psychologists at York University and the Ontario Institute for Studies in Education, respectively, examine one of the more demanding sides of literate competence; the use of writing for systematically exploring ideas in a conventional literary form, the essay. They propose that the generative power of writing arises from the the potential dialectic not between writers and imagined readers but between the requirements of belief and the requirements of the conventions of text. In a series of experiments they explore the possibility of aiding this dialectic by providing either diagnostic cues for editing essays or planning cues for generating essays. The experiments determine the effects of these procedures on the writing practices of young children. The results are promising in that such devices do in fact alter the quality of children's written products. Yet young writers, they note, have difficulty in honoring the multiple constraints of written texts; they achieve coherence at the expense of reflection or vice versa. The fruitful interplay of the two sets of requirements, those of prior knowledge and those of written text, is what makes writing skill worthwhile and yet elusive.

Part IV: Literacy and reading. Reading is, of course, the fundamental form of literate competence. Just what is involved in reading an alphabetic orthography? Not only must a reader work out the relations between sound and form in order to read, as pointed out in the chapter by Ferreiro, but once worked out the orthographic form may affect the perception of sounds, words, sentences, and the like. The two-way relation between phonology and orthography is the focus of the chapters in this part.

Linnea Ehri, a psychologist at the University of California at Davis, examines several important ways in which learning to read a written text influences speech. Her central argument is that written language provides a model for the explicit (visible) representation of speech. Primary aspects of the written form are the representation of lexical units by means of isolated words and of phonological units by means of letters. In a series of experiments, both her own and those of others, Ehri shows that children detect, judge, and remember the oral forms by means of their written representations. Thus if they know that a word is spelled *pitch*, they think that is has a /t/ sound in it; if they know that a word is spelled *rich*, they think that it does not. Yet linguists tell us that the ending sounds are in fact identical. Most of these effects occur when words and sounds are analyzed as separate units — listening to particular words outside their contexts of normal speech. It remains to be seen if the impact of the written form intrudes into ordinary discourse. It is possible, for example, that so-called polite forms or formal language reflect the written norm quite directly.

Roderick Barron, a psychologist at the University of Guelph, further examines the relations between spelling and sound in literacy. He argues and provides evidence for the view that skilled readers build up two sets of linguistic representations, one phonological and the other orthographic, and that these two sets of representations interact in reading and spelling. While spelling and sound diverge to a considerable extent in English orthography, becoming literate requires a flexible use of both visual–orthographic and auditory–phonological knowledge. Poor readers, on the other hand, appear to use primarily their visual representations for reading and their auditory ones for spelling.

Charles Read, a linguist at the University of Wisconsin, shows the complex interaction between phonetics, phonology, and orthography that influences children's beginning spelling in English, Dutch, and French. His primary conclusion is that there is an important inter-action between pronunciation and orthographic knowledge. On one hand, children are most likely to invent spellings that omit certain phonemes, such as preconsonantal nasals (the /m/ in *bump*, for example) because in the phonological form that nasal consonant is very brief. A similar pattern has been found in Dutch and French, indicating that spelling patterns reflect availability in underlying phonological form. On the other hand, children's subsequent success in hearing these sounds depends upon their acquaintance with the orthography, as Ehri points out.

Paul Kolers, a psychologist at the University of Toronto, comments on the papers of Ehri, Barron, and Read from the perspective of his work on the psychological processes involved in skilled reading. He criticizes both Barron and Ehri for not going far enough in recog-nizing the autonomy of written language from speech. Readers, he argues, can pay attention to any level of structure, including those that are purely visual, such as typeface. He suggests that written and spoken language are different media possessing somewhat distinctive forms, serving different functions, and involving different conven-tions. To treat writing as simply derivative of speech, he goes on to say, would be a serious error. This is a view Kolers shares with both Barron and Ehri and with most of the other writers in this volume.

The volume is completed by an annotated bibliography prepared by Ron Scollon, an anthropological linguist at the University of Alaska, which includes the major books and papers that serve as a foundation for the growing interdisciplinary study of literacy. A few entries have been added by the editors.

Some conclusions

Any act of reading, even reading papers of the quality of the chapters described above, involves some assimilation to existing schemata, as Bartlett would have said. Some of the summarizing conclusions I shall mention were forced on me by the arguments and data outlined above and some were already present before I began reading and editing these chapters. I began with the conviction that oral language was different from written language in important respects and that those differences would help account for the difficulties some children have in becoming fully literate. That belief was sustained and elaborated by most of the chapters in this volume. That is not to say that the modality is what matters, although that is part of it; rather, it is to say that some forms of discourse are particularly suited to one or the other medium of expression, speaking or writing, and that those modes involve distinctive linguistic formulations – simple versus complex clauses, rough versus precise wording, vernacular versus technical terms, specialized versus unspecialized discourse structures, and so on. The structure of language, however, is open enough that specializations of language worked up for the process of writing may be added to the language – relativization is a case in point – and the option then becomes available, if awkwardly, for speech. Anything that can be written can, it seems, be spoken; both modes utilize the same linguistic structures. The differences, then, are primarily of two sorts: In speaking we exercise a somewhat different set of lexical and syntactic options than we do in writing. Secondly, people who do a lot of reading and writing, or who have parents who do a lot of reading and writing, acquire the set of linguistic options required for written texts. Central to this enlarged set of linguistic options relevant to reading, in addition to a more differentiated vocabulary, are devices, such as conjunctions, for integrating ideas into complex clauses and devices for integrating sentences into complex linguistic forms, such as stories, essays, and the like. These are the sets of linguistic options that schools attempt systematically to inculcate into children, and these are the options that the children of highly literate parents seem to pick up in learning to talk in the first place.

Part of the elaborated language that is involved in literacy is the logical machinery required for specifying the relations between ideas in an argument or between episodes in a narrative. These structures are in turn useful for the formation and expression of thought. Another part of that elaborated language is the language for talking about language, the metalanguage. *Word*, *sound*, and *sentence* are conspicuously related to reading. But so are the more general terms for referring to what was *said*, the speech-act verbs, and to what was *meant*, the mental-state verbs. It is this set of terms, and the concepts they represent, that give literate thought some of its characteristics of reflectivity, criticalness, and literalness.

But the fact that literacy involves a more elaborated and highly syntactically organized language should not lead us to overlook the richness of oral language. While literate forms of expression lead us to "spell things out" one at a time, oral forms do a myriad of things at once – express propositions, illocutionary force, speaker stance, social stance, emphasis, nuance, and so on. Hence, the analysis of an oral transcript is both illuminating and humbling. The difference between speech and written texts is that the latter tend to be much more specialized. And as Robin Horton (1970) once pointed out, as symbols become better for one purpose, the less useful they are for anything else. As a general all-purpose tool, ordinary oral language has a competitor neither in writing nor in computer technology.

Both oral and written language involve the mastery and use of conventions ranging from the letter (or sound) to the syntax to the meaning to the discourse. And as several of the chapters in this volume show, the conventions of speech interact with those of writing. But writing has a second effect on conventions that depends not on the simple technological fact of writing but on the altered social world to which writing contributes. Speech is most commonly generated for a single listener or small group of listeners. The linguistic communities sharing these conventions are relatively small and constitute a dialect group. Writing, because of its transportability, can and usually does reach a larger audience, an audience describable as a reading public. This reading public is larger than the oral dialect group. For language to work for this larger group, it is necessary to ensure that the same sets of conventions are used – conventions of pronunciation, meaning, and the like. Because of their broader base, literate conventions are accorded both prestige and authority. And they are taught to children. On the one hand, their mastery devalues the oral dialect; on the other, through them the child gains access to a larger social world, an access gained in part through abandoning the linguistic practices of the more local dialect group.

Finally, the effects of literacy on intellectual and social change are not straightforward. As we noted at the outset, it is misleading to think of literacy in terms of consequences. What matters is what people do with literacy, not what literacy does to people. Literacy does not cause a new mode of thought, but having a written record may permit people to do something they could not do before – such as look back, study, interpret, and so on. Similarly, literacy does not cause social change, modernization, or industrialization. But being able to read and write may be vital to playing certain roles in an industrial society and completely irrelevant to other roles in a traditional society. Literacy is important for what it permits people to do – to achieve their goals or to bring new goals into view.

REFERENCES

Bacon, F. *Novum organum.* 1620. Reprinted in S. Warhaft (Ed.), *Francis Bacon: A selection of his works* (College Classics in English, H. N. Frye, Ed.). Toronto: Copp Clark, 1965.

Eisenstein, E. *The printing press as an agent of change: Communications and cultural transformations in early-modern Europe.* Cambridge: Cambridge University Press, 1979.

Havelock, E. *Origins of Western literacy.* Toronto: Ontario Institute for Studies in Education, 1976.

Horton, R. African traditional thought and Western science. In B. R. Wilson (Ed.), *Rationality.* Oxford: Blackwell, 1970.

Innis, H. *Empire and communication.* Oxford: Oxford University Press, 1950.

McLuhan, M. *The Gutenberg galaxy: The making of typographic man.* Toronto: University of Toronto Press, 1962.

Understanding media: The extensions of man. New York: McGraw-Hill, 1964.

Popper, K. *Objective knowledge: An evolutionary approach.* Oxford: Clarendon Press, 1972.

Watt, I. *The rise of the novel: Studies in Defoe, Richardson, and Fielding.* Berkeley: University of California Press, 1957.

Whitehead, A. N. *Adventures of ideas.* Cambridge: Cambridge University Press, 1933.

PART I

Literacy and society

2

On the printing press as an agent of change

ELIZABETH L. EISENSTEIN

In this chapter I plan to discuss my recent book, *The Printing Press as an Agent of Change* (1979). The choice of this title posed problems that I will take up a little later. First I want to say something about the choice of topic – about how I first became concerned with the historical consequences of printing. This takes me back to 1963, when my curiosity was provoked (and I use the word *provoked* deliberately) by reading Marshall McLuhan's *Gutenberg Galaxy* (1962).

While studying and teaching Western European history, I had become increasingly dissatisfied with prevailing explanations for the political and intellectual revolutions of early modern times. Mc-Luhan's work pointed to a dimension that seemed to be left out of conventional historical accounts. By bringing the fifteenth-century communications shift into the picture, I thought it might be possible to develop more adequate explanations for certain puzzling aspects of early modern European history. But *The Gutenberg Galaxy* was written by a man who condemned historical inquiries as obsolete and who presented five hundred years of unevenly phased change as a single event. Before other matters could be considered, I needed more specific historical information on the advent of printing and on some of its initial effects. (I was thinking then, and still am thinking now, only of Western Europe. The advent of printing in China or Korea presents fascinating problems, but they lie outside my area of concern.) What were some of the new cultural features introduced by typography in Western Europe in the fifteenth century? How did other authorities view the consequences of the communications shift?

Anticipating that I would need to make a strenuous effort to master a large and growing literature, I set out to investigate what had been written on this obviously important topic. To my surprise,

I found that there was not even a small literature available for consultation. All authorities seemed to agree that major consequences were entailed, but all stopped short of spelling out just what these consequences were. There was not a single book or even a sizable article that attempted to survey or summarize the main consequences of the advent of printing.

Though I recognized that it would take more than one book to remedy this situation, I felt that a preliminary effort, however inadequate, was better than none and so embarked on a decade of study to acquaint myself with the special literature on early printing and the history of the book. Here, indeed, I did find a very large literature, one I am still struggling to master. In the course of studying this unfamiliar material, I discovered (as all neophytes do) that what seemed relatively simple at first became increasingly complex on closer examination. The advent of printing was in itself a complicated innovation involving an ensemble of many different changes. As for its consequences, they seemed to be even more variegated as well as elusive and difficult to summarize. It was particularly difficult to avoid oversimplification in preliminary papers and articles. Whenever I tried to encapsulate my findings in the form of a thesis statement or terse formulation, I found I was dissatisfied with the result. Here I feel a conflict between an obligation to provide a few key statements that will sum things up and an even more compelling obligation to convey my sense that any simple or single formula will be misleading at best.

To illustrate what I mean, let me offer one example of a formula that has been imputed to me. The advent of printing, the formula goes, moved Western Europe "from image culture to word culture." Now I did imply that some such formula might work, but I failed to note that its reverse was also true: that a movement from word to image was being encouraged by the same process and at the same time.

Let us look at this example a little more closely. The formula "image to word" appeared in a seminal article on literacy and education by Lawrence Stone (1969). His point was well taken. A latent iconoclasm was reinforced and the medieval justification for allowing graven images in church was weakened by print. Pope Gregory the Great had held that statues were useful as "Bibles for the illiterate." Sixteenth-century reformers such as Calvin could insist on Bible reading as a duty required of every man and could dispense with religious statuary altogether. As Frances Yates points out in her fascinating study *The Art of Memory*, the more information storage and retrieval was handled by printed reference works, the less need there was for vivid images to serve as memory aids (1966). The increasing number of encyclopedias in book form diminished the need for cathedrals to serve as encyclopedias in stone.

But the "image to word" formula holds good only for a limited set of phenomena. After all, printing also endowed graven images with a new lease on life. As the work of Albrecht Dürer, Lucas Cranach, and others suggests, print stimulated the inventive faculties of Protestant as well as Catholic image makers. Even Protestant icono-clasts made use of picture books and exploited caricatures and cartoons. Printed publicity, furthermore, helped win new celebrity for painters and draftsmen no less than for playwrights and poets.

The formula seems even less applicable when one considers the contributions made by printed images to the natural sciences. In such fields as anatomy, geography, and astronomy the influence of printing led away from using words, away from ambiguous culturally bound verbal statements toward clear and precise pictorial and mathematical ones. By making it possible to duplicate maps, graphs, tables, and charts, print revolutionized communications within the Commonwealth of Learning. The creation of a more uniform pic-torial and mathematical vocabulary made it possible to bypass the confusion engendered by linguistic multiformity, by translation prob-lems, and by diverse names for constellations, landmasses, flora, or fauna.

When attempting to explain the rise of modern science, then, one must be prepared not just to discard the formula but to turn it around. In this area, print led toward an increased use of the image and a diminished use of the word.

This example may serve to remind us that print not only encour-aged the spread of literacy among people who had no access to manuscripts but also affected communications among the literate professional elites. Image worship gave way to bibliolatry among the masses of faithful in Protestant lands. At the same time, men of learning (whether Protestant or Catholic) often became less certain than earlier scholars had been about the literal meaning of the sacred word. This point is rarely noted, partly because printing is connected almost exclusively with evangelical and popularizing trends – with vernacular Bibles and the spread of literacy. Little or no attention has been given to the internal transformations within a Common-wealth of Learning where the Latin Bible had long been studied but complete polyglot versions had never been seen. My book attempts to rectify this imbalance by placing special emphasis on changes that affected literate elites – men of learning and letters who had previously relied on scribal transmission and who gravitated to printshops almost as soon as the first presses appeared.

This special emphasis on conditions within the Commonwealth of Learning runs counter to current trends. My concerns are different from those of Africanists, anthropologists, and students of popular culture who also deal with communications and textual transmission. Whereas they are interested in the shift from an oral culture to a literate one, I am concerned (primarily although not exclusively) with the shift from one kind of literate culture to another. When Jan Vansina, who is both an anthropologist and a historian of precolonial Africa, explores "the relationship of oral tradition to written history," he naturally skips over the differences between written history produced by scribes and written history produced in printing shops (1965). When Western European historians explore the effect of printing on popular culture, they naturally focus attention on the shift from an oral folk culture to a print-made one. In both cases, attention is deflected away from the main issues I want to explore. These issues are so unfamiliar that some readers of my early articles jumped to the mistaken conclusion that I was dealing with the same issues that Vansina does.

This misunderstanding is difficult to forestall. For one thing, the advent of printing did encourage the spread of literacy at the same time that it changed the way written texts were handled by already literate groups. For another, even literate groups had to rely much more upon oral transmission in the age of scribes than they did later on. Many features characteristic of oral culture, such as the cultivation of memory arts and the role of a hearing public, were also of great significance among scribal scholars. Problems associated with oral transmission thus cannot be avoided even when one is dealing with literate groups. Nevertheless, the experience of the scribal scholar was different from that of his preliterate contemporaries; the advent of printing had an effect on Latin-reading professors that was different from its effect on unlettered artisans. To leave out the former and consider only the latter is to lose a chance to help explain major intellectual transformations of early modern times.

In dealing with these transformations one cannot ignore how printing spurred the spread of literacy. But to me the most neglected important aspect is not the spread of literacy but how printing altered written communications within the Commonwealth of Learning. Thus when I refer (as I often do) to an "unacknowledged revolution,"

I am thinking not of an oral culture but of a scribal culture being replaced.

The first part of my book is aimed at identifying the main features of this "unacknowledged revolution." Here it proved difficult to strike the right balance between the enthusiasts who believe printing changed everything and the skeptics who hold it changed nothing. The enthusiasts take the claims made in prefaces by early printers and editors too literally. They ignore the fact that early prefaces, like advertising copy written today, promised much more than early printers actually delivered. The skeptics overreact to the boasts and false claims made by early printers: They often unfairly judge early printed products by twentieth-century standards, and they tend to exaggerate the capacity of medieval copyists to arrest scribal corruption and to anticipate trends that arose only after printing.

Of course, we need to take stock of the changes that manuscript book production underwent during the millennium before printing shops appeared. Certainly there is good reason to be cautious about overestimating the initial changes wrought by print and good reason to issue a warning against taking the claims of early printers at face value. It is also important to be alert to the resemblance between late manuscripts and early printed books. There is much wisdom in Rudolf Hirsch's statement: "The road from manuscript to print was continuous *and* broken." (1967). Still, I feel that a well-grounded fear of exaggerating the break should be coupled with more concern about underrating its true dimensions. It is common at present to describe the appearance of urban booksellers and lay stationers in the twelfth century as a revolutionary change and the appearance of the first printers in the fifteenth century as evolutionary change. To place a "book revolution" in the twelfth century while denying that there was one in the fifteenth century (Saenger, 1975) does not preserve historical perspectives but rather sets them askew.

The new powers of the press are especially likely to be underestimated when printing is placed in the framework provided by the history of the book. For instance, the masterful survey of the first three centuries of printing by Febvre and Martin (originally published in 1958) has been misleadingly entitled *L'Apparition du Livre* (*The Coming of the Book* in recent English translation, 1976). By Gutenberg's time, the book had been in circulation for a thousand years or more, depending on whether one starts with the codex or goes back to the earlier scroll. What is new in fifteenth-century Western Europe is not "l'apparition du *livre*" but "l'apparition de l'*imprimerie*."

Largely because of this consideration, I decided it was best to take as my title *The Printing Press as an Agent of Change*. Bearing in mind Marc Bloch's dictum that "the good historian is like the giant of the fairy tale. He knows that wherever he catches the scent of human flesh, there his quarry lies" (1953), I would have liked to have underlined the human element in my title by taking the early printer as my "agent of change." Yet although I do think of certain master printers as being the unsung heroes of the early modern era, and although they are the true protagonists of my book, impersonal processes involving transmission and standardization must also be given due attention. Of course, not one tool but many were involved in the new duplicating process. The term *printing press* in the context of the book serves simply as a convenient label – a shorthand way of referring to a larger cluster of specific changes that entail the use of movable metal type, oil-based ink, and so forth. The point of departure, in any case, is not the invention of one device in one Mainz shop but the establishment of many printing shops in many urban centers throughout Europe over the course of two decades or so. This entailed the appearance of a new occupational culture associated with the printing trades. New publicity techniques and new communication networks also appeared. By placing less emphasis on the advent of the book and more on the advent of printing shops in many towns throughout Europe between the 1460s and 1480s, I think we will be better situated to appreciate the revolutionary aspects of the shift.

The first part of my book is aimed at bringing these revolutionary aspects more clearly into view by considering the new functions performed by early printers, not just as businessmen but also as editors, translators, lexicographers, and cultural impresarios. Economic historians correctly assign printers a prominent position among the early capitalists of Western Europe, and their entrepreneurial role is certainly significant. Early printers, however, were more at home in the world of books than were other capitalists. They engaged in new cultural as well as new economic activities. They acted as press agents for men of learning and letters, served as sponsors of scientific research, and sometimes engaged in new forms of data collection themselves. Thus the printing shop did more than issue products that enriched libraries and literary diets. It provided a new setting for intellectual activity. It served as a kind of institute for advanced learning (as a "laboratory of research," in Myron Gilmore's phrase, 1952), which rivaled the older university, court, and academy and which provided preachers and teachers with opportunities to pursue alternative careers. Martin Lowry's (1979) biography of Aldus Manutius the sixteenth-century Venetian printer who used the dolphin and anchor as his trademark, describes the Aldine printing shop of the 1500s, with its household of some 30 people, as "a now almost incredible mixture of the sweatshop, the boarding house and the research institute." This statement nicely sums up the hybrid character of the establishment set up by many master printers in early modern Europe.

The new functions performed in early printing shops are too often overlooked by sociologists of knowledge. Karl Mannheim, for example, singles out the intelligentsia as a unique social group because they are cut off from "direct access to any vital and functioning segment of society. . . . The secluded study and dependence on printed matter afford only a derivative view of the social process. No wonder that this stratum remained long unaware of the social character of change. . . . The proletariat had already perfected its own world view when those late comers appeared on the scene" (1956).

For Mannheim, "the rise of the intelligentsia marks the last phase of the growth of social consciousness." In my view, however, he has put first things last. Many inhabitants of the early modern Republic of Letters spent more time in the printing shop than in secluded studies. They were thus in direct contact with a "vital and functioning segment of society." Printing shops were more sensitive registers of political, economic, religious, and cultural developments than any other kind of shop in early modern Europe. Authors who literally "composed" their works with a composing stick in hand were not uncommon in the age of Erasmus – nor in that of Benjamin Franklin. The historical and social consciousness of men of letters and learning in early modern Europe seems to me to have been well in advance of that of other groups. The conditions Mannheim describes may have become operative after the advent of the steam press in the early nineteenth century. Before then, however, men of learning were in close touch with mechanics and merchants. Often, indeed, the genteel publisher and the mechanic printer were one and the same man. This hybrid figure presided over the rise of a lay intelligentsia that then developed a world view of its own.

The question of how printing may have affected prevailing world views is taken up in the second part of my book. It deals in turn with the three major intellectual movements of early modern times: the Renaissance, the Reformation, and the Scientific Revolution. It attempts to show how the communications shift entered into each of these movements by changing the way classical, scriptural, and scientific traditions were transmitted and were received.

A special problem is posed by the Renaissance because the advent of printing comes well after the beginning of the classical revival in Italy. The first phase of the Italian Renaissance must be placed within the context of scribal culture and seen to predate printing by a century-and-a-half.

Accordingly, one should take as a starting point the self-conscious revival that was launched by scribal scholars in Italy well before the first printing shop appeared in Mainz. Then one may pose the question: How was the ongoing Italian revival affected by being perpetuated in print? In its early phase, the Italian Renaissance was like the Carolingian or twelfth-century revival in that it depended on the limited and highly perishable resources of scribal culture. The preservative powers of print transformed the Petrarchian revival. Thus, for the first time, Greek studies could be pursued independently of the survival of enclaves of Greek immigrants in the Mediterranean world. It became possible to carry on Greek studies in northern Europe, across the Alps, across the Channel, and eventually even overseas. For the first time, a permanent process of recovery was launched so that the accumulation of ancient texts and artifacts became continuous.

By thus assigning special significance to the continuous process of recovery launched by printing, one may explain the anomalous association of the fall of Constantinople with a revival of learning. Until the 1450s the destruction of a major center of manuscript records had always been associated with the onset of a "dark" age. The dispersal of Greek scholars and Greek manuscripts after the Ottoman takeover, however, was associated not with the beginning of a dark age but with a prelude to a golden one. This reversal becomes less puzzling when one takes into consideration the movement of Greek scholars and manuscripts not only into Western classrooms and libraries but also into newly established printing shops, such as Aldus' Venetian firm.

Other problems associated with the Renaissance also may be clarified by considering the preservative powers of print. For example, the preservation of artists' and writers' personal records together with their portraits and works contributed to certain aspects of Renaissance and individualism. New forms of publicity helped to move "the drive for fame" into high gear. It also seems likely that the limited resources of scribal culture inhibited perception of anachronism and that the preservative powers of print entered into the growing sense of distance through time and the new historical consciousness that is a hallmark of modern thought.

In Renaissance studies there is a tendency to neglect the effects of printing because Gutenberg came so long after the Petrarchian revival was launched. In Reformation studies the topic is not neglected, but I think it is brought in too little and too late. Thus printing and Protestantism are conventionally linked by the spread of Lutheran broadsides and Bibles after 1517, but little attention is devoted to the output of Bibles and other printed matter before that date. As I see it, printing acted both as a prerequisite for and a precipitant of the Lutheran revolt. New issues posed by printing had begun to divide Western Christendom and force churchmen to adopt new positions well before the Ninety-five Theses were nailed, mailed, or issued in print.

In considering how printing affected a traditional Christian faith, I became increasingly aware that a two-way process was at work. Here as elsewhere, a McLuhan formula seems misleading. The message and medium must be kept apart to see how they interact. Beginning with Gutenberg's Bibles and indulgences, the old messages and the new medium acted upon each other. A traditional drive to spread the Gospel and to convert the infidel helped power the early presses. In this connection, the enthusiastic welcome given to printing by Western churchmen before the Reformation needs more attention. Prelates welcomed printing as a "divine art"; popes regarded it as a God-given weapon in the crusade against infidel Turks. Early examples of how Western Europeans coupled claims of technological superiority with assertions of moral and spiritual superiority may be found in the anti-Ottoman propaganda of the late fifteenth century (Atkinson, 1935). (When Protestants hailed printing as a divinely ordained weapon against the pope they were simply playing variations on an earlier Church-sponsored theme.) In addition to special Christian motives and long-lived apostolic drives, Bible printing was powered by the capitalist urge to expand markets, outdo competitors, and increase book sales. The new combination of evangelism and capitalism made for a powerful, irreversible movement that threatened traditional priestly prerogatives in an unprecedented way.

The changes wrought by printing on an older scriptural tradition were so far-reaching that orthodoxy as well as heresy was inevitably transformed. The use of the new medium to implement old aims carried some religious reformers such as Erasmus so far beyond traditional limits that in retrospect they seem to have performed revolutionary roles. The most conservative theologian, obedient layman or tradition-bound pope could not avoid departing from medieval precedent even in the act of defending the status quo. The positions adopted by the Catholic Church at Trent reflected changes engendered by print no less than did those taken by the Protestants. Still, a common interest in the spread of vernacular Bibles and lay literacy did link Protestants more closely than Catholics with the interests of printers-at-large. Providing breviaries for priests, manuals for confessors, and textbooks for seminarians kept certain privileged Catholic firms prosperous; but the censorship regulations issued by Counter-reformation churches curtailed the open-ended expansion of lay book markets and diversification of output that was occurring in Protestant regions, to the disadvantage of Catholic printers.

The new device of the Index of Prohibited Books boomeranged, producing an intriguing, asymmetric effect in pattern of the European printed book trade. Just as being banned in Boston helped American book sales in states other than Massachusetts during the 1930s and 1940s, inclusion of a title on the Index heightened risks and lowered profits for Catholic printers while having the reverse effect upon Protestant ones. Authors such as Rabelais, Boccaccio, Machiavelli, and Aretino who were by no means favored by Protestant pastors nevertheless were promoted by Protestant publishers, who thus endowed Protestant literary culture with a strangely secular and libertine flavor.

As the peculiar workings of the Index may suggest, it is a mistake to assume that printers invariably depended on directives from above – that they merely reflected prevailing orthodoxies and served as press agents for whatever power was in command. No doubt they provided publicity for ruling princes and prelates; they also exploited publicity for their own ends. Because they shared common interests with early Protestants, they flocked to Wittenberg and Geneva almost as soon as Luther and Calvin arrived. But they also gravitated to other towns, such as Basel and Frankfurt, where religious zeal was more subdued. Some printers helped to fan the flames of religious warfare by mounting propaganda campaigns. Others contributed to a clandestine propagation of cosmopolitan and tolerant creeds. An affinity for so-called Nicodemite positions, which masked inner dissent by outward conformity to established churches and secular officials, marked many of the most prosperous and celebrated sixteenth-century firms. Independent of secular dynastic interests and religious orthodoxy alike, these firms served as sanctuaries for refugees of diverse faiths and represented a special kind of "Third Force" in early modern Europe.

Here again it seems important to consider the scholarly elites as well as mass movements and popular trends. Greek or polyglot Bibles clearly lacked the widespread appeal that vernacular Bibles had. Nevertheless, they did encourage the formation of polyglot house-holds in the shops of certain merchant publishers. More than mere toleration of Greeks, Jews, and other émigré scholars was entailed for those master printers who supervised scholarly versions of sacred works. The homes of these men resembled miniature international houses for months on end. (Henri II Estienne provided a celebrated example when, he described the household in which he grew up: Representatives of 10 different nationalities sat around the table of his father, Robert Estienne. Even the servants spoke Latin, so Henri says, for it was the only tongue shared by all [Armstrong, 1954].) The new industry thus encouraged not only the formation of financial syndicates and far-flung trade networks similar to those established by merchants in the cloth trade during early modern times. It also encouraged the formation and articulation of a special ethos that was ecumenical, irenic, and tolerant without being secular; genuinely pious yet opposed to fanaticism; often combining outward conformity to established churches and regimes with inner fidelity to heterodox creeds. Thus some of the views that later became characteristic of the Enlightenment were first shaped in certain sixteenth-century printing shops under the aegis of merchant publishers who plied their trade during the religious wars.

The last section of my book is devoted to the relationship between printing and modern science. Here again my approach differs from conventional treatments. The usual interpretation stresses popular-izing themes (such as the rise of the vernaculars, the appearance of artisan authors, and new varieties of science writing reflected in the term *popular mechanics*). Printing is seen to have encouraged a new genre of vernacular technical literature outside the university, even though Aristotle still reigned supreme in traditional Latin lectures (Drake, 1970). There is much evidence to support this interpretation. Printing did make it possible for craftsmen, artisan engineers, "reckon masters," barber surgeons, painters, and potters who had not mas-tered Latin to contribute to public knowledge. By elaborating on this point one can draw useful connections between Protestantism and early modern science. The authorization of vernacular Bibles can be linked to the encouragement of vernacular technical literature. In seventeenth-century England during the Civil War, for example, the cause of Englishing Bibles and lawbooks expanded to include Englishing medical prescriptions as well. (The radical Puritan was so far in advance of his times that three centuries later Latin medical prescriptions have not yet been Englished for us all.)

I am sympathetic (at least as an occasional patient) to the Puritan enthusiast who believed medicine should be deprived of its aura of mystery, and I think it is important to note how data collection was spurred by the vernacular translation movement. But I am also persuaded that this particular theme has been overplayed. Vernacular translation had little to do with the major landmarks in early science: *De Revolutionibus, De Fabrica, De Motu, Principia* – each one in Latin, each by an academically trained professional. In this light it seems misguided to follow the Marxists in setting an avant-garde of capitalists and mechanics against a rearguard of Latin-reading clerks. This alignment does little to clarify late medieval science and much to obscure the new interchanges fostered by print.

Divisions between town and gown, scholar and craftsman, university and workshop were significantly diminished by printing. One point worth noting is that preachers and teachers were often more inclined to resort to publicity and help with vernacular translation than were guildsmen who were trained to be secretive about tricks of their trade. But one should not place too much emphasis on the issue of vernacular versus Latin, for this issue distracts attention from other important changes wrought by print. As Galileo himself says, the Book of Nature is written neither in Latin nor in the vernacular; rather "it is written in the language of mathematics, and its characters are triangles, circles, and other geometric figures without which it is humanly impossible to understand a single word of it." (Galilei, 1623/1956).

This brings me back to the point I made earlier about a decreasing reliance on ambiguous words. The duplication of visual aids reduced time spent on slavish copying of tables, charts, and maps. It also provided a new basis for agreement about precisely observed natural phenomena. Corrupted texts and drifting records could be discarded and fresh ventures in collaborative data collection launched. Technical literature inherited from Alexandria was subjected to the same kind of scrutiny in the sixteenth century that the scriptural tradition was. Much as Erasmus set out to redo St. Jerome, so too Copernicus set out to emend Ptolemy. Both men launched revolutions they did not foresee. The fate of the medieval Vulgate, which was undercut by vernacular translations on the one hand and by polyglot versions on the other, was paralleled by the fate of Alexandrian textual traditions derived from Ptolemy and Galen. But whereas polyglot editions made Scripture (the words of God) seem more multiform, repeatable visual aids made nature (the works of God) seem more uniform. It can thus be argued that printing played a significant part in weakening confidence in scriptural revelation while strengthening trust in mathematical reasoning and man-made maps.

In presenting a case for the transforming powers of print I have had to consider objections from critics who are worried about monovariable interpretations and technological determinism. I believe it is possible to make a good case for multivariable explanations even while stressing the effects produced by a particular invention; clearly, the mixture of the many motives that converged in the printing shop provided a much more powerful impetus than any single motive, whether spiritual or material, could have provided by itself. I have already noted how old missionary impulses were combined with new profit-seeking entrepreneurial drives. Presses also served to implement equally powerful drives for power and for fame. By providing rulers with their own independent propaganda machines, printing offered a way for them to extend their charisma and to emancipate their realms from dependence on clerical copyists and scribes. Among artisans and guildsmen printing acted by a kind of marvelous alchemy to transmute private interest into public good. It catered to both selfish and altruistic motives, encouraging instrument makers to serve the cause of public knowledge by making their inventions known and at the same time to serve themselves by attracting purchasers to their shops. In short, the use of early presses by Western Europeans was "overdetermined" by many different forces that had been incubating in the age of scribes. In a different cultural context, the same technology might have been used for different ends (as in Korea) or it might have been unwelcome and not used at all (as in many regions outside Europe where Western missionary presses were the first to be installed).

Such speculation suggests the importance of considering the institutional context of any technological innovation. Yet the fact remains that once presses were established in numerous European towns, the transforming powers of print did begin to take effect. And as far as I can see, the transformations that began in fifteenth-century Europe are still under way.

Because contrary views have been expressed, it seems necessary to point out in conclusion that the process that began in the mid-fifteenth century has not ceased to gather momentum in the age of the computer printout and the television guide. Since the advent of movable type, an enhanced capacity to store and retrieve, preserve and transmit has kept pace with (and has perhaps outstripped) an enhanced capacity to create and destroy. The somewhat chaotic appearance of modern Western culture owes as much, if not more, to the duplicative powers of print as it does to the harnessing of new powers in the past century. A continuous accumulation of printed materials has certain disadvantages. Each generation of artists seems to suffer from an increasingly oppressive "burden of the past." Among scholars, problems of overload have become acute. The voracious appetite of Chronos was feared in the past; a monstrous capacity to disgorge poses more of a threat at present. Still the capacity to scan accumulated records also confers certain modest advantages. We may examine how our predecessors read various portents and auguries and compare their prophecies with what actually occurred. We may thus discern over the past century or so a tendency to write off by premature obituaries the very problems that successive generations have had to confront.

This impulse to end tales that are still unfolding owes much to the prolongation of nineteenth-century historical schemes, especially those of Hegel and Marx that point dialectical conflicts toward some ultimate goal. Hegelian grand designs do not allow for the possibility of an indefinite prolongation of fundamentally conflicting trends – of a continuing opposition of thesis against antithesis with no synthesis in sight. Yet we still seem to be experiencing the contradictory effects of a process that fanned the flames of religious zeal and bigotry even while it fostered a new concern for ecumenical concord and toleration, a process that more permanently fixed linguistic and national divisions even while it created a cosmopolitan Commonwealth of Learning and extended communications networks that now encompass the entire world.

At the very least, I hope my book indicates the premature character of prevailing historical grand designs by showing that the gulf separating the age of scribes from that of printers has not yet been fully probed. The continuous, unevenly phased, and persistently accelerating process of recovery and innovation that began in the second half of the fifteenth century still remains to be described.

ACKNOWLEDGMENT

This chapter is based on an Engelhard Lecture on the Book presented at the Library of Congress on September 3, 1977, and subsequently published as "In the Wake of the Printing Press," *Quarterly Journal of the Library of Congress*, 1978, 183–197.

REFERENCES

Armstrong, E. *Robert Estienne, Royal Printer*. Cambridge: Cambridge University Press, 1954.

Atkinson, G. *Les nouveaux horizons de la Renaissance française*. Paris: Droz, 1935.

Bacon, F. *Novum organum*. 1605. Reprinted in S. Warhaft (Ed.), *Francis Bacon: A selection of his works* (College Classics in English, H. N. Frye, Ed.). Toronto: Copp Clark, 1965.

Bloch, M. *The historian's craft*. Trans. Peter Putnam. New York: Knopf, 1953.

Drake, S. Early science and the printed book: The spread of science beyond the universities. *Renaissance and Reformation*, 1970, *6*, 43–52.

Eisenstein, E. L. *The printing press as an agent of change*. Cambridge: Cambridge University Press, 1979.

Febvre, L., & Martin, H. J. *The coming of the book*. Trans. David Gerard, ed. G. Nowell-Smith and D. Wootton. London: NLB, 1976.

Galilei, G. The assayer. 1623. Reprinted in *Discoveries and opinions of Galileo*. Trans. Stillman Drake. Garden City, N.Y.: Doubleday, 1956.

Gilmore, M. *The world of humanism, 1453–1517*, Vol. 2, *The rise of modern Europe*. New York: Harper, 1952.

Havelock, E. *Prologue to Greek literacy*. Toronto: Ontario Institute for Studies in Education, 1976.

Hirsch, R. *Printing, selling, and reading, 1450–1550*. Wiesbaden: Harrassowitz, 1967.

Horton, R. African traditional thought and Western science. In B. R. Wilson (Ed.), *Rationality*. Oxford: Blackwell, 1970.

Innis, H. *Empire and communication*. Oxford: Oxford University Press, 1950.

Lowry, M. *The world of Aldus Manutius: Business and scholarship in Renaissance Venice*. Ithaca, N.Y.: Cornell University Press, 1979.

McLuhan, M. *The Gutenberg galaxy: The making of typographic man*. Toronto: University of Toronto Press, 1962.

Understanding media: The extensions of man. New York: McGraw-Hill, 1964.

Mannheim, K. *Essays on the sociology of culture*. Ed. Ernest Manheim and Paul Kecskemeti. London: Routledge & Kegan Paul, 1956.

Saenger, P. Colard Mansion and the evolution of the printed book. *Library Quarterly*, 1975, *45*, 405–18.

Stone, L. Literacy and education in England, 1640–1900. *Past and Present*, 1969, *42*, 78.

Vansina, J. *Oral tradition: A study in historical methodology*. Trans. H. M. Wright. Chicago: Aldine, 1965.

Yates, F. A. *The art of memory*. London: Routledge & Kegan Paul, 1966.

3

Atlantans, Centaurians, and the litron bomb: some personal and social implications of literacy

IAN WINCHESTER

When one contemplates what we have in the West because of literacy, the story seems enormously complicated and our judgments of the results of its possession inevitably mixed. First of all is the question of what we have as a result of literacy in the possession of a small elite. Then we have the question of what we have because this elite expanded and the varieties of interests served by literacy expanded. And finally we have the question of what we have because of universal minimal literacy since 1850 or so. It is also not clear whether we should consider the expansion of schooling and higher education since the Second World War as a new era with new and special consequences.

There are three things that we have in the West due to the earlier, elite phase of literacy and that we would not have without that literacy. The first of these is Western religion in its theological form: the interrogation of God. The second is Western science in its systematic theoretical and experimental or observational form: the interrogation of Nature. And the third is the interrogation of human nature by means of Western literature. There are very likely connections to be traced between these three and Western art, architecture, music, and mathematics, as well as between them and the notion of elite literacy from perhaps 1100 onward and certainly from the Renaissance, if we neglect the contribution of Greece. But I think that anyone denying the relationship between literacy and religion, science, and literature in the West would have a much more difficult argument to make than he would with respect to the other major categories of great traditions, with the exception of mathematics.

The possession of universal minimal literacy wedded to the continuance of an elite literacy since 1850 seems to have provided essentially the basis for Western industrial organization and, closely allied with this, Western government organization. Indeed, in some cases, the industrial and governmental organization are one and the same. What also seems clear is that neither the possession of elite nor of universal literacy favors, in and of itself, any one form of government over another. All that it favors, it would seem, are certain grades and complexity of organization. Literacy makes a radical difference to the complexity of organization that humans can manage. But systematization and complexity can be equally at the service of a variety of tyrannies as of open societies.

There are two ways that we, imbedded as we are in a literate culture, can come to grips with the question of whether or not the same major developments in tradition could have been brought about in a totally oral culture, however long it would have taken. The first way is to try to construct scenarios with considerable plausibility in which theological religion, natural science, and interrogative oral literature are imagined to have developed. Then we should see if we can give any a priori reasons why these scenarios cannot in fact ever be instantiated or at least under what *different* (but nonliterate) conditions they might be.

The second way we might approach the question of whether we could have done it orally is to imagine in some systematic way the removal of our literate capacity step by step while our society carries on just as it is for a time. The question becomes, then, one of estimating just how long it could carry on in that fashion.

I shall turn to each of these exercises in theoretical history, or subjunctive conditional history, in just a moment. However, before I do, I should allay the fears of the experimentalists that I have anything against real experiments in general, or that I think thought experiment is always and everywhere to be preferred. It is just that I think that in history, or historical sociology, both experiment and, for that matter, observation are logically out of the question. Nor do I think that we can, for example, isolate the Tasaday of North Borneo for a few millennia and wait to see if they develop oral Western theology, science, and literature or the equivalent (whatever that might be). Thus I think that we really have only these two basic ways of coming to grips with the question of what the *necessary* connection between Western theology, science, and literature is. To this I will now turn.

Oral interrogative theology, science, and literature

Under what conditions can we imagine a purely oral culture producing Western science, theology, and literature? Well, one plausible suggestion is as follows:

There is a race of humans on Atlantis who have minds of a mnemonist. That is, their memories are effectively unlimited, both in time and extent. Furthermore, they live, on the average, a very long time, roughly a thousand years. Otherwise, they are very much like the run of ordinary humans in appearance and with the extreme of abilities to be found in otherwise ordinary people.

The Atlantans, as I have envisaged them, seem plausibly like just the sort of people who might have been up to developing our theology, science, and literature, especially if we add that they have virtually no capacity for boredom. This seems to be so because the main feature that seems to connect literacy to the great Western traditions is the requirement that there be, in some sense, objective knowledge (in Karl Popper's phrase). That is, we would need the logical equivalent of knowledge depositories, of an Alexandrian library, because of the consequences of death being the end of personal knowledge. No one of us can hope to know all the things there are to know. So that, given limited memories, and even more limited time, we are always in danger of losing what we know unless we have objective knowledge depositories. And, at least up until now, these were centrally connected with our literacy, in particular our production of books and manuscripts, in such a way that anyone properly instructed in the reading of the appropriate *kind* of book or manuscript could, at least in principle, recover the objective knowledge – even though no living human knew it. This, of course, is a description of the major task of the early universities of Padua, Paris, and Oxford – the recovery of objective knowledge from ancient sources, possessing only the literate key to the knowledge, namely a knowledge of Greek and Arabic and Latin.

Now our Atlantans are, at least in principle, walking, talking books, much like Hal the computer in *2001*. They can interrogate one another for very long periods of time on any topic. And since they all possess infallible memories and live a long time and do not get bored, then it seems quite plausible that they might very well develop analogs to our great traditions . . . provided, that is, that they are in other respects very much like us. They would have to have a considerable interest in things other than remembering. But since remembering for them is like breathing, they presumably can put a great deal of time into rational discussion, composing (which they do not have to write down), and experimenting with nature, as well, presumably, as building all sorts of interesting technical devices. Whenever they wish to know something that somebody else knows, they merely have to go and talk with that person (who never gets bored in the retelling). Of course, for such a system to work, since the diversity of personal knowledge that must be objectively available is very great, certain Atlantans specialize as indexes. Others specialize as abstracts. And yet others pride themselves as being living bibliographies of those who know and what they know, although not themselves interested in the knowledge itself. Indeed, one Atlantan city is known as the Library. Here over 1 million Atlantans live whose job it is to make themselves available day or night to other Atlantans who want to know a piece of objective knowledge. The organization is highly hierarchical, since nobody wants to wait about more than a decade to meet the one Atlantan who knows what, for example, Athos (who just died) knew about the bud worm. Indeed, in order to speed up the location process, the Atlantans in the Library have special patterned, so-called catalog colors to make easy identification of their location possible. It is very boring, even for an Atlantan, to have to go down the street asking randomly everyone you pass where you can find the person who knows what Athos knew about the bud worm. Indeed, in the worst of bad luck it might take a million (or by that time more) handshakes.

For a people who live so long one would not expect the Atlantans to be obsessed by death and the preparations for it. But, in fact, the Atlantans are, because before they die it is their duty to empty their entire memories into those of other Atlantans so that nothing will be lost. For so complicated a culture, it is unclear just what is crucial and what is not. Consequently the Law of Demise, as it is called, was passed in order that nothing of objective value be lost. Thus, while the first 500 years of an Atlantan's life are spent pleasantly enough learning, composing, experimenting, and what not, the last 500 are spent in preparation for death according to the rule that it takes just as much time to tell what you know as to come to know what you know.

The Atlantan society, though it prevailed for many thousands of years and, by means of its advanced technology, was able to live a life of isolation and peace, collapsed quite suddenly. It is said that a visitor from China one day landed in the Library and was astonished to find how long it took to find anything out. So he showed the Atlantans how to write down an index and number all the people who lived there. The Atlantans quickly saw the advantages of the system and, being reasonable people, quickly admitted the superiority of the Chinese with whom they then intermarried freely. All that is left of this remarkable people, I am told, is a mnemonist or two in

China and, occasionally, in bordering countries where the Atlantans also wandered.

The scenario of the Atlantans could, of course, be developed considerably further than I have done. In each case the line of development would be to show that even for such a remarkable people, with infinite memories and long lives, literacy in our sense would have overwhelming organizational advantages.

Before I turn to the other way to think about the necessary connection between literacy and our great traditions let me just give a passage from Whitehead's *Adventures of Ideas* (1933) that seems to me to summarize with exemplary clarity the point I have been making:

However far we go back in recorded history, we are within the period of high grade functioning of mankind, far removed from mere animal savagery. Also, within that period it would be difficult to demonstrate that mankind has improved upon its inborn mental capacity. Yet there can be no doubt that there has been an immense expansion of the outfit which the environment provides for the service of thought. This outfit can be summarized under the headings, modes of communication, physical and mental, writing, preservation of documents, variety of modes of literature, critical thought, systematic thought, constructive thought, history, comparison of diverse languages, mathematical symbolism, improved technology providing physical ease. This last list is obviously composed of many partially redundant and overlapping items. But it serves to remind us of the various ways in which we have at our service facilities for thought and suggestions for thought, far beyond those at hand for our predecessors who lived anywhere from two to five thousand years ago. Indeed the last two hundred years has added to this outfit in a way which may create a new epoch unless mankind degenerates. Of course, a large share of this outfit had already accumulated between two and three thousand years ago. It is the brilliant use which the leading men of that millennium made of their opportunities which makes us doubt of any improvement in the native intelligence of mankind (p. 55).

Consequences of the systematic removal of our collective literature capacity

Whitehead's remarks serve to remind us just how much has been accumulated by means of literacy and its organization in the service of thought. Consequently, the question of the maintenance of that literacy and its organization is rightly the central theme of our school and university systems. It seems to me that much of the fuss in recent years made over "the basics" is connected with the deep intuition that the decline of which Whitehead speaks as a possibility is very easy to bring off and that the maintenance of our literate traditions and their furtherance is not at all easy. If this is so, then it is not so surprising that educational reformers, sounding like prophets crying in the wilderness, hearken back to themes of the 1850s.

At the present we seem on the brink of a whole new technology that may seem to make the whole "outfit which the environment provides for the service of thought" obsolete. Thus, we might suggest, any prophet seriously concerned with the possibility of our populations in the West declining seriously in their capacities to read well and with understanding, to write exactly and grammatically, to perform arithmetical operations accurately and rapidly, is simply outdated. Undoubtedly such a prophet will also emphasize the danger to the body social from a corresponding decline in orderly and mannerly conduct. The reasons that such a prophet will give will likely be of the following sort:

Our culture depends largely on literate means for its self-propagation. These are the things that enable us, in the end, to teach, to transmit to us all, what it takes genius to arrive at. They are also among the preconditions for the exercise of genius.

Our prophet might then go on:

I say "among," because of course there are others. But it takes little reflection to see that the propagation of science would be impossible without the mastery of these three skills (or four, if mannerly conduct is included). The propagation of religion and art would be very much more difficult – though not absolutely impossible. But what would certainly disappear would be our thinking about them, since oral transmission would be too cumbersome and out of the question entirely.

Of course, our prophet would have to qualify his meaning somewhat here in perhaps the following way to escape the most obvious objections:

By saying this, I do not mean to imply that (remarkable) isolated individuals cannot get along without mastery of reading, writing, and arithmetic provided these are otherwise widespread. But our culture cannot. No more than it can dispense with civil and mannerly conduct.

So much for our prophet. But prophets are more often than not false. How might we estimate the truth of his remarks? We cannot, for example, point to the backwardness of illiterate cultures as proof, however suggestive this may seem. Indeed, in contemplating the Atlantans we have considered the possibility that an illiterate culture need not necessarily lack science, high literature, or anything else (although extreme longevity and infinite memory are special attributes, to be sure).

There are two ways we can try to think about the impact on our present Western society of the general or complete removal of the literacy we now have. The first is to conduct a thought experiment (or series of such) in which we imagine we have systematically removed various features and levels of literacy. We then try to estimate what would remain possible for us; how much of our civilization would, in fact, be intact. The second way is to imagine what kind of advances in technology, if any, would enable us to dispense with a particular kind or level of literacy without provoking fundamental changes in our society.

A reduction-of-literacy thought experiment

Let us suppose, in the first instance, that an Alpha Centaurian equivalent of the neutron bomb is to be exploded over the Earth. The effect of this bomb is to wipe out entirely an individual's capacity to read and write, although it leaves everything else intact, including memory. The litron bomb, the Alpha Centaurians have found, leaves everything as it was, but paralyzes a civilization nonetheless. Their only reason for dropping the litron bomb on the Earth is scientific curiosity. Deeply influenced by the Centaurian equivalent of Karl Popper, they believe in ever wider and more severe testing of their bold conjectures. In deciding upon this scientific attack on Earth the Centaurians argued as follows:

The Earthlings communicate either orally or by means of written symbols that either represent this oral speech or comprise an analysis of it. They have organized their present-day business and government affairs, their scientific and technological research, their religions (at least partly), and their literature such that at any one time that which is known, their objective knowledge is never known by any identifiable set of individuals. Instead, it resides in knowledge repositories (libraries, books, manuals, computer storage discs and tapes) and is only recoverable ultimately by means of a grasp of natural languages and their written form. The effect of a well-timed litron bomb should be to sever the link between what they collectively and what they individually know. This will lead to a quiet and certain collapse of their civilization.

The Earth Defense System, however, is quite aware of this exercise in cosmic academic freedom run riot and at the Supreme Defense

Council discusses its options. The president of the council rises and speaks as follows:

There is no stopping the overwhelming scientific curiosity of the Centaurians. But we do know that one of three main things can happen when the bomb goes off. Either our literacy is universally wiped out and we are left with a total literate incapacity; or our most highly literate are wiped out, since the susceptibility of an individual to the effects of the bomb is proportional to the degree of literacy. [Here the president lowered his voice and said under his breath: And then we'll know who was right in the Leavis–Snow controversy.] In this event our civilization will be in the hands of the nearly illiterate and middle management. Or, if by some stratagem or miscalculation the litron bomb has a random though devastating effect, we may be left with a tiny minority of the highly literate and an equal number of all the other grades of literacy, but with the vast majority reduced to talking to one another.

In the event of a highly literate elite being left, the rebuilding of our civilization, or at least its maintenance, seems a likely long-term possibility. The effect will be like an enormously extended postal strike. There will, of course, be normal service for the few. But these literate few will bear the brunt of the maintenance of civilization. So they will need the rewards that come with a stranglehold on knowledge and the means of destruction.

In the event that it should be the highly literate that are wiped out (in their literate parts, that is) the recovery of our knowledge will be a very slow and uncertain matter indeed. We will find ourselves in much the same state as the world after the destruction of the library at Alexandria . . . hundreds of dark years until we can regain (if we ever do) anything like our previous state.

But the most disturbing possibility is that of the complete success of the litron bomb, the complete loss of literacy for now and all future generations on Earth. We would still retain the knowledge we have, of course. But it would henceforth have to be orally transmitted. And its propagation and expansion and retention orally seems to pose some very great organizational problems. Furthermore, if numeracy is included in the destructive impact of the litron bomb, then the problem is many orders of magnitude greater. For, although we shall have telephones, we will not be able to either look up a number or dial or touch-tone one. Similarly all of our calculators and to a considerable degree our computers will be useless to us. We can, of course, before the darkness ensues, attempt to convert all our devices to responding to sound rather than touch. Thus all our indexes will have to be orally imbedded in some memory system not dependent on letters or numbers in written or printed form. We are praying that simple on–off states in switching devices are not treated by the litron bomb as 1 and 0. Because if the effect of the bomb is in fact by means of attacking all overt or covert binary devices, then our digital computer technology is as much at risk as are our brains. We cannot believe at this date that this is so, since we have no idea how our brains handle data, particularly literate data. But should the mechanisms prove to be similar for digital devices and our own brains, then our indexing and calculating problems are immense.

I have already ordered a calling up of all "calculating boys" and "calculating girls" to be pressed into defense service. They are to learn to do their calculating only from oral cues if they presently do not do so. Similarly I have our armies scouring the world for mnemonists to function as indexes and libraries. We shall, of course, have to provide these vital individuals with special privileges, since their future tasks will be so onerous. Also, we are presently compiling a version of *Who's Who* called *Who Knows What* to be memorized in the first instance. And taxi drivers are being specially trained to find addresses over the entire world in the absence of maps and written addresses.

Finally, I am having three billion "Tell a Friend What You Know Tonight" buttons made up to launch this world wide oral knowledge campaign.

I need not say what is obvious to you – that many groups on Earth are in favor of the litron bomb and its effects. These people believe in the essential privacy of knowledge and in its privileged access to the knower. I'm afraid we shall have to round them all up and put them, at least for the time being, in detention camps where they will be given generous doses of truth serum and made to watch Ibsen plays.

Of course, a litron bomb can take many forms. It need not be sent to us by the Alpha Centaurians. We are perfectly capable of fashioning one for ourselves. There have been such bombs in the past. There will probably be such bombs in the future. Two obvious historical instances are the burning of the library at Alexandria and subsequent loss of the Hellenistic culture, with only a slow and partial recovery after 1100 or so due to the interaction of Arabic and Christian cultures in southern Europe, and the decline of Islam itself under the dual impact of war and religious fundamentalism in the middle medieval period. The only thing we have not devised so far is a permanent paralysis of our literate powers.

While any decline in the general levels of literacy and numeracy is probably reprehensible in the short run, and while any significant decline in the levels of literacy of the literate elite is probably reprehensible in the short and the long run, one can also imagine advantages of the shaking-up effect that one or other of these declines might have. For example, the loss or partial loss of objective knowledge, where such a knowledge serves or is thought to serve an important social end, could mean not only the rediscovery of old modes of thought but the invention of new modes that far surpass the old ones in force and generality. Something like this must be attributed to the Renaissance and to its scientific aftermath. It is possible that it was the very incompleteness of the material recovered from the ancient world that enabled Kepler, Copernicus, Galileo, and Newton and a spate of others to boldly fashion their own methods of observation, their own cosmological and physical problems, and their own methods of argument, both logical and mathematical.

In our own age there has been considerable discussion surrounding the question of a possible literacy decline due to both changes in teaching emphases and changes in attitudes toward children. This discussion has been widespread in the Western world and may be, at least in part, correlated with what is an objective fact, namely, the decline in the relative economic importance of the West. The only Western nation truly to keep up and perhaps enhance its economic position is an honorary Western nation only, namely, Japan. One might therefore speculate that it is not literacy that is in decline in the West, but the taste for perpetual innovation in technology – one of the clearly driving features of the rapid economic advance of Germany and the United States in the period spanning the Great Exhibition of 1850 and the Second World War. This brings us to our second major topic.

The impact of literacy on the individual

Whatever may be the relationship between literacy and the taste for perpetual technical innovation in a society generally, the relationship between these two things for an individual may be very complicated indeed. Literacy at all levels, including the highest and broadest, seems to be perfectly compatible with a taste for speculative innovation as well as with a taste for the working out of infinite technical details. Which of these two modes is dominant determines the flavor of the science and scholarship of an age. In a speculative age the pedantic scholar is a drudge and a bore. In an age engaged in amassing detail and in working out implications, the speculative set of mind is seen as unreliable. Of course, every age in fact has mixed modes of these. But there is always one emphasis or the other whether we talk of an age generally or of a particular discipline or a particular individual. In this century, physics, linguistics, and philosophy have oscillated strikingly between the innovative, speculative mode and the working out of details. If it could be shown that an increase of literacy at whatever level has the effect of changing an individual's taste with respect to either of these two modes, we would be able to claim a striking individual consequence of literacy.

It is part of the dispute between Karl Popper and Thomas Kuhn that while they both believe in the importance of literacy, they identify literacy with quite different modes of thought. Thus we find Popper identifying as the root of literate rationality, bold conjecture and refutation by argument – the literary mode of part of Western scientific thinking since Plato. Kuhn, on the other hand, emphasizes the Aristotle-inspired working out and recording of details *ad infinitum* on the basis of some paradigmatic approach to some subject matter. The crux of their dispute, at least from the vantage point of high-grade literacy, is which mode of literacy ought to be passed on in order best to further progress in an academic discipline.

The impact of a high level of literacy on an individual is probably of three major kinds. First is its role in freeing the mind to dwell on generalities by freeing the memory of details. The details can be written down, cataloged, indexed, placed on file cards. Second is its role in enabling the simultaneous consideration of many things. Marshall McLuhan argued in *Understanding Media* (1964) that an oral culture is a culture of simultaneity and that recent developments in electronic media by encouraging simultaneity, were tending to return us all to an oral mode of thought. In fact, this seems to be a sheer mistake. What is emphasized in an oral culture and by electronic media such as television is immediacy, not simultaneity. What the literate culture, at least in its high-grade forms, has permitted is the simultaneous consideration of multiple influences on any abstract referent, quite independent of immediacy. This is most obvious in the cases of mathematics and physics. But it seems equally obvious, after a moment's reflection, to be true in the case of literature as well. A printed document can be read and understood in much the same way regardless of the place or time in which it is read. Of course, I can conceive of lots of odd documents and situations that require qualification to the generalization here. But the point is that they have to be odd. It is exactly the reverse in the case of the oral presentation of a sequence of sentences in an ordinary setting, charged as the setting is with the emotions and the uniqueness of the moment, Here it is the odd case and the setting that enable the objectification of the material presented: the lecture in mathematics or physics, the description and naming of the patterns of the heavens, the presentation of formal, logical arguments and their refutation.

The third impact that high-grade literacy has on the powers of thought of an individual is in its permitting the indefinite extension of argument. This may be merely a function of limited human memory in the normal case, or it may be something more. In any event, it becomes possible for an argument to extend over 10, 20, 300, or 1,000 pages. And it permits the leisurely consideration and reconsideration of that argument. A history book may be a species of single argument to a single point, just as a single mathematical theorem may take 300 pages to expound and prove. Perhaps with a certain simple augmentation of our powers of memory such things could be done orally. But unless this infinite memory was effortless, our powers of critical appraisal of such argument would be likely to remain rudimentary in the extreme.

In summary, then, the impact of high-grade literacy on the thought of an individual is of three kinds: It frees the mind to dwell on generalities by freeing it from remembering necessary but encumbering details; it enables the simultaneous consideration of numerous connections; and it permits the indefinite extension of argument.

The impact of elementary literacy

There is no reason to suppose that literacy, in its elementary forms, has any of these three effects. A child who can read a few words or sentences in a Dick and Jane primer is not significantly different, except in that particular respect, from one who cannot as yet do so. In fact, at the elementary levels, the mind is so engaged with the sheer effort of sounding out a word or of recognizing it, or of printing it in something like an acceptable spelling, that no dwelling on anything but the immediate situation is possible. Even when a certain fluency of reading and writing is achieved, the three main advantages of high-grade literacy do not automatically follow. Although high-grade literacy presupposes elementary literacy, it does not reduce to it by any means. Indeed, being able to enjoy the advantages of high-grade literacy is so little an automatic matter that a long and arduous apprenticeship is involved, usually in a discipline of the kind that the universities encompass. And even then these advantages become automatic only in the context of that discipline.

Elementary literacy does, of course, enable many things that could not otherwise be easily managed without other, more complicated technical aids. A message to be understood by somebody else at a later date is the most obvious elementary example. Here we have the possibility of making an oral message time-independent. Until the advent of the miniature cassette recorder, the written message was the only way of doing this. Also elementary literacy, to the degree that spelling and sentence form are standardized, contributes to objectifying what was said. (See Chapter 13.) The immediate situation

and emotional tones of an utterance are removed and the interpretation of the utterance approaches more nearly a standard interpretation. It is only in the deliberate poetic use of written language that
this process is reversed.

It is not such a stupid prejudice to think that people who have
become literate in this elementary sense have been thereby changed
in certain socially useful ways. In particular, there appears to be a
natural analogy between the standardization and orderliness of
elementary literacy and the standardization and orderliness required
of an elementary industrial worker. There is, I think, considerable
truth to the notion that the mass movement to universal elementary
literacy that swept Europe and North America from the 1850s until
the Second World War was connected with such an analogy being
drawn – sometimes explicitly – by school promoters (Prentice, 1977).

In our own age this thinking has been carried to the whole world
by UNESCO, which began its campaign to wipe out illiteracy world-
wide in 1965. In a paper I presented to a conference at the University
of Leicester on the general topic of literacy, education, and society
in post-Reformation Europe, I judged UNESCO's premises as follows:

Perhaps the most striking feature of UNESCO discussion on literacy since
1965, when a campaign to wipe out world illiteracy got going, is that it is
remarkably little based on either experiment or historical precedents. Rather,
in spite of Adam Curle's careful warnings in 1964, action seems as much
based on self-evident axioms and hope as on anything else. UNESCO assumes
that literacy is a good thing – more latterly, functional literacy. Furthermore,
in no clearly defined or understood way poverty, disease, and general
backwardness are believed self-evidently connected with illiteracy; progress,
health, and economic well-being are equally self-evidently connected with
literacy. UNESCO is committed to what amounts to a modernization theory
to the effect that economic progress follows upon a change in the man from
illiterate to literate, preferably in one generation, and, even better, in the
very same man. It is presupposed that such a change will lead, if not
immediately then inevitably, to such changes and values in a society that
economic progress – and in its train good health, longevity, and, perhaps
peace – is possible. (Winchester, 1980)

In the remainder of that paper I went on to argue that, at least in
European experience, universal elementary literacy was not connected with the industrialization of the nations of Europe as cause,
but rather as effect in the first instance. The increased capacity of
European nations to pay the costs of schooling because of their
industrializing activities and the ideals that the aftermath of the

French Revolution had spread to the distant corners of the continent tended to make universal elementary literacy plausible as a national goal. Of course, once school systems were in place, the very emphasis on regularity and order required by the process (as it was then conceived) of inculcating literacy may have rendered people much easier and more successful factory fodder.

It is possible that the UNESCO literacy promoters are aware that at least historically they have put the cart before the horse. And it is also possible that, like our own nineteenth-century school promoters, their concern was largely with what they expected to be deep personal changes in those who learned to read and write in a school setting that emphasized order and method. As Susan Houston (1974) has argued, in Ontario the main concern of nineteenth-century school promoters was to wipe out "crime, poverty, and ignorance" at one blow by means of their literacy campaign. The UNESCO rhetoric is very similar to the mid-1800s' rhetoric.

Do we have any historical reasons to think that any changes were made in individuals just by the fact that they learned to read and write and count in an elementary fashion? Carter Njovana's (1981) recent study of the impact of elementary schooling on Botswana's traditional society is one among many recent efforts that suggest that even the elementarily literate person in a traditional society is more likely to leave his local village and migrate to a city seeking work than his illiterate neighbor. I have recently been looking at Swedish migration into towns in the late eighteenth and early nineteenth centuries, a time when the entire Swedish population could read with some fluency. The migration rates are astonishingly high in a society that used the religious monopoly on literacy to maintain social control of a remarkably rigid kind. This sort of historical evidence certainly suggests some differences between the literate and the nonliterate as regards their picture of the world and their possibilities in it, at least on the average. However, the difference may be as much related to the content of what was conveyed in the process of becoming literate as in the mere possession of the elementary literate skills themselves. Also, the astonishingly high per capita migration rates of Swedes to the United States and Canada after the 1850s may have been due, at least in part, to their having no great difficulties imagining a new world and a new beginning as well as their having no difficulty reading the propaganda blurbs circulated by the steamship companies.

These sorts of historical considerations suggest a kind of social and individual impact of elementary literacy. But again, the impact may be entirely due to the kind of content which that kind of literacy made available. If even that could be shown, that would be sufficiently remarkable.

I will summarize my remarks in this chapter by roughly reversing the order of the argument. First of all, we have to distinguish between high-grade literacy and elementary literacy in the sense that high-grade literacy presupposes elementary literacy but does not reduce to it. Elementary literacy is being able to read or to read and write or to read and compose in ordinary ways. High-grade literacy is what university disciplines are all about. The possession of elementary literacy in an individual is not likely in and of itself to have any special effects. However, it does enable, when exercised, such things as time-independent communication with others and, by means of the content potentially made available, could lead to a change or expansion of an individual's picture of the world.

The impact of high-grade literacy on an individual is enormous, for its possession enables the individual to escape from the tyranny of memory as regards details, permitting, at least in principle, the dwelling on generalities, the simultaneous consideration of numerous logical and empirical connections, and the indefinite expansion of argument. But to gain these benefits, long and arduous training in the bookish disciplines is necessary. Thus the importance of the university.

The social consequences of elementary literacy as such are not well understood. Certainly universal elementary literacy will not, in and of itself, lead to industrialization or the banishment of crime and poverty. Once industrialization has taken root, however, its further expansion may be connected with a society's having a population with at least an elementary level of literacy.

The social consequences of high-grade literacy are immense because of the impact high-grade literacy has both on the individual and on the possibilities for social organization that the presupposed elementary literacy (not necessarily widespread) permits. The essential social value of high-grade literacy, however, lies in its ability to make objective knowledge, including science and literature, available, in principle at least, to anybody with elementary literacy who is willing to make the effort to upgrade his or her knowledge and who has the wit to do so.

Because of these individual and social benefits that literacy really does convey to us, the impact of a litron bomb would be rather devastating. However, an oral society with remarkable powers of memory and great longevity could conceivably create a world much clumsier, but in many other respects very similar to our own.

REFERENCES

Houston, S. The impetus to reform: Urban crime, poverty, and ignorance in Ontario, 1850–1875. Ph.D. dissertation, University of Toronto, 1974.

McLuhan, Marshall. *Understanding media: The extensions of man.* New York: McGraw-Hill, 1964.

Njovana, C. A. Perceptions of educational objectives: Problems and solutions in Botswana. Ph.D. dissertation, University of Toronto, 1981.

Prentice, A. *The school promoters: Education and social class in mid-nineteenth century Upper Canada.* Toronto: McClenland and Stewart, 1977.

Whitehead, A. N. *Adventures of ideas.* Cambridge: Cambridge University Press, 1933.

Winchester, I. How many ways to universal literacy? Paper, presented at the conference on "Literacy, Education, and Society in Post-Reformation Europe, with Special Reference to Swedish Sources," University of Leicester, March 1980.

4

The concept of literacy in print and film

MICHAEL COLE and HELEN KEYSSAR

Preliminary comments

Literacy is conventionally understood as the ability to use graphic symbols to represent spoken language. Literacy so conceived is one important class of mediated human activity. It is a form of literacy based on print. In addition, in ordinary language, literacy often refers to the ability to interpret or negotiate understanding within any mode of communication. Thus we speak of film literacy or music literacy or computer literacy, and we mean by these terms the ability to understand and explain film or music or computers. When someone says that she is musically illiterate, we think we know what she means; she cannot make knowledgeable interpretations of events presented in the medium. Insofar as the ability to *use symbols* is essential to literacy, then it is clear that the second, increasingly commonsense notion of the concept is inaccurate or incomplete. To reconcile the technical and everday notions of literacy, the whole notion of the relation between use of a medium of communication and "literacy" in that medium must be modified. Otherwise we cannot coherently understand literacy as an activity common to media other than print.

Webster's provides a dual definition of *literate*. To be literate is to "be able to read and write," but it is also to be "well versed in literature or creative writing." This contrast implies that there is more than one pattern of interacting with text, just as there is more than one way that text relates to its referents; moreover, these different patterns of interaction implicate different consequences. In this chapter, we begin to generate a concept of literacy that is sufficient and appropriate to a variety of media in relation to their contexts of use. We then pose questions about the applicability of this concept of literacy to media other than print. The subject of our investigation is the boundaries within which different forms of mediated human activity share a *common* structure such that increasing use of that structure to interpret communicative events represents greater literacy in the medium.

Starting from our current understandings of the consequences of engaging in activity involving print, we consider the extent to which there exists a general theory of mediated activity within which print, film, drama, television, and other "media" constitute particular configurations. By contrasting some shared understandings about print literacy and understandings about other forms of mediated human activity, we gain three kinds of benefits: (1) Our knowledge of print literacy might be applied to help us understand mediated activity involving other media; (2) accepted generalizations about the nature of other mediated activities might give us insight into print literacy; and (3) we might make progress toward a general theory of mediated human activity.

Given our basic concern with the application of a concept of literacy to media other than print, it would be appropriate to discuss any and all types of media. In this chapter, we have chosen to focus our attention on film and, to a lesser degree, on theater, both because these forms appear to challenge some common assumptions about literacy and because issues relevant to film literacy illuminate both the concept of literacy itself and fundamental questions about mediation in contemporary societies. That film and theater are *directed*, that is, call forth overtly an act or series of acts of mediation, is particularly important, because it emphasizes the interactive and partial natures of these forms. Problems of interpretation, of audience, of historical context, and of point of view come forward immediately when we approach the idea of film literacy. In addition, the physical resemblance of the projections of film to "the real world" presents key questions about the process by which the spectator interacts with the medium.

To some degree, the specific instances of film and theater that we will discuss are coincidental and arguably eccentric as choices for analyses. Our discussion began with an old chestnut; how can a play written four hundred years ago be said to create the same response in a modern audience that it did (say) in Shakespeare's day? Our explorations of possible responses led to the discovery that we had had parallel experiences with the text of Shakespeare's *Romeo and Juliet* and the Franco Zeffirelli film drawn from that text. Somewhat later, we discovered antithetical responses to Robert Altman's film *Nashville*, provoking us to consider the possibility of different kinds or degrees of film literacy. The relative accessibility of Zeffirelli's *Romeo and Juliet* contrasted forcefully with the relative inaccessibility of *Nashville*. This contrast provoked our discussion of the relevance of filmic modes of narration and point of view, each of which has instructive parallels in literacy theory. We turn to these films in this chapter not because either or both are archetypical or perfect as objects for analyses of film literacy but because together they constrained and revealed central questions about our concepts of literacy.

In pursuing this line of inquiry, we are mindful of important work that explores differential forms (or bias) of activity associated with different media (Barthes, 1977; Burke, 1973; McLuhan, 1962; Salomon, 1979; and many others). At the same time, statements about properties specific to a medium *imply* that there is a general theory applying to all media, such that special cases and their relationships to each other can be systematically understood. We want to continue the inquiry into the nature of that theory. As an entry point, we will summarize what we consider to be a working consensus concerning some important features of mediated activity involving print. Next we will propose some very general propositions concerning mediated human activity, and we will briefly apply these principles to print. Then we will present informal accounts of our individual reactions to reading *Romeo and Juliet*, the Zeffirelli film, and the film *Nashville*. Finally, we will use the contrast between film and print as mediated activities to articulate the relevance of a unified communications framework for understanding of specific "media effects."

A rough consensus concerning print

During recent decades there has been much and varied scholarly activity intended to describe and explain the impact of print literacy on individuals, the activities they engage in, and the societies they live in. Coming from such diverse sources as art history (Schmandt-Besserat, 1978), anthropology (Goody, 1977), history (Ong, 1971), and psychology (Bruner & Olson, 1977–78; Scribner & Cole, 1981), we find general adherence to the following summary of the consequences of literacy.

The introduction of literate devices into a society changes the actual and possible interactions between people and the world. These changes can occur at all levels of aggregation of human activity. That is, they can be found in the kinds of trade that people can engage in, the size of the social units that can reasonably be held together, the way that the transmission of culture is organized for the young, and so forth.

Insofar as thinking is understood to be "the process of internalizing the ways of acting, imagining and symbolizing that exist in [one's] culture" (Bruner, Olver, & Greenfield, 1966), changes in trade and political organization (that is, changes in people's normal intercourse with each other and their environments) will go hand in hand with changes in intellectual processes (Goody, 1977).

When characterizing the mental concomitants of changes in human interaction wrought by interaction with literate technologies, special attention is focused on those interactions where the given literate technologies are central components – for example, systems of accounting (Schmandt-Besserat, 1978; Goody, 1977), laws and rules, the transmission of important cultural knowledge (Havelock, 1976), and knowledge-seeking activities (McLuhan, 1962). This is not to say that interactions where no literate device is present will not be affected by the presence of literacy in a society; such changes in the social order are strongly assumed to be present and crucial to understanding the consequences of literacy. However, in terms of *psychological process* hypotheses, interactions directly involving literate technologies are the primary focus.

Within those contexts, where the technology of writing is an element in the interaction, literacy is conceived to exert its effect by producing a *functional reorganization* of the system of activities; it is in freeing language of its spatial and temporal restrictions that literacy has its primary effects. Crudely put, literacy is said to act primarily through its ability to hold information intact over periods of time and to transmit information faithfully over distance.[1] Using the relevant psychological terminology for the moment, literacy functions to change the relation between memory and such processes as attention, inference, and classification. Unloosed from the mental burden of remembering, people are freer to put more mental resources into reasoning about the information at hand, logical syllogisms can be used to clarify relations among propositions, and taxonomically organized category systems are rendered "visible."

There is also agreement that the causal impact of literate technology is not unidirectional from technology to activity. Activities provide greater and lesser opportunities for particular literate technologies to be effective. As recounted in Goody (1977) or Schmandt-Besserat (1978), the interplay of socioeconomic and literate–technological forces represents a classical case of dialectical interacting systems that are always incipiently in a process of change.

Unresolved issues. Our ability to give a general account of the consequences of literacy for which there is rather widespread agreement
provokes us to turn our attention to the many issues in dispute within
this general concensus. To what extent does literacy do more than
enable certain functional reorganizations of activity? Does it also bias
the structure of the interactions of which it is a part (Olson, 1977;
McLuhan, 1962)? How general are the changes wrought by literacy
within a literate culture or literate individuals (Scribner & Cole,
1981)? What are the social and economic conditions necessary for
literacy to enter into the ongoing organization of activities in a
productive way (Scribner, 1981)? To what extent can the changes
wrought by literacy be considered to reflect a general direction in
human history or individual development (Goody, 1977)?

It will not be easy to resolve disputes over these questions, in part
because they are interconnected with each other in just the ways that
print is interconnected with the individuals and societies that use it.
One course is to propose general principles that might apply, with
appropriate transformations, to any form of mediated activity. We
take this to be the effort of such writers as McLuhan (1962). Another
important endeavor is to work out a number of cases in great detail,
seeking in each case to explicate general mechanisms as well as
possible. Such work exists, as our brief review indicates. If the first
approach strikes the average academic as speculation, often tending
to the wild side, the second strikes the general reader as unnecessarily
detailed and labored. In the remainder of this chapter, we will
attempt to avoid tendentious detail, yet keep our generalizations
tethered to, if not tied down to, grounded arguments and concrete
instances.

Some common propositions about mediated human activity

While there is no prototheory of mediated human activity in the
sense that there is a prototheory of print literacy, there are several
key propositions concerning mediated activity that enjoy wide accep-
tance. The following propositions appear most powerful to us at the
present stage of our thinking.

Proposition 1. Of the knowledge we have of the world very little comes
from scenes in which we have literally participated. In this sense, we
have little direct experience of the world. Rather, much (some would
say all) of our knowledge is obtained *indirectly*. It is not *immediately*
experienced; rather, it is *constructed* – it is *mediated*.

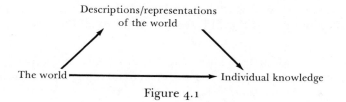

Figure 4.1

This understanding is represented differently by different writers in different traditions. Whether from semiotics, literary criticism, or psychology, this basic idea can be represented in terms of Figure 4.1. In this figure, individual knowledge is depicted as arising from direct experience of the physical world ("raw experience") and from indirect knowledge (mediated experience) that comes through prior representations. Even in scenes where we may be considered immediate participants, interaction may be considered mediated insofar as understandings coded in language constrain activity or one or more "media" are instrumental to the activity (Percy, 1975; Olson, 1976).

Proposition 2. Insofar as our knowledge is mediated, it is an *incomplete* rendition of the original event. This incompleteness arises from two primary sources:

First, any representation/description of the world is necessarily an incomplete rendition (re-presentation) of the original. It is not only that a picture is worth a thousand words, but that no amount of talk (and no picture) can completely replicate the events it represents; the most precise verbal or visual presentation of the world is limited by the resources of the actor and the forms of the medium.

Second, an account arising from any interaction between people is incomplete, because a communicative verbal formulation is always and necessarily a compromise between what the speaker experienced and what can be coded in terms of prior knowledge of the world such that part of the referred-to events are now understood in common (Holquist, 1981). This incompleteness has many ramifications, among them the very possibility of distinguishing the self and others, which is the very motivational force of communication itself.

These two sources of incompleteness interact to increase the overall uncertainty in the system of mediation as it relates to the match between some supposed state of reality ("the original") and some understood version of it (the mediated representation-as-understood). From this incompleteness issues a central paradox common to all forms of mediated human activity: It is very hard to figure out what is going on in the world, but we all do so all the time.

Proposition 3. Mediated knowledge is not only incomplete; it is incomplete in ways that reflect the selective factors operating at the time of the events that were encoded. In this respect, mediation always reflects a point of view. It is in this sense "biased" to coincide with the systems of understandings that guided its selection process. These systems are shaped by prior history and current context and are intimately tied to language.

Insofar as mediation is successful, we are led to say that something has been established in common between a state of the world (raw experience) and the individual, or between two individuals: We say that *communication* has occurred. Here we take *communication* in its root sense of "putting in common."[2]

Applying our three propositions to print

No extended discussion of print literacy is necessary because one or more of our basic propositions has been presupposed in much of the research we summarized in the earlier section on writing. However, it may prove useful to reformulate the consensus concerning print literacy in the current framework, at least with respect to its psychological consequences, which are our chief concerns here.

1. *Indirectness.* The basically mediated nature of literate activity is taken for granted. Not even pictographic systems of writing are considered direct copies of the referents of writing.

2. *Incompleteness.* Discussion here focuses on the way in which different models of representation (orthographies) interact with language forms and the communication demands in society to produce different systems of literacy (Glushko, 1979; Hatano, 1982; Scribner & Cole, 1981). So, for example, a syllabic script like Vai may be optimal with respect to speed of acquisition and adequate to its terms. Yet its ·syllabic structure may reduce its intelligibility outside close social bonds, reducing the possibilities of wider use (Scribner & Cole, 1981).

3. *Selectivity.* The selectivity in the way that writing systems permit or promote various representations and processing skills has also evoked discussion; argument centers on the nature of the selection constraints that different technologies of representation and reproduction foster. (Some, like Havelock, 1976, argue that

the special representative powers of the alphabet enable totally new forms of thought; see also Olson, 1977.)

This discussion could be expanded at this point to explore print literacy in terms of our three propositions about mediated activity. Instead we will apply them to the notion of literacy in film and then return to print in a more general theoretical context.

Literacy and film

The concept of literacy has frequently been applied to media other than print.[3] But theory in this area is still in its infancy, and contradictions abound. Thus, while film theorists may discuss the knowledge that enables various "readings" of a flim, Seldes (1960) can assert that "there is no illiteracy in film." When such contradictory statements in otherwise reasonable discourse arise we immediately begin to reexamine our initial assumption. It is really useful to speak of "reading film"? Does the concept of literacy apply untransformed?

As a means of sharpening the issues, we will recount episodes that illustrate our concerns with the applicability of concepts from the study of print to the study of film. We chose these encounters not for their decisiveness with respect to a comprehensive theory; we have no such theory to offer. But we believe that they raise significant questions that such a theory should address and suggest some problems and approaches that could usefully be applied to the study of print literacy.

"Romeo and Juliet." Both authors of this chapter encountered Shakespeare's *Romeo and Juliet* first in a printed version and much later in a film directed by Franco Zeffirelli. Kayssar, a literature major on her way to a career in drama, came to the play with a different orientation than Cole, whose liberal arts education led to a career in psychology. But their reactions to the printed play and then the film, as recalled in the discussions that provoked this chapter, were similar in many respects.

Cole summarized his experience as follows: Romeo and Juliet are sufficiently universal symbols in our society that it is impossible for me to remember my first encounter with the *idea* of Romeo and Juliet. It was a part of doing something else. In high school, however, I clearly remember encountering Shakespeare's play in a literature class. My main response to reading it was slight annoyance. I found Shakespearean English difficult to understand; I looked upon Romeo and Juliet as a couple of headstrong teenagers who killed themselves.

Now, wiser about, if not freer from, the fear of disapproval of my opinions about Romeo and Juliet, I will add that I thought they were real dopes to do it.

The situation did not change much for many years. As I became more sophisticated in the ways of academe, I learned that *Romeo and Juliet* is considered a *tragedy*, a form of play in which human frailties lead to a lot of unhappiness for decent people. Since the only character fault I attributed to Romeo and Juliet was stupidity (not a trait calculated to evoke strong efforts at empathy), I wondered at the play's reputation. *Othello* terrified me. I readily accepted it as a tragedy, not as a teenage romance.

Thus prepared, I went to see Zeffirelli's filmed version of *Romeo and Juliet*. It was a revelation in the sense that it made manifest for me *precisely* the tragic possibilities of all-consuming passion, and it did so in terms that felt very certain and were certainly very strong. I was captured first by the fight among the boys. As the action took its course, and the dangers to which the lovers were exposing themselves became (as they say) apparent to me, I became more and more uncomfortable, reaching a point where I wanted to reach out and say, "No! Stop! Don't do it!"

Keyssar summarized her experience as follows: I was not attracted to the play, the characters, or the world of *Romeo and Juliet* when I first encountered it in a high school literature class nor when I encountered it for the second time in college. The Shakespearean verse did not in itself confound me (I was trained to read poetry), but little in the language or my instruction about the play engaged me. My early encounters with the play – both my own readings and what my teachers said about it – stressed the antagonism between the two families. I found that all rather foolish; I also found it unconvincing that these two young people would end up dead because of their parents' stupidity.

Some years after my first encounter with *Romeo and Juliet* I, too, saw the Zeffirelli film of the play, and I, too, was engaged by the film in a way I had not thought was possible. The physical beauty and sensuality of the images of the young lovers were so strong that the possibility of their deaths was unbearable. I have almost no memory of their families from the film; the warring Capulets and Montagues were treated by Zeffirelli just as my naïve readings had suggested they should be – as the aggravating cultural context. Zeffirelli captured my attention from the beginning by setting the world of *Romeo and Juliet* in the adolescent world of Romeo, his friends, and his foes, not in the culture of their parents. I did not particularly like or admire Romeo, but I was drawn to his vitality and the vigor of his relationship to his male friends. And that energy was easily reattached to Juliet. I felt myself caught in their fervor of reckless abandon, and while I, as spectator, like Mike, wanted to say, "Stop!" I also wanted neither of them to stop because to stop was to arrest their passion as well as mine.

In the simplest terms, I was also attracted by *Romeo and Juliet*'s unabashed eroticism. I, too, felt that pain, that sense of irretrievable loss, that has something to do with the art of tragedy, because the film made me feel what death was all about: It was about absence, and I recognized that absence because the human beings on the screen had been made so present to me.

A second case: "Nashville." How are we to understand the different experiences that resulted from the two forms in which we encountered *Romeo and Juliet*, the written script and the film?

Perhaps a sheer increase in "immediacy" is the reason; we were helped to a Shakespearean response by the physical, evocative properties of color film. McLuhan's distinction between hot and cool media might be a sufficient summary of the two kinds of experience. Perhaps the increasing complexity of each of our own lives over time enabled a more mature interpretation. Perhaps. But these are insufficient constraints on our speculation. To complicate matters, and constrain ourselves, we will include two more accounts, this time of our viewing of Robert Altman's film *Nashville*.

Cole saw *Nashville* in the company of Keyssar in the context of teaching a course on film. He spent a considerable time trying to figure out what was happening. A lot of American popular culture was displayed on the screen, both music and menace. He admired a variety of technical filmmaking achievements. He smiled at the irony of the songs. But he did not like the film, and he felt that he didn't understand it. He came away remembering swatches of action and character. He doubted, as he does on such occasions, that there was all that much to understand. It was not a particularly pleasant experience.

Keyssar's reaction was significantly different. She was exhilarated from the opening credits to the closing boom. She heard the introductory voice-over as a barker's voice announcing a central event of the film, the political campaign. When a garage door covered with the political candidate's logo was raised, she interpreted it as "the curtain going up." Drama is her thing; she liked the gesture.

As the film continued, she noted elements in the film that are not a part of Cole's account. A sign saying "THE BANK" is partially obscured so that it reads "HE BANK"; almost everything in the film is colored red, white, and/or blue; other colors, yellow in particular, take on a coherent signification specific to and mediated by this film.

Keyssar found herself caught up in the kaleidoscopic pattern of the situations portrayed in the film so that the film as a whole became a moving experience. Cole was never comparably engaged. Both were made uncomfortable by a scene in which a vulnerable girl is manipulated into doing a strip tease before a room full of Nashville businessmen. Both reacted with ironic understanding as the strip scene is intercut with a sequence in which an archetypically laid-back male singer croons to five different women, each of whom momentarily believes that the singer is addressing her – and then perceives differently. Cole and Keyssar then held in common some perceptions of and responses to much of *Nashville*, but the differences in their experience were as marked as the differences between their readings and viewings of *Romeo and Juliet*.[4]

Applying the basic propositions to film

In order to keep this discussion of the basic propositions relevant to the initial print orientation of this essay, we will select applications that seem to us to speak most directly to questions of the consequences of literacy and to the notion of literacy itself.[5]

Is not film immediate? The strong sense of direct access to events represented in film is the central phenomenon of film theory. Barthes (1977) accounts for this sense of directness by referring to photographic images as *analogons*. An analogon is an image the structure of which replicates raw experience in ways that provoke specieswide recognition. In a restricted sense, film, based on photography, is comprised of a set of analogons for which "there is no necessity to set up a relay, that is to say a code, between the object and its image" (Barthes, 1977, p. 16). In this same restricted sense, film could be considered directed, unmediated access to some event.[6]

This sense of immediacy, whatever its applicability to a small photographic image, is too restricted to apply fruitfully to a film. A film, taken from beginning to end, cannot be considered an analogon precisely because the entirety is comprised of pieces, which are, at a minimum, a reduction of the whole. It is possible, of course, to place a camera at a fixed position and cause it to film a geographically and temporally restricted event. But this is not what filmmakers do. In an earlier era of filmmaking Pudovkin (1929/1970) declared the need for "clear selection, the possibility of the elimination of those insignificances that fulfill only a transition function and are always inseparable from reality, and of the retention only of climactic and dramatic points" (p. 93). Arnheim (1957) makes the same point: "From the time continuum of a scene [the filmmaker] takes only the parts that interest him, and of the spatial totality of objects and events he picks out only what is relevant. Some details he stresses, others he omits altogether" (p. 89).

These comments make clear the several important respects in which film is distinctly *not* an analgon, in Barthes's sense, and not a direct mode of communication in terms of our basic propositions concerning mediated activity:

1. Even a single, continuous piece of film is a selection because it does not provide its own context.
2. While it might be said that analgons "interpret themselves," an entire film does not; when a film does seem to "interpret itself," – that is, when analgons become signs – we can expect to find that the filmmaker's and viewers' notions of "relevance" of the analgons (in Arnheim's sense) coincide.
3. Instead of an analgon, a film is a complex *arrangement* of images that often transforms the interpretations of events represented, thereby changing the meaning of the analgons, considered as a system.
4. The necessary coexistence of selection and arrangement imply a "point of view" to the *entity* produced. In short, communication via film, no less than other forms of communication, is mediated.

What might film literacy be?

The notion of literacy applied to film must refer to more than the ability to recognize analgons. Film literacy is the ability to obtain meaning from the arrangements constructed by the filmmaker, in addition to the meaning obtainable "directly" from analgons. Borrowing from modern semiotic theorists, we will refer to recurring patterns of arrangements as codes.

A *hierarchy* of codes?

Film images are not the experience of the world reduced to the *image*. We know this to be true in a formal sense, but it is palpably true in the efforts of filmmakers to make films correspond more closely to real experience, as in the creation of 3-D films with complex sound systems (or in imaginative flights like Aldous Huxley's suggestion for "feelies").[7]

While the creation of 3-D films is a public manifestation of the shortcomings of film-as-unmediated-experience, a far more refined set of ideas concerning mediating mechanisms in film has grown up in the work of film innovators and film theoreticians. It has struck us in reviewing this work that it is possible to "rank" various film techniques for how closely they approximate a direct transmitter of their real-world referent.[8] We identify the following categories of image-making techniques that are prevalent in film and that seem to offer important distinctions with respect to the kind of mediated activity involved.

1. Archetypal codes. Here we have in mind images that are believed to evoke particular responses universally by virtue of primitive, universal, symbol systems. These may be produced either by techniques such as the use of camera angle (shooting up produces the sense of power in the superior part of the image) or by movement patterns of the actors (head bowed in mourning) (Ivanov, 1976).[9]

2. Psychophysical codes. Here we have in mind techniques such as the zoom, the closeup, and rapid cutting. These techniques all mimic in some way an aspect of our normal perception of the world such that (for example) a closeup arouses both the sense of attending to detail and the illusion of physical closeness. Yet research with children shows that totally naïve children who can follow the main story outline do not correctly interpret sequences where these devices play a prominent role (Salomon, 1979), indicating that some form of mediated interpretation is necessary. This same research indicates that these psychophysical codes are easily mastered; a little experience with television is enough to master them.

3. Cultural codes. A cultural code is an image that evokes a set of culturally linked concepts, although these concepts may not be directly named in the film. The red–white–blue versus yellow–blue color scheme in *Nashville* provides an excellent example of what we mean by a cultural code; red–white–blue signifies the Unites States, patriotism, the flag, and so on. In contrast, the color yellow is emptied of its conventional cultural signification of cowardice and reestablished as a new code specific to the film. When these codes are not explicitly tied to the film's story line, they may not be explicitly noted by the viewer.[10]

4. *Media and genre codes.* A clear example of such a code is the garage door going up at the beginning of *Nashville*. The "unmediated" interpretation of this event (e.g., the commonsense interpretation given it by Cole) is a garage door going up; Keyssar's interpretation (curtain going up) relies upon a system of events from theater, from which film is historically derived and with which film retains strong intellectual and stylistic ties.

5. *Theoretical codes.* It is difficult to be explicit about what we mean by a theoretical code. An accessible starting point is Metz's notion of the "language" of film, by which he means that system of codes that allows us to connect the various images that are *presented* and to *re*-present them to ourselves in the form of our interpretation of the film. The term *language* needs to be placed in quotation marks in this context because, as Metz (1974) points out, "It is not because the cinema is language that it can tell us such fine stories, but rather it has become language because it has told such fine stories" (p. 47).

In the telling of stories, the different kinds of codes provide us with different kinds of meaning, corresponding to different systems of constraints arising from the film and the audience, as our examples have shown. Recognizing that the interpretation of film cannot rest on any one system of codes in isolation gives us another link to the concept of literacy – for example, the ability to interpret the *system of codes* that the film offers. But as Metz's characterization of the origin of film language indicates, we cannot investigate that system independent of "the stories" that are its driving force. We must, in short, take into account the narrative that provides the environment for the system of codes.

Narrative structure

Earlier we spoke of *codes* as structures of meaning arising out of particular arrangements of photographic images. Starting, as we did, from Barthes's characterization of a photograph, discrete images and sounds appeared to be the obvious unit of analysis. But an individual image or sound may not be a viable or relevant basic unit of film. The term *analgon* might be usefully applied, in Barthes's sense, to units larger than a single photographic frame. *The shot* (a single, continuous piece of footage) is often considered a basic, meaning-bearing unit.

For purpose of this discussion, it is useful to point out that *events* have some of the properties of analogns; when the structure of an event in a film replicates the structure of our everyday experience, we "re-cognize" it; we have a ready-made interpretation or "schema" for it. These directly understood events are basic to our understanding of film literacy because these events provide the meaning structure within which the filmmaker can construct and embed codes.

The past decade has produced a significant body of psychological research on the way the processes of the comprehension and remembering of stories depend upon the structure of the events within them. Narratives characterized by structural features that deviate from the event structures of everyday life are more difficult to understand, more difficult to remember later, and less pleasant to interact with than stories that adhere to a relatively well specified (and perhaps universal) story schema (See Mandler, 1979, for a review). Thus, for example, a narrative in which there are several parallel developments, in which there are multiple points of view, in which the goals of the protagonists are not specified, or in which the temporal sequence of events is scrambled can be expected to be difficult to interpret; it may also be rated as low in quality by the majority of an ordinary audience. In simple terms, we find it unpleasant to struggle, and, failing to understand, we have a difficult time keeping things straight.

The codes we have been discussing are all experienced by the viewer in a context of the narrative portrayal of ongoing events. So film viewing can be seen to involve two mutually embedded systems of understanding. On the one hand are a set of codes that apply to processes common across events within a film and potentially common across films as well. On the other hand, we have our everyday schema for events in the world: people acting to get things done. These two aspects of knowledge and human interaction form the basis for our interactions with a film.[11]

This contrast is useful for interpreting the different responses of Cole and Keyssar to the two films. In *Romeo and Juliet* we have a conventionally structured narrative, one that we have some knowledge about even before we enter the theater; the narrative has become a part of our language and culture. Even if the "story" of Romeo and Juliet is unknown to us before entering the theater, after viewing the film we will be able to present some diachronic retelling of the film's tale. The varieties of film codes all work in support of a story that we understand; in Zeffirelli's film, they work powerfully indeed.

Romeo and Juliet presents an important contrast to *Nashville* in this respect. Each contains narrative elements, each gives rise to categories of understanding of a broad nature, and each suggests a significance that transcends the narrative. But they differ in their underlying strategies of creating meaning. *Romeo and Juliet* works *through* narrative to embody categories of understanding that operate on us very powerfully. We ponder the mystery of Shakespeare's ability to create a story powerful enough to transcend centuries.

Nashville works *through* a concept (a theory, if you prefer). The fragments of narrative interwoven into its structure are elements in the tapestry of that concept. The concept itself is difficult to formulate. Nashville is the name of a place, Romeo and Juliet are people. The film is not intended as a documentary about the place.

Nashville defies our tendency to make a temporally coherent story out of what we are seeing. Altman wants us to read the codes synchronically, without benefit of a strong narrative structure to carry us along. *Nashville's* narrative, narrowly understood, is about a political rally; there are within it many intertwining narratives whose connections to each other are not made obvious causally or temporally, except insofar as the cultural setting and the "political rally" narrative suggest connections. Their connection, we want to argue, is conceptual. Upon first viewing, it is very difficult to keep straight what is happening or to retell the "story." In short, *Nashville* fits the description of a poorly structured narrative. We can expect it to cause difficulties of recall, and hence difficulty in linking (already difficult-to-interpret) events late in the film to events early on. We can also expect the effort to be frustrating, producing negative feelings about the film.[12]

Insofar as a viewer knows a variety of film codes ("curtain going up," for example) he or she has greater access to the general system of constraints that are structuring the narrative. We can expect such viewers to "take more out of" narratively less coherent films and to find them less frustrating. In fact, Keyssar's reaction shows that for some the film can be gripping. Cole's reaction, on the other hand, is a clear case where the film codes were not sufficiently well understood to allow a satisfying interaction with the object.[13]

Comparing print and film

The points of contrast between the notions of literacy in print and film are evident. At the same time, there is an overriding similarity;

literacy in both print and film refers to the ability to reconstruct narrative, some account of the sequence of events or items of information, or to construct some concept relating diverse episodes. Yet print and film clearly represent different "systems of literacy," different "galaxies," to use McLuhan's term. Depending upon the overall communicative task of which they are a part, we can expect film and print to display different strengths and weaknesses as communicative devices. Exploring this galaxy is a risky business. There is a tendency, on the one hand, to become so fascinated with the intricacies of individual systems that the larger systems that form and reform them drop from view. It is equally tempting to become so entranced by one's depth of focus that the description that comes back is hardly encompassable in human narrative, fragmenting language and theory into an uneven mosaic (McLuhan being the outstanding case in point).

Given the dangers, we want to illustrate some of the ways that our comparison has influenced us to think about literacy in our respective areas of concern.

The social roles of print and film

In thinking about film and print as systems of mediation, we find it useful to consider them in very broad social–functional terms, focusing upon their respective roles in human affairs. Writing systems grew up initially as devices for counting and naming with a gradual expansion of economic production and trade. The spread of writing to supplant oral information-storage devices for narrative is a very recent innovation connected with the invention and spread of *alphabetic* writing systems. When combined with an efficient way of representing number, writing served as the central tool of physical science theory, upon which the political power and economic attainments of the last 1,000 years have been built.

The research on "consequences of literacy" reviewed earlier in this chapter focuses understandably on the combined social, theoretical, and psychological changes that literacy has produced in those arenas of life where it has long been recognized as instrumental to well-being. But this emphasis on socioeconomic instrumentality seems to have restricted both the notion of literacy and the domains to which these theoretical insights can be applied. Forgotten are the consequences of extending writing systems to represent prose that is *not* exclusively intended to operate in the political–economic–technical arena. We need to recall that the earliest extension of alphabetic technology to prose was to write down the *Iliad* and the *Odyssey*. A brief consideration of the social function and technologies of these epics suggests that they lie partly in the domain of "instrument" and partly in the domain that we will call, for lack of a better term, "entertainment." On the one hand, Homer was treated as a kind of oral encyclopedia of Greek culture, the "text" that all Greek children needed to learn (Havelock, 1976). Many kinds of instrumentality appear here: teachings about the tactics of battle, the proper behavior of soldiers, kin obligation, as well as complex theory of the origins of the world and the Greeks' place in it. While we may be unable to appreciate the didactic utility of knowing who went to Troy with how many men and horses, we can readily appreciate the relevance of the accounts of bravery, loyalty, friendship, and fear – they remain a central part of our own cosmology.

From scholarly detective work (Lord, 1960) and fictional recreation (Renault, 1978) we know something about the nature of the occasions when such epics were performed. We know that their "recitation" was a musical as well as an oral construction; the tales-as-produced were complicated combinations of politics, poetry, and music, formula-bound memory and occasion-specific construction. We also know that they were intended to *entertain* as well as *instruct*. In fact, it can be plausibly argued that is precisely the mixture of these two functions that vexed Plato in the *Republic*. Contemporary research on the consequences of literacy seems to have retained Plato's distaste for literacy in which entertainment elements are central. We don't approve of mixing business and pleasure.

From the current perspective this bifurcation of functions and theories is not likely to be productive. While each new medium may evolve in the context of a specific sphere of human activity, it is erroneous, in fact and in theory, to accept uncritically the "doing–appreciating" antinomy. The ancient and active fields of rhetoric and literary criticism have long been as concerned with the qualities of the doing as with the narrowly utilitarian characteristics of inter-action via writing. Aristotle's *Rhetoric* nicely conjoined these concerns, even as Plato's *Republic* was driving a wedge between them. The theory of literacy implicit in the *Rhetoric* focuses on increasing the degree of structuring that the reader can take from text; at the same time, Aristotle develops a theory of what the writer can build into that for specific communicative purposes (Keyssar, 1977). Very similar efforts and converging theories are to be found in the arts as well (Gombrich, 1960; Arnheim, 1957). In the best of this tradition, "being well versed in" is seen as one aspect of the larger doing, as when Kenneth Burke (1973) speaks of literature as "equipment for living." By providing models of strategic encounters between people and their predicaments, literature provides us with "recipes" for dealing with life. In this respect, film and print share many common characteristics.

Concluding comments

These comments bring us back to our earlier assertion that we have found it useful to think of media effects within the common framework provided by the idea of a system of mediated human activity. Each medium thus provides diversity within a large but constrained set of possibilities. In contrasting the two systems of film and print, we constantly find ourselves forced to specify in some detail both the technologies' potential for creating shared meaning and the sociocultural circumstances that make certain orders of meaning valuable.

Because the psychophysical properties, social functions, and specific modes of training for print and film are different, the resulting configurations of activities that can be said to constitute literacy in each medium will necessarily differ. To many, the difference may appear so large that attempts at establishing an overall framework such as we are working toward may appear to put an intolerable burden on the scholar, who must learn the intimate details of several different systems of activity that are similar only at an abstract level.

We seek to see films better, yet not only scholars but most spectators resist analysis of films. Our attraction to films has to do with their ability to transport us away from our ordinary lives, yet films are a potent source of gossip and impetus to conversation in our everyday interactions with social peers. As equipment for living, film is at once more accessible and more difficult to contain than print. We believe that the differences between the "appreciation" and "action" orientations of the media as "equipment for living" raise questions about the very nature of literacy.

Because both the social functions and the training of literacy in print and in film are distinct activities, what we mean by literacy in each medium cannot be reduced to psychophysical properties of the interactions. Yet the boundaries in each area are neither firm nor uncrossed. The problem inheres in the different kinds of questions we ask about literacy in each domain and the limits we encounter when formulating answers to them. Insofar as different academic disciplines map onto the "doing" and "being able" notions of literacy, the methodology of one discipline may not even be able to ask a kind of question that another can.

Literacy extends people's ability to share meaning in their joint endeavors. In this deep sense, it gives human beings access to other minds. Media, the objects and distinctive patterns of interaction that mediate our activity, are equipment for living in association with one another and with our pasts and futures. A general theory of literacy implies a general theory of mediated human activity; if we expand our notion of literacy to include nonprint media, it is impossible to consider post–Cro-Magnon human interaction without some form of literacy. If we consider the media as equipment for living, the problem is more complex. For the richness of our lives depends not only on how much equipment we carry with us, but how we use that equipment and in what contexts it is relevant. The chisel in the hands of a sculptor is different than the chisel in the hands of a bricklayer, but it is not clear that one uses the tool *better* than the other. The first step, and one that continues to meet with resistance, is to recognize and work with films such as *Romeo and Juliet* and *Nashville*, as well as printed books, as equipments for living. This is not to reduce meaning to usefulness but to enlarge our concepts of "meaning" and "usefulness."

ACKNOWLEDGMENT

Support for the preparation of the manuscript and part of the work on which it is based was provided by the Carnegie Corporation.

NOTES

1. The whole issue of "faithfully" is raised rarely in the literature, but it is crucial to Havelock's (1976) argument about what kinds of activities constitute full literacy.
2. When we speak of "putting in common with raw experience" it sounds a little strange, and perhaps stranger to think of this as communication. But in fact "creating something in common with states of the world" is a critical part of that kind of commonness for oneself that psychologists term "thinking."

   Moreover, there are additional propositions that we could offer. We limit ourselves here to pointing out that these propositions concerning mediated activity imply that power is a central issue in communication, a point that is brilliantly emphasized by Bakhtin (1973; see also Holquist, 1981).

3. This idea is reflected in the title of Monaco's *How to Read a Film* (1981). Metz's *Film Language* (1974) contains useful summaries of the achievements of film theoreticians and semioticians pursuing this idea.
4. For a more formal analyses of these films see Keyssar (in press).
5. In the course of our work we have discovered that it is Proposition 1 that merits most discussion, because all central issues in the study of mediated activity flow from it.
6. The fact that a sense of immediacy is central to film theory produces a curious paradox, for we know that it rests on an illusion. We laugh on those occasions when people are "fooled" into confusing film and reality at the same time that we recognize such "confusion" as a central resource for communication via film.
7. The recent film *Polyester* has implemented part of Huxley's vision.
8. The same kind of attempt can be found in Salomon (1979), Eisenstein, (1947), and elsewhere.
9. We should make it clear that we are not claiming the truth of the theory that generates these categories. However, many scholars have found it useful to posit panhuman cognitive universals, and the applications of these ideas has an honorable history in film theory.
10. The issue of what influence cultural codes exert in cases where they could not be explicated by viewers is a large area of uncertainty in both film theory and cognitive psychology. For example, Cole could retrospectively acknowledge a lot of red, white, and blue in *Nashville* even though he did not formulate that relationship during the film. What intermediate state characterizes this knowledge?
11. We are here reinventing the contrasts, central to linguistic theory, literary theory, and cognitive psychology, between surface structure and deep structure, forms and meaning, paradigmatic and syntagmatic, synchronic and diachronic, *langue and parole*, and metaphor and metonome that are central to the study of all mediated systems of activity.
12. That a film like *Nashville* may be a popular success despite these difficulties is a testimonial to both the alternative sources of meaning in film and audiences' sophistication in interpreting film.
13. It is worth noting that experiments that attempt to get college students to use arbitrary "grammatical" relations in structuring a set of meaningless lexical tokens have shown the process to be exceedingly difficult and confusing (Miller, 1967).

REFERENCES

Arnheim, R. *Film as art*. Berkeley: University of California Press, 1957.
Bakhtin, M. M. *Marxism and the philosophy of language*. Trans. L. Matejka & I. R. Titunik. New York: Seminar Press, 1973.
Barthes, R. *Image, music, text*. New York: Hill & Wang, 1977.

Bruner, J. S., & Olson, D. R. Symbols and texts as the tools of intellect. *Interchange*, 1977–78, *8*(4), 1–15.

Bruner, J., Olver, R., & Greenfield, P. *Studies in cognitive growth*. New York: Wiley, 1966.

Burke, K. *The philosophy of literary form: Studies in symbolic action*. Berkeley: University of California Press, 1973.

Cavell, S. *The world viewed: Reflections on the ontology of film*. New York: Viking Press, 1971.

Cole, M., & The Laboratory of Comparative Human Cognition. Intelligence as cultural practice. In R. Sternberg (Ed.), *Handbook of human intelligence*. Cambridge: Cambridge University Press, 1981.

Eisenstein, S. *Film sense*. New York: Harcourt, Brace & World, 1947.

Glushko, R. J. Cognitive and pedagogical implications of orthography. *Quarterly Newsletter of the Laboratory of Comparative Human Cognition*, 1979, *1*(2), 22–26.

Gombrich, E. H. *Art and illusion: A study in the psychology of pictorial representation*. New York: Bollinger Foundation, 1960.

Goody, J. *The domestication of the savage mind*. Cambridge: Cambridge University Press, 1977.

Hatano, G. Cognitive consequences of practice in culture specific procedural skills. *Quarterly Newsletter of the Laboratory of Comparative Human Cognition*. 1982, *1*, 15–18.

Havelock, E. A. *Origins of Western literacy*. Toronto: Ontario Institute for Studies in Education, 1976.

Holquist, M. The politics of representation. In S. S. Greenblatt & J. Hopkins (Eds.), *Allegory and representation*. Baltimore: Johns Hopkins University Press, 1981.

Huxley, A. *Brave new world*. New York: Harper & Row, 1946.

Ivanov, V. V. *Essays on the history of semiotic in the U.S.S.R.* Moscow: Nauka Publishers, 1976. (In Russian)

Keyssar, H. I love you. Who are you? The strategy of drama in recognition scenes. *PMLA*, March 1977, pp. 297–306.

Robert Altman's *Nashville*: New roots for the nation. *Prospects*, in press.

Lord, A. B. *The singer of tales*. Cambridge: Harvard University Press, 1960.

McLuhan, M. *The Gutenberg galaxy: The making of typographic man*. Toronto: University of Toronto Press, 1962.

Mandler, J. M. Categorical and schematic organization in memory. In C. R. Puff (Ed.), *Memory organization and structure*. New York: Academic Press, 1979.

Metz, C. *Film language: A semiotics of the cinema*. Trans. Michael Taylor. New York: Oxford University Press, 1974.

Miller, G. A. *The psychology of communication*. New York: Basic Books, 1967.

Monaco, J. *How to read a film: The art, technology, language, history, and theory of film and media*. New York: Oxford University Press, 1981.

Olson, D. R. Culture, technology, and intellect, In L. B. Resnick (Ed.), *The nature of intelligence*. Hillsdale, N. J.: Erlbaum, 1976.

From utterance to text: The bias of language in speech and writing. *Harvard Educational Review*, 1977, *47*, 257–281.

Ong, W. J. *Rhetoric, romance, and technology: Studies in the interaction of expression and culture*. Ithaca, N.Y.: Cornell University Press, 1971.

Percy, W. *The message in the bottle: How queer man is, how queer language is, and what one has to do with the other*. New York: Farrar, Straus & Giroux, 1975.

Pudovkin, V. I. *Film technique and film acting*. 1929. (Reprinted by Grove, New York, 1970.)

Renault, M. *The praise singer*. New York: Pantheon, 1978.

Salomon, G. *Interaction of media, cognition, and learning*. San Francisco: Jossey-Bass, 1979.

Schmandt-Besserat, D. The earliest precursor of writing. *Scientific American*, 1978, *238* (6), 50–59.

Scribner, S. Studying working intelligence. In B. Rogoff & J. Lave (Eds.), *Everyday cognition: Its development in social context*. Cambridge: Harvard University Press, 1981.

Scribner, S., & Cole, M. *The consequences of literacy*. Cambridge: Harvard University Press, 1981.

Seldes, G. *The public arts*. New York: Simon & Schuster, 1960.

Sontag, S. *Against interpretation*. New York: Delta, 1966.

5

Cognitive consequences of communication mode: a social psychological perspective

ROCCO FONDACARO and E. TORY HIGGINS

Literacy may be defined as the ability to read and write a simple message (cf. Harman, 1970). In considering the cognitive consequences of literacy, one approach has been to compare the responses of people who have the ability to read and write simple messages with the responses of those who do not have this ability. This has been the traditional approach and has involved historical, cross-cultural, and developmental comparisons of literate and illiterate samples. An alternative approach is to select a literate sample of people and compare their responses when they do and do not use their ability to read and write simple messages – that is, compare their responses when communicating in the written versus the oral mode of communication. One advantage of this second approach is that one can more easily control for confounding variables, such as schooling and historical variables, that have plagued the more traditional studies of the cognitive consequences of literacy. This second approach is the one taken in the present chapter. For our purposes, then, the question becomes "What are the cognitive consequences of communication mode?" In addition, our particular concern is with the consequences of communication mode for the communicator, rather than for the recipient, and especially the consequences for communicators' evaluations, judgments, and memory of other people. Therefore, the specific question we wish to address is "What are the social cognitive consequences of communication mode for the communicator?"

Unfortunately, there has been little research on the cognitive consequences of communication mode for the communicator, and even less on social cognitive consequences. Thus, our discussion of this issue is necessarily preliminary and speculative, and is meant simply to provide a framework and rationale for future empirical investigations of this issue. In doing so, we also intend to introduce a "social psychological" perspective on the cognitive consequences of literacy by considering the role of social psychological factors as independent, dependent, and mediating variables. We begin by briefly summarizing our general conception of interpersonal communication and review some evidence of the impact of communication in general on communicators' social cognitions. We then consider various ways in which communication is different in the written versus the oral mode and discuss how these differences might influence communicators' social cognitions. Finally, we attempt to demonstrate, in a "metaanalytic-like" way, some of the social cognitive consequences of communication in different modes.

Communication and the "communication game"

Communication is an interpersonal enterprise. At some level, it is a transaction between a transmitter and a receiver that seeks to establish some kind of commonality (cf. Rommetveit, 1974), such as commonality about some message referent or the definition of physical and/or social reality (Ruesch & Bateson, 1968). Indeed, verbal communication is characterized by both an information-transmission feature involving the conveyance of the logical or propositional content of the message and a social relations feature involving the definition of the interpersonal relationship or social structural context of the communicants inherent in the message (cf. Olson & Hildyard, 1981; see also Higgins, 1981). Together, these two features determine the "meaning" of the message.

In social psychology, the study of verbal communication processes has traditionally relied upon a general information-transmission approach (cf. Higgins, Fondacaro, & McCann, 1981) that has inspired research primarily in referential communication (cf. Glucksberg, Krauss, & Higgins, 1975; Mehrabian & Reed, 1968) and persuasive communication (cf. Eagly & Himmelfarb, 1978; McGuire, 1969, 1972). The emphasis in this research has been on message accuracy, comprehensibility, and validity, and it has stressed the importance of such mediating processes as attention, verbal and perceptual comparison, comprehension, retention, and role taking. The research paradigms reflecting the information-transmission approach typically motivate communicators and recipients to transmit or know the truth about some message referent or to transmit or hold the correct attitude or opinion with regard to some issue. Thus, researchers have focused primarily on the information-transmission feature of verbal communication to the exclusion of the social relations feature. (Olson and Hildyard, 1981, have made similar observations.)

We have noted elsewhere (Higgins et al., 1981) that this unidimensional focus in verbal communication research has led to conceptualizations of speaker and listener processes as being essentially similar – that communication involves a general set of communication skills and rules, such as role taking and taking into consideration the needs of one's communication partner (cf. Flavell et al., 1968; Higgins, 1977). However, the expected positive relation between speaker and listener effectiveness implied in the information-transmission approach tends not to be obtained in research specifically correlating speaker and listener effectiveness scores (cf. Brilhart, 1965; Heider, 1971; Johnson & Gross, 1968; Krauss & Glucksberg, 1969; Strickler, 1975). Effective speakers are not necessarily effective listeners. Moreover, theoretical analyses of speaking and listening suggest that while some skills may be generally similar (e.g., comparisons of similarity between message content and potential targets may be required by both speakers and listeners), underlying cognitive processes (e.g., those associated with production by speakers and those associated with comprehension by listeners) are different for speakers and listeners (cf. Bloom, 1974; Higgins et al., 1981; Huttenlocher, 1974).

Certainly, the information-transmission approach has been heuristic and has contributed significantly to the social psychology of communication, but many aspects of the communication process are overlooked by this approach. Many of those aspects are associated with the social relations feature of communication. For example, cultural conventions for appropriate language use with different message topics and in different social situations, interpersonal or social exchange goals other than information transmission (i.e., "face" goals, "social reality" goals, and "social relationship" goals), and distinctions between speaker and listener roles are not captured by the traditional information-transmission approach.

An approach that does encompass these social relations aspects, as well as those factors mediating accurate information transmission, conceives of communication as a "game." This approach reflects an integration and elaboration of approaches derived from the fields of speech communication, philosophy, linguistics, and sociology. Although the assumptions of the "communication game" approach are presented elsewhere (Higgins, 1981; Higgins et al., 1981) and will not be recounted in detail here, let us first note briefly that the approach conceptualizes communication as "purposeful social inter-

76

ROCCO FONDACARO AND E. TORY HIGGINS

action occurring within a socially defined context, involving inter-
dependent social roles and conventional rules, stratagems, and tactics
for making decisions and obtaining various goals" (Higgins, 1981, p.
346). Consequently, the efficient transmission of information is only
one aspect of communication. Also important are socially determined
processes of conflict resolution and decision making with respect to
goal maximization and rule and strategy utilization (Higgins et al.,
1981).

The transmission of information, either to inform or to persuade,
is a major purpose of communication. Moreover, the factors mediating effective information transmission (i.e., labeling, verbal comparison, attention, comprehension, retention, and role taking) are
included within the "communication game" framework. In addition,
the rules of communication include, for example, prescriptions that
messages be accurate, understandable, and valid and that both
communicators and recipients take into consideration the characteristics of their communicative partner. Other factors, however, are
also important in communication, such as fulfilling communication
roles, defining the communication situation, judging message appropriateness, judging motives and intentions, and responding to confirmation or disconfirmation of cultural expectations. In addition,
there are several general rules of the "communication game" that
incorporate both information-transmission aspects and social relations aspects of communication (Higgins et al., 1981).

Communicators should do the following:
1. Take the audience's or recipient's characteristics into account.
2. Convey the truth as they see it.
3. Try to be understood (be coherent and comprehensible).
4. Give neither too much nor too little information.
5. Be relevant (stick to the point).
6. Produce a message that is appropriate to the context and
   circumstances.
7. Produce a message appropriate to their intent or purpose.
Recipients should do the following:
1. Take the communicator's or source's characteristics into account.
2. Determine the communicator's intent or purpose.
3. Take the context and circumstances into account.
4. Pay attention to the message and be prepared for receiving it.
5. Try to understand the message.
6. Provide feedback concerning message interpretation.

These lists are not intended to be complete. There may be other
rules underlying effective communication. Neither is it the case that

communicants must be consciously aware of these rules. One's ability to be an effective communicator may derive from a socialized but tacit knowledge of communication rules. And, of course, it is not likely that a communicant will be able to follow simultaneously all of the rules. Some rules must take precedence over other rules. This is partly because following all the rules would be cognitively unmanageable and because particular rules will often be incompatible with one another as well as with certain goals one wants to achieve at the moment. For example, telling the truth can conflict with a speaker's "social relationship goals" by angering the listener or it can conflict with a speaker's "face goals" by embarrassing the speaker.

The weight given to different goal-related rules is affected by both social situational or cultural contingencies and individual needs and desires. For example, there are cultural rules of social interaction for communicants that reflect various demographic and social relationship factors, such as age, gender, status, and power. Deference and politeness must often be reflected in communicative behavior and may conflict with such speaker rules as "tell the truth as you see it" or listener rules such as "provide feedback to the speaker about his or her interpretation and understanding of the message." For instance, in the interests of politeness, listeners may not interrupt a speaker's elaborated explanation of some point even when comprehension has been achieved.

Social cognitive consequences of the "communication game"

As can be seen from even this brief summary of the "game" properties of communication, verbal communication is embedded within a complex system of task (i.e., information transmission) *and* sociocultural contingencies. Let us sample, somewhat arbitrarily, from among the many aspects of the communication game in order to demonstrate some of the implications of this approach for social cognition (see Higgins, 1981, for a more comprehensive discussion).

Communicator rule 1 states that communicators should take the recipient's characteristics into account. Research indicates that communicators do, indeed, modify messages to suit the recipient (cf. Flavell et al., 1968; Glucksberg et al., 1975; Mehrabian & Reed, 1968), even when the relevant characteristic is the recipient's attitude toward the message referent (Higgins & Rholes, 1978; Manis, Cornell, & Moore, 1974; Newtson & Czerlinsky, 1974). Higgins and Rholes (1978), for example, showed that a communicator will modify his or her description of a person to suit the evaluative tone of the recipient's

Table 5.1 *Reproduction distortions*

Message recipient's opinion	Message		No message	
	Positive distortions	Negative distortions	Positive distortions	Negative distortions
Like	2.4	0.0	.8	.6
Dislike	.3	1.9	.8	.5

Source: Higgins & Rholes (1978).

attitude toward that person. For instance, if the target person's behavior was ambiguously described by the statement "By the way he acts one can readily see that Donald is well aware of his ability to do many things well," communicators were likely to label this person as "confident" when the recipient was said to like Donald but as "conceited" when the recipient was said to dislike Donald. Overall, in their messages about the target person, communicators were likely to include more positive labels when the recipient liked the target person than when the recipient disliked the target person.

Since communicators believed that the recipient's task was to identify the target person, modifying their messages about him would presumably facilitate this referential communication task by evaluatively bringing their message of Donald in line with the recipient's impressions of Donald. One might therefore expect that communicators would be aware of their message modification, and thus it would have little effect on their own personal impressions of Donald. On the other hand, previous research suggests that message modification to suit an audience can have consequences for communicators (cf. Manis et al., 1974; Zimmerman & Bauer, 1956). Indeed, communicators' memories and evaluative judgments of the target person were significantly affected by their message modification in the Higgins and Rholes (1978) study. Specifically, there was a significant tendency for communicators' reproductions of the initial essay about Donald to be evaluatively distorted in the direction of their recipients' attitudes. In addition, this effect was only observed in conditions where subjects actually wrote a message. It was not found in another condition in which subjects only intended to write a message (see Table 5.1). Similarly, communicators' own attitudes toward Donald became more consistent with the attitude of their recipients, but only when they actually produced a message. Further, a positive correla-

tion was found between the evaluative tone of communicators'
messages and the evaluative tone of their reproductions, with the
size of the correlation increasing over time (from $r = +.18$ when
there was a 20-minute delay between message and reproduction to
$r = +.74$ when there was a 2-week delay).

The results of a recent study indicate that communicators will also
modify their message to suit the information needs of their recipient
(Higgins, McCann, & Fondacaro, 1982). In this experiment, communicators modified their message about a target person as a function
of the amount of information about the target person that they and
their recipients held in common. Communicators and recipients were
put in separate rooms connected by a one-way intercom. The
communicators were asked to *describe* and *interpret* for the recipient
information they received about a target person. All subjects then
read the same essay about the target person, but were told that their
communicative partner had received either basically the *same* or
different information about the person. After reading the essay, but
prior to any communication, subjects were asked to reproduce the
essay exactly, word for word. Following the communication, all
subjects were again asked to reproduce the essay.

From a communication game perspective, it would be expected
that when recipients had different information about Donald, communicators should emphasize description over interpretation of the
target person information in order to provide the recipient with a
complete and accurate account of the target person. When recipients
had basically the same information about the target person, however,
communicators should emphasize interpretation over description of
the target person information in order to produce a message that
would not be redundant with respect to what the recipient already
knew and that would convey a particular viewpoint. Consistent with
these expectations, communicators' messages in the "different" condition involved significantly less change (i.e., less distortion or deletion) and less evaluative polarization of the original target person
information than communicators' messages in the "same" condition.
That is, communicators were more careful to "stick to the facts" in
the "different" condition.

Consistent with the results of our earlier study (Higgins & Rholes,
1978), there was also evidence that communicators' messages about
the target person influenced their own memory of the original
stimulus information. The reproductions of communicators in the
"different" condition involved less change and less evaluative polarization after message production than before message production,

whereas the reproductions of communicators in the "same" condition involved more change and more evaluative polarization after message production than before message production. Thus, message modification does affect communicators' memory for the person described. Communicators who "stick to the facts" in their messages about a target person subsequently have more accurate memories of that person. Further supporting the conclusion that message modification is the critical determinant of the changes in person memory is the fact that recipients' pre- and postmessage reproductions did not vary in terms of the same–different manipulation.

Let us now consider the opposite side of the communicative coin. Recipient rules 1 and 2 state that recipients should take the communicator's characteristics, motives, and intentions into account. Although it is not necessarily the case that recipients will be able to recognize a communicator's actual motives or intentions, the demands of the recipient's role will lead the recipient to make such inferential judgments about the communicator.

The recipient's judgments of the communicator, as well as the recipient's interpretation of the message, will derive from various cues in the communicative situation. For example, if recipients know that the communicator is aware of their attitude toward the message referent, then they should be less willing to accept, or may even discount, a similar attitude when reflected in the communicator's message. Research has shown that subjects who are asked to judge a communicator's true opinion after reading a message on an issue that was directed to an audience holding an extreme position on the issue will "correct" their judgment away from the opinion of the audience (Newtson & Czerlinsky, 1974). Recipients, by the same token, are also more likely to perceive that the attitude conveyed in a message accurately reflects the communicator's true position if the expressed opinion is either contrary to the recipient's attitude or against the communicator's best interests or if the recipient has "overheard" the message (cf. Eagly, Wood, & Chaiken, 1978; Mills & Jellison, 1967; Walster & Festinger, 1962). In terms of attribution theories (Heider, 1958; Jones & Davis, 1965; Kelley, 1967), recipients are less likely to explain the reasons for a communicator's expressed opinion in terms of the communicator's dispositions or personality if they perceive that situational pressures or constraints have shaped the message. As has just been suggested, the recipient's attitude is just such a situational constraint.

It is unclear whether the effectiveness of a persuasive message is enhanced or inhibited by a recipient's awareness of the communicator's persuasive intent (cf. McGuire, 1966). Recipients may respond differently, however, if they believe that a communicator's expressed opinion, say on some political issue, is motivated by a desire to defeat them (competitive orientation) as opposed to gaining their support (cooperative orientation). Such differences in perceived communicator intent may derive from other communicator characteristics. A communicator who is a member of a different political group may be ascribed a competitive persuasive intention, which is likely to produce reticence and little yielding to the message by recipients.

Interpreting messages as well as responding to them can also be affected by the recipient's judgments of the communicator's intentions and characteristics (cf. Asch, 1952). The particular social and physical frame of reference for a communicative interaction and the communicator's characteristics may affect message interpretation. To take a Canadian example, following recent federal and provincial oil-pricing conferences, one would likely interpret the statement "The talks went very well" differently if said by an Albertan representative or by a federal government representative.

In sum, recipients, like communicators, must take their partner's characteristics into account. Judgments about a communicator's characteristics and communicative intent can affect a recipient's judgments about the communicator's true attitudes and beliefs, and this, in turn, can affect the way in which recipients respond to and/or interpret the message. Thus, the social relations aspect of verbal communication has social cognitive consequences for recipients as well as communicators.

Finally, let us consider the social cognitive implications of a difference in the rules for communicators and recipients. Communicators should "try to be understood (be coherent and comprehensible)" and recipients should "be prepared for receiving the message." While these different rules seem complementary for successful communication, following them is likely to produce differences between communicators and recipients in their impressions of the message referent (Higgins et al., 1981; Higgins et al., 1982). Because communicators must produce clear and coherent messages, they should polarize and distort stimulus person information more than recipients who are supposed to be open to change and prepared for a wide range of possible information in the message. Indeed, there is abundant evidence in the "cognitive-tuning" literature that supports this prediction (e.g., Cohen, 1961; Leventhal, 1962; Powell, 1974; Zajonc, 1960). However, in addition to these normative rules associated with the communicator and recipient roles, the procedure of

many cognitive-tuning studies has led recipients, but not communicators, to expect to receive additional information about the stimulus
person. Since subjects are more likely to integrate information about
a stimulus person into a unified impression when they believe they
have all the relevant information than if they know they will be
receiving additional information, this difference in expectations could
account, in part, for the results of previous cognitive-tuning studies.
Differences in expectations about receiving additional information,
as well as the role-prescribed goals of communicators and recipients,
were independently manipulated as a second part of the Higgins et
al. (1982) study.

After subjects were assigned the role of communicator or recipient,
half the communicators and half the recipients were told they would
later receive additional information about the target person ("expectation" condition). The remaining communicators and recipients
were told nothing at all ("no expectation" condition). All subjects, in
fact, received only the initial essay describing the target person. Prior
to any communication all subjects were asked to write down their
impressions of the target person. These premessage impression
measures are most comparable to the measures taken in previous
cognitive-tuning studies.

Impressions were scored in terms of the number of positive and
negative trait terms spontaneously labeling the various behavioral
descriptions of the target person. Across all conditions, impressions
reflected a strong positivity bias (positive labels, $M = 2.5$; negative
labels, $M = 1.5$). The positivity bias, however, was not present in all
conditions (see Table 5.2). Consistent with previous cognitive-tuning
studies, the "no expectation" communicators showed a positivity bias
whereas the "expectation" recipients did not. Communicators in the
"expectation" condition, however, also positively distorted their
impression even though they expected additional information. Of
course, even when communicators expect additional information,
they must still produce a clear and coherent message for the recipient.
Consistent with this interpretation, communicators' subsequent messages achieved coherence through positive polarization (positive
labels, $M = 2.3$; negative labels, $M = 1.7$). Interestingly, recipients
who did not expect additional information about the target person
produced impressions that were as positively distorted as those of
communicators. It would appear that while the communicators'
positivity bias in impressions was determined by their following a
communicative rule (i.e., be concise, clear, and coherent), the recip-

Table 5.2. *Impression labeling*

Communication role	Expectation			No expectation		
	Positive label	Negative label	Positive–negative difference	Positive label	Negative label	Positive–negative difference
Communicator	2.6	1.5	1.1***	2.7	1.5	1.2*
Recipient	2.2	1.9	.3[a]	2.3	1.1	1.2**

* $t = 2.53$, $p < .05$, two-tailed.
** $t = 2.85$, $p < .02$, two-tailed.
*** $t = 2.98$, $p < .01$, two-tailed.
[a] $t < 1$, $p > .30$, two-tailed.
Source: Higgins, McCann, & Fondacaro (1982).

ients' positivity bias was determined by whether they expected additional information about the target person.

From even this brief summary of some of the implications of the "communication game," it is clear that the social relations aspect of interpersonal communication can have cognitive consequences for both communicators and recipients. What is less clear and, unfortunately, has received little empirical attention is whether the consequences vary as a function of communication mode. As stated earlier, our aim here is simply to consider in a preliminary manner how the social cognitive consequences of communication for the communicator may vary as a function of communication mode. To accomplish this aim, we must first consider some ways in which oral and written communication are different. In doing so, it is not our intent to review exhaustively all the possible differences between oral and written communication, nor even to review all those differences that could have social cognitive consequences for the communicator. Moreover, for those oral–written differences we do discuss, we are not suggesting that these differences are absolute or universal. With respect to the social relations aspect of communication, especially, few features of oral and written communication are mutually exclusive. Rather, our concern is with differences between oral and written communication as typically or characteristically performed – exemplified, for instance, by the differences between face-to-face conversation and writing a report.

Differences between oral and written communication

We will briefly consider three basic variables with respect to which oral and written communication differ: production, social context, and goals.

Production

Permanence and ease of review. As pointed out by Horowitz and Newman (1964), Portnoy (1968), and others (see, for example, Chafe, Chapter 6), the record of a written message is relatively permanent and easily available, whereas an oral message is relatively transient and easily forgotten. There are various features of the oral channel that increase the difficulty of reviewing and evaluating one's message. First, much more information is produced per unit of time in oral communication (cf. Horowitz & Newman, 1964; Vygotsky, 1962). In one of our own studies (Higgins, 1973), we found that the mean number of bits of information produced per minute by communicators from grades 4, 5, 6, and 8 in a referential communication task was 6.5 in the oral channel versus only 1.6 in the written channel. Second, there is a tendency in speaking to avoid an "embarrassing silence"; thus, speakers tend to produce a relatively continuous flow of words.

Ease of review, in turn, should influence other aspects of production. For example, one might expect that the easier it is to review one's message, the easier it would be to construct an efficient, concise, nonredundant, and informative message. Indeed, the written messages in our earlier study (Higgins, 1973) were significantly more efficient and concise, as well as less redundant. For the younger schoolchildren, the written messages also contained more bits of information than the oral messages, which is reasonable since one would expect that ease of review would be especially important for younger schoolchildren. In order to test directly whether ease of review was a determining factor of information output for younger schoolchildren, we conducted a follow-up study in which the opportunity to review one's message in the oral and written channels was varied (see Higgins, 1978). This was accomplished through the use of a dictaphone in the oral condition and the use of a "guide" in the written condition that allowed the communicator to write only one line at a time and covered all lines previously written. The fourth graders' messages in both channels contained significantly more information when message review was facilitated, and there was no communication mode difference in information output when ease of review was controlled for.

Speed and deliberation. Producing a written message is a much slower process than producing an oral message. As mentioned earlier, we found that schoolchildren produced four times as many bits per minute in the oral than in the written channel. Written communication is also more deliberate, which would contribute to the lesser production of errors in written than in oral messages (see Chafe, Chapter 6). Indeed, two of the traditional distinctions between oral and written communication, as summarized by Moscovici (1967), suggest that written communication requires more effort than oral communication. First, more complex neuromuscular processes and greater conscious effort are required for writing than for speaking. Second, speaking is a relatively familiar, well-practiced process, whereas writing is a rarely exercised mode of expression and thus requires conscious, concentrated adaptation to a communication mode that is only occasionally used. Vygotsky (1962) draws a similar contrast in explaining why written skills develop more slowly than oral skills among schoolchildren. Moreover, Horowitz and Berkowitz (1964) and Horowitz and Newman (1964) have suggested that the greater effort required to produce a written message may be one reason why written messages are relatively concise and efficient.

Social context

Another traditional distinction between oral and written communication summarized by Moscovici (1967) is that spoken messages typically presuppose the presence of another person (or persons), whereas written messages typically address an absent audience. Thus, the entire range of gesticulatory and mimetic signs that can be used in speaking are inapplicable to written communication. Vygotsky (1962) has emphasized the importance of the situational context for the production of a message, and he characterizes the written message as a "monologue" and the spoken message as a "dialogue." Without precise knowledge of the audience or immediate, simultaneous feedback from the audience, Vygotsky argues, the writer is obliged to use words and syntax more accurately, deliberately, and elaborately. In conversation, the participants function as an immediate, concrete environment for one another.

There may also be more variation in the social context, and thus more variation in sign–social context relations, for oral messages. Because the audience is more general and fixed for written communication, there may also be less shifting and reorganization of the communicants' social relationship during the interchange (see Erickson, 1981). Conversation is an ongoing social interaction, a cooperative interchange. Because of the continuous, simultaneous adjustment involved in conversation, the message is more jointly produced than in written communication. As Moscovici (1967) points out, each instance of both oral and written communication inheres in a specific social situation that influences the communicator's behavior, with the norms of a particular situation being extended to the speech. Oral communication tends to occur in less formal situations and across a broader range of situations than written communication. Indeed, Moscovici (1967) found that spoken messages produced in more formal, less conversationally natural situations (e.g., back-to-back communication) had a structure that was more similar to the structure of normal written messages than to the structure of oral messages produced in natural face-to-face interaction. In addition, because the production of written messages typically occurs in different social and task contexts than the production of oral messages, different social roles and self-identities may become associated with these two channels. In fact, it is difficult to distinguish the effects of literacy per se from the effects of exposure to those novel social roles and self-identities that are associated with the acquisition of literacy.

Goals

It may be that oral and written communication generally emphasize different goals. It has been suggested that in most conversational language the social aspects of meaning are primary to the logical or propositional aspects of meaning (e.g., Olson & Hildyard, 1981). Because written communication does not involve face-to-face inter-action, cooperative interchange, or simultaneous feedback from a coacting audience, it may be that the relative emphasis on these two aspects of meaning is different, perhaps even reversed. After all, the norms associated with the social role of communicator in a conver-sation include responding to ongoing, concurrent feedback from the audience and coordinating the message output to the audience's responses, whereas this is generally not the case for written com-munication. In terms of the "communication game," therefore, it may be that greater weight is given to "social relationship" goals, "face" goals, and "social reality" goals in oral than in written com-munication, whereas greater weight is given to "information-trans-mission" goals or "task" goals in written than in oral communication. The fact that there is likely to be less shifting and reorganization of the communicants' social relationship during written than during oral communication also suggests that written communicators may pay less attention to the social relation aspects of communication. In addition, communicators may more readily associate social goals with oral than with written communication because children's first lan-guage is oral and the social uses of utterances initially receive greater weight than the literal meanings (cf. Shatz, 1978; Bates, 1976).

The results of some recent studies by Chaiken and Eagly (1976) on the relation between communication modality and message per-suasiveness are consistent with the notion that social relationship goals are more important in oral than in written communication. They found that the likableness of the communicator was a major determinant of the impact of a persuasive message when the message was oral but not when it was written. Moreover, the recipients had more thoughts about the communicator (e.g., "He seems unfriendly"), as opposed to thoughts about the message content (e.g., "The economic advantage of the trimester seems reasonable"), when the message was oral than when it was written. Thus, it appears that there was greater communicator orientation (i.e., social goals) than message orientation (i.e., task goals) for oral than for written communication.

It has also been suggested (cf. Chafe, Chapter 6) that whereas there is a greater concern with evidentiality in written than in oral communication, there is greater self-involvement in oral than in written communication. In part because of the production differences between oral and written communication described earlier (e.g., effort and ease of review), one would also expect a greater emphasis on conciseness in written than in oral communication. One would also expect that these production differences would lead oral communicators to employ redundancy more than written communicators. In addition, the immediate presence of an audience in oral communication should result in greater weight being given to attention control features in oral than in written communication.

Social cognitive consequences of differences between oral and written communication

The differences between oral and written communication described above have a number of implications for communicators' social cognitions. Given the current lack of empirical evidence concerning this issue, our discussion of these implications is necessarily speculative. Hopefully, our discussion will provide some hypotheses for future investigations. In considering this issue, we will focus on the potential consequences of communication mode for the following general mediating variables: memory, motivation and commitment, and self-perception.

Memory for the message

As discussed earlier, there is considerable evidence that message modification can subsequently influence communicators' own evaluations, judgments, and memory of the message topic or referent (cf. Higgins, 1981; Higgins et al., 1982). Presumably, this occurs for at least two reasons. First, the labeling involved assigns meaning to the message referent or target stimulus by connecting it to the cognitive category designated by the label. Once a communicator has selected a label, the label becomes part of the available information about the stimulus that can be subsequently recalled. In fact, the stimulus is likely to be reconstructed in recall so as to be consistent with the features of the category designated by the label (cf. Bartlett, 1932; Bourne, Ekstrand, & Dominowski, 1971; Neisser, 1967). Often this can result in the original stimulus information being distorted in recall. Since communicators will vary their message labeling to suit their interactive goals, communicators with different goals are likely later to remember the original stimulus information differently. Another reason why message modification could affect recall is that communicators may also modify the details of the stimulus information when constructing their message in order to suit their interactive goals, as well as to be consistent with the implications of their message labels. When later asked to recall the original stimulus information, communicators may instead recall the modified details contained in their message.

Both these reasons for message modification effects on the communicator require that communicators remember their message. That is, memory for the message is a critical determinant of the social cognitive consequences of communication. Thus, to the extent that memory for the message varies as a function of communication mode, the social cognitive consequences of communication should vary as a function of communication mode, with the consequences being greater for whichever mode results in better memory for the message. Given that written messages, as discussed earlier, are easier to review, take more effort to produce, and are both more concise and more permanent, they should be better remembered than oral messages. Thus, the social cognitive consequences of communication should be greater for written messages than for oral messages.

Motivation and commitment

The social cognitive consequences of communication should also be greater when communicators are motivated and committed to respond subsequently in a manner that is consistent with the beliefs or information contained in their message. One would expect for a number of reasons that communicators of written messages would be more committed to their message than communicators of oral messages. First, written messages are more permanent, and thus it is easier for others later on to make the communicator accountable for the statements contained in the message. Second, written messages are more likely to have an authority register (cf. Olson, 1977), which obligates the communicator to defend the message statements. Third, oral messages involve more direct cooperation between communicator and recipient, with the final message being more of a joint product. Thus, communicators of oral messages may feel less personal commitment and responsibility for the message.

For all the above reasons, then, communicators of written messages should be more committed to their message. If this is so, then written messages should have more impact on communicators than oral messages. There is considerable evidence in the cognitive dissonance literature, for example, that as commitment increases, there is an increase in dissonance and in the tendency to reduce dissonance by changing cognitions so as to increase internal consistency (cf. Brehm & Cohen, 1962). For instance, if a communicator freely advocates a counterattitudinal or dissonant position on some issue, the tendency for the communicator later to change his or her original position on the issue to be in closer agreement with the communicated position increases as commitment to the message increases. Moreover, the motivation to reduce dissonance depends upon the extent to which the communicator feels personally responsible for the message (cf. Wicklund & Brehm, 1976). There is also evidence that commitment is important when communicators advocate a proattitudinal or consonant position on an issue. Kiesler (1971), for example, has shown that communicators who are told to advocate their own opinion on an issue are more resistant to subsequent counterattacks on their position if the circumstances of message production increased their commitment to their message. In addition, communicators tend to become more extreme in their position when they are more committed to their message.

Finally, the greater effort to produce written than to produce oral messages could also have motivational implications. Studies of "effort justification" in the dissonance literature have found that when people voluntarily expend considerable effort on a difficult or unpleasant task they are motivated to find a justification for their effort (cf. Wicklund & Brehm, 1976). One possible justification is to conclude that the task was intrinsically worthwhile or important. Thus, when communicators freely advocate a counterattitudinal position, they may be more likely to consider their message worthwhile and important when it is produced in the written channel than when it is produced in the oral channel.

Self-perception

Message modification should also have greater social cognitive consequences to the extent that communicators believe that their message truly and accurately reflects their own personal knowledge, beliefs, or attitudes. Communicators, after all, should be more willing to use their past statements as a current basis for making judgments and for reconstructing past events if they believe the statements were accurate. Once again, there are a number of factors that could cause written communicators to be more confident than oral communicators that their message accurately reflects their true beliefs. First, we suggested earlier that the social aspects of meaning and social goals of communication (e.g., social relationship goals) are given more weight in oral than in written communication, whereas the propositional aspects of meaning and task goals are given more weight in written than in oral communication. Thus, it should be less obvious retrospectively to written communicators than to oral communicators that their past message might have sacrificed the "truth" for the sake of other goals. Second, the authority register, deliberateness, and greater accountability of written messages, as well as the greater association of written messages with formal tasks and professional identities, may increase the apparent credibility and objectivity of written messages so that even communicators are more confident of the accuracy of written messages than of oral messages. Certainly, recipients are more likely to believe that a statement is the truth when it is written than when it is spoken.

A third factor that could affect communicators' judgment of the "truth" of their messages is the social context of message production. As discussed earlier, the audience for which the message is modified is more specific, concrete, immediate, and salient in oral communication than in written communication. The potential influence of the audience on message content at the time of production should be more obvious, therefore, in oral communication than in written communication. In addition, subsequent memory for the audience and its possible impact on message content should be greater in oral communication than in written communication because the audience was more salient during production and is more likely to be part of the communicator's episodic memory for the message production event. For both these reasons, oral communicators should be more likely than written communicators to consider the audience as a possible external cause of the message content. According to self-perception or self-attribution theory (cf. Bem, 1972; Kelley, 1971), the role of a given cause in producing a given effect is discounted if other plausible causes are present, and there is considerable evidence to support this proposition (cf. Schneider, Hastorf, & Ellsworth, 1979). Thus, if one plausible cause of the content in a communicator's message is his or her audience's pressures and demands for a particular content, then the role of the communicator's true beliefs in producing the message may be discounted. That is, the communicator may not consider the message to be an accurate reflection of his or her true beliefs, and this is more likely to occur in oral communication than in written communication.

Summary

Surprisingly, the preceding account of the social cognitive consequences of various communication mode differences seems to converge to a single general conclusion: Message modification should have a greater impact on communicators' social cognitions when communication is written than when it is oral. This conclusion was suggested by every factor that we considered. A couple of caveats are in order, however. First, there may be a number of factors that we did not consider that would suggest an opposite conclusion. We were not consciously selective or biased, however, in the factors we discussed. Second, our conclusion concerns the impact of message modification per se and *not* the overall impact of engaging in communication. We are simply suggesting that the impact of *a particular amount of message modification* will be greater for written communication than for oral communication. But the overall impact of engaging in communication obviously depends also on how much message modification actually occurs. It may be that there is typically a greater amount of message modification in oral communication than in written communication. In fact, the communication mode differences described earlier (e.g., relative emphasis on social goals versus task goals, immediacy of audience, etc.) suggest, if anything, that there would be greater message modification in oral communication. Thus, it is difficult to predict which mode of communication generally has a greater impact on the communicator.

Social cognitive consequences of communication mode: a preliminary investigation

We would like to conclude this chapter by comparing some of the social cognitive consequences of message modification for oral communicators versus written communicators. Our approach in this regard may be described as "pseudo-metaanalytic." That is, the data for oral communicators come from a different experiment than the data for written communicators, although both experiments were dealing with social cognitive consequences of message modification. Both experiments are grounded in the "communication game" conceptual framework (cf. Higgins, 1981) and are alike in many critical respects. The data bases being compared, however, consist of subjects sampled from geographically and historically independent populations of university students. Our analysis of differences between oral-mode and written-mode communication will involve *z* tests and *t* tests for comparing means from independent samples. The results of these comparisons are somewhat tenuous, of course, and should be treated with caution. Our intention is merely to demonstrate some "face validity" for our earlier speculations and, perhaps, to provide some impetus for further research on communication mode and social cognition.

Subjects and procedures. We suggested earlier that message modification should have a greater impact on communicators' social judgments and memories when communication is written than when it is oral. In order to begin to test this general hypothesis, the messages and reproductions of 28 communicators were sampled from two experiments. Both experiments examined the social cognitive impact of modifying messages about a stimulus person to suit the recipient's attitude toward the stimulus person. In the first experiment (Higgins & Rholes, 1978), communicators produced *written* messages for recipients who purportedly either liked or disliked the person being described. In the second study (McCann, Fondacaro, & Higgins, in preparation), which was a replication and extension of the first experiment, communicators *orally* transmitted their messages about the stimulus person. To obtain equal groups of communicators that varied in their communication mode, 14 communicators were randomly selected from the subjects in each experiment.

The experiments were quite similar conceptually and operationally, but there were some procedural differences. Communicators in both studies were provided with an essay describing a hypothetical stimulus person named Donald and were instructed that their task was to describe Donald to another person who was familiar with Donald. The Donald essays used in the two experiments were functionally identical (see Higgins & Rholes, 1978, for details). The essays were composed of 12 behavioral descriptions, including 4 positive descriptions, 4 negative descriptions, and 4 evaluatively ambiguous descriptions. After reading the Donald essay, communicators delivered a message describing Donald for a recipient who purportedly either liked or disliked Donald.

At this point the procedures vary somewhat between the two experiments in ways other than communication mode. In the Higgins and Rholes (1978) study, the communicators' attitudes toward Donald and reproductions of the original Donald essay were obtained either immediately following their message or 2 weeks later. In the McCann et al. (in preparation) replication study, the initial oral message was followed by a second oral message to a different recipient who also purportedly liked or disliked Donald. Half the communicators described Donald for two recipients having the same attitude toward Donald (i.e., like–like, dislike–dislike) and half the communicators described Donald for recipients having different attitudes (i.e., like–dislike, dislike–like). The attitude and reproduction memory measures were obtained immediately following delivery of the second message or after a week's delay. For the present analysis, the immediate–delay factor was collapsed across in the selection of both the oral and written subjects.

The inclusion of the second message in the replication study affected the selection of oral communicators for the present analysis. In order to avoid a potential bias in favor of our hypothesis, the 14 oral communicators were randomly selected from only those communicators who delivered messages to recipients who either both liked or both disliked Donald. If anything, this restriction in selection could bias the results of our analysis in a direction *opposite* to our hypothesis, because when communicators produce messages for two recipients with the same attitude toward Donald, the second message is likely to reinforce the first. Moreover, in order to increase comparability with the written-mode communicators, only the second message of each oral communicator was used, which means the memory measure was closer in time to the message. Thus, this test of our hypothesis is fairly conservative because the differences in procedure favor a stronger effect of oral communication.

Measures. The messages describing Donald and the reproductions of the original Donald essays were obtained for all 28 communicators. The oral messages had been recorded and were transcribed before being content-analyzed. The messages and reproductions were coded in terms of three content categories: the number of positive, negative, and ambiguous essay descriptions included in an undistorted or "unchanged" manner; the number of essay descriptions included but positively distorted; and the number of essay descriptions included but negatively distorted. Interrater agreement was over 89% for all coding categories.

For each communicator, the percentage of overall evaluative distortion of messages and reproductions was also calculated. This index is obtained by subtracting the sum of all the unchanged negative descriptions and those descriptions that were negatively distorted from the sum of all the unchanged positive descriptions and those descriptions that were positively distorted, and then dividing this difference by the sum of all the descriptions included in the output. The arcsine transformations of these proportions (preserving the positivity or negativity of their sign unless stated otherwise) were used in all analyses.

Other measures of interest here are the number of words in each message and the communicators' attitudes toward Donald, the message referent. In both experiments, attitudes toward Donald were expressed by communicators on 11-point bipolar liking scales.

Results. We predicted that, all things being equal, written communication is likely to have greater social cognitive consequences for a communicator than oral communication. Before testing this hypothesis, let us consider some of the message variables that we suggested earlier were related to the social cognitive impact of messages, such as differences in conciseness and efficiency of the message, amount of message modification, and communicator commitment to the message.

Concise and efficient communications are likely to be more memorable than communications that are less concise and efficient. They are more coherent, better integrated, and more highly organized. Memorable messages, in turn, are likely to have greater influence on subsequent judgments and recall of the message referent than less memorable messages. A very rough indication of conciseness and efficiency is provided by considering the number of words required to transmit a certain amount of information. A comparison of the mean number of Donald descriptions included in the messages of oral communicators ($M = 5.39$, $\sigma^2 = 3.4$) with the mean number of descriptions in messages of written communicators ($M = 6.0$, $\sigma^2 = 3.9$) revealed no difference in amount of information transmitted by communicators, $t_{26} < 1$, n.s. However, oral communicators used over twice as many words as written communicators ($M = 298.8$, $\sigma^2 = 14,818$, and $M = 135.4$, $\sigma^2 = 1,836$, respectively), $t_{26} = 4.74$, $p < .01$, to produce equally informative messages about Donald. The messages of written communicators, therefore, appear to be considerably more concise and efficient than the messages of oral communicators. Thus, according to our earlier arguments, written communication should have a greater impact than oral communication.

Our major hypothesis, as stated earlier, was that "the impact of a particular amount of message modification will be greater for written communication than for oral communication." The amount of message modification can be determined by examining the number of "unchanged" Donald descriptions included in a message and by examining the percentage of *absolute* distortion in a message. A mean comparison of both these indices indicates essentially no difference in the amount of message modification between oral- and written-mode communications in the present data. Oral communicators did include slightly fewer unchanged descriptions ($M = 3.64$, $\sigma^2 = 3.23$) in their messages than did written-mode communicators ($M = 4.43$, $\sigma^2 = 3.39$), but this difference was not reliable, $t_{26} = 1.15$. With regard to the absolute distortion of the messages, an analysis using the arcsine transformations of the absolute proportion of distortion revealed a mean distortion of 39% in oral messages relative to a mean distortion of 37% in written messages, $t_{26} < 1$, n.s. Thus, it appears, overall, that oral and written communicators modified their messages about Donald to the same extent. As stated above, as long as there is an equivalent amount of message modification in oral and written communication, there should be a greater impact for written messages than for oral messages.

We also suggested that commitment to one's message should increase the impact of the message on subsequent social cognition. We speculated that communicators of written messages would be more committed to their messages than communicators of oral messages. One indicator of the degree of commitment to a message is the correlation between the percentage of positive or negative distortion of the message and the communicator's attitude toward the message referent. Not surprisingly, an initial comparison of mean liking ratings of Donald revealed no difference between the attitudes of oral communicators ($M = -.29$, $\sigma^2 = 6.92$) and written communicators ($M = .57$, $\sigma^2 = 8.24$), $t_{26} < 1$, n.s. Unexpectedly, the mean correlation between message distortion and attitude toward Donald tended to be slightly higher for oral-mode communicators ($r = .56$, $p < .03$) than for written-mode communicators ($r = .41$, $p < .07$), suggesting somewhat more affective commitment on the part of oral communicators to their message. These correlations, however, did not differ significantly ($z = .34$, n.s.).

The differences between oral and written communication in conciseness and efficiency, amount of message modification, and com-

Table 5.3. *Comparison of the correlations between communicators' messages and reproductions for the oral and written modes*

| | Communication mode | | |
Measure	Oral r	Written r	Z difference
Unchanged descriptions	.11	.32	.54
Positively distorted descriptions	−.19	.84**	−3.31*
Negatively distorted descriptions	.31	−.11	−.96
Overall evalutive distortion	.15	.45*	.77

Note: N = 14.
* *p* = .05, one-tailed.
** *p* < .01, one-tailed.

municator commitment to message, as we suggested earlier, may be useful for predicting which communication mode should result in the greater social impact for communicators. Although these three factors, in the present analysis, do not unambiguously point to the superior potency of one mode of communication or the other, the overall pattern of results would lead us to predict greater impact of message modification following communication in the written mode.

Communicators' reproductions of the original stimulus information about Donald can reflect social cognitive impact, where the amount of impact is indicated by the amount of correspondence between communicators' messages and reproductions. The correlations between the descriptions that were unchanged, positively distorted, or negatively distorted in communicators' messages and reproductions reflect the amount of impact of message modification. The best single measure of social cognitive impact is the correlation between overall evaluative distortion in communicators' messages and reproductions. Table 5.3 presents the correlations between messages and reproductions for oral and written communicators, separately. For three out of four of the measures (unchanged descriptions, positively distorted descriptions, overall evaluative distortion), the correlation between the messages and reproductions of written communicators was stronger, although only the oral–written difference for positively distorted descriptions was significant ($p < .01$) given the small subject sample. Although these results are only suggestive, the general pattern is consistent with our earlier hypothesis that the impact of a particular amount of message modification will be greater for written communication than for oral communication.

General summary

We have attempted to address the specific question "What are the social cognitive consequences of communication mode for the communicator?" We began by showing that following the rules for socially appropriate and effective communication has important consequences for the way communicators think and feel about their communicative partner and about the topic of communication. Several differences between oral and written communication were then considered, and preliminary speculations concerning the impact of communication mode on communicators' social cognitions were presented. Finally, we concluded by comparing the evaluations and memories of the message topic for oral communicators versus written communicators. The results of this comparison generally supported our speculations and expectations. All other things being equal, the social cognitive consequences of communication tend to be greater for written than for oral communication.

REFERENCES

Asch, S. E. *Social psychology*. Englewood Cliffs, N.J.: Prentice-Hall, 1952.

Bartlett, F. C. *Remembering*. Cambridge: Cambridge University Press, 1932.

Bates, E. *Language and context: The acquisition of pragmatics*. New York: Academic Press, 1976.

Bem, D. J. Self-perception theory. In L. Berkowitz (Ed.), *Advances in experimental social psychology* (Vol. 6). New York: Academic Press, 1972.

Bloom, L. Talking, understanding, and thinking. In R. L. Schiefelbusch & L. L. Lloyd (Eds.), *Language perspectives: Acquisition, retardation, and intervention*. Baltimore: University Park Press, 1974.

Bourne, L. E., Ekstrand, B. R., & Dominowski, R. L. *The psychology of thinking*. Englewood Cliffs, N.J.: Prentice-Hall, 1971.

Brehm, J. W., & Cohen, A. R. *Explorations in cognitive dissonance*. New York: Wiley, 1962.

Brilhart, B. L. The relationship between some aspects of communicative speaking and communicative listening. *Journal of Communication*, 1965, *15*, 35–46.

Chaiken, S., & Eagly, A. H. Communication modality as a determinant of message persuasiveness and message comprehensibility. *Journal of Personality and Social Psychology*, 1976, *34*, 605–614.

Cohen, A. R. Cognitive tuning as a factor affecting impression formation. *Journal of Personality*, 1961, *29*, 235–245.

Eagly, A. H., & Himmelfarb, S. Attitudes and opinions. *Annual Review of Psychology*, 1978, *29*, 517–554.

Eagly, A. H., Wood, W., & Chaiken, S. Causal inferences about communicators and their effect on opinion change. *Journal of Personality and Social Psychology*, 1978, *36*, 424–435.

Erickson, F. Timing and context in everyday discourse: Implications for the study of referential and social meaning. In W. P. Dickson (Ed.) *Children's oral communication skills*. New York: Academic Press, 1981.

Flavell, J. H., Botkin, P. T., Fry, C. L., Wright, J. W., & Jarvis, P. E. *The development of role-taking and communication skills in children*. New York: Academic Press, 1968.

Glucksberg, S., Krauss, R. M., & Higgins, E. T. The development of referential communication skills. In F. Horowitz, E. Hetherington, S. Scarr-Salapatek, & G. Siegel (Eds.), *Review of child development research* (Vol. 4). Chicago: University of Chicago Press, 1975.

Harman, D. Illiteracy: An overview. *Harvard Educational Review*, 1970, *40*, 226–243.

Heider, E. R. Style and accuracy of verbal communications within and between social classes. *Journal of Personality and Social Psychology*, 1971, *18*, 33–47.

Heider, F. *The psychology of interpersonal relations*. New York: Wiley, 1958.

Higgins, E. T. A social and developmental comparison of oral and written communication. Ph. D. dissertation, Columbia University, 1973.

Communication development as related to channel, incentive, and social class. *Genetic Psychology Monographs*, 1977, *96*, 75–141.

Written communication as functional literacy: A developmental comparison of oral and written communication. In R. Beach & P. D. Pearson (Eds.), *Perspectives on literacy*. Minneapolis: College of Education, University of Minnesota, 1978.

The "communication game": Implications for social cognition and persuasion. In E. T. Higgins, C. P. Herman, & M. P. Zanna (Eds.), *Social cognition: The Ontario Symposium*. Hillsdale, N.J.: Erlbaum, 1981.

Higgins, E. T., Fondacaro, R., & McCann, C. D. Rules and roles: The "communication game" and speaker–listener processes. In W. P. Dickson (Ed.), *Children's oral communication skills*. New York: Academic Press, 1981.

Higgins, E. T., McCann, C. D., & Fondacaro, R. The "communication game":
Goal-directed encoding and cognitive consequences. *Social Cognition*,
1982, *1*, 21–37.
Higgins, E. T., & Rholes, W. S. "Saying is believing": Effects of message
modification on memory and liking for the person described. *Journal of
Experimental Social Psychology*, 1978, *14*, 363–378.
Horowitz, M. W., & Berkowitz, A. Structural advantage of the mechanism
of spoken expression as a factor in differences in spoken and written
expression. *Perceptual and Motor Skills*, 1964, *19*, 619–625.
Horowitz, M. W., & Newman, J. B. Spoken and written expression: An
experimental analysis. *Journal of Abnormal and Social Psychology*, 1964, *68*,
640–647.
Huttenlocher, J. The origins of language comprehension. In R. L. Solso
(Ed.), *Theories in cognitive psychology*. Hillsdale, N.J.: Erlbaum, 1974.
Johnson, R. L., & Gross, H. S. Some factors in effective communication.
Language and Speech, 1968, *11*, 259–263.
Jones, E. E., & Davis, K. E. From acts to dispositions: The attribution process
in person perception. In L. Berkowitz (Ed.), *Advances in experimental
social psychology*. New York: Academic Press, 1965.
Kelley, H. H. Attribution theory in social psychology. In D. Levine (Ed.),
Nebraska Symposium of Motivation, 1967, *15*, 192–238.
    Attribution in social interaction. In E. E. Jones, D. E. Kanouse, H. H.
Kelley, R. E. Nisbett, S. Valins, B. Weiner (Eds.), *Attribution: Perceiving
the causes of behavior*. Morristown, N.J.: General Learning Press, 1971.
Kiesler, C. A. *The psychology of commitment*. New York: Academic Press, 1971.
Krauss, R. M., & Glucksberg, S. The development of communication:
Competence as a function of age. *Child Development*, 1969, *40*, 255–256.
Leventhal, H. The effects of set and discrepancy on impression change.
Journal of Personality, 1962, *30*, 1–15.
McCann, C. D., Fondacaro, R., & Higgins, E. T. Effects of alternation in
message modification on memory and liking for the person described:
A replication and extension. Manuscript in preparation.
McGuire, W. J. Attitudes and opinions. *Annual Review of Psychology*, 1966,
17, 475–514.
    The nature of attitudes and attitude change. In G. Lindzey & E. Aronson
(Eds.), *The handbook of social psychology* (2nd ed.), Vol. 3, *The individual in
a social context*. Reading, Mass.: Addison-Wesley, 1969.
    Attitude change: The information-processing paradigm. In C. G. Mc-
Clintock (Ed.), *Experimental social psychology*. New York: Holt, Rinehart
and Winston, 1972.
Manis, M., Cornell, S. D., & Moore, J. C. Transmission of attitude-relevant
information through a communication chain. *Journal of Personality and
Social Psychology*, 1974, *30*, 81–94.
Mehrabian, A., & Reed, H. Some determinants of communication accuracy.
Psychological Bulletin, 1968, *70*, 365–381.

Mills, J., & Jellison, J. M. Effects on opinion change of how desirable the communication is to the audience the communicator addressed. *Journal of Personality and Social Psychology*, 1967, *6*, 98–101.

Moscovici, S. Communication processes and properties of language. In L. Berkowitz (Ed.), *Advances in experimental social psychology*, 1967, *3*, 225–270.

Neisser, U. *Cognitive psychology*. New York: Appleton-Century-Crofts, 1967.

Newtson, D., & Czerlinsky, T. Adjustment of attitude communications for contrasts by extreme audiences. *Journal of Personality and Social Psychology*, 1974, *30*, 829–837.

Olson, D. R. On the language and authority of textbooks. *Journal of Communication*, 1977, *27*, 10–26.

Olson D. R., & Hildyard, A. Assent and compliance in children's language. In W. P. Dickson (Ed.), *Children's oral communication skills*. New York: Academic Press, 1981.

Portnoy, S. A comparison of oral and written verbal behavior. Ph. D. dissertation, Columbia University, 1968.

Powell, F. A. Cognitive tuning and differentiation of arguments in communication. *Human Communication Research*, 1974, *1*, 53–61.

Rommetveit, R. *On message structure: A framework for the study of language and communication*. New York: Wiley, 1974.

Ruesch, J., & Bateson, G. *Communication: The social matrix of psychiatry*. New York: Norton, 1968.

Schneider, D. J., Hastorf, A. H., & Ellsworth, P. C. *Person perception* (2nd ed.). Reading, Mass.: Addison-Wesley, 1979.

Shatz, M. Children's comprehension of their mothers' question-directives. *Journal of Child Language*, 1978, *5*, 39–46.

Strickler, R. D. A developmental study of the relationship between speaker and listener abilities in referential communication. Ph.D. dissertation, Columbia University, 1975.

Vygotsky, L. S. *Thought and language*. Cambridge: MIT Press, 1962.

Walster, E., & Festinger, L. The effectiveness of "overheard" persuasive communications. *Journal of Abnormal and Social Psychology*, 1962, *65*, 395–402.

Wicklund, R. A., & Brehm, J. W. *Perspectives on cognitive dissonance*. Hillsdale, N.J.: Erlbaum, 1976.

Zajonc, R. B. The process of cognitive tuning and communication. *Journal of Abnormal and Social Psychology*, 1960, *61*, 159–167.

Zimmerman, C., & Bauer, R. A. The effects of an audience on what is remembered. *Public Opinion Quarterly*, 1956, *20*, 238–248.

PART II

Literacy and language

6

Linguistic differences produced by differences between speaking and writing

WALLACE L. CHAFE

In an earlier paper (Chafe, 1982) I discussed two major dimensions that distinguish written language from spoken language, so far as the linguistic properties of these two styles are concerned. I suggested that these dimensions are determined by two basic differences in the writing and speaking processes. The fact that writing is a slow, deliberate, editable process, whereas speaking is done on the fly, leads to a difference that I called the integrated quality of written language as opposed to the fragmented quality of spoken. The fact that writing is a lonely activity whereas speaking typically takes place in an environment of social interaction causes written language to have a detached quality that contrasts with the involvement of spoken language. I listed and illustrated some of the major linguistic features that are manifestations of integration or fragmentation and of detachment or involvement. I also gave some preliminary counts of the occurrences of these features in dinner table conversations and academic prose, counts based on some initial data collected in a research project designed to investigate such differences.

More data, and more thought on these matters, have led to a richer conception of the ways in which written language and spoken language are different. The earlier classification of the relevant linguistic features along the dimensions of integration and involvement was helpful up to a point, but fell short of providing a complete framework for the differences that have been emerging. Here I will present a somewhat more elaborate classification that, although not the final word, comes closer to accounting for our findings. I will mention various broad categories of differences and will list some, but not all, of the linguistic features belonging to each category. I will not here give figures on the relative occurrences of these features in the several kinds of written and spoken data we have collected, reserving such tabulations for a final, more extensive report. The findings and examples below come from 20 subjects who provided us with spoken samples of dinner table conversation and more formal lectures and with written samples of letters and academic prose.

Idea units

Some of the differences between written and spoken language can be understood only with reference to the notion of idea units. Spontaneous, unplanned spoken language is produced in a series of spurts, for which the term *idea unit* has seemed appropriate. A prototypical idea unit has the following properties: (1) It is spoken with a single coherent intonation contour, ending in what is perceived as a clause-final intonation; (2) it is preceded and followed by some kind of hesitation, ranging from a momentary break in timing to a filled or unfilled pause lasting several seconds; (3) it is a clause — that is, it contains one verb phrase along with whatever noun phrases, prepositional phrases, adverbs, and so on are appropriate; and (4) it is about seven words long and takes about two seconds to produce. Idea units do not always conform to this prototype, but on the whole they are clearly identifiable elements of spoken language, and deviations from the prototype are usually explainable in interesting ways. (For further discussion of idea units, their properties, and their significance, see Chafe, 1980.)

It is rewarding to hypothesize that an idea unit contains all the information a speaker can handle in a single focus of consciousness. That is, there is a limit to the amount of information on which a person's attention can be focused at one time. An idea unit expresses the amount of information a person can comfortably pay attention to and verbalize. Trying to handle more information causes trouble, both conceptually and linguistically. (Cf. the "one-clause-at-a-time hypothesis" of Andrew Pawley and Frances Syder, 1983, who show the kinds of difficulties that arise when people try to compose more than a clause at a time.) Another way to put this is to say that an idea unit expresses what is held in short-term memory at a particular time, that short-term memory contains approximately the amount of information that can comfortably be expressed with about seven words of English, and that the content of short-term memory changes about every two seconds, so far as linguistic evidence can tell us.

One of the major characteristics of written language is that it is produced very slowly in comparison with spoken language. There are two reasons for this slowness. To begin with, we really have no choice in the matter. We have to write more slowly than we speak because of the mechanical constraints of writing itself. Not even typing brings us up to the speed of speaking, and presumably the differences between written and spoken language originally developed in the context of handwriting, which is very much slower than speaking. But not only do we have to write more slowly, it would seem that often we want to as well. The fact that we do not need to worry about keeping a listener's attention by talking at a normal speech rate means that we have plenty of time to think about how to put language together. Writing is in fact free of the constraints imposed by the limited temporal and informational capacity of focal consciousness; we have time to let our attention roam over a large amount of information and devote itself to a more deliberate organization of linguistic resources.

One might predict from this that written language, freed from the constraints that produce idea units in spoken language, would not exhibit idea units at all. For some written language that is true. It is hard to find anything like idea units within a passage like the following sequence of 34 words:

Most efforts of psychologists within this tradition have been concentrated on looking for evidence demonstrating the psychological reality of one or another hypothesized underlying representation or of one or another type of linguistic rule.

But, in fact, the most readable writing shows idea units rather clearly. Readable writers seem to organize their material intuitively into this format, using punctuation marks to show idea unit boundaries, or to show the same intonational and hesitational patterns that in spoken language would signal idea unit boundaries.

Two speculations on why the most effective written language should exhibit idea units are worth mentioning. First, written language is historically secondary to spoken language in the sense that very few people in human history have been literate and that even now, with literacy widespread, people still spend much more time talking than writing. It is not surprising that something as basic to spoken language as its organization into idea units should be carried over into writing. Written language is not a brand-new kind of language, but a kind that was founded on the resources of spoken language and that has in the meantime developed certain expanded possibilities. Second, the existence of idea units in written language probably aids considerably the process of reading. When people listen to spoken language, they are in the habit of assimilating information in chunks of idea unit size. As readers, they are probably more comfortable when they are presented with something similar. Or at least it can be suggested that the readability of written language is enhanced by its organization into idea-unit-like segments. It is interesting to note that, while writing is much slower than speaking, reading is usually a little faster. Thus, the amount of information that can be dealt with in a single focus of consciousness is an important consideration in the reading process, and writing that is sensitive to the reader must take that limitation into account. Effective written language, in short, contains idea units because it would otherwise be difficult to assimilate.

Our finding has been that when idea units can be identified in written language, they tend to be significantly longer and more complex than those of spoken. The mean number of words per idea unit in written language appears to be about 11, as compared with about 7 for spoken. The reason, I am suggesting, is that a writer has more time and more devices to use to pack more information into an idea unit: more time in its initial production as well as more time for the luxury of going back and rewriting it. In addition, it is probably relevant that a reader can scan a larger chunk of language than a listener in the same amount of time. Thus, if the mind is actually predisposed to jump from one focus of consciousness to another about every two seconds, a reader can take in more information in that time than a listener. If there is also a limit on how much information can be processed in that time, perhaps writing cannot push the limit too far without forcing a reader to stop and reread. In other words, the best writer may be one who pushes the 7 words per idea unit of spoken language only up to about 11. Readability may be jeopardized by going significantly beyond that. A sequence like the 34-word passage quoted above is simply hard for a reader to assimilate.

Devices for idea unit expansion

It is interesting, then, to discover what devices written language uses for expanding the size and complexity of idea units. I list below the most common of these devices and give examples of each.

(1) Nominalizations, by which verbs like *tend, prefer, speak, refer*, and *use* or adjectives like *abstract* become noun phrases that can then be the arguments of other verbs or the objects of prepositions:

One *tendency* of interest in our narratives is the *preference* of both English and Japanese *speakers* for *referring* to entities by *using* words of an intermediate degree of *abstractness,*

(2) Attributive (preposed) adjectives, by which predications are turned into modifications:

These *communicative* tasks must be discovered by *detailed ethnographic* observation.

Each individual probably develops a partially *unique* set of *linguistic* processes.

(3) Preposed present participles, by which verbs become attributive adjectives:

It is possible that this microcosm functions as an *organizing* framework for further conceptual material.

The *resulting* assertion sounds quite odd.

(4) Postposed present particles, which allow such deverbal modifiers to be followed by direct objects and more:

The infant's knowledge of the world is based initially on innate reflex mechanisms *relating* particular sensory inputs to particular motor actions.

Such an investigation should give insight into . . . the factors *influencing* the loss or retention of that status throughout a discourse.

(5) Preposed past participles:

The sight of an object brings about *directed* looking.

There are *unrestored* ruins there which support this belief.

(6) Postposed past participles:

Some people *labeled* in this way are similar to those in category III.

I was able to understand more intuitively the nature of the linguistic devices *used* by these three speakers.

(7) Prepositional phrases, which writers often use exuberantly:

By this we mean that the goal *of* our ethnographic inquiry is the discovery *of* certain strategic encounters that mirror the progress *of* individuals *through* certain social institutions.

(8) Constituents conjoined in pairs:

Their *explanations and comments* often were revelations to me.

. . . based partly on his own *continuous and largely unconscious* efforts to impose patterns on the linguistic input he receives from other speakers.

(9) Constituents conjoined in series:

Much of syntactic structure as acquired by children is a consequence of *pragmatic and discourse functions, stages of sensori-motor and cognitive development, the development of processing capacities, social development, and various aspects of meaning.*

(10) Complement clauses:

Certain interesting aspects of the situation indicate *that we are not witnessing obligatory synchronic rules at all in the younger speakers.* Her realism involves the refusal *to recognize that literary language has no referent.*

(11) Restrictive relative clauses:

The rules developed here have environmental constraints *that are important to some speakers but non-applicable for others.*

(12) Adverbial phrases of various kinds:

These groups are, of course, labelled *quite profusely* outside of this particular environment. These two unusual processes entered the language *only a century ago.*

(13) Indirect questions:

It is important to ask *whether a given theory deals only with the kinds of cognitive skills that children acquire normally.* . . . since it reveals much in a general way about *how he or she looks.*

(14) Indirect quotations:

Lakoff says *that a sentence like 6b presupposes that Esther Williams is not a fish.* Some speakers say *they heard someone say once that this referred to reeds in the lake there.*

All these devices are more common in writing than in speaking. All of them contribute to the elaboration of idea units that the writer, with a leisure unavailable to the speaker, is able to indulge in.

Integration of idea units into sentences

In spoken language idea units are typically strung together in a chain, with a relatively small amount of subordination. The complex arrangements of clauses characteristic of written language are rarely exploited. Speakers do not have the time or mental resources to compose them. Idea units may be independent:

> And my room was small.
> It was like . . . nine by twelve or something.
> It seemed spacious at the time.
> I came home,
> I was really exhausted,
> I was eating a popsicle,
> I was sitting there in my chair,

Or they may be linked by coordinating conjunctions, by far the most frequent of which is *and*:

> And it's very well equipped.
> You know the kitchen,
> and and it's got a dishwasher,
> and it's got all kinds of you know mixers and plates
> and you know every kind of equipment you need.
> And and staple things.

Thus, idea units in spoken language tend to be not only shorter, but also more independent of each other than those in written language.

The increased amount of time available to a writer, the editability of writing, and probably also the increased speed with which a reader can scan a piece of writing make it possible for a writer to arrange sequences of idea units in ways that are impossible for a hard-pressed speaker on the run. A writer can produce well-rounded sentences that for a speaker are usually impossible. As I have discussed elsewhere, sentences in spoken language are often difficult to identify, and their function is problematic (Chafe, 1980). They are probably not units of cognitive processing and memory, as idea units appear to be. They seem rather to function as ad hoc super–idea units, concocted on the spot, whose terminations are based on passing and changeable judgments of coherence. Sentences in written language, on the other hand, can be sculptured by the writer into complex products of more deliberate, leisurely creation. The principal devices for doing this that we have observed in our data include:

(15) Dependent clauses (by far the most frequent device), introduced by a variety of subordinating conjunctions – for example, *after, although, as, as if, as soon as, because, before, if, in order to, once, since, so that, unless, until, when, whereas, while*:

> *Once a child was called on*, he or she went to the front of the room.

> I shall talk about two styles . . . *as if they were discrete entities*.

(16) Appositives expressed in separate idea units:

> The dinner took place in the home of Kurt, *a native New Yorker living in Oakland, California*.

> This suggestion finds some support in studies of children's "egocentric" speech as well as adults' "inner speech," *cases in which the speaker is not concerned with the needs of a listener*.

(17) Participial clauses:

> Realism, *granting the difference between representative and the thing represented*, is concerned with the nature and quality of representation.

> *Described in this way*, the use of nominal vs. pronominal reference seems to be an appropriate area for psycholinguistic investigation.

To summarize, spoken language consists typically of chains of relatively brief, relatively independent idea units. Written language not only has longer idea units, but places them in various relations of dependence.

Information flow

Another difference between written and spoken language that can be attributed to the different ways in which they are produced in time has to do with features of spoken language that are present because a speaker is putting out information at a rapid rate and needs to monitor and attempt to control its flow. Here we are concerned with features of a type that are prevalent in spoken language, but virtually absent from written. They are features of two kinds, in a sense positive and negative consequences of producing language on the fly. The positive consequences are devices that control the flow of information, like sluice gates in the stream of speech. Included here are words and phrases such as *anyway, by the way, for one thing, let's say, now, oh, OK, well,* and *why*:

(18) Flow-monitoring devices:

> And *anyway* it was a lot of people.
> *Well, now* when . . . just starting this week . . . for the first time.

The more negative consequences of the rapid rate of speaking are the numerous "disfluencies" in spoken language: false starts, afterthroughts, repetitions, corrections, and fumblings:

(19) Disfluencies:

> No but I mean there are . . . there are some people I can toler . . . old people I can tolerate.
> Cause . . . um . . . there were . . . four fam . . . four? Yeah four families.

I would not want to emphasize the negative qualities of these disfluencies so much as to point out their contribution to a lively, ongoing, creative use of language. We do not normally perceive them as deficiencies in language production, unless a speaker is unusually inarticulate. We tune them out, and are surprised when the prevalence of disfluencies in normal speech is pointed out.

Spoken language, then, shows various devices for the control of information flow and various disfluencies attributable to the rapid pace of speaking. These phenomena are present only in writing that mimics the process of composing speech – for example, to some extent in informal letters. In most writing, though the writer may have come up with false starts and afterthoughts on the way to the finished product, it is only that product we see. Spoken language shows us a great deal about the processes of its own creation. Written language generally hides such processes from us and shows us only the polished result.

Innovation and conservatism

Written and spoken language actually differ with respect to another scale of time as well. So far we have considered only the effects of small-scale time, that involved in the production of idea units and sentences: time on the scale of minutes or seconds or fractions of seconds. But there is also a difference on the scale of years or centuries or even millennia. Spoken language as a thing in itself disappears almost as soon as it is produced; written language can last indefinitely. Furthermore, something written down can be examined as a static object. Specimens of it can be analyzed at the

analyst's leisure, and grammars can be written to describe what it is
like, or what it ought to be like. Norms for written language become
codified and taught. Nothing equivalent happens for speaking. In
fact, only since the recent advent of the tape recorder has it been
possible leisurely to examine the nature of spoken language. Before
that there was, and still is in many circles, a strong inclination to
equate language with written language. Understandably enough. It
was the only kind of language that was there to be seen. The result
of this situation has been a tendency for written language to be in
some respects more conservative, to change less rapidly, than spoken.
Its codification, the establishment of norms, has made written language the repository of more stabilized linguistic traits, traits that
spoken language is freer to replace through normal processes of
change.

   The English lexicon consists of three kinds of items: those that are
used predominantly in speaking, those that are used predominantly
in writing, and those (the largest group) that are neutral with respect
to this distinction. Examples of predominantly spoken vocabulary,
where often new senses have developed for old words, are items like
the following:

(20) Colloquial vocabulary:

   guy [vs. neutral *man* or *person*]
   stuff [vs. neutral *material*]
   scary [vs. neutral *frightening*]

Words like the following are used mostly in writing:

(21) Literary vocabulary:

   display [vs. neutral *show*]
   state [vs. neutral *say*]
   heed [vs. neutral *pay attention to*]

   When it comes to the study of *grammatical* innovation and conservatism in spoken and written language, I can do no more than provide
a few suggestive examples. We all know that spoken English makes
use of grammatical devices that are not accepted in written English.
Some of them could conceivably become a respectable part of our
language's future. Some are now considered "errors" in traditional
English grammar; others are regarded as sloppy ways of talking. But
all of them could be thought of simply as ways in which the language
is changing, so that, if spoken English were left to its own develop-

ment, they might sooner or later become an institutionalized part of its grammar. What follows is an illustrative sampling of such devices:

(22) Indefinite "this":

I'm doing *this* big thing with Bill.
I woke up with *this* headache.

(23) A pronoun referring to an event or state, rather than to a nominal referent:

That in itself was scary [where *that* refers to fainting in the shower].

(24) A pronoun with no established referent:

It's actually going to be more like eight to one [where *it* has no clear referent].

(25) Singular verb agreement with a plural noun:

There's so many things that could be done with those [instead of *there are*].

(26) A clause-final preposition:

And he started after the guy I was *with*.

(27) A trailing conjunction:

You want to look at everything else that bears on what it might possibly be *and*.
It was too big for him *but*.

(28) A topic:

But *a friend of mine*, he had a student,
The whole sequence I can describe to you.

(29) An antitopic:

Never been to a wedding dance. *Neither of us*.
It was almost like eating from morning till evening. *These enormous meals*.

(30) A contraction:

It's the first time *she's* ever done it.
We'll see how it works out.

On the conservative side, written language preserves various constructions rarely used in spoken. Among those we have found are:

(31) A past perfect:

I *had not decided* to use this conversation in particular.

(32) A subjunctive:

Realism insists that representation in art *be* "true" and not "false."

(33) A postposed adjective:

This information is not necessarily derivable from other appellations *equally appropriate* in an absolute sense.

(34) *No* used as an adjective:

And in *no* instance is the discrepancy between basic and subordinate level responses significant.

(35) A postposed reflexive pronoun:

She was well aware that the work of art is not reality *itself*.

All in all, then, spoken language seems to be the locus of ongoing language change, whereas written language preserves a more conservative vocabulary and grammar.

Involvement and detachment

So far we have considered those differences between written and spoken language that can be attributed to the slowness, editability, and permanence of writing, as opposed to the speed and evanescence of speaking. But there are other differences between speaking and writing, among them the fact that speakers are usually in face-to-face interaction with their interlocutors, whereas writers are usually isolated from their audiences, both spatially and temporally. The result is an opposition that I have referred to as the involvement of spoken language versus the detachment of written. But there are really three kinds of involvement: involvement of the speaker with himself, that is, ego involvement; involvement of the speaker with the hearer, that is, concern for the dynamics of interaction with another person; and involvement of the speaker with the subject matter, that is, an ongoing personal commitment to what is being talked about.

Ego involvement shows up most obviously in the use of first-person pronouns – *I, me, we, us, my, our, mine, ours* – but also in the use of phrases like *I mean, I don't know,* and *as I say,* as well as in references to the speaker's mental processes: -

(36) Ego involvement:

I mean like everyone was shocked.
And so *I thought* hm that's strange you know.

Involvement with the hearer may take the form of using a second-person pronoun, addressing the hearer by name, responding to a hearer's question or posing one, making a request, asking for confirmation with *right?* or *OK?* or especially using the ubiquitous *you know* (see the preceding example):

(37) Involvement with the hearer:

I mean *you* should do that.
Well we've won a whole lot . . . *right?*

Finally, there is the use of devices that express a speaker's lively interest in the subject matter being communicated. A speaker may exaggerate, exclaim, use expressive vocabulary, introduce the historical present, use direct quotations, or sprinkle his or her discourse with vivid particles like *just* and *really*:

(38) Involvement with the subject matter:

You can always write *dozens* of articles.
The first three days of it were *really* grueling.

Written language is correspondingly detached. A writer is typically less concerned with ego expression, less concerned with any direct interaction with the audience, and less immediately involved with the subject matter. There are a few overt indications of greater detachment on the part of writers. One is the use of passives:

(39) Passives:

I will demonstrate that, in this case, these processes *have been freed* from earlier constraints.
Thus the styles of the participants *can only be judged* as they surfaced in interaction with these other participants.

Another is the use of subjects that are abstract noun phrases or abstract clauses:

(40) Abstract subjects:

> While *such unavoidable lack of objectivity* is indeed a danger . . .
> Then *this limitation* will surely play a part in determining the nature of the "rules" for reference in any language.

Speakers, in short, are typically wrapped up in the speech situation and in their topic. Writers, no matter how committed, do not usually maintain an involvement of the same degree.

Evidentiality

All languages seem to have various ways of expressing the attitudes speakers or writers have toward the knowledge they are communicating. Such attitudes have to do, for example, with the reliability of that knowledge, the reasoning that led to it, or the kind of data on which it was based. Phenomena of this kind have been classed within linguistics under the heading "evidentiality" (Chafe and Nichols, in press). What is of interest to us here is that spoken and written English treat evidentiality somewhat differently. I have discussed this matter in more detail elsewhere (Chafe, in press) and will only summarize here what I have found.

It would appear that spoken–written differences in the expression of evidentiality can be attributed to both the temporal and the interactive aspects of speaking and writing. The greater time available to writers means that they can deliberate longer regarding the status of their knowledge, and in fact writers show a concern for certain kinds of reliability and certain kinds of reasoning that speakers are not so much concerned with. Furthermore, the permanence of written language means that writers need to worry about possible future criticism of their output in ways that a speaker does not. But it is also relevant that the interactive nature of speaking results in speakers paying more attention to their direct experience and to the ways in which language reflects their experience. In being more detached from their subject matter, writers evaluate its reliability in a more detached way.

One type of evidentiality has to do precisely with a speaker or writer's assessment of the reliability of the knowledge being communicated, the degree to which it can be taken as fact. Most knowledge is communicated as if it *were* factual, and, in English at least, it is only in a minority of cases that the question of reliability enters the picture at all or is linguistically signaled. Ways in which reliability is communicated include the use of adverbs like *maybe*, *probably*, and *certainly* and of modals like *may* and *might*. The following two examples are from spoken language:

(41) Reliability of knowledge:

> We kept thinking *maybe* they'd be stationed at the Presidio.
> The one thing that *might* shed light on it was something about requests.

Written language uses these same devices plus a few others that occur rarely in speaking – for example *possibly, undoubtedly,* and *surely*:

> The answer *undoubtedly* varies from one situation to another.
> . . . then this limitation will *surely* play a part in determining the nature of the "rules" for reference in any language.

There is, however, an interesting difference between spoken and written language with respect to the marking of reliability. Speakers seem to be concerned almost exclusively with the likelihood of something being true or not true. The choice is a categorical one, and spoken language simply expresses the probability of something being one way rather than another. Writers, on the other hand, have time to recognize that truth itself may be relative, that what is being communicated may itself be more or less true and not just true or not. There is a concern for statistical reliability that is rarely present in spoken language. This concern is manifested in evidentials like *basically, essentially, generally, in some sense, invariably, normally, primarily,* and *virtually*:

> The need for a personal name is *normally* felt at the time of a person's birth.
> . . . where players on the field chatter *primarily* in formulas.

Beyond the expression of reliability, a second type of evidentiality marks knowledge as having been arrived at through some kind of reasoning. Spoken language emphasizes inductive reasoning – inference based on some kind of evidence – which it marks most commonly with the modal *must*, but also with expressions like *seem to, evidently,* and *be obvious*:

(42) Induction:

> It *must* have been a kid.
> It was just *obvious* I couldn't work.

Written language, especially academic prose, marks inductive reasoning less and deductive more. In particular, writers use expressions like *should* and *presumably* to predict that something is or will be the case although there is no direct evidence for it. Deductive reasoning, one might suppose, requires the greater time for imaginative thought that writing provides, time to formulate hypotheses and deduce their consequences:

(43) Deduction:

Longer processing times *should* be associated with better performance.

. . . though adults *presumably* are capable of purely logical thought.

A third type of evidentiality marks knowledge more specifically as having been derived from a particular kind of evidence, usually either from sensory evidence or from hearsay. English has devices of this sort that occur sporadically in our spoken data, but not at all in the written. Sensory evidence leading to highly reliable knowledge may be expressed directly in spoken language with the verbs *see*, *hear*, and *feel*:

(44) Sensory evidence:

I *hear* her taking a shower.

Lesser reliability is indicated with the expressions *look like*, *sound like*, and *feel like*:

It *sounds like* she's taking a shower.

Hearsay evidence, the evidence provided by another person's utterances, may be expressed in spoken language by phrases like *it seems* or *supposed to*:

Well Schaeffer *it seems* had just found the latest article from the Smithsonian.

I think it's *supposed to* be the most expensive place in Europe to live.

Writers do not often mention sensory or hearsay evidence, but in academic prose information derived from another source is of course provided by citations of relevant literature, as may be seen passim in any academic paper.

The fourth and last kind of evidentiality I will mention comes under the category of "hedges" (Lakoff, 1972). Here the concern is not with the reliability of knowledge itself, but with the extent to which a given piece of knowledge matches an available category — the extent to which it is adequately coded, for example, by some word or phrase. Spoken language makes frequent use of *sort of* and *kind of* for this purpose:

(45) Hedges:

He started *sort of* circling.

"Circling," we understand, may not have captured exactly what the speaker had in mind, but it was the best she could come up with under the time pressure of conversation. These expressions are rare in written language, in which reliability is more of an issue than categorization. Writers have more time to find the right word or phrase and seldom need to hedge their choices. They are more prone to wonder whether, or to what extent, their statements may be true.

In summary, spoken and written language both show a concern for the reliability of knowledge. Written language, however, shows more awareness that truth is not just categorical, but a matter of degree. So far as reasoning is concerned, spoken language signals induction more often, written language deduction. Evidence and hearsay are signaled more often in spoken language, except for the frequent literature citations in academic writing. Hedging, in the sense of signaling the inadequacy of the choice of some word or phrase to convey exactly what the speaker had in mind, is characteristic of speaking but not of writing.

Conclusions

I began by describing the idea units that recent research has shown to be fundamental units of spoken language, the linguistic expression of speakers' focuses of consciousness as their thoughts move forward through time. I noted that idea units may also be present in written language, where they are usually longer, presumably because writers have more time to pack more information into them and because readers are able to scan more information in a given time period. I then showed how idea units are loosely chained together in spoken language to form sentences, the boundaries of which are often ambiguous and unclear, and how writers have more time to integrate the idea units within sentences into more complex constructions. A final result of the fast pace of speaking versus the deliberateness of writing is the prevalence in the former and the absence in the latter of devices marking information flow, as well as the numerous disfluencies so characteristic of spoken language.

On a larger time scale we can consider the evanescence of speaking and the permanence of writing, a difference that leads to the preservation of more conservative traits in the latter, spoken language being the principal site of ongoing language change, both lexical and grammatical. Written language holds onto older traits longer; spoken language is constantly introducing new ones.

The fact that speakers are usually face to face with their audiences while writers are usually isolated leads to manifestations of involvement in spoken language that contrast with the detachment of written. There is involvement with the speaker's own ego, with the process of interaction with the hearer, and with the subject matter. Written language lacks these manifestations of involvement and shows signs of detachment from such concerns.

Finally, I discussed some differences between a speaker's and a writer's attitude toward the knowledge being communicated, as expressed in various evidential devices. In judging the reliability of their knowledge, speakers restrict themselves to the likelihood of something being categorically true or not, whereas writers often allow for degrees of truth, for statistical probability. In reasoning, speakers rely on induction whereas writers have the leisure for hypothesis formation and deduction. Speakers sometimes throw in markers of sensory or hearsay evidence, whereas writers only admit hearsay in the form of citations. And the hedging of categorizations is restricted to spoken language.

These generalizations apply best to the extremes of spoken and written language that we have investigated, dinner table conversation and academic prose; they must be qualified for more formal styles of speaking as well as for more casual styles of writing. As yet we have hardly investigated at all the occurrences of these features in aesthetic literature, where we expect to find different authors exploiting them differently for different purposes. In a later report we will also trace the genesis of these differences in the speaking and writing of elementary school children, making use of data from third and sixth graders that parallel the adult data discussed here.

ACKNOWLEDGMENTS

This project has been supported by Grant NIE-G-80-0125 from the National Institute of Education. I am grateful to Jane Danielewicz and Pamela Downing for their collaboration.

REFERENCES

Chafe, W. L. The deployment of consciousness in the production of a narrative. In W. L. Chafe (Ed.), *The pear stories: Cognitive, cultural, and linguistic aspects of narrative production.* Norwood, N.J.: Ablex, 1980.

Integration and involvement in speaking, writing, and oral literature. In D. Tannen (Ed.), *Spoken and written language.* Norwood, N.J.: Ablex, 1982.

Evidentiality in conversational English and academic prose. In W. L. Chafe & J. Nichols (Eds.), *Evidentiality: The linguistic coding of epistemology.* Norwood, N.J.: Ablex, in press.

Chafe, W. L., & Nichols, J. (Eds.). *Evidentiality: The linguistic coding of epistemology.* Norwood, N.J.: Ablex, in press.

Lakoff, G. *Hedges: A study in meaning criteria and the logic of fuzzy concepts.* Chicago Linguistic Society, Vol. 8, 1972.

Pawley, A., & Syder, F. Natural selection and syntax: Notes on adaptive variation and change in vernacular and literary grammar. *Journal of Pragmatics*, 1983, 7, 551–579.

7

Relative focus on involvement in oral and written discourse

DEBORAH TANNEN

Introduction

Most research on spoken versus written language has analyzed casual conversation as spoken language and expository prose, or what Olson (1977) calls "essayist literacy," as written. This is not by chance. There is something typically spoken about face-to-face conversation and something typically written about expository prose. These genres typify but do not exhaustively characterize spoken and written discourse. In recent writings (Tannen, 1982a, 1982b, 1983) I have demonstrated that both spoken discourse and written discourse exhibit combinations of features that have been identified with spoken and written language, respectively, or, more generally, with an oral and a literate tradition. I have previously called these features *oral and literate strategies*.

I have suggested, furthermore, that these features do not reflect orality versus literacy per se. Rather, what I was calling oral strategies and others have called features of orality or of spoken language in fact are the result of relative focus on interpersonal involvement. And what I was calling literate strategies and others have called features of literacy or of written language are actually the result of relatively less focus on interpersonal involvement, with consequently more focus on the information conveyed. Thus, the terms *oral strategies* and *literate strategies* are misnomers. For this reason, I would like now to move away from them and refer instead to features reflecting relative focus on interpersonal involvement.

The significance of relative focus on involvement is not an arbitrary or trivial notion, nor is it limited to issues of orality and literacy. One of the reasons it is appealing as an explanatory hypothesis is that it accounts for variation in all forms of discourse, including conversation. The framework of relative focus on interpersonal involvement is related to a framework that runs through the recent work of many scholars on interaction – the universal simultaneous but conflicting human needs to be connected to others and to be independent. This has been discussed in linguistics under the rubric of universal politeness phenomena (R. Lakoff, 1973, 1979; Brown & Levinson, 1978) and as the cline of person (Becker & Oka, 1976) and in sociology as deference (Goffman, 1967).

The concept of relative focus on involvement is related to what Bateson (1972) describes as the double bind in communication – a phenomenon that he introduced to account for pathology but that, Scollon (1982) demonstrates, characterizes all human communication. As rephrased by Becker (1982), humans continually subject each other to simultaneous conflicting messages to the effect that "You are like me" and "You are not me," or, put another way, "I want to be close to you" and "I want to be separate from you." These two conflicting messages necessarily grow out of the conflicting human needs to be connected to other people and to be distant from them – that is, not to be engulfed by closeness.

Indeed, humans are not the only creatures caught in this double bind. Bettelheim (1979) cites the example of porcupines who seek shelter in a cave during a cold winter. They huddle together for warmth, but their quills prick each other, so they pull away. Then they get cold again. They must continually adjust their closeness and distance in order to balance their simultaneous but conflicting needs to be close to each other and not to get pricked.[1]

The need to serve these conflicting goals motivates linguistic choices. For example, indirectness is used in conversation to avoid imposing one's wants or opinions on others; and much of casual conversation has little significant information to impart but is important because it shows connection. In Bateson's terms, it carries a metamessage of rapport: The fact that it is said communicates that the speaker wants to be involved with the addressee.

In this chapter I first outline the evolution of my own thinking about oral and written discourse, then describe and further discuss the features that grow out of relative focus on involvement (previously called "oral strategies" and "literate strategies"), explain how they grow out of relative focus on involvement, and demonstrate that they cut across spoken and written modes, using examples from my own and others' research. Finally, I suggest that the features reflecting relative focus on involvement seem to underlie successful production and comprehension of discourse in both spoken and written modes.

From oral/literate tradition to involvement

My use of terms has evolved from *oral and literate tradition* (Tannen, 1980a) to an *oral/literate continuum* (Tannen, 1980b, 1982b), to *oral and literate strategies* (Tannen, 1982a, 1983), to *features of involvement focus versus content focus*,[2] to my present notion of *features reflecting relative focus on involvement*.

In the process of analyzing narratives told in English and Greek about the same film I found myself faced with a "So what?" problem. I had identified certain differences between Greek and American narratives – for example, the Greeks tended to approach the narrative as a storytelling task whereas the Americans tended to approach it as a memory task, with complex discourse consequences in both cases – but I could not figure out the significance of these differences. John Gumperz suggested that I turn to research on oral versus literate tradition and directed me to Goody and Watt (1963). Eureka! This seemed to explàin the differences I had found. One after another of the discourse phenomena in the Greek and American narratives could be explained by the hypothesis that the Greeks were using narrative strategies associated with oral tradition – for example, selecting an overall theme of the film, including only those details that contributed to the theme, making use of culturally familiar explanations, personalizing, and philosophizing – whereas Americans were using strategies associated with literate tradition – for example, listing details for correctness, fussing over temporal accuracy, critiquing the filmmaker's skill, and analyzing the film as an artifact (Tannen, 1980b.)

Soon I had immersed myself in the literature on this topic (for example, Olson, 1977; Goody, 1977; Ong, 1967, 1977; Havelock, 1963; Kay, 1977; Cook-Gumperz & Gumperz, 1981). The oral/literate dichotomy had the power and fascination of a revelation.

Looking back on research I had done on conversational discourse, I saw that this too could be explained by the oral/literate dichotomy. Analyzing taped, transcribed spontaneous conversation among friends, I had discovered that certain speakers tended to use such conversational strategies as cooperative overlap, that is, talking at the same time without interrupting; exaggerated paralinguistic features such as dramatic changes in rate of speech, loudness, and pitch; and frequent storytelling in which the point of the story is dramatized rather than stated and tends to be about personal feelings. These and other conversational strategies could be seen as sacrificing the explicit and clear statement of information for the demonstration of interpersonal involvement. (This phenomenon will be illustrated presently. See also Tannen, 1981, 1984.) Thus I began to think in terms of an oral/literate continuum.

It occurred to me, then, that the broad perspective of research on oral and literate tradition went far to account for features that had been identified as associated with spoken versus written (Chafe, 1982; see also Chapter 6) and unplanned versus planned discourse (Ochs, 1979). However, as my students and I systematically looked for these features in spoken and written narratives, it became clear that some written genres – for example, literary prose – combined features of spoken with features of written discourse (Tannen, 1980b, 1982b).

For example, the analysis of a personal narrative first told and then written by the same narrator suggested that written literary narrative combined what Chafe calls features of integration expected in writing with features of involvement expected in speaking. Therefore, it seemed preferable to refer to oral and literate strategies that could be used either in speaking or writing (Tannen, 1982a, 1983).

In all these discussions, I stressed that the key differences motivating discourse are not orality versus literacy per se but rather relative focus on interpersonal involvement and relative focus on content or information conveyed. In a sense, my use of *oral* and *literate* in referring to these features reflected my own heuristic process – it was through research on oral and literate tradition and spoken and written language that I had come to identify the significance of relative focus on interpersonal involvement. However, terminology tends to reify concepts. Since what is really significant is not the distinction between orality and literacy per se but rather relative focus on involvement, I would now like to adopt terminology that places that key dimension in the foreground.

Two features of relative focus on involvement

Two hypotheses have been advanced to account for differences that have been observed between spoken and written discourse. I will refer to them as the contextualization hypothesis and the cohesion hypothesis. I will consider each in turn, determining whether it is in fact descriptive of spoken versus written discourse and considering it in terms of relative focus on involvement.

The contextualization hypothesis

Many scholars have characterized spoken discourse as highly context-bound and written discourse as decontextualized. Thus, a speaker can refer to the context of immediate surroundings visible to both speaker and hearer who are copresent in time and place. For example, I could say, "Look at this!" relying on hearers to see what *this* refers to. Second, speakers are free to be minimally explicit because if the hearer(s) are confused, they can ask for clarification on the spot. Finally, speakers frequently share social background and hence many assumptions about the world, their mutual or respective histories, and so on.

In contrast, according to the contextualization hypothesis, a writer and reader are generally separated in time and place, so immediate context is lost. Second, the reader cannot ask for clarification when confused, so the writer must anticipate all likely confusion and preclude it by filling in needed background information and as many as possible of the steps of a logical argument. Third, because the writer and reader are likely to share minimal social context, the writer can make fewer assumptions about shared attitudes and beliefs.

Clearly, in such a schema, what is thought of as spoken discourse is spontaneous face-to-face conversation, and what is thought of as written discourse is expository prose. For these genres it is informative to point out that spoken language is highly context-bound, while written appears to be less so. Of course, the notion that written discourse – or any discourse – is actually decontextualized is at best an exaggeration. Many scholars, including Fillmore (1979a), Nystrand (1982), and Rader (1982), have demonstrated that no piece of discourse can be understood without prior knowledge of many kinds of contexts. Hymes (personal communication) points out that to verify this one need only read a scholarly article in a discipline other than one's own. Hence, I suggest that the features described grow out of the respective genres and their own contexts rather than out of the spoken and written modes per se.

In face-to-face spontaneous conversation such as that which occurs at a dinner table, the fact of speaking to each other is often more important than the information or messages conveyed. Moreover, most of what is said in social settings is relatively insignificant, as teenagers are quick to notice in their parents' conversations. But that is not to say that the utterances are not important. Quite the contrary: They communicate what Bateson (1972) calls metamessages – statements about the relationship between interactants. Far from being unimportant, metamessages are the necessary basis for any interaction. Typical are such metamessages as "I am [or am not] well disposed toward you," "I'm teasing you," and the like.

Expository prose is a special genre in which the message (as distinguished from the metamessage) is relatively important. Thus Kay (1977) points out that what has been associated with writing, what he calls "autonomous language," has come with technological advancement. A complex technological society has need for much communication, typically among strangers, in which interpersonal involvement is ostensibly beside the point and communication is more efficiently carried out if such involvement is conventionally ignored. When carried over to face-to-face communication, however, such conventional ignoring of interpersonal involvement may be seen as peculiarly American or Western. It tends to create misunderstandings when American businessmen and diplomats try to ignore personal involvement and get right down to business with their Japanese, Arab, or Greek counterparts, for whom the establishment of personal relationships must lay the groundwork for any business or diplomatic dealings.

It is not a coincidence that the genres of casual conversation on the one hand and expository prose on the other have been associated with spoken and written language, respectively. There is something typically written about message-focused communication, for it is the innovation of print that made it common to communicate on a large scale with others who are not in one's immediate context. And there is something typically oral about interpersonal involvement. In communication with others with whom one has a close social or personal relationship, it is hard to focus on information exclusively, because the importance of the relationship is too keenly felt to be ignored. This involvement is reflected in the conventional wisdom that one should not take driving lessons from a spouse or parent, or by the fact that any comment can touch off a fight between speakers or any comment can seem particularly charming, depending on the place of the interaction in the history of the relationship between participants.

Nonetheless these two genres, conversation and expository prose, are by no means exclusive. It is possible and indeed common to have written communication in which it hardly matters what the content is; the fact of communication is paramount – for example, in some personal letters, where it is just as possible to write a lot of nothing as it is to whisper sweet nothings, with just as much satisfaction for all concerned. Note-passing in school and at lectures can fall into this category as well. Similarly, it is possible, indeed common, to have communication that is message-focused in an oral mode, as in lectures and radio or television broadcasts (though contemporary radio and television broadcasts, including the news, seem to be getting more involvement-focused and less message-focused). It seems, moreover, that ritual language in traditional society has some of the features usually associated with written texts: The speaker performs a chant or ceremony that was composed long ago by authors far away, addressed to a large and impersonal audience (Chafe, 1982).

A key dimension distinguishing discourse types, then, is whether it is one-way or two-way communication, and this dimension is closely associated with relative focus on involvement, as contrasted with relative focus on information (in Bateson's terms, the metamessage and message, respectively).

One more observation is in order about the close connection between interpersonal involvement and speaking, on the one hand, and focus on information and writing, on the other. The slowness of writing makes it an ill-formed medium for the communication of nonsignificant messages. I have experienced this in communicating with deaf people, wherein writing is the only medium available for communication. Straightaway, I find myself choosing not to communicate all sorts of relatively unimportant asides because they do not seem worth the trouble of writing.[3] Yet it is just such seemingly meaningless interchange that creates social relationships. That is precisely why deafness is such a terrible handicap: It is socially isolating.

Cohesion in spoken and written discourse

A second major observation that has been made about spoken and written discourse – one that indeed seems to be an outgrowth of spoken versus written modes and that accounts for the second major strategy difference I refer to – is the observation that in spoken discourse, cohesion is accomplished through paralinguistic and prosodic cues, whereas in written discourse cohesion must be lexicalized (Chafe, 1982; Cook-Gumperz & Gumperz, 1981; Gumperz, Kaltman, & O'Connor, 1984; Ochs, 1979).

In speaking, everything that is said must be said in some way: at some pitch, in some tone of voice, at some speed, with some expression or lack of expression in the voice and on the face of the speaker. All these nonverbal and paralinguistic features reveal the speaker's attitude toward the message – what Labov (1972) identified as "evaluation" in narrative – and establish cohesion, that is, show relationships among ideas, highlight relative importance, foreground or background certain information, and so on. Just as in a social setting one cannot not communicate – the act of keeping silent within the frame of interaction communicates something (Bateson 1972) – one cannot speak without showing one's attitude toward the message and the speech activity.

In writing, on the other hand, the nonverbal and paralinguistic channels are not available. You may wrinkle your brow until it cracks while you write, but this will not show up on the written page. You may yell or whisper or sing as you compose sentences, but the words as they fall on the page will not reflect this. Print, and to a lesser extent handwriting, is a great leveler; it reduces or inflates all utterances to lines of equivalent evaluative status on a page. Writers try to overcome this limitation by using such devices as capitalization, underlining, italics, exclamation points, and the like.

Therefore, in writing, the relationships between ideas, and the writer's attitude toward them, must be lexicalized. This can be done in a number of ways, including (1) explicit statement (for example, the contrast between smiling, smirking, or chuckling while speaking, as opposed to writing, "In a humorous vein . . ."; or winking while speaking as opposed to writing, "I don't mean this literally"); (2) careful choice of words with just the right connotations; or (3) complex syntactic constructions and transitional phrases. Thus a number of linguists have found that in spoken narrative – and here the genre is important – ideas are strung together with no conjunctions at all or the minimal conjunction *and* (Chafe, 1982; Kroll, 1977; Ochs, 1979). In contrast, written narrative uses conjunctions such as *so* and *because*, which express the relationship between ideas and subordinate constructions that foreground and background information as is done paralinguistically in speaking.

Thus we may think of discourse in which meaning and attitudes are expressed paralinguistically, nonverbally, or indirectly as being typically spoken, that is, using strategies that are basic to face-to-face conversation and possible only in spoken discourse. These strategies, furthermore, build on interpersonal involvement, since filling in unstated information and relationships between propositions, as well as deducing evaluation from voice quality and other paralinguistic features, requires the hearer to share prior communicative experience and background knowledge and to do some of the work of sense making, all of which create a feeling of involvement. In contrast, discourse that relies on lexicalization of meaning and relationships between propositions either is written or uses strategies that are frequently found in written discourse. And note that lexicalization is message-focused; it draws less on the reader's shared social knowledge and makes the reader do less of the work of sense making. However, written discourse may try to create the effect of face-to-face interaction as novelists do when they add to dialogue such comments as "She said with a wink."

Involvement focus and information focus in discourse

The observation that spoken discourse can exhibit strategies generally associated with either an oral or a literate mode can be traced back to what Bernstein (1964) calls restricted and elaborated codes. Bernstein found that children's discourse, as elicited by experimental tasks, fell into two stylistic types, which he identified as different "codes." For example, in describing a picture, a child using restricted code might say, "They hit it through there and he got mad." A child using elaborated code might say, "The children were playing ball and hit the ball through the window. The man who lived in the house got mad at them." The second version is easier to understand, but only when the picture is not in view, that is, when the immediate context is not shared. To speak an "elaborated code," that is, to fill in referents and contextual information when it is provided by the immediate context, may be perceived as a denial of shared context and might elicit an offended protest: "I've got eyes. I can see that." It would be perceived as appropriate only in contexts that require such otherwise redundant information, as for example some school or school-like tasks.

Bernstein did not associate these two codes with orality and literacy, but this correspondence is pointed out by Cook-Gumperz and Gumperz (1981), Hill and Varenne (1981), Kay (1977), and Olson (1977).

I would now like to cite some of my own and others' work to demonstrate that both written and spoken discourse can reflect both features typically associated with speaking and those typically associated with writing – that is, features of relative focus on involvement. I will show examples of such features first in spoken and then in written discourse.

Focus on involvement in conversation

Let us assume that involvement is marked by discourse that is highly context-bound, that requires maximal contribution from the audience in supplying background information and doing interpretive work, and that depends upon paralinguistic and nonverbal channels rather than lexicalization for cohesion and evaluation. Message-focused discourse relies less on immediate context, it requires less audience contribution in supplying necessary information and connections, and it achieves cohesion through lexicalization.

In my own research on conversation I have identified systematic differences in features I refer to, collectively, as conversational style. These can be understood as different ways of observing relative focus on interpersonal involvement.

In one extended study, I tape-recorded and transcribed two-and-a-half hours of naturally occurring conversation at Thanksgiving dinner among six friends of various ethnic and geographic backgrounds. I identified the linguistic and paralinguistic features that made up participants' speaking styles in this setting, focusing on such features as pacing, rate of speech, overlap and interruption, intonation, pitch, loudness, syntactic structures, topic, storytelling, irony, humor, and so on (Tannen, 1984). I found that many of these features clustered in the styles of participants such that three of the participants seemed to share what might be called one style. (This, of course, is an idealization; each person's style is a unique cluster of devices used in particular ways.) In contrast, the other three clearly did not share this style (that is, they did not use the features identified in the ways the others did, and they did not interpret those features in the way the others intended them). I have called this identifiable style high-involvement, since many of the features that characterize it can be understood as placing emphasis on interpersonal involvement, or the interpersonal dynamic of the interaction. Those who did not share this style expected strategies that may be seen as more message-focused (some would say literate-like) in the sense that they placed more emphasis on the information conveyed.

One way this pattern emerged was in attitude toward and tendency to use overlapped or simultaneous speech. Three of the participants in the conversation I studied were "cooperative overlappers." That is, two or more of them often talked at the same time, but this did not mean that they weren't listening to each other, and it did not mean that they wanted to grab the floor – that is, to interrupt. Often, a listener talked at the same time as a speaker to show encouragement, or showed understanding by uttering "response cries" (Goffman, 1981), or told mini-stories to demonstrate understanding, or finished the speaker's sentences to demonstrate that the listener knew where the sentence was headed. All of this overlapping gives the speaker the assurance that he or she isn't in the conversation alone. In addition, the active listeners often asked questions eliciting information the speaker obviously would have told anyway, not to indicate that they thought the speaker wasn't going to tell, but to assure the speaker that the information was eagerly awaited.

The preference for overlapping talk in some settings has been reported among at least some members of numerous ethnic groups: Armenian, Italian-American, black American, West Indian, Cape Verdean, to name just a few. The preference for overlapping talk sacrifices the clear relay of information for the sake of showing conversational involvement. In that sense, it is typically interactive, valuing the need for interpersonal involvement more highly than the need for the information conveyed. The speakers who exhibit overlapping speech in a casual setting probably do not use it, or use less of it, in such settings as interviews or receiving instructions in which information is relatively more important. But when speakers use this device with others who do not expect or understand its use in this way, the effect is quite the opposite. The other speaker feels interrupted and stops talking. An ironic aspect of this style clash is that the interruption is actually created by the one who stops talking when he or she was expected to continue.

Another aspect of effects of differing focus on involvement that emerged in this study of conversational style is the way speakers got to the point of their personal narratives and what the points of their stories were likely to be. In the conversation of speakers whose style I have characterized as involvement-focused (1) more stories were told; (2) the stories were more likely to be about personal experiences; (3) the point of the story was more likely to concern feelings about those experiences; and (4) perhaps most important, the point of the story was generally not lexicalized but was dramatized by replaying the speaker's reaction or creating a similar reaction in the audience by mimicry of the characters in the narrative.

These differences in storytelling styles left all participants feeling a bit dissatisfied with the narratives told in the style other than their own. All participants tended to react to stories told by different-style speakers with a variant of "What's the point?" – the rejoinder Labov (1972) has aptly called "withering."

The following is an example of a story told during Thanksgiving dinner by Steve:

(1) Steve: I have a little seven-year-old student ... a little girl who wears those. ...... She is too much.
p

(2) Deborah: She wears those? [*chuckle*]
Steve: Can you imagine? She's seven years old, and she
acc
sits in her chair and she goes .... [*squeals*
acc--------]
and squirms in his seat]

(3) Deborah: Oh:: Go::d. ... She's only SEVen?

(4) Steve: And I say, well ... hów about let's do sò-and-so.
And she says ... Okay::. ... Just like thát.
acc--------] [*squealing*]

(5) Deborah: Oh::::
p

(6) David: What does it méan.
p, acc

(7) Steve: It's just so ... she's acting like such a little girl already.
p

where

- ⁄ indicates primary stress
- \ indicates secondary stress
- underline indicates emphatic stress
- CAPITALIZATION indicates most emphatic stress
- . (period) indicates sentence-final falling intonation
- ? (question mark) indicates rising intonation
- ⌈ indicates high pitch on phrase
- ⌈⌈ indicates very high pitch on phrase
- *acc* indicates accelerando (speeding up)
- *p* indicates pianissimo (spoken softly)
- : indicates elongation of vowel sound
- ... indicates half-second pause (each extra dot = another half-second pause)
- [brackets on two lines indicate simultaneous speech: two speakers talking at once

It is clear from the transcript that the two listeners, David and I, have different reactions to the story. In (3) and (5) I show, through paralinguistically exaggerated responses, that I have appreciated the story. In contrast, David states in (6) that he doesn't understand what the story is supposed to mean – or at least that he is not satisfied with the way Steve told it. When I played this segment of the taped conversation to David later, he said that Steve hadn't said what it was about the girl's behavior that he was trying to point out. Moreover, when Steve answered David's question in (7), he didn't explain at all; David observed that "such a little girl" to him means "such a grownup," whereas Steve meant "such a coquette." David seemed to feel that Steve wasn't telling the story right; he should have said what he meant. To Steve, the point was obvious, having been dramatized, and should not be stated.

Elsewhere in the transcript David relates his experiences, and there the reactions of Steve and the other overlap-favoring stylists indicate that they feel David is stating the obvious and not getting to the point quickly enough.

By expecting the point of a story to be made explicit, and by finding events more important than characters' feelings, some of the participants in this conversation were exhibiting expectations that speech make use of strategies typically associated with writing, that is, strategies that focus more on information and less on involvement. By expecting the point of a story to be dramatized by the speaker and inferred by the hearer, and by finding personal feelings more interesting than events, the other speakers were exhibiting typically oral or involvement-focused strategies.

It is particularly significant that the speakers in my study who used involvement-focused strategies are highly literate. Many of the studies that have distinguished between oral and literate strategies in spoken style (including Cook-Gumperz and Gumperz, 1981; Michaels and Cook-Gumperz, 1979; and Michaels and Collins, 1984) have done so to explain the failure of children of certain ethnic groups, often black, to learn to write and read well. The speakers I have found using involvement-focused strategies in speaking are New Yorkers of Eastern European Jewish background, a cultural group that has been documented as having (like black cultural groups) a highly developed oral tradition (Kirshenblatt-Gimblett, 1974), but also a highly developed literate one – in fact, one of the longest literate traditions of any cultural group. And far from having a history of failure in school, children from this community have traditionally performed successfully at literate tasks. Thus, individuals and groups are not either oral or literate. Rather, people have at their disposal and are inclined to use, in speech or in writing, combinations of strategies that have been associated with oral or written modes but that are more accurately understood as reflecting relative focus on involvement.

A final example of how both involvement- and information-focused strategies surface in spoken discourse comes from an analysis of fluency. Fillmore (1979b) distinguishes four types of oral fluency, characterized by the abilities to do the following:

1. Talk at length with few pauses
2. Have appropriate things to say in a wide range of contexts
3. Talk in semantically coherent, reasoned, and dense sentences
4. Be creative and imaginative with language.

I suggest that the first two of these types of fluency are associated with involvement-focused strategies. That is, they grow out of inter- active or social goals, when the message conveyed is less important than the metamessage conveyed by the fact and manner of talk. In contrast, the last two are message-focused types of fluency; the third depends on intratextual relationships, and the fourth builds on words as carrying meaning in themselves rather than triggering social meaning.

Focus on involvement in written discourse

If one thinks at first that written language and spoken language are very different, one may think as well that written literary discourse – short stories, poems, novels – are the most different from casual conversation. On the contrary, imaginative literature has more in common with spontaneous conversation than with the typical written genre, expository prose.

If expository prose is minimally dependent on immediate context and maximally dependent on lexicalization – that is, the writer demands the least from the reader in terms of filling in referents, background information, crucial premises, cohesive relationships, and evaluation, then literary discourse is also maximally contextual- ized, not in the sense of depending on immediate context but by requiring the reader (or hearer) to fill in maximal background and other elided information. The best literary work is the one that suggests the most to readers with the fewest words. Rader (1982) demonstrates this, suggesting that maximal contextualization is not incidental to the nature of literature but rather is basic to it. The goal of the creative writer is to encourage readers to do as much filling in as possible. The more the reader supplies, the more she or he will believe and care about the message in the work. As Rader puts it, "The reader of a novel creates a world according to the instructions given" (p. 195).

The features thought of as quintessentially literary are, moreover, basic to spontaneous conversation and less developed in written expository prose. A few such features are repetition of sounds (alliteration and assonance), repetition of words, recurrent metaphors and other figures of speech, parallel syntactic constructions, and compelling rhythm. (This hypothesis is suggested in Tannen, 1982a, and elaborated in Tannen, 1984. See also Friedrich, 1979.)

Analyzing a transcript of ordinary conversation among family members, Sacks (1971) shows that in determining why a speaker chose a particular variant of a word – for example, *because, cause,* or *cuz* – an analyst should look to see if the variant chosen is "sound coordinated with things in its environment." In the case Sacks presents, a speaker said (referring to fish being eaten), "cause it comes from cold water." A few moments later, the same speaker said, "You better eat something because you're gonna be hungry before we get there." In considering why the speaker chose *cause* in the first instance and *because* in the second, Sacks notes that *cause* appears in the environment of repeated /k/ sounds in *comes* and *cold,* whereas *because* is coordinated with /bi/ (i.e., "bee") in *be hungry* and *before.*

Sacks goes on to suggest that another speaker chose a rather stilted expression, "Will you be good enough to empty this in there," because at that point in the talk there are a number of measure terms (i.e., an extended metaphor) being used, seen in this expression in *empty* and in nearby sentences in the words *more* and *missing.* Hence the choice of *good enough,* in which the measure term *enough* is metaphoric. (Sacks's lecture notes are rich with examples of poetic processes in ordinary conversation.)

Examples of parallel constructions in natural conversation are also ubiquitous. Speakers frequently set up a syntactic construction and repeat it for several sentences. A brief example will be taken from a narrative I have analyzed elsewhere, comparing spoken and written versions of the same story (Tannen, 1982a). In a spontaneous casual conversation, the speaker emphasized the linguistic ability of a coworker by saying, "And he knows Spanish, and he knows French, and he knows English, and he knows German. And *he* is a *gentleman.*" The rhythm of the repeated constructions sweeps the hearers along, creating the effect of a long list, suggesting that he knows even more than the four languages named. (Such parallel constructions are probably also an aid to speech production, since the repeated construction can be uttered automatically while the speaker plans new information to insert in the variable slot. It is a technique public speakers use frequently.) Furthermore, the speaker can use the established rhythm of the repeated construction to play off against, as in the phrase that follows the parallelism: "And *he* is a *gentleman.*"

Contrast this with the way the same narrator conveyed the same idea when she wrote the story down: "He knows at least four languages fluently – Spanish, French, English, and something else." This sentence is orallike, or involvement-focused, in its use of the phrase *something else* in place of the name of a fourth language, creating a feeling of immediate narration. The writer could have taken as much time as she needed to think of the fourth language and add it, or choose an alternative grammatical structure and revise the text to read – for example, "including. . . ." But with regard to rhythmicity created by parallel constructions, the written statement exhibits the feature Chafe (Chapter 6) calls "integration," which he finds typical of expository prose, conflating the parallel constructions by eliminating the repeated parts. The result is a sentence that is more word-efficient but rhythmically less involving (and, one might say, less moving).

Rhythm, then, is a fundamental feature of the oral strategy of parallel constructions. Erickson and his collaborators (Erickson & Shultz, 1982) and Scollon (1982) have demonstrated that rhythm is basic to participation in face-to-face conversation. Erickson has shown that ordinary conversation can be set to a metronome, and verbal and nonverbal participation takes place on the beat. In order to show listenership and to know when to talk, one must be able to pick up the beat. In conversation with speakers of different cultural back-grounds, or speakers who tend to take turns more slowly or quickly than one is used to, one cannot tell when others are finished and therefore cannot judge when to start or stop speaking. The effect is like trying to enter a line of dancers who are going just a bit faster or slower than one expects; one has to either drop back or break in, spoiling everyone's rhythm.

Thus rhythm is basic to conversational involvement in the most mechanical sense. It contributes in conversation, as it does in music, poetry, and oratory, to the impact of the discourse on the audience. The rhythm sweeps the audience along and convinces them by moving them emotionally. Saville-Troike (1982) quotes Duncan (1962) to the effect that Hitler, in his preface to *Mein Kampf*, apologizes for writing a book, since he believes that people are moved not by writing but by the spoken word, and that "every great movement owed its growth to great orators, not to great writers."

Why is it that literary language builds on and perfects features of mundane conversation? I believe it is because literary language, like ordinary conversation, is dependent for its effect on interpersonal involvement. It fosters and builds on involvement between speaker and hearer rather than focusing on information or message. It also depends for its impact on the emotional involvement of the hearer. In contrast, expository prose, associated with literate tradition in the way we have seen, depends for its impact on impressing the audience with the strength and completeness of its argument, that is, with aspects of the lexicalized message. In fact, responses to all discourse are probably emotional, just as Olson (1977) points out that most people cannot distinguish between logical arguments and arguments with which they agree. But in justifying their responses to expository prose, most American readers are likely to maintain that they find the argument logical, not that they like the way it sounds. Nonetheless, some awareness of the power of rhythm and sound play can be seen in the observation "It has a nice ring to it," sometimes used to suggest that "it" must therefore be right.

Reading and writing as involvement-focused skills

A particularly fascinating aspect of the notion of involvement- and information-focused strategies is the possibility that the former, which have been associated with spoken language, may be the most efficient for both writing and reading. Successful writing, which seeks to lexicalize necessary background and cohesive relationships, requires not production of discourse with no sense of audience but rather the positing of a hypothetical audience in order to fulfill its needs. This is the sense in which writing is decontextualized: The context must be posited rather than being found in the actual setting. A better term would be *recontextualized*. The ability to imagine what a hypothetical reader needs to know is an interactive skill. Similarly, reading is a matter of decoding written words – a message-focused skill. But the act of reading efficiently is a matter not so much of accurate decoding, though this is part of it, but of discerning a familiar text structure and hypothesizing what information will be presented, so that it can be efficiently processed when it comes. By making maximum use of the context of prior texts, to use Becker's term, good readers use highly context-sensitive skills, strategies that I am suggesting are interactive or involvement-focused.

Preparation for literacy in oral discourse in school

Cook-Gumperz and Gumperz (1981) suggest that children make a "transition to literacy" when they go to school. Michaels and Cook-Gumperz (1979) analyze in detail an oral discourse activity in a first-grade classroom that prepares children for a literate approach to information: "sharing time." Here children are expected to address the entire class and tell about one thing that is very important. Although the children are communicating face to face and share context in many ways, the teacher encourages them to express known information in order to give a "complete" discourse appropriate to sharing time. Michaels and Collins (1984) give the example of a child who brought to class two candles she had made in day camp and began to talk about them "using highly context-bound expressions and gestures." She said, for example, "This one came out blue and I don't know what this color is." The teacher encouraged the child to produce a more literate-style discourse: "Tell the kids how you do it from the very start. Pretend we don't know a thing about candles." The teacher's use of "from the very start" and "Pretend . . ." emphasizes the counterintuitive nature of such elaborated-style discourse in face-to-face interaction. The injunction to "pretend we don't know a thing about candles" sets up the reader-as-blank-slate idealization that underlies much expository writing.

Michaels and Cook-Gumperz found that children in the class they observed fell into two groups with respect to how well they performed during sharing time, how much reinforcement they received from the teacher, and consequently how much practice in literate-style discourse they received. Some children were more likely to lexicalize connections in order to focus on the main point, whereas others were more likely to accomplish this cohesion by special intonation patterns that, tragically, the teacher was not able to recognize, since she and these students came from different cultural backgrounds.

In order to document these differences better, Michaels and her coworkers showed the children a short film (as it happens, the same film used to elicit the narratives analyzed in my previously mentioned comparison of Greek and American discourse) and had them tell what they saw in the film. These experimentally elicited narratives also exhibit what Michaels and Collins (1984) call oral-based and literate-based strategies in spoken narratives. In the film a man is shown picking pears. A boy comes along, takes a basket of pears away on his bike, and later falls off his bike. Three other boys help him, and he gives them three pears. At the end, the three boys, eating their pears, walk past the man who was picking them in the first scene. These scenes were designed to set up an encoding problem: In describing the last scene, narrators must identify the man as the same one who appeared in the first scene.

Michaels and Collins characterize one group of children as literate-style speakers (I will call them message-focused), who used complex syntactic constructions and lexicalization to identify the man. A second group, characterized as oral-style speakers (in my terms, involvement-focused ones) used special intonation patterns. Thus, a message-focused speaker says, "there was a man that was picking some pears." Notice that the speaker introduces the man by using an independent clause, "there was . . . ," and then identifies him by using a relative clause, "that was picking some pears." In contrast, an involvement-focused speaker introduces the same character by using two independent clauses: "It was about this man. He was, um . . . um . . . takes some, um . . . peach – . . . some . . . pears off the tree." (Readers will notice that the second child is less fluent, but that is not significant for the phenomenon under discussion.)

Even more striking than the use of two independent clauses as opposed to an independent and a subordinate clause is the way these two speakers identify the man when he reappears in the last scene. The message-focused speaker uses a restrictive appositive, a relative clause beginning with "who": ". . . and then . . . they . . . walked by the man who gave . . . wh–who was picking the pears." In contrast, the involvement-focused speaker again uses two independent clauses, identifying the man as the same one previously mentioned by using a special intonational contour on the word *man*: ". . . and when that . . . when he pa:ssed, by that ma:n, . . . the man . . . the ma:n came out the tree." It is the special intonational contour on *man* that signals "You know which man I mean – the one I mentioned before."[4]

Although prosodic cues cannot specify which other man is intended, they can indicate that some particular other man is meant, and this is sufficient to lead a listener to infer which other man that is. (In this case, only one other man has been mentioned.) Thus the two children use different strategies to establish cohesion. Their spoken styles reflect relative reliance on context and paralinguistic cues (hence audience involvement) or on lexicalization (hence message focus).

Finally, these spoken styles have important consequences for written competence. Michaels and Collins compared fourth-grade children's speech styles with their writing styles by having them watch the same film and then both tell and write a narrative account of it. Style differences appeared in the oral narratives of the fourth graders, very much like those described for first graders; furthermore, the children who lexicalized cohesion in speaking also wrote unambiguous prose, whereas the children who relied on paralinguistic channels in speaking were more likely to write a text that was ambiguous. In other words, these children neglected to compensate for the loss of the paralinguistic channel in writing by lexicalizing connections that were signaled paralinguistically in speaking.

For example, a fourth grader who uses complex syntactic constructions and other message-focused devices in speaking uses similar devices in writing, resulting in unambiguous prose. In reintroducing the pear picker, this child begins a new paragraph and writes. "The man collecting fruits noticed. . . ." In contrast, a fourth grader who uses paralinguistic signaling rather than lexicalization to establish cohesion in speaking produces, in writing, prose that is ambiguous concerning which character he is referring to. He writes, "This man was picking pears and this boy was riding by on his bike and he saw the pears. . . ." There is nothing in the text to disambiguate *he*: Does it refer to the man or the boy? (Of course, the reader can make a good guess based on prior contextual knowledge, but that is another matter.) Thus the children's spoken discourse styles have significant consequences for their acquisition of literacy.

Conclusion

I have suggested that previous work on oral and literate tradition and spoken versus written language has led to two hypotheses. The first, that written language is decontextualized whereas spoken is context-bound, seems to grow out of the types of spoken and written discourse that were examined: face-to-face conversation on the one hand and expository prose on the other. I suggest that the identified differences result not so much from the spoken and written modes as from relative focus on interpersonal involvement typically found in conversation and relative lack of focus on involvement in favor of a focus on information or message typically found in expository prose.

The second hypothesis that had been previously put forth is that spoken language establishes cohesion by use of paralinguistic and nonverbal signals, whereas written language depends more upon lexicalization. This is indeed an outgrowth of spoken versus written modes of discourse. Nonetheless, various uses of contextualization and relative reliance on lexicalization can be manipulated both in speaking and in writing in order to produce discourse that is maximally or minimally involving of the audience. Finally, I have suggested that oral strategies may underlie successful discourse production and comprehension in the written as well as the oral mode, insofar as it requires drawing on prior experience, which in the case of written discourse includes the experience of prior written texts. All of these phenomena have implications for interpersonal communication, an understanding of discourse production and comprehension, and the acquisition of literacy.

ACKNOWLEDGMENTS

I would like to thank A. L. Becker for invaluable comments on an earlier draft and David Olson for a careful editorial reading that led to numerous improvements. This chapter is an extensive revision of a talk presented at the conference Literacy in the 1980's at the University of Michigan, June 1981, published as Tannen (1983), used by permission of the Modern Language Association.

NOTES

1. I am grateful to Pamela Gerloff for calling my attention to this reference. Bettelheim cites Schopenhauer as the source of the simile.
2. Becker helped me to see that relative focus on content is an artifact of relative focus on involvement and that the notion of "content" invokes the conduit metaphor in communication (i.e., messages are placed in a container and sent by conduit to a receiver who extracts them from the container; cf. Lakoff & Johnson, 1980), the connotations of which I wish to avoid.
3. This is true of any situation in which there is an impediment to effortless communication – for example, when someone has laryngitis, is in another room, or is not fluent in the language spoken. Since I am hearing-impaired, I am frequently reminded of this when a request for repetition elicits the maddening "It wasn't important."
4. Not only am I substituting my terms *involvement-focused style* and *message-focused style* in place of Michaels and Collins's terms, but I am also substituting my own simplified transcription system for theirs, since theirs contains more information than is needed for the argument I am making here.

REFERENCES

Bateson, G. *Steps to an ecology of mind*. New York: Ballantine, 1972.
Becker, A. L. Beyond translation: Esthetics and language description. In H. Byrnes (Ed.), *Contemporary perceptions of language: Interdisciplinary dimensions* (Georgetown University Round Table on Languages and Linguistics, 1982). Washington, D.C.: Georgetown University Press, 1982.
Becker, A. L., & I Gusti Ngurah Oka. Person in Kawi: Exploration of an elementary semantic dimension. *Oceanic Linguistics*, 1976, *13*, 229–255.
Bernstein, B. Elaborated and restricted codes: Their social origins and some consequences. *American Anthropologist*, 1964, *66*(6), Pt. 2, 55–69.
Bettelheim, B. *Surviving*. New York: Knopf, 1979.
Brown, P., & Levinson, S. Universals in language usage: Politeness phenomena. In E. Goody (Ed.), *Questions and politeness*. Cambridge: Cambridge University Press, 1978.

Chafe, W. Integration and involvement in speaking, writing, and oral literature. In D. Tannen (Ed.), *Spoken and written language: Exploring orality and literacy.* Norwood, N.J.: Ablex, 1982.

Cook-Gumperz, J., & Gumperz, J. J. From oral to written: The transition to literacy. In M. F. Whiteman (Ed.), *Variation in writing.* Hillsdale, N.J.: Erlbaum, 1981.

Duncan, H. D. *Communication and the social order.* London: Oxford University Press, 1962.

Erickson, F., & Shultz, J. *Gatekeeping in counseling interviews.* New York: Academic Press, 1982.

Fillmore, C. J. Innocence: A second idealization for linguistics. *Proceedings of the Fifth Annual Meeting of the Berkeley Linguistics Society,* 1979a.
  On fluency. In C. J. Fillmore, D. Kempler, & W. S.-Y. Wang (Eds.), *Individual differences in language ability and language behavior.* New York: Academic Press, 1979b.

Friedrich, P. Poetic language and the imagination: A reformulation of the Sapir hypothesis. In *Language, context, and the imagination: Essays by Paul Friedrich* (selected and introduced by A. S. Dil). Stanford, Calif.: Stanford University Press, 1979.

Goffman, E. *Interaction ritual.* Garden City, N.Y.: Doubleday, 1967.
  Response cries. In *Forms of talk.* Philadelphia: University of Pennsylvania Press, 1981.

Goody, J. *The domestication of the savage mind.* Cambridge: Cambridge University Press, 1977.

Goody, J., & Watt, I. The consequences of literacy. *Comparative Studies in Society and History,* 1963, *5,* 304–345.

Gumperz, J., Kaltman, H., & O'Connor, M. C. Cohesion in spoken and written discourse. In D. Tannen (Ed.), *Coherence in spoken and written discourse.* Norwood, N.J.: Ablex, 1984.

Havelock, E. *Preface to Plato.* Cambridge: Harvard University Press, 1963.

Hill, C., & Varenne, H. Family language and education: The sociolinguistic model of restricted and elaborated codes. *Social Science Information,* 1981, *20*(1), 187–227.

Kay, P. Language evolution and speech style. In B. Blount & M. Sanches (Eds.), *Sociocultural dimensions of language change.* New York: Academic Press, 1977.

Kirshenblatt-Gimblett, B. The concept and varieties of narrative performance in East European Jewish Culture. In R. Bauman & J. Sherzer (Eds.), *Explorations in the ethnography of speaking.* Cambridge: Cambridge University Press, 1974.

Kroll, B. Combining ideas in written and spoken English. In E. O. Keenan & T. Bennett (Eds.), *Discourse across time and space. Southern California Occasional Papers in Linguistics,* 1977, *5,* 69–108.

Labov, W. *Language in the inner city.* Philadelphia: University of Pennsylvania Press, 1972.

146   DEBORAH TANNEN

Lakoff, G., & Johnson, M. *Metaphors we live by*. Chicago: University of Chicago Press, 1980.
Lakoff, R. The logic of politeness, or minding your p's and q's. *Papers from the Ninth Regional Meeting of the Chicago Linguistics Society*, 1973, 292–305.
Stylistic strategies within a grammar of style. In J. Orasanu, M. Slater, & L. L. Adler (Eds.), *Language, sex, and gender. Annals of the New York Academy of Science*, 1979, *327*, 53–78.
Michaels, S., & Collins, J. Oral discourse style: Classroom interaction and the acquisition of literacy. In D. Tannen (Ed.), *Coherence in spoken and written discourse*. Norwood, N.J.: Ablex, 1984.
Michaels, S., & Cook-Gumperz, J. A study of sharing time with first grade students: Discourse narratives in the classroom. *Proceedings of the Fifth Annual Meeting of the Berkeley Linguistics Society*, 1979, 51–80.
Nystrand, M. Rhetoric's "audience" and linguistics' "speech community": Implications for understanding writing and text. In M. Nystrand (Ed.), *What writers know: The language, process, and structure of written discourse*. New York: Academic Press, 1982.
Ochs, E. Planned and unplanned discourse. In T. Givon (Ed.), *Discourse and syntax*. New York: Academic Press, 1979.
Olson, D. From utterance to text: The bias of language in speech and writing. *Harvard Educational Review*, 1977, *47*(3), 257–281.
Ong, W. J. *The presence of the word*. New Haven: Yale University Press, 1967. *Interfaces of the word*. Ithaca, N.Y.: Cornell University Press, 1977.
Rader, M. Context in written language: The case of imaginative fiction. In D. Tannen (Ed.), *Spoken and written language: Exploring orality and literacy*. Norwood, N.J.: Ablex, 1982.
Sacks, H. Mimeographed lecture notes, March 11, 1971.
Saville-Troike, M. *The ethnography of communication*. London: Blackwell, 1982.
Scollon, R. The rhythmic integration of ordinary talk. In D. Tannen (Ed.), *Analyzing discourse: Text and talk* (Georgetown University Round Table on Languages and Linguistics, 1981). Washington, D.C.: Georgetown University Press, 1982.
Tannen, D. A comparative analysis of oral narrative strategies. In W. Chafe (Ed.), *The pear stories*. Norwood, N.J.: Ablex, 1980a.
Implications of the oral/literate continuum for cross-cultural communication. In J. Alatis (Ed.), *Current issues in bilingualism* (Georgetown University Round Table on Languages and Linguistics, 1980). Washington, D.C.: Georgetown University Press, 1980b.
New York Jewish conversational style. *International Journal of the Sociology of Language*, 1981, *30*, 133–139.
Oral and literate strategies in spoken and written narratives. *Language*, 1982a, *58*, 1–21.
The oral/literate continuum in discourse. In D. Tannen (Ed.), *Spoken and written language: Exploring orality and literacy*. Norwood, N.J.: Ablex, 1982b.

Oral and written discourse

147

Oral and literate strategies in spoken and written discourse. In R. W.
Bailey & R. M. Fosheim (Eds.), *Literacy for life: The demand for reading
and writing.* New York: Modern Language Association, 1983.
Conversational style: Analyzing talk among friends. Norwood, N.J.: Ablex, 1984.

8

Are there really no primitive languages?

IVAN KALMÁR

Of Plato and swineherds

"When it comes to linguistic form, Plato walks with the Macedonian swineherd, and Confucius with the head-hunting savage of Assam." The statement by Sapir (1921, p. 219) has ingrained itself into the collective conciousness of the linguistic profession as almost a solemn declaration of faith. It is taken to be axiomatic that there are no primitive languages.

The subtle violence of Sapir's quote, associating as it does Plato with swine and Confucius with cannibalism, was undoubtedly due to his contempt of the nineteenth-century moralist for whom "high culture" stood in sharp contrast to the uncouth customs of the savage.

Among ninteenth-century scholars, that enthnocentric, moralist view was strengthened by the evolutionary writings of Darwin. The first to write a "Darwinist" pamphlet on linguistic evolution was the comparative philologist August Schleicher. In a pamphlet claiming that Darwinian-type evolution was actually discovered by philologists first, Schleicher for the first time presented to the scientific public the thesis of evolution from isolating through agglutinative to inflectional languages (1869, pp. 50–54). The idea caught on and became one of the main features of nineteenth-century linguistic and anthropological thought. But it was not a fully original idea. As far back at least as Hegel's *Philosophy of History*, the "advanced" Indo-European languages were thought to have achieved a clarity of expression through inflectional categories that was denied to languages of other types (Hegel, 1953, p. 28). And Wilhelm von Humboldt had already speculated on the relative degrees of intellectual development (*geistige Entwicklung*) evidenced by isolating, agglutinative, and inflectional languages (1971). Schleicher's "merit" was merely to arrange in an evolutionary line what seemed to

Humboldt to be independent if not equally valid manifestations of the human language-forming capacity. This language-forming capacity was a manifestation of the human *Geist*, or spirit, so central a force in the German idealist view of progress.

It is true that Schleicher cited neither Humboldt nor Hegel, but rather claimed to lay down parallels between comparative–historical philology and Darwin's view of natural history. Yet there is no indication in his pamphlet that he grasped one of Darwin's central points. Modern evolutionists point out that according to Darwin evolution was not goal-directed, not progressive, and not a product of the striving of *Geist*, but rather a product of natural selection among randomly produced variants (Gould, 1977, esp. Chap. 1). As such it gave support to a materialist rather than idealist view of change. Schleicher gives no sign that he understood the role of random variation in a Darwinian theory.

At any rate, critics of linguistic evolution attacked not its Darwinian underpinnings, but rather its idealistic implications about the progress of *Geist* as found in Humboldt's work. It was the view of evolution as intellectual progress that eventually damned the whole thesis of evolution in language to universal, though unexamined, condemnation.

The earliest criticism of the Schleicher–Humboldt scheme did not, at first, rule out linguistic evolution as such. Some nineteenth-century observers rejected Schleicher's objectification of language as an organism capable of autonomous development. According to Gaston Paris, language could not develop on its own, but only as a result of "the physiological and psychological laws of human nature" (1868, p. 242) because it is nothing apart from the people who use it. Paris's objection, however, hardly precludes linguistic evolution; it would simply require the evolution of language to be explained in terms of the evolution of "human nature."

A more influential objection, which appeared fairly early in the nineteenth century, was that the Schleicher–Humboldt scheme was racist. Hans Arsleff (1979) details some of the relevant arguments of Madvig, Whitney, and Bréal. Following the "classical" view of the Port Royal grammarians, these scholars rejected the notion of a direct relation between language form and categories of thought. Rationalists all, they believed such categories to be universal, though some languages might not express all of them in overt form. They did not, however, argue against linguistic evolution. They objected only to equating stages in languages with important stages in thought.

The most influential critique of linguistic evolutionism came not from European rationalists, but from Americans researching their continent's aboriginal languages.

The father of such research, Franz Boas, who was undoubtedly deeply versed in the language scholarship of his native Germany,[1] appears to have accepted the Humboldtian proposition that language form and thought reflect one another:

When we say *The eye is the organ of sight*, the Indian may not be able to form the expression *the eye*, but may have to define that the eye of the person or of an animal is meant. Neither may the Indian be able to generalize the abstract idea [*sic*] of an eye as the representative of a whole class of objects, but may have to specialize with an expression like *this eye here*. (1911, p 60)

However, this is only as long as there is no need for generalization. When necessary, languages will develop the requisite forms:

I have made this experiment, for instance, with the Kwakiutl language of Vancouver Island, in which no abstract term ever occurs without its possessive elements. After some discussions, I found it perfectly easy to develop the idea of the abstract term in the mind of the Indian, who will state that the word without a possessive pronoun gives a sense, although it is not used idiomatically. I succeeded, for instance, in this manner, in isolating the terms for love and pity, which ordinarily occur only in possessive forms, like his love for him or my pity for you. (1911, p. 60)

Boas, then, still accepted that there are "primitive languages" (he did use the term), and even that they reflect primitive thought. But he argued, possibly against a straw man, that this did not mean racial inferiority of the speakers. They can become less primitive and change their language.

It fell to Edward Sapir, a student of Boas, to develop Boas's antiracist sentiment to the point that required a complete denial of the existence of primitive languages. Sapir's comparison of Plato to a swineherd would undoubtedly even today irk any professor of philosophy, but it became canon in linguistics.

There the matter came to rest. Since then there has been little serious discussion of linguistic evolution. Introductory textbooks simply repeat that primitive languages do not exist and leave it at that. An exception is J. Greenberg's essay "Language and Evolutionary Theory" (1957, Chap. 5). Greenberg defines *evolution* as a gradual process toward greater efficiency in the fulfilment of some function by the evolving entity: "efficiency is meaningful only in terms of some function to be performed" (1957, p. 61). He identifies communication as the main function of language. Greenberg recognizes that changes in society and in technology have radically altered the communication environment. But this, he believes, has led only to changes in the means of communication and in the social distribution of linguistic skills, not in language itself. In effect, Greenberg's article simply restates Sapir's thesis.

During the course of history from earliest times through the appearance of agriculture, of the state, of writing, of mass communication technology, it seems to be universally agreed, language has stayed essentially the same, except for changes in the lexicon.

A reappraisal

The unanimity on this point is surprising. The case against language evolution is, after all, not all that convincing. A priori, it would seem more likely than not that languages do evolve. If we agree with Durkheim that language is a social institution, then we would expect it to evolve as all other such institutions do. Culture as a whole has been understood to be something that evolves. The idea of cultural evolution goes back at least to Hegel, and through Kroeber (1944) and Steward (1955) has been as much an unquestioned part of social–anthropological lore as the no-primitive-languages dictum has been part of linguistics. Marriage, the economy, political organization, music, art all adapt to changing conditions. Why not language?

Perhaps the answer may be found in Lenneberg's representation of language as innate (1967). According to Lenneberg we learn language as we learn to walk, with only minor input from the social environment. This view, however, reduces differences between languages to the same status as differences between a Canadian's and an Ethiopean's gait. There can be little doubt that history will consider such a conclusion a reductio ad absurdum. One may accept that at some "deep" level all languages are the same and that this deep level is innate and thus universal. But one still has to account for the significant differences from language to language, "superficial" as they may be. Do these differences represent evolution? Lenneberg's position, whether correct or not, does not preclude a positive answer.

But is it not true that linguistic evolution cannot be demonstrated? So far, very little effort has been put into demonstrating it. Schleicher's typology was presented more than a hundred years ago. One cannot refute a general idea because of objections to just *one* formulation of it. Since the time of Schleicher until recently, all the effort went into denying, rather than demonstrating, evolution.

Recently, however, some studies have appeared that can be interpreted from an evolutionary perspective. If "evolution" is taken in its broadest sense, that is, "qualitative change," then we may include here recent studies of case marking that claim that the path of change always leads from ergativity to accusativity, and not vice versa (see several of the papers in Plank, 1979). But Greenberg is probably right that such a broad definition of evolution can trivialize the issue. It is better to limit one's attention to evolution as adaptation of a structure to the environment. One may even agree with Greenberg that such adaptation should facilitate a particular function.

An example of adaptation to changing functions of language is Givón's view of the "pragmatic mode." The pragmatic mode characterizes the earlier stage of development. The two types of "mode" have the following characteristics (Givón, 1979, p. 223):

Pragmatic Mode	*Syntactic Mode*
a. Topic–comment structure	Subject–predicate structure
b. Loose conjunction	Tight subordination
c. Slow rate of delivery (under several intonation contours)	Fast rate of delivery (under a single intonational contour)
d. Word order is governed mostly by one *pragmatic* principle; old information goes first, new information follows	Word order is used to signal *semantic* case functions (though it may also be used to indicate pragmatic–topicality relations)
e. Roughly one-to-one ratio of verbs to nouns in discourse, with the verbs being semantically simple.	A larger ratio of nouns to verbs in discourse, with the verbs being semantically complex
f. No use of grammatical morphology	Elaborate use of grammatical morphology
g. Prominent intonation – stress marks the focus of new information; topic intonation is less prominent	Very much the same, but perhaps not exhibiting as high a functional load, and at least in some languages totally absent

The pragmatic mode, from which the syntactic developed, characterizes "Pidgin versus Creole, Child versus Adult, and Informal versus Formal language" (p. 223). It is thus "a feature of extant human language as we know it" (p. 304). Givón shows how the pragmatic mode develops diachronically into the syntactic (Sec. 7.9). The syntactic mode is "the last *phylogenetic* stage in the evolution of human language" (p. 304, emphasis in original). Moreover, the development of the syntactic mode from the pragmatic – syntacticization – correlates with the development of "societies of strangers" from "societies of intimates." The society of strangers is represented by literate, "more complex" societies like those where "English, Hebrew, Spanish, Japanese, or French" are spoken. In contrast, societies of intimates are "traditional, rural, nonliterate, preindustrial." Givón points out that the use of indefinite subjects is one of the syntacticized constructions that "tend to be found mostly in literate, more complex societies." And even more unequivocally, Givón states that

as serious, unbiased (i.e., non-Eurocentric) typological accounts of diverse languages become more available, it slowly becomes clear that certain *types of languages* – those which have only coordination ("clause chaining") but no subordination (Longacre, 1979; Thurman 1978) – are found *only* in preliterate "societies of intimates." (1979, p. 306, emphasis mine)

We shall return later to the issue of subordination as a symptom of evolution. For now, suffice it to say that the above statements appear to place Givón firmly on the side of linguistic evolution.[2]

The relevance of written and other permanent texts

One potentially fertile source of information on linguistic evolution is the growing field of literacy studies, to which this volume is one of many contributions. The consensus emerging from these studies is that (1) spoken and written languages are significantly different and (2) the differences between spoken and written language are due to the social context of written as opposed to spoken communication. Practically all commentators point to the decontextualization of written messages as one important factor: The reader, unlike the hearer, may be removed from the sender of the message in space and in time. Chafe adds another consideration: The writer, but not the speaker, has more time to work on his message – to complicate its structure, perhaps to revise and embellish it. The result is that written language is structurally more integrated compared to the fragmented nature of spoken language (see Chapter 6).

We may stay with Chafe for examples of how these contextual factors determine the characteristics of spoken and written language, respectively. In Chafe's written texts there were $11\frac{1}{2}$ times as many nominalizations as in his oral samples, 4 times as many participles, and 4 times as many attributive adjectives.

It is legitimate to ask whether, given the above results, languages like English have not adapted to the appearance of writing, that is, whether they have not *evolved* as a result of literacy.

There are at least two grounds for a negative answer. First, even preliterate speakers are said to exhibit the complex of features characteristic of writing on occasions of ritual oratory. Chafe suggests that in many ways ritual speech is like writing:

> Rituals, on the other hand, are performed and listened to over and over again. As a result they contain language that has been formalized and polished, even over many centuries, contrasting with the spontaneity and roughness of conversation. We might then expect to find in ritual language something like the integration of written language, as opposed to the fragmentation of spoken. It is also the case that the performer of a ritual is removed from his audience in a way that parallels the solitude of a writer. What he performs is a monologue, with minimal feedback and no verbal interaction. (1982, p. 49).

Second, the idea of written language as representing an advanced stage of evolution is weakened by the fact that all the results so far show only statistical differences between speech and writing. Written English has *more* nominalizations than spoken English, but spoken English has some nominalizations, too. The differences in frequency that there are may be attributed to *parole*, not *langue*.

These objections do not preclude an investigation of linguistic evolution as a correlate of writing. They do, however, require a streamlining of the topic that such investigation ought to be concerned with.

First, we may have to widen the search for environmental stimuli to linguistic evolution, from writing to other forms of discourse. It may be that before the appearance of writing, the development of forms of oral communication that are in some ways similar to writing can elicit linguistic change. For the features of written discourse that language adapts to may perhaps already be found in some spoken styles.

Chief among such features are *integration* – the tight organization of devices that result from the deliberate planning of discourse – and *decontextualization* – the spatiotemporal divorce of the sender and the receiver of communication. We must face the empirical, ethnographic task of determining the extent to which integration and decontextualization occur in spoken language. We ought to look for them first of all in "oral literature."

As a preliminary investigation we might use the following typology of texts as an index of integration and decontextualization: *spontaneous texts*, *composed texts*, and *permanent texts*.

Spontaneous texts are unplanned productions not intended for reproduction, like most normal conversation. Composed texts are prepared in advance.

Among the Inuit, the native people of northern Canada and Alaska, people used to sit together in silence, concentrating on the forces that would make a poem "come to them." Then they broke out reciting a text that they perceived as a spontaneous inspiration (Freuchen, 1961). It seems unlikely that such poems were composed.

The Seneca oratory described by Chafe is more likely to be composed in advance of its performance, although probably not word for word. The epic tales of the Somali or the Macedonian, and probably of the prebiblical Israelite and pre-Homeric Greek, are clearly composed texts, based largely on repeated formulaic phrases. Here composition should result in a good deal of integration. As the performer of an epic tale is able to recite it in any environment, such tales are also decontextualized.

The maximum of premeditated integration and of decontextualization occurs in truly permanent texts. The prime examples are written compositions: They can be read anywhere, they are permanent in the sense that they essentially permit an unlimited number of identical decodings – one reading is essentially like any other. In a permanent text, language for the first time becomes truly divorced from the speaker and the listener. A written text truly "exists" apart from the act of its writing and reading. However, not all permanent texts are written. Certain prayers, for example, are remembered and recited almost verbatim even in many preliterate societies.

Every human society, of course, produces spontaneous texts. Also, every society has some form of permanent texts. The simplest form is that of spells. A typical spell in a primitive society is found among the Inuit, who purchased magical spells at a good price from each other and then kept them secret until sold again (Rasmussen, 1930). Such spells are often incomprehensible and always very short. Moreover, they are often secret rather than intended for public recitation. Hence it is unlikely that they are substantial enough to precipitate any qualitative change in the language.

A second form of permanent text that appears to be common to all societies is that of chants and songs. We must be cautious here, however. The ethnographic literature seldom reports more than one performance of a song. Given the improvisational nature of much of primitive poetry and music it is not impossible that songs, too, are partly improvised, although some invariance of the text is of course necessary. That is, they are *composed* but not *permanent* texts. However that may be, songs in simple hunting and gathering societies are to my knowledge always either incantations – sung spells in effect – or short refrains inserted inside a spoken narrative. Hence, again they are too insignificant to generate new linguistic features.

Significant nonspontaneous texts appear only when short songs change into longer stories, which may well be sung or chanted. Such narrative texts are repeated essentially verbatim and may have a religious character. They always tell of divine acts or heroic exploits that explain and/or justify social structure. Any society with a lineage system of organization will find such texts educational. And indeed, we find that West Africans sometimes sit together all day reciting memorized texts dealing in part with their ancestry. Records of descent lines are also common in the oldest sections of the Bible. There is not enough evidence to determine if these are merely composed or truly permanent texts. In either case, they are one form that may contribute to the appearance of qualitatively different linguistic devices.

In more specialized societies, nonspontaneous narrative texts tend to be developed into a multitude of genres, and of course this process is accelerated by the introduction of writing. But the beginnings appear, according to my hypothesis, in a lineage-based society concerned with a record of its members' ancestry. This requires a society at least at the level of tribal organization. Such a society may or may not develop a significant body of composed or permanent texts. A society organized only at the band level, however, does not need them and will not develop them.

If this hypothesis is empirically confirmed, it would mean that the appearance of nonspontaneous texts depends on the attainment of a certain level of evolution in the social organization of the speaker community.

This hypothesis of the genesis of text permanence may then be added as an independent adjunct to my more basic hypothesis that new linguistic features arise in language as a result of the appearance of nonspontaneous narrative texts. And we expect further changes with the appearance of truly permanent texts made possible by writing. This is an evolutionary hypothesis in Greenberg's sense: Language becomes more efficient in serving the new means of communication. If, furthermore, genesis of the permanent narrative text is caused by changes in the social environment, then the evolutionary nature of our basic hypothesis is both firmer and more interesting.

We have refocused the scope of our investigations from writing to the appearance of any type of composed and permanent text. Now let us deal with the second problem posed earlier, namely that speech–writing differences are statistical rather than categorical. That is, while some features are found more often in written text, there are no features that occur only in writing. Hence the difference may just be one of *parole*, not *langue*.

To date, not enough research has been done to settle this issue satisfactorily. In languages with a long history of writing, features of written language will inevitably creep into speech, with the result that speech differs from writing only statistically. In fact, such a state is typical of an "evolved" language. What is needed to resolve this issue is a thoroughgoing comparison of languages without a long history of nonspontaneous narrative texts, on the one hand, with those with a tradition of such texts, on the other. The evolutionary hypothesis will be strengthened if the comparison unearths significant differences in linguistic structure. It would be strengthened even more if we caught a language in the very act of evolution – that is, if we could show how an "evolved" feature appears just at the time a language is developing a significant body of nonspontaneous texts.

Although this chapter reports work that is under way, I shall indicate the feasibility of its program by a small sample of the data on the evolution of linguistic structures under the impact of writing.

A comparison of evolved and primitive languages: subordination

I have indicated that there is a gradient of text permanence between languages in which there is little or no composed oral literature (no epics or memorized perorations of any length) and those with a large body of permanent, written texts. To simplify the argument, let us call languages at the first extreme "*primitive*" and the others "*evolved*." (As in social anthropology, *primitive* here means simply "in an early stage." The thesis that a primitive language is of inferior worth will not be revived by any thinking linguist today. It is not even necessary that a primitive language be less complex than an advanced one. Adaptation to changing extralinguistic factors is all that is at stake.)

There may be many features not found in primitive languages that are found in evolved ones, and vice versa. Chafe's "integrative devices" and the characteristics of Givón's "syntactic mode" are among the good candidates for evolved linguistic structure. As I intend, in this chapter, merely to illustrate and not fully to defend the possibilities of an evolutionary view of language, I select just one feature found in both Chafe's and Givón's work, clause subordination. Primitive languages do not have subordinate clauses; instead they use a bound morpheme, a word, or a phrase. If a clause is in any sense subordinated to another, then it is subordinated only in meaning but not in form.

By clause subordination, of course, I refer to overt, "surface structure" subordination. One can always derive a word or a phrase from an inferred underlying clause and thereby trivialize the difference between languages with and without the overt version of the structure in question. Such a procedure may be fully justified when one's goal is a universal grammar. A universal grammar, by glossing over surface distinctions, does not, however, explain them. It would leave begging the question of the limited occurrence of the "surface" subordinate clause. Hence I leave all consideration of inferred "deep" grammar aside and take overt surface structure grammatical features at their face value.

Clearly, it is "surface structure" subordination that Meillet (1952) and his editors had in mind when they remarked that Australian languages had no subordinate clauses (p. 707). More interestingly, Meillet claimed that the Uralic languages spoken by Siberian hunters (like the Samoyed) resembled proto-Uralic in their lack of subordination, while others did develop it (p. 309 et passim). Similarly, paleo-Siberian languages seem to lack subordination (Skorik, 1974).

In addition to Australia and Siberia, "hunter–gatherer" societies using language without permanent narrative texts are found in some parts of Africa and in the Americas. Snyman's studies suggest that Bushman has no overtly marked subordinate clauses (1970), although a more thorough study of this and other languages is needed to confirm this point. In the languages of American peoples such as the Ojibway, who live at the band level of organization, many modally marked clause types are traditionally described as "dependent." In fact, they are able to figure as independent clauses, and their "subordination" is only semantic. Even languages spoken by Native American peoples with more complex societies seem to lack subordination. I have already mentioned Chafe's comment on the total lack of formal devices of integration in Seneca (Chafe, 1982). The same is true of many of the "dependent" clauses of Inuktitut, the language of the Inuit, where certain mode suffixes can often be translated by English subordinating conjunctions like *when, because,* or *while,* and yet in a preponderance of cases the same suffixes occur on the main verb of an independent clause where such a clause does not express essential information (Kalmár, 1982).

Yet subordination does occur in a multitude of today's languages. This may be due to the disappearance of most band societies and the appearance of types of social organization conducive to composing texts, from lineage-based chiefdoms to the state. Originally, it may well be that even Indo-European languages did not utilize subordination. Benveniste (1957), for one, argues that proto-Indo-European did not have a relative clause. It is quite likely that the number of subordinate clause types grew as narrative developed and accelerated with the advent of writing. Typical is the development of subordination in Greek, which hardly existed in Homer but was well developed in the classics (Goodwin, 1912).

Though much research remains to be done, it appears that subordination does not occur in modern primitive languages nor in the primitive ancestors of evolved languages, whereas it clearly occurs with all its complexity, including the comparatively rare relative clause, in the best-known literary languages, including not only Indo-European languages but also Chinese (see, e.g., Li and Thompson, 1976, p. 482, on *de*) and Japanese (Kuno, 1973, Chaps. 4, 5).

Is subordination now appearing in Inuktitut?

It would indeed be helpful to "catch" an evolved feature like subordination as it first appears in a language where permanent texts are just taking hold. Two tentative examples may be given from Inuktitut, one involving a complement clause and one a relative clause.

Inuktitut was originally a group of hunter–gatherer dialects without significant nonspontaneous texts, but its 100-year-old writing system has in the last few years grown from an exclusively religious vehicle into the medium of a rich bureaucratic literature and some belles lettres.

The normal equivalent of a complement clause in Inuktitut can be expressed as a morpheme within the boundaries of a verb: There are the suffixes -*guuq* (it is said that, he/she/they say that), -*tuqaq* (it seems that), -*palatsi* (it sounds like), and perhaps some others. In such cases the resulting word is like a complex sentence with a complement clause. Witness the following examples (Harper, 1979):

qangatasuug   tikkinniartu-ruuq
airplane   will arrive -(form of *guuq*)
"He said that the airplane would arrive"

illaqu -palatsi-juq
laugh-   -(3rd person)
"It sounds like he/she is laughing"

Here the suffix *-guuq* or *-palatsi* functions like a main verb in a less polysynthetic language. In fact, Woodbury (1975) derives suffixes with such a function from underlying main verbs.

Where the main-verb equivalent is not coded as a member of the closed set of Inuktitut suffixes, the language still does not resort to overt clause subordination. In direct quotations, for example, the quotation is juxtaposed to the "he says" clause, as in the following example:

inuit	*iqqiliilu*	*igiravigiyangit*	*gavamakkut*
Inuit	Indians	their movement	government

miksaanut	*inuit*	*nunangini*
about	Inuit	in their land

saginippaugattauvuq	*nipinut*	*kanatam*
is one of the strongest	to voices	in Canada

ullumi	*taimatuq*	*uqalauqtuq*
today	so	spoke

Luis	*amalat*
Louis	Hamelin

"The Inuit and Indian movement in the North is one of the strongest voices in Canada today, says Louis Hamelin." (*Inuit Today*, 6(5), 16)

Here we have the mere apposition of two independent clauses with perhaps semantic subordination of one to the other, but no overt "surface structure" subordination marked in form. A similar use occurs with an indirect quote:

. . . *titiralauqtut*	*tapsumunga*
they wrote	to this

inuliriyikkut	*angayuqqaarmaringanut*
office in charge of the Inuit	to its minister

vaaran	*almant*	*tapsuminga*
Warren	Almand	this (ACC)

qauyisaqtitsiquyablutik[3]	*nunatsiap*
they made him investigate (INF)	NWT's

gavamangunnik . . .
its government (ACC)

"... asked the minister of northern affairs Warren Allmand to order an investigation into the NWT government." (*Inuit Today*, 6(5), 16)

As traditional Inuit did not often feel a need, in their small societies, to identify a speaker, the morpheme *guuq* generally did the job. Direct quotations and indirect quotations such as the above were rare. However, they are increasing as a result of modernization and the decontextualized nature of writing, taking a little from the importance of polysynthetic morphology and adding a little to syntax.

As this development takes place, subordinate clauses may appear. There are indications of this in the relatively prolific Inuit press such as *Inuit Today*, the magazine of the Eskimo Brotherhood of Canada. These are bilingual publications where the Inuktitut is a translation of the original English.

In the examples given below, the English original appears at the bottom in parentheses.

An example of a construction resembling a true complement clause is found in the Eskimo Brotherhood's manual, *Inuit and the Law* (1974):

katimayinkut	*isumagariaqarmata*
councillors	have to think

kikulimaanut	*atuqtauyut*
by everyone	is used

aaqiqsimattiaq-t-u-mik
properly fix -PART-intr.-acc. (p. 14)

"The members of the Council bear the important responsibility to ensure that proper services are provided." (The councillors have to make sure that what the public needs is provided.)

Here the writer has used an accusative case construction as the object of the verb *isuma* (think). The head of the object phrase, that is, *aaqiqsimattiaqtumik*, is in the "participle" form ("what is properly fixed"), which permits the attachment of the accusative case suffix *-mik*. The more traditional thing to have done would have been to say *aaqiqsimattiaqtuni*, using a verb form meaning roughly "(while) they fix properly," as in the indirect quotation illustrated above. By nominalizing the verb via the participle suffix and then adding the accusative case, the writer has introduced true formal subordination to the main verb *isuma* (think). The accusative phrase, however, is probably not a real clause. For, as I argue next, a word in the participle mode is not a clause. (In Canadian Eskimo, the use of the accusative in this way has not been reported until now. In Greenlandic, with a literature going back to the seventeenth century, accusative complements have been known since Kleinschmidt, 1851/1968, p. 85.)

It has in fact been claimed that a participle is used analogously to an English relative clause. The participle is formed with the suffix *-t/-y*, as in

    katima-yi   -u -y   -ut
    meet -engaged in-BE-PART-they

    "council members"

This may modify a noun, as in

    inuit   *katimayiuyut*
    "The Inuit   who are council members"

It has been claimed, most notably by Creider (1978), that participles used in this manner are relative clauses. However, such constructions differ from what we normally mean by "relative clause" in significant ways. First, there is no relative pronoun. Second, there is no "movement" of the relativized element. These two facts alone made Woodbury doubt that the participle could really, as he nevertheless assumed it did, constitute a relative clause (1975, p. 20). They are also partly responsible for Creider's claim that the Inuktitut "relative clause" is grammatically independent of the main clause and hence not a true subordinate clause! The third problem in claiming that the Inuktitut construction is a true relative clause is that it usually consists of a single word in traditional Inuktitut. For example, I have not found a single multiword example in Rasmussen's 1930 *Iglulik and Caribou Eskimo Texts*. Longer examples appear only in very recent texts. Creider's examples are longer, but they are very recent and all of them have been elicited.

Moreover, the participle as a word class has important uses other than in the equivalent of relativization. It can be used more or less as a main verb (cf. Harper, 1979, p. 9):

    qulaani   inguyaliru   -yug
    up there   be hovering   -he, PART   (Rasmussen, 1930)

    "He was hovering up there"

And the participle is also used like an adjective:

saakuluk   qaquq-tuq
saucer   white-it, PART

"White saucer," "The saucer is white"

arnaq   quviasuk-tug
woman   happy -she, PART

"Happy woman," "The woman is happy"

In fact there is no reason, at least at the surface structure level with which we are concerned here, to consider the Inuktitut participle to be anything but a generalized adnominal modifier that, given the circumstances, may take on the semantic function of a true participle, an adjective, a relative clause, or even an out-of-focus verb. One cannot speak of it as a subordinate clause *in form*: It is merely a word or possibly a phrase.

Yet there is a possibility that the relative clause is developing in written Inuktitut, although not from the participle. Rather, it seems to be springing from an altered use of the demonstrative *taanna* and its variant *taana*.

Literally meaning "this," *taanna*, like *this* in informal English, often singles out a previously unidentified person. In the following excerpt it appears to function as a true relative pronoun:

. . .taimataq   uqalauqpug   Luis   amalat
    so   spoke   Louis   Hamelin

taanna   ilinniarvigjuarmiutaq   silaturiarvingmi
this   member of university   in nature research

atilingmi   lavalmi   kapaak   sitimi
in one called   Laval   Quebec   in city

". . . says Louis Hamelin [who is a member] of Laval University in Quebec City." (*Inuit Today*, 6 (5), 16)

Here, *taanna* appears to have the same function as the English relative pronoun *who*. To my knowledge, this type of construction has not previously been noticed in the linguistic literature. It seems to be a genuine innovation, hardly a borrowing from English. My informant, however, did not find it unusual.

Clearly, what is needed is a thorough study of written texts in Inuktitut and other such "newly written" languages and to see if my isolated examples represent a pattern. I hope to have pointed in the direction of the rewards that may be expected from such an endeavor.

Conclusion

In this chapter, I have sketched the argument that linguistic evolution is logically possible and has not been disproved, that linguistic evolution may be triggered by the appearance of substantial permanent, and especially written, texts. Further, proof of linguistic evolution ought to be sought in a far-ranging comparison of languages with and without a long history of writing (or other permanent texts) and in a study of languages where writing is only now making its impact, where its effects on linguistic structure may be observed as they appear.

ACKNOWLEDGMENTS

I am grateful for comments by W. Chafe, T. Givón, W. McKellin, and D. Olson, whose suggestions have led me to revise several sections of the chapter. What remains is entirely my own responsibility.

NOTES

1. I am preparing a study of the nineteenth-century German-Jewish scholars M. Lazarus and H. Steinthal, where important influences on Boas are discussed.
2. However, Givón remains skeptical about the thesis of evolution in extant languages (personal communication).
3. Verbs like *qauyisaqtitsiquyablutik* have been termed *infinitive* by Kleinschmidt, presumably on account of their translation into Germanic. Yet it is clear from Kleinschmidt's own discussion that this is a minor and relatively infrequent use of such forms (1851, p. 92). Much more often the "infinitive" expresses "simultaneous" or some other background events taking place off the main track of a narrative. And sometimes it occurs on its own – a fully independent clause. (The arguments for treating the "infinitive" as an independent clause are detailed in Kalmár, 1982.) Hence if one looks at the Inuktitut sentence rather than its translation one recognizes it as a conjunction of two independent clauses, with the meaning

"They wrote to the minister of northern affairs, Warren Allmand, *and* asked him to investigate the NWT government."

REFERENCES

Arsleff, H. Bréal vs. Schleicher: Linguistics and philology during the latter half of the nineteenth century. In. H. M. Hoenigswald (Ed.), *The European background of American linguistics: Papers of the Third Golden Anniversary Symposium of the Linguistic Society of America*. Dordrecht: Foris, 1979.

Benveniste, E. La phrase rélative, problème de syntax générale. *Societé Linguistique de Paris, Bulletine*, 1957, 53, 39–54.

Boas, F. Introduction. In *Handbook of American Indian languages*. Bureau of American Ethnology Bulletin 40. Washington, D.C.: U.S. Government Printing Office, 1911.

Chafe, W. L. Integration and involvement in speaking, writing, and oral literature. In D. Tannen (Ed.), *Spoken and written language*. Norwood, N.J.: Ablex, 1982.

Creider, C. The syntax of relative clauses in Inuktitut. *Études/Inuit/Studies*, 1978, 2, 95–110.

Freuchen, P. *Book of the Eskimos*. Cleveland: World, 1961.

Givón, T. *On understanding grammar*. New York: Academic Press, 1979.

Goodwin, W. W. *Syntax of the moods and tenses of the Greek verb* (Rev. ed.). London: Macmillan, 1912.

Gould, S. J. *Ever since Darwin: Reflections in natural history*. New York: Norton, 1977.

Greenberg, J. *Essays in linguistics*. Viking Fund Publications in Anthropology 24. New York: Wenner-Gren Foundation for Anthropological Research, 1957.

Harper, K. *Suffixes of the Eskimo dialects of Cumberland Penninsula and North Baffin Island*. Canadian National Museum of Man, Mercury Series, Canadian Ethnology Service Paper no. 54. Ottawa: National Museum of Canada, 1979.

Hegel, G. W. F. *The philosophy of Hegel*. Ed. C. J. Friedrich. New York: Modern Library, 1953.

Humboldt, W. v. Linguistic variability and intellectual development. 1831. (Reprinted by Miami Linguistic Series No. 9, University of Miami Press, Coral Gables, trans. G. C. Buck & F. A Raven, 1971.)

Kalmár, I. The function of Inuktitut verb modes in narrative. In P. Hopper (Ed.), *Tense-aspect: Between semantics and pragmatics*. Amsterdam and Philadelphia: John Benjamins, 1982.

Kleinschmidt, S. *Grammatik der grönländischen Sprache*. Berlin: Walter de Gruyter, 1851. (Reprinted by George Olms Verlag, Hildesheim, 1968.)

Kroeber, A. *Configurations of culture growth*. Berkeley: University of California Press, 1944.

Kuno, S. *The structure of the Japanese language*. Cambridge: MIT Press, 1973.

Lennenberg, E. H. *Biological foundations of language*. New York: Wiley, 1967.

Li, C. N., & Thompson, S. A., Subject and topic: A new typology of language. In C. N. Li (Ed.), *Subject and topic*. New York: Academic Press, 1976.

Longacre, R. The paragraph as a grammatical unit. In T. Givón (Ed.), *Syntax and semantics*, Vol. 12, *Discourse and syntax*. New York: Academic Press, 1979.

Meillet, A., & Cohen, M. (Eds.). *Les langues du monde*. Rev. ed. Paris: Centre National de la Recherche Scientifique, 1952.

Paris, G. Review of *La theorie de Darwin: De l'importance du langage pour l'histoire naturelle de l'homme* by A. Schleicher [translation of Schleicher (1869)]. *Revue Critique d'Histoire et de Litterature*, 17 October, 1868, pp. 241–244.

Plank, F. *Ergativity: Towards a theory of grammatical relations*. London: Academic Press, 1979.

Rasmussen, K, *Iglulik and Caribou Eskimo texts*. Report of the Fifth Thule Expedition, 1921–23, Vol. 7, No. 3. Copenhagen: Gyldendalske Boghandel, Nordisk Forlag, 1930. (Microfiche edition: IDC, Poststrasse 9, Zug, Switzerland.)

Sapir, E. *Language: An introduction to the study of speech*. New York: Harcourt, Brace & World, 1921.

Schleicher, A. *Die darwinsche Theorie und die Sprachwissenschaft*. Weimar: Bohlau, 1869.

Skorik, P. Ja. *Sklonenie v paleoaziatskix i samodijskix jazykax*. Leningrad: Nauka, 1974.

Snyman, J. W. *An introduction to the !Ku (!Kung) language*. Cape Town: Balkema, 1970.

Steward, J. H. *Theory of culture change*. Urbana: University of Illinois Press, 1955.

Thurman, R. Clause chains in Chuave. M.A. thesis, UCLA, 1978.

Woodbury, A. C. Ergativity of grammatical processes: A study of Greenlandic Eskimo. M.A. thesis, University of Chicago, 1975.

9

The story schema: universal and culture-specific properties

WILLIAM F. BREWER

The first section of this chapter outlines a theory of stories that deals with some important properties of the genre of popular stories in Western literature. The second section describes a recent series of experiments suggesting that this structural–affect theory of stories accounts for a number of aspects of the story schema in English-speaking readers. The next two sections provide an analytic framework that can be used to examine the conventionalized aspects of stories and then apply this framework to cross-cultural investigations of oral literature. The final section presents some hypotheses about the nature of the universal and culture-specific aspects of stories from the oral tradition and contrasts these features with those of written stories from Western popular literature.

A theory of stories

The basic theory of stories sketched here has been presented in Brewer and Lichtenstein (1981, 1982, in preparation). This theory relates particular text structures to particular affective states and then relates the affective states to story intuitions and overall judgments of liking. The goal of the theory is to give an account of the story schema of literate English-speaking adults.

The narrative component

In the narrative component of the theory we distinguish between event structure and discourse structure. The *event structure* that underlies a narrative consists of a series of events arranged in temporal order with respect to some real or imaginary world. The events are structured through the use of plan schemata and causal schemata (Schank & Abelson, 1977; Schmidt, Sridharan, & Goodson,

1978). The schemata that underlie narratives are presumably the same ones that are used to structure the observed actions of objects and people in the ordinary world (see Brewer & Dupree, 1983; van Dijk, 1975; Lichtenstein & Brewer, 1980).

Discourse structure refers to the sequential arrangement of events in the narrative. For a given event sequence there will be many possible discourse sequences. The term *discourse* is meant to be modality-free: The discourse order of a written narrative is the particular arrangement of the events in the text, the discourse order of an oral narrative is the particular arrangement of the events in the spoken presentation, and the discourse order of a motion picture is the particular arrangement of the events in the film.

The distinction between event and discourse is a traditional one in structuralist theories of literature. The Russian Formalists were very clear on this issue and referred to the two levels as the *fabula* and the *sjuzet*, respectively (see Chatman, 1978, for a review).

The author of a narrative has enormous freedom to omit or rearrange events in the discourse. A theory of the reader's narrative schema should give an account of the psychological processes that the reader uses to go from the presented discourse organization to the underlying event organization (see Brewer, 1980, 1982). Thus, for example, it would give an account of the effects of flashbacks on text comprehension. There is as yet no detailed account of the narrative schema for English (however, see Johnson & Mandler, 1980, for a start).

The affective component

The affective component attempts to capture the fact that stories are intended to entertain and that they carry out this function by evoking affects such as suspense and surprise. As part of a general theory of aesthetics, Berlyne (1971) has attempted to relate several general patterns of emotional response to pleasure and enjoyment. In particular, Berlyne has postulated that enjoyment is produced by moderate increases in arousal ("arousal boost") or by a temporary sharp rise in general arousal followed by arousal reduction ("arousal jag"). If both processes operate together, then pleasure is produced both by the rise in arousal and by the subsequent drop in arousal ("arousal −boost−jag"). The affective component of the story theory attempts to apply this more general hedonic theory to the domain of stories.

The structural–affect component

The structural–affect component of the theory relates particular discourse structures to particular affective states produced in the reader. This component of the theory has been greatly influenced by contemporary structural approaches to literary theory (e.g., Barthes, 1974; Chatman, 1978; Culler, 1975; and Sternberg, 1978).

In several recent papers (Brewer & Lichtenstein, 1981, 1982, in preparation) we have proposed three major discourse structures (surprise, suspense, curiosity) that we claim underlie the structure of a large proportion of popular stories from Western culture. Each of these discourse structures is based on a different arrangement of the discourse with respect to the underlying event structure; each is designed to produce a particular affect.

Surprise. An event structure capable of producing surprise must contain *critical expository* or *event* information early in the event sequence. This information is critical in the sense that it is necessary for the correct interpretation of the event sequence. In a surprise discourse structure, the author withholds this critical information from the beginning of the discourse structure without letting the reader know that something has been withheld. Then, at the end of the discourse, the author reveals the information, and the reader is surprised. The surprise is resolved when the reader successfully reinterprets the event sequence in light of the unexpected critical information. An example of a minimal surprise discourse structure is: "Marian walked into her bedroom. She opened her closet door to reach for her nightgown and saw a hand holding a knife." In the underlying event sequence, the person with the knife entered the closet before Marian walked into her bedroom. However, the author has deliberately withheld this critical information from the discourse in order to produce surprise in the reader.

Suspense. An event structure capable of producing suspense must contain an *initiating event* or *situation*. An initiating event is an event that could lead to significant consequences (either good or bad) for one of the characters in the narrative. The event structure must also contain the outcome of the initiating event. In a suspense discourse structure the discourse is organized with the initiating event early in the discourse. The initiating event causes the reader to become concerned about the potential outcome (see Jose & Brewer, in press).

Then the discourse typically contains some additional material in order to prolong the suspense; and finally the outcome is given, resolving the suspense for the reader. Thus, in a simple suspense discourse structure, the order of events in the discourse maps the order of events in the event structure.

An example of a minimal suspense discourse structure based on the above event sequence is: "The psychopath hid himself in the closet. Marian slowly climbed the stairs to her bedroom. Marian walked into her bedroom. She opened her closet door to reach for her nightgown and saw a hand holding a knife. She slammed the closet door and escaped out the front door." Note that it is the *reader's* affect that is crucial. In this example the character is presumably feeling little or no affect while walking up the stairs, yet the reader is in suspense. If the author chooses to reveal the initiating information to both the character and the reader, then both the character and the reader will experience some form of affect.

Curiosity. An event structure capable of producing curiosity must include a *significant event* early in the event sequence. In a curiosity discourse structure the significant event is withheld from the discourse, but (unlike the surprise discourse structure) it provides enough information about the earlier event to let the reader know that the information is missing. This discourse structure leads the reader to become curious about the withheld information. The curiosity is resolved by providing enough information in the later parts of the discourse for the reader to reconstruct the omitted significant event. The classic mystery story is a good example of the curiosity discourse structure. The discourse typically opens with the discovery of the crime, and the rest of the discourse provides information designed to allow the reader to reconstruct the significant events that occurred just before the opening of the discourse (i.e., how the crime was committed and who the criminal was). Figure 9.1 illustrates the three event-structure/discourse-structure relationships and gives the predicted affective curve for each.

The enjoyment component

We have focused on the discourse organization component of an overall theory of narrative appreciation. In particular we have extended the work of Berlyne (1971) and have hypothesized that readers will enjoy narratives organized to produce surprise and resolution, suspense and resolution, or curiosity and resolution

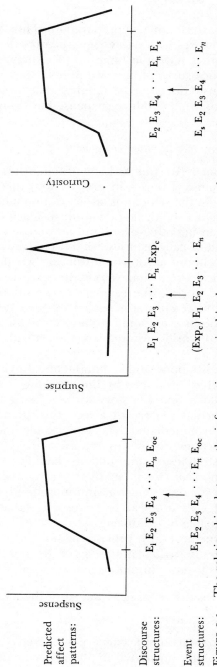

Figure 9.1. The relationships between the information required in the discourse structures, the sequencing of this information in the event structures, and the predicted patterns of affective response for suspense, surprise and curiosity. *Key:* E_i = initiating event or situation; E_{oc} = outcome event; Exp_c = critical expository information required for correct interpretation of events $E_1 \ldots E_n$; E_s = significant event.

(Brewer & Lichtenstein, 1981, 1982, in preparation). Thus, we predict readers will prefer narratives with discourse structures that produce surprise to narratives that have the same event structures but are not organized to produce surprise; and we predict they will prefer narratives with suspense discourse structures that produce and resolve suspense to those that produce suspense but do not resolve it.

The story intuition component

We have recently claimed (Brewer & Lichtenstein, 1981, 1982, in preparation; Lichtenstein & Brewer, in preparation) that the three discourse structures from the structural–affect component form the major part of the concept *story* for literate adult speakers of English. Thus, narratives with an initiating event and an outcome (suspense discourse structure) will be called stories, whereas narratives without an initiating event or without an outcome will not be called stories. Narratives with a critical event and resolution (surprise discourse structure) will be called stories, whereas narratives without a critical event or with no resolution will not be called stories; and similarly, narratives with a significant event and resolution (curiosity discourse structure) will be called stories, whereas narratives without one or the other will not.

We argue that story intuitions (unlike judgments of liking) are not based on the actual affect produced by the narrative. Clearly, one can know that a particular text is a story without liking the text or directly feeling a particular pattern of affect. Instead, we propose that story intuitions are mediated by two possible mechanisms: knowledge of story discourse structures and meta-affect. The structural hypothesis suggests that story intuitions are based on the reader's knowledge of the canonical discourse structures for stories. The meta-affect hypothesis suggests that story intuitions are based on the reader's meta-knowledge about the affective responses that the events in the narrative are capable of producing.

In summary, the structural–affect theory of stories relates particular discourse structures to particular affective states and then relates both these components to story intuitions and story enjoyment.

Empirical results relating to the story theory

Event structure

The hypothesis that goal-directed events are interpreted in terms of plan schemata was strongly supported by the experiments reported in Lichtenstein and Brewer (1980). In that study subjects were asked to view videotapes of goal-directed events (such as an actor setting up a slide projector) and then to recall what they had seen. We developed a theory of the psychological representation of goal-directed events in terms of plan schemata and then tested the theory with the recall data. The data clearly support the hypothesis that observed goal-directed actions are interpreted in terms of plan schemata. Events that were higher in the goal hierarchy were recalled better than events lower in the hierarchy; actions in canonical schema order were recalled better than actions not in canonical order, and actions presented in noncanonical order tended to shift in recall to their canonical positions.

Narrative structure

The hypothesis that event structures underlie narratives was also examined in the study by Lichtenstein and Brewer (1980). In order to relate our findings with observed events to linguistic narrative structures, we wrote out narratives that described the videotaped events. We then carried out recall studies with these narratives and obtained essentially the same results that we had obtained with the recall of the videotaped events. Hence we argued that both observed goal-directed events and written narratives are understood and recalled by means of the same plan schemata.

Inasmuch as our findings for the recall of natural goal-directed events and for narratives were essentially the same as those in the story recall literature deriving from the story grammar tradition (Mandler, 1978; Mandler & Johnson, 1977; Rumelhart, 1977; Stein & Nezworski, 1978; Thorndyke, 1977), we argued that these studies are best interpreted as studies of memory for goal-directed events and studies of narrative structure, and *not* as studies of the structure of stories. Thus, for example, the finding that actions higher in the goal hierarchy are better recalled than actions lower in the hierarchy (Rumelhart, 1977; Thorndyke, 1977) is probably due to nonlinguistic plan schemata operating in recall. However, those studies that manipulated the order of events in the discourse with respect to the order of events in the event structure (Mandler, 1978; Stein & Nezworski, 1978; Thorndyke, 1977) can be viewed as investigations of narrative structure, with the general finding that narratives are easier to understand and remember if the discourse order maps the event order. A more detailed discussion of the reinterpretation of

story grammars and plan-based theories of stories can be found in
Brewer (1980) and Lichtenstein and Brewer (in preparation).

Structure and affect

Data from two recent studies (Brewer & Lichtenstein, 1981, in
preparation) examined the relationship between discourse structures
and affective states. In these studies we asked subjects to start reading
a narrative, and then we stopped them at fixed points in the narrative
and asked them to make judgments about their affect (i.e., degree
of suspense, surprise, curiosity). The results were in strong agreement
with the structural–affect component of the story theory. Narratives
without an initiating event evoked little suspense. Narratives with
suspense discourse organization caused a strong rise in suspense and
a drop at the point of resolution. Narratives with surprise discourse
organization caused a strong rise on the surprise scale at the point
where the critical information was introduced into the discourse.
Narratives with curiosity discourse organization structures caused a
rise in curiosity when information about the significant event was
introduced and a sharp drop in curiosity when the significant event
was revealed in the discourse structure. See Figure 9.2 for an example
of the suspense and surprise curves for one narrative from Brewer
and Lichtenstein (1981).

Story intuitions

Data from the two studies just outlined (Brewer & Lichtenstein, 1981,
in preparation) also supported the story intuition component of our
theory. In addition to asking the subjects to make affect ratings, we
also asked them to rate the narratives on the degree to which they
were stories or nonstories. The data were in good agreement with
the theory outlined earlier. Narratives without an initiating event or
without an outcome were not considered to be stories. However
narratives with suspense discourse structures, surprise discourse
structures, or curiosity discourse structures were all considered to be
stories.

Thus, the findings from a variety of studies suggest that the
structural–affect theory of stories is capable of handling a wide
range of data concerning event structure, discourse structure, affective curves, and story intuitions. However, this theory was designed
to deal with written stories from Western culture and has been tested

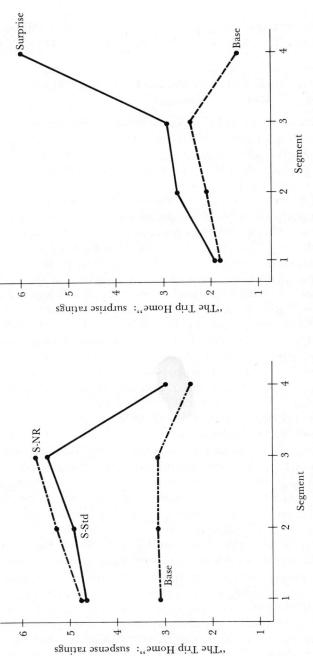

Figure 9.2. Mean suspense and surprise ratings for four different versions of "The Trip Home" (modified from Brewer & Lichtenstein, 1981). Key: Base = no initiating event or outcome event; S-Std = initiating event and outcome event included; S-NR = initiating event but no outcome event; Surprise = critical information at end of discourse.

with readers from the same culture. The next section will explore the implications the theory has for the cross-cultural study of stories.

Cross-cultural nature of the story schema: empirical findings

There have been two recent empirical studies directed at the issue of the universality of the story schema, and they arrive at opposite conclusions. Kintsch and Greene (1978) conclude that story schemata are culture-specific, while Mandler et al. (1980) conclude that there is a universal story schema.

Kintsch and Greene investigated the issue by having University of Colorado undergraduates write summaries of four Western short stories (from the *Decameron*) and four native Alaskan narratives. They found that the undergraduates could write better summaries of the Western short stories than they could of the Alaskan narratives. In a second experiment Colorado undergraduates were asked to recall a Western fairy story and an Apache story. Recall was better for the fairy story. In light of the fact that Kintsch and Greene used only members of one culture for this study, it is an incomplete experimental design. Without data from Alaskan and Apache subjects showing the reverse pattern of results, one cannot know if the findings were due to a mismatch between the subjects' story schema and the texts or if the particular non-English texts chosen were simply intrinsically harder to recall for individuals from any culture. Nevertheless, Kintsch and Greene conclude that the data show that story schemata are culture-specific.

Mandler et al. (1980) studied the issue by having American children and adults and Liberian children and adults listen to and recall four Western folktales and one Liberian folktale. They found that the amount and pattern of recall for the two groups were quite similar. They suggest, on the basis of these findings, that the structure of folktales may be a cultural universal.

The basic problem with these empirical studies is that they are based on theories of stories that do not distinguish between event structure, narrative structure, and story structure. The results of a cross-cultural study using stories are not analytic unless the study is designed to distinguish between these three types of information. If one carries out a cross-cultural study using stories as stimuli and finds a difference between culture X and culture Y, then one does not know if the two cultures differed at the level of event and plan schemata, at the level of narrative schemata, or at the level of story schemata.

The next section of the chapter attempts to use the analytic framework developed for studying stories in Western culture to examine the issue of the cultural specificity or universality of the story schema. This approach has the advantage of bringing a theory to bear on the problem, but the disadvantage of letting a laboratory scientist loose in the complex world of cross-cultural anthropology.

The story schema: culture-specific properties

Events

Clearly, the members of a particular culture have knowledge of a wide variety of culture-specific goal-directed actions – for example, hosting a potlatch ceremony, operating a Xerox machine, sending a drum message. Knowledge of this type is one very important aspect of an individual's culture, but it must be carefully distinguished from narrative and story schemata. Consider the following thought experiment: An American college undergraduate and a member of the Txikaos tribe from the Amazon Basin watch two different goal-directed actions: (a) someone setting up a slide projector and (b) someone preparing materials for a complex Txikaos religious ceremony. If we then ask the two individuals to explain the two actions to us or to recall the two action sequences, we would almost certainly get enormous culture-specific differences. Each individual would be attempting to apply plan schemata to both actions, but would not be successful for the cross-culture actions because they would not fully understand the particular goals and intentions of the actors in the cross-culture episode. If we described the two action sequences in narrative form and carried out a recall study, we would expect similar culture-specific results, yet this difference would be due to the culture-specific nature of the underlying goal-directed actions and would tell us nothing about the cultural specificity of narrative or story schemata.

In fact, Steffensen and Colker (1982) have recently carried out a version of this design with narrative materials. They asked Australian Aboriginal women and women from the United States to recall two narratives: One narrative described a child becoming sick and being treated by Western medical practices, and the other described a child becoming sick and being treated by Aboriginal native medicine. They obtained the expected culture-specific results, with each group showing much better recall for the same-culture narrative than for the cross-culture narrative. Each group was using culture-specific knowledge about the intentions and goals of the actors to interpret the action sequences described in the narratives.

Narratives

Culture-specific aspects of narrative are characteristics of narratives that hold for all narratives of a culture (both story and nonstory) or for a class of nonstory narratives.

Labov (1972) has given an example that might fit this criterion. Labov had middle-class white speakers and inner-city black speakers each relate a personal experience. In analyzing these narratives Labov noted one important difference in narrative form. He found that middle-class white narrators tended to use "external evaluation": They interrupted the narrative and made explicit comments about their feelings or emphasized the point they were trying to make. The inner-city black narrators tended to use "internal evaluation": They did not interrupt the narrative, but got information across by using exact quotations or by describing an external action that would act as a sign of an internal state. This distinction is similar to the distinction between "telling" and "showing" in written narratives (see Booth, 1961, chapter 1). Labov's data thus suggest that there are cultural differences in narratives of personal experience with respect to how the narrator chooses to convey certain types of information to the listener.

Tannen (1980) has compared narratives told by Greek speakers and English speakers describing a short film. She reports a variety of culture-specific narrative choices by the two groups; for example, the Greek narrators tended to include more specific judgments about the actions of the characters. Thus, it seems likely that additional cross-cultural work will show a variety of culture-specific characteristics in the narrative schema.

Stories: oral

In this section an attempt is made to identify the culture-specific characteristics of stories that are true reflections of story structure and not merely reflections of culture-specific event structure or narrative structure. The characteristics of stories from oral traditions will be examined first.

The oral tradition of nonliterate cultures typically includes a wide variety of genres – folktales, myths, legends, proverbs, riddles (Bascom, 1965; Ben-Amos, 1981; Brunvand, 1968; Finnegan, 1970). Essentially all cultures have one or more narrative genres designed primarily to entertain (Bascom, 1965, p. 4; Brunvand, 1968, p. 103; Finnegan, 1967, p. 60; Dégh, 1972, p. 60; Smith, 1940, p. 64). The cross-cultural analysis in this chapter focuses on the broad class of *stories*, where the term is taken to include all long narratives designed primarily for entertainment (see Brewer & Lichtenstein, 1982, pp. 477–478).

The purpose of this analysis of stories from oral traditions is to uncover the aspects of these narratives that are specific to stories – that is, culture-specific *story conventions*, defined as features more frequently found in stories than in ordinary spoken language or other specialized genres. Table 9.1 provides an overall framework for the study of story conventions. Along the left side of the table are the basic story elements: opening, setting, characters, events, resolution, epilogue, closing, and narrator. Across the top of the table are the basic discourse options: The discourse can include a particular story element or omit it; the element can be made explicit in the discourse or included in some more indirect fashion; for a given story element the type can vary; the point in the discourse when an element is first introduced can vary; an element can be repeated or not in the discourse; the discourse order can be the same as the underlying event order or can differ.

Reflecting the basic story elements across the basic discourse options produces, to a first approximation, an inventory of possible story conventions. In the rest of this section the oral traditions from a diverse set of cultures are examined in order to see what different types of story conventions have been observed and thus to determine the characteristics of culture-specific story schemata.

Opening. Conventionalized story openings occur throughout the world (Finnegan, 1970, pp. 379–380; Jacobs, 1964, p. 334). Some of these openings use conventionalized setting information such as the "He lived there" of the Clackamas Indians of the American Northwest or "Once upon a time" from the Western oral tradition (Thompson, 1977, p. 457). Others are so formulaic that they have no other meaning; for example, the Zuni story opening is said to be untranslatable (Tedlock, 1972, p. 123).

Setting. In order to show that setting information is story-specific it is necessary to show that its occurrence in stories differs from its

Table 9.1. *Possible story conventions*

Story elements	Discourse option				Discourse order	
	Presence/ absence	Explicitness	Type	Initial introduction	Repeated/ not repeated	Mapped/ reordered
Opening	X	X	X			
Setting (time and location)	X	X	X	X	X	
Characters	X	X	X	X	X	
Events	X	X	X	X	X	X
Resolution	X	X	X	X	X	X
Epilogue (morals, evaluations, and explanations)	X	X	X	X		
Closing	X	X	X			
Narrator	X	X	X			

occurrence in nonstory narratives. Jacobs gives some good examples from American Indian cultures. He states that in some of these oral traditions there was a small set of obligatory forms of location and/or time from which the setting must be selected. Thus for a particular culture the setting might have to include "he left the village" (1964, p. 335). The Kham of Nepal actually have an explicit verb form that distinguishes setting information from event information, though it is not clear if this is story-specific (Watters, 1978). It appears that many North American Indian cultures omitted descriptive setting information relating to nature (Jacobs, 1964, p. 336; Shimkin, 1947, p. 341). Dégh notes that the conventionalized setting of European folktales is in the Middle Ages (1972, p. 64).

Characters. There are clear differences in conventionalized characters across cultures. Thus the protagonist of trickster stories is a coyote among North American Indians (Thompson, 1977, p. 319), a rabbit among cultures in Central Africa, and a spider in West Africa (Finnegan, 1970, p. 337). A number of authors have suggested that little detail describing characters is given in stories from the oral tradition: the Limba of West Africa (Finnegan, 1967, p. 52), the Zuni of the American Southwest (Tedlock, 1972, p. 130). There are a variety of conventional ways of introducing the characters of stories. The Longuda of Nigeria (Newman, 1978, p. 103) and the Khaling of Nepal (Toba, 1978, p. 158) both require that all the characters be introduced at the beginning of the story. The Hanga of Ghana conventionally introduce the villain before the hero (Hunt, 1978, p. 241), while among the Sherpa of Nepal the order of character introduction is victim, villain, hero (Schöttelndreyer, 1978, p. 253). A very common characteristic of oral traditions is the repetition of character types (e.g., three brothers, three monsters). The number of repetitions varies from culture to culture. It is five for the Clackamas of the Pacific Northwest (Jacobs, 1959, p. 224); it is four for the Navaho (Toelken, 1981, p. 167); and it is three for stories in the Western oral tradition such as "The Three Bears" (Olrik, 1909/1965). The order of introduction for a set of repeated characters is often conventional. A very common pattern is for the conventionalized number of brothers to be introduced (and carry out their actions) in order from oldest to youngest, with the youngest finally successful. This pattern occurs in the Navaho (Toelken, 1981, p. 167), the Nez Percé (Stross, 1972, p. 110), the Clackamas (Jacobs, 1959, p. 227), and the Western oral traditions (Olrik, 1909/1965, p. 136).

Events. In order to show that some aspect of story events is conventionalized one must show that they differ in some way from the events actually occurring in the culture. Thus, the fact that seal hunting occurs in Eskimo stories more often than it does in Apache stories says nothing about conventionalized Eskimo story events. Nevertheless, in most cultures there are story characters who carry out superhuman acts – killing monsters, moving huge objects, visiting the heavens. A number of writers have noted that events are chosen for inclusion in a story for their dramatic or entertainment value (Finnegan, 1967, p. 60; Fischer, 1963, p. 237; Shimkin, 1947, p. 332; Smith, 1940, p. 67). Frequently there are conventionalized event sequences known as *motifs* (see Thompson, 1977). Thus Zulu stories conventionally disposed of villains by giving them a bag of snakes and scorpions to open (Finnegan, 1970, p. 381). Many American Indian groups used a motif in which the hero ascended to the sky by a ladder made of arrows (Jacobs, 1964, p. 337). In stories from the Western oral tradition there is the motif of rescuing the princess from the dragon or the motif of danger from wishes that come true (Thompson, 1977, pp. 24, 134).

Examination of the ordering of events in oral traditions shows much repetition and parallel development. Thus, the protagonist will carry out one act, then a second similar act; or the protagonist can repeat exactly the same act. If there are several characters with similar roles, one attempts to carry out an act (and often fails), then the second character attempts the same act, and so on. For discussions of these issues see Dégh (1972, p. 61), Finnegan (1967, p. 89), Fischer (1963, pp. 249–252), Olrik (1909/1965, pp. 132–134), Shimkin (1947, p. 340), and Stross (1972, pp. 109–112). A number of investigators have stated that in stories from oral traditions the discourse order always follows the event order (Finnegan, 1967, p. 49; Fischer, 1963, p. 249; Jacobs, 1959, p. 213; Olrik, 1909/1965, p. 137); however, other investigators have reported the occurrence of flashforwards and flashbacks in stories from oral traditions – for example, the Shoshone (Shimkin, 1947, p. 339) and the Toura of West Africa (Bearth, 1978, p. 215). It is not clear if these discourse – event order conventions are story conventions or general narrative conventions.

Resolution. Fischer (1963, p. 237) has stated that all stories in oral traditions have a "dramatic" structure (i.e., Brewer & Lichtenstein's suspense discourse structure) and that they include some form of resolution of the conflict. However, there are some counterexamples. Thus, the Limba of West Africa have a subgenre of "dilemma" stories in which conflict is created and deliberately not resolved (Finnegan, 1967, p. 30). It is not clear if there are conventions about stories resolving with "good" outcomes. Certainly a number of stories from oral traditions have "bad" endings from the point of view of a Western reader.

Epilogue. In many oral traditions stories contain a conventionalized epilogue that makes a meta-comment on the story, gives a summary, or gives some postresolution information about the characters. For example Clackamas stories had an obligatory explanatory segment (Jacobs, 1959, p. 247). Limba stories could have a moral, a generalizing comment, or an explanatory segment (Finnegan, 1967, p. 88). Shoshone stories could have an explanatory segment or additional information about the characters (Shimkin, 1947, p. 334). Hanga stories gave either a summary or a moral, or both (Hunt, 1978, p. 240). Some Sherpa stories included a moral and then a summary of the events from the story relevant to the moral (Schöttelndreyer, 1978, p. 265).

Closing. Conventionalized closings occur very widely. They vary from the simple "it is finished" of the Limba (Finnegan, 1967, p. 87) and "they lived happily ever after" of the Western oral tradition (Thompson, 1977, p. 457) to the enigmatic Shoshone "Coyote way out there is tracking through slush" (Shimkin, 1947, p. 335). In one type of closing for stories of the Fali of West Africa the linguistic form is not formulaic; instead a conventionalized event must be described – several dogs of different colors going hunting, killing game, and eating it (Ennulat, 1978, p. 148). My personal favorite is the conventionalized closing used by the Kamba of East Africa. "May you become rich in vermin in your provision-shed, but I in cows in my cattle-kraal" (Finnegan, 1970, p. 380).

Narrator. In an oral tradition the individual telling the story is obviously the narrator. But the issue is actually somewhat more complex than that. The individual telling the story can be merely a vehicle or can intrude into the narrative and provide information and make evaluative comments. It is not completely clear from the few accounts that discuss the issue if there are story-specific narrator conventions, but it seems likely. Dégh (1972, p. 61) states that in telling European folktales there were conventionalized forms of narrator intrusion. The Khaling of Nepal have a number of linguistic devices (e.g., locative adverbs) that must be used when the narrator interrupts the sequence of events in the narrative (Toba, 1978, p. 160). Limba narrators have a word form that they use to indicate that they are about to give the audience information not yet known to the characters (Finnegan, 1967, p. 76). The Syuwa of Nepal show an interesting relation of narrator to narrative. The Syuwa language has a sentence-final particle that is used to indicate whether the speaker witnessed the information or the information is second-hand and unverified. In telling stories Syuwa narrators use the unverified marker for the initial sentence but then can shift to the speaker-witnessed form for the rest of the story (Höhlig, 1978, pp. 23–24).

Vocabulary and syntax. In addition to the conventionalized story elements discussed above there are frequently conventionalized vocabulary, morphology, and syntax (see Jacobs, 1964, p. 332; Tedlock, 1972; Toelken, 1981). However, these more purely linguistic aspects of stories in oral traditions will not be covered in this chapter.

The purpose of this analysis of stories in oral literature across cultures has been to gain some understanding of the nature of culture-specific story schemata. The framework provided by Table 9.1 and the cross-cultural evidence outlined in this section give a good indication of the types of information about content and form that are represented in culture-specific story schemata.

Stories: written

In this section an attempt is made to specify some of the types of information that are part of the story schema for Western written stories. In keeping with the analysis of stories from the oral tradition the focus will be on long narratives designed primarily for entertainment – for example, spy novels, mystery novels, westerns, science fiction, and popular short stories. The analysis will not cover "literary" genres. In fact, it seems unlikely that most members of Western culture have been exposed to enough examples of literary texts to have developed a schema for these genres.

Opening. One very obvious difference between written stories and oral stories is that written stories do not have a conventionalized opening. Even the most formulaic genres do not have a fixed linguistic form that must appear at the beginning of the story.

Setting. The placement of setting information in written stories has apparently undergone a change since the late 1800s. In earlier novels (e.g., those by Fielding, Scott, and Trollope) it was conventional to place much setting information at the beginning of the discourse (Sternberg, 1978). However, in more recent fiction it has become conventional to omit the initial setting and distribute the information throughout the discourse. In fact, O'Faolain (1963) has argued that the convention of opening a discourse with an event (e.g., "She saw him put it in his pocket") is one of the most striking characteristics of modern fiction. The type of setting used is also often conventionalized. Thus, classic mystery stories are conventionally set in the English countryside. In popular literature the American West of the late 1800s has become a conventionalized setting, while New England mill towns of the same period have not.

Characters. The number and order of introduction of characters does not appear to be a frequently conventionalized aspect of written stories. However, the types of characters are highly conventionalized. In order to show that a character type has become conventionalized it is necessary to show that individuals of that type portrayed in stories can be distinguished from the society's general stereotypes of that type of individual. Thus detectives with extraordinary powers of reasoning are almost certainly conventionalized characters in Western written stories, because our cultural stereotype of real-world detectives does not include such extraordinary powers of reasoning. Which types of individuals are chosen for inclusion is also conventionalized – note the names of several specific Western genres: detective stories, spy stories, cowboy stories. In principle one could have a genre in which a tree is discovered to be dead, the arborist is called, and through extraordinary powers of reasoning the arborist discovers what caused the tree to die; but in practice the detective has become a conventionalized character and the arborist has not.

Events. Many writers have noted that a basic characteristic of the events in written stories is that they are selected to provide conflict (Brooks & Warren, 1979, p. 36; Jaffe & Scott, 1960, pp. 2–3; Perrine, 1970, p. 43). The order of events in the discourse of written stories often does not map the order of the underlying events. Both O'Faolain (1963) and Sternberg (1978) suggest that presenting events in the discourse out of their underlying order is an important convention of modern fiction. It is these event-related aspects of written stories that form the core of Brewer and Lichtenstein's structural–affect theory of stories.

Western written stories also show conventionalized motifs: first contact with an alien species in science fiction, the Russian scientist who wishes to defect in the spy novel, the gun duel on Main Street in the Western.

Resolution. A number of writers have noted that the underlying structure of most written stories is a buildup of tension that is resolved near the end of the discourse (Brooks & Warren, 1979, p. 36; Altenbernd & Lewis, 1969, p. 23). Perrine (1970, pp. 44–48) notes that "inexperienced" readers have trouble appreciating modern literary works that do not resolve. There have been, in recent years, some shifts in the conventions about outcome valence of stories (i.e., a good or bad ending). Up through the 1950s a good outcome was conventionalized for many written genres – for example, spy stories, westerns, adventure stories. However, more recently this story convention has become less rigid, and stories with bad endings sometimes occur in these genres (Cawelti, 1976, p. 42). Perrine (1970, p. 47) comments that the frequent use of bad outcomes in modern literature is another factor that causes inexperienced readers to have problems appreciating these works. Thus, it appears that in modern entertainment fiction the "happy ending" has shifted from a rigid story convention to a somewhat weakened convention.

Epilogue. The explicit use of summaries or morals is not a convention of popular written stories, though there is some use of epilogues to give additional information about the course of events after the resolution of the basic conflict.

Closing. Apparently, modern written stories do not show an obligatory closing form. A quick sample of 20 recent paperback books (5 science fiction, 5 mystery, 5 spy, 5 best-sellers) from our shelves at home showed no use of the formulaic closing "The End."

Narrator. The intrusiveness of the narrator in written stories is another convention that has shifted in written stories. During the 1800s an intrusive narrator was the conventional form. However, by the turn of the century the convention shifted and the use of unintrusive narrators became conventional (O'Faolain, 1963, p. 52; Scholes & Kellogg, 1966, p. 268). Perhaps among the most elaborate sets of conventions in written stories are those related to point of view. In written stories there have evolved a variety of techniques that involve the information available to the narrator, the location of the narrator, and the visibility of the narrator (Booth, 1961; Friedman, 1955).

Story schema. In comparing the Western written story to the oral story it appears that the written story shows less conventionalization with respect to number of story elements and the fixed location of story elements, although it does have much conventionalized content (i.e., types of setting, characters, events, and resolutions). In written stories discourse organization tends to replace repetition as a device for producing affect.

The story schema: universal properties

In this section the issue of story universals is considered. Clearly this is a speculative business. The logic of uncovering culture-specific aspects of stories is much clearer. One finds two cultures with different story conventions and contrasts them. The logic of uncovering story universals is much less certain. One examines the similarities across cultures and makes an inductive leap. Nevertheless, the attempt must be made if we are to have a comprehensive theory of stories.

As with the analysis of culture-specific universals, one must distinguish phenomena occurring at the level of events, at the level of narrative, and at the level of stories.

Events

Whereas many contents of goal-directed actions will be culture-specific, the underlying use of plan schemata to understand human actions must be a universal. I find it hard to imagine a human culture in which individuals do not interpret human actions in intentional form.

Narrative

It seems clear that members of all cultures will need to be able describe action sequences in linguistic form, so narrative will be a universal form of discourse. In narratives designed primarily for comprehension, the order of events in the discourse will map the order of the underlying events, and some setting information will be placed at the beginning of the discourse. Both these conventions should reduce the cognitive load for the narrative understander and are derived from more general restrictions on human beings as information processors.

Stories: oral

This subsection includes an attempt to identify universals in stories in oral traditions that are separate from the event universals and narrative universals. First, it appears that all cultures have a genre of long prose narratives told primarily for entertainment (Boas, 1925, p. 329; Bascom, 1965, p. 16; Fischer, 1963, pp. 237, 241). It seems likely that the entertainment is produced by the activation of affective states such as suspense, surprise, curiosity, humor, sexual arousal, and anger. However, the universal status of these particular affective states in oral stories clearly needs investigation. Similarly, the status of the particular devices used in stories to produce affect needs to be studied cross-culturally (see Finnegan, 1967, p. 61).

The use of conventionalized opening and closings seems to be a universal (see Dégh, 1972, pp. 60–61; Finnegan, 1970, pp. 379–380; Jacobs, 1964, p. 334; Olrik, 1909/1965, pp. 131–132). Certain types of characters may occur in all cultures. Thus, talking animals may be universal characters (Boas, 1925, p. 333), and the hero figure may also be universal (Fischer, 1963, p. 255). It may be that characters in the oral tradition show limited characterization (Finnegan, 1967, p. 52; Tedlock, 1972, p. 130) or that the characterization is done by "showing," not by "telling" (Olrik, 1909/1965, p. 137). Another possible universal is that characterization is carried out in terms of extremes (e.g., extremely strong, or beautiful, or evil). The repetition of characters may be a universal feature of stories in the oral tradition (Jacobs, 1964, p. 334; Olrik, 1909/1965, p. 133).

The choice of events to produce particular affective states may be a universal (Fischer, 1963, p. 237), and the repetition of events in stories seems to be universal (Boas, 1925, p. 330; Dégh, 1972, p. 61; Fischer, 1963, p. 251; Olrik, 1909/1965, pp. 132–133).

The oral tradition versus the written tradition

In this section the universals postulated to occur in stories in the oral tradition are compared with the features found in stories from the Western written tradition and an attempt is made to give an account of the differences.

One major difference between the written and oral traditions is genre specialization. Many oral narratives appear to be carrying out a wide variety of functions at the same time. Thus, a single oral narrative may be doing what Western literature would do through a novel, a dirty joke, a history text, a scientific journal article, a religious text, and a philosophical essay (see Finnegan, 1967, pp. 31, 63; Fischer, 1963, p. 258). Literacy, the printing press, and specialization of function in Western society have allowed the development of highly specialized genres. Along with the specialization of discourse force (e.g., to inform, or to entertain, or to persuade) has gone specialization of discourse form (see Brewer, 1980). Thus written texts include specialized forms such as the "pyramid style" of the newspaper article, the formulaic headings of the scientific journal article, and the inverted order of the mystery story.

The occurrence of conventionalized openings and closings in stories from the oral tradition may reflect the difference between having a live narrator versus an "abstract" narrator in a written story. The teller of an oral story has to distinguish narratives told for entertainment from the teller's everyday discourse, and the conventionalized opening and closing may serve this function. This hypothesis is supported by Davenport's gloss for the story opening used in the Marshall Islands. "This is a fairy tale; it may or may not have happened long ago; it is not to be taken seriously; it is not always supposed to be logical" (1953, p. 224). It is also supported by the Rattray's translation of the opening of Ashanti stories. "We do not really mean, we do not really mean (that what we are going to say is true)" (1969, p. 55). In written stories this type of information is given by the book cover, by the knowledge of where the book was obtained, and by other indicators of genre.

The differences in characterization between oral and written stories may also be due to the fact that stories in the oral tradition are performed, not read. In decontextualized written stories the character information has to be placed in the discourse, but in oral stories the performer can act out characters' emotions and internal states, so that such information need not be placed explicitly in the discourse (see Finnegan, 1967, p. 52; Fischer, 1963, p. 237).

Finally, the occurrence of repetition at a number of levels in oral stories may be a story device that is particularly successful at producing suspense in an oral performance (Davenport, 1953, p. 226; Finnegan, 1967, p. 79; Jacobs, 1959, p. 224; Olrik, 1909/1965, p. 133; Toelken, 1981, p. 167), or it may help the narrator's fluency

(Jacobs, 1964, p. 335) or serve to reduce the memory load for both performer and the audience (Finnegan, 1977, chap. 3).

Overall, these differences between oral and written stories can be seen as similar to the distinction Chafe (1982; Chapter 6) makes between integration and involvement in language. The decontextualized nature of written stories leads to complex characterization and point-of-view development. The use of the written mode makes possible the elaboration of these devices and also allows complex rearrangements of the discourse order (flashbacks and flashforwards).

In contrast, the performed nature of oral stories leads to the need for conventionalized openings and closings and to the use of repetition to overcome memory limitations. The ability of the performer to dramatize some aspects of the information reduces the need to place this information explicitly in the discourse.

Conclusions

The purpose of this chapter has been to uncover basic properties of the story schema. An analytic framework has been proposed that distinguishes between event schemata, narrative schemata, and story schemata. This approach provides considerable clarification of the difficult issues in this area. Applying the framework to the oral tradition in a variety of cultures provides an initial account of the nature of universal and culture-specific story schemata. Culture-specific story schemata for stories from the oral tradition tend to include a wide variety of conventions regarding the occurrence and discourse order of such story elements as openings, characters, events, epilogues, and closings. Story schema universals in oral traditions reflect more abstract characteristics of stories, such as the use of affect to produce enjoyment and the use of repetition and parallel structure.

By contrasting the findings for oral tradition with those for Western written genres it is possible to highlight the story conventions of Western written stories. The story schema for written stories tends to include fewer conventions about the number and fixed discourse order of story elements. However, like the story schema for oral stories, it does appear to include a number of conventions about the type of settings, characters, and events that are included in stories. The written story schema tends to use discourse organization instead of repetition to produce affect (see Brewer & Lichtenstein, 1981, 1982, in preparation) and to include explicit character description and elaborate development of narrator point of view. Finally, it is possible to account for some of the differences between the story schema for oral and written stories by taking into account the fact that oral stories are performed by narrators whereas written stories are experienced in a decontextualized setting.

May you become rich in vermin in your provision-shed, but I in cows in my cattle-kraal.

ACKNOWLEDGMENTS

This research was supported in part by the National Institute of Education under Contract No. HEW-NIE-C-400-76-0116. I would like to thank Ellen Brewer, Janet Dougherty, Claire Farrer, Anne Hay, Paul Jose, Ed Lichtenstein, Muriel Saville-Troike, and Patricia Tenpenny for comments on an earlier draft of this paper.

REFERENCES

Altenbernd, L., & Lewis, L. L. *Introduction to literature: Stories* (2nd ed.). New York: Macmillan, 1969.

Barthes, R. *S/Z*. New York: Hill & Wang, 1974.

Bascom, W. The forms of folklore: Prose narratives. *Journal of American Folklore*, 1965, *78*, 3–20.

Bearth, I. Discourse patterns in Toura folk tales. In J. E. Grimes (Ed.), *Papers on discourse*. Dallas: Summer Institute of Linguistics, 1978.

Ben-Amos, D. (Ed.). *Folklore genres*. Austin: University of Texas Press, 1981.

Berlyne, D. E. *Aesthetics and psychobiology*. New York: Appleton-Century-Crofts, 1971.

Boas, F. Stylistic aspects of primitive literature. *Journal of American Folklore*, 1925, *38*, 329–339.

Booth, W. C. *The rhetoric of fiction*. Chicago: University of Chicago Press, 1961.

Brewer, W. F. Literary theory, rhetoric, and stylistics: Implications for psychology. In R. J. Spiro, B. C. Bruce, & W. F. Brewer (Eds.), *Theoretical issues in reading comprehension*. Hillsdale, N.J.: Erlbaum, 1980.

Plan understanding, narrative comprehension, and story schemas. *Proceedings of the National Conference on Artificial Intelligence*, 1982, 262–264.

Brewer, W. F., & Dupree, D. A. Use of plan schemata in the recall and recognition of goal-directed actions. *Journal of Experimental Psychology: Learning, Memory, and Cognition*, 1983, *9*, 117–129.

Brewer, W. F., & Lichtenstein, E. H. Event schemas, story schemas, and story grammars. In J. Long & A. Baddeley (Eds.), *Attention and performance 9*. Hillsdale, N.J.: Erlbaum, 1981.

Stories are to entertain: A structural–affect theory of stories. *Journal of Pragmatics*, 1982, *6*, 473–486.

A structural–affect theory of the reader's story schema. In preparation.

Brooks, C., & Warren, R. P. *Understanding fiction* (3rd ed.). Englewood Cliffs, N.J.: Prentice-Hall, 1979.

Brunvand, J. H. *The study of American folklore: An introduction*. New York: Norton, 1968.

Cawelti, J. G. *Adventure, mystery, and romance*. Chicago: University of Chicago Press, 1976.

Chafe, W. L. Integration and involvement in speaking, writing, and oral literature. In D. Tannen (Ed.), *Spoken and written language*. Norwood, N.J.: Ablex, 1982.

Chatman, S. *Story and discourse*. Ithaca, N.Y.: Cornell University Press, 1978.

Culler, J. *Structuralist poetics*. Ithaca, N.Y.: Cornell University Press, 1975.

Davenport, W. H. Marshallese folklore types. *Journal of American Folklore*, 1953, *66*, 219–237.

Dégh, L. Folk narrative. In R. M. Dorson (Ed.), *Folklore and folklife: An introduction*. Chicago: University of Chicago Press, 1972.

Ennulat, J. H. Participant categories in Fali stories. In J. E. Grimes (Ed.), *Papers on discourse*. Dallas: Summer Institute of Linguistics, 1978.

Finnegan, R. *Limba stories and story-telling*. Oxford: Clarendon Press, 1967.

Oral literature in Africa. Oxford: Clarendon Press, 1970.

Oral poetry. Cambridge: Cambridge University Press, 1977.

Fischer, J. L. The sociopsychological analysis of folktales. *Current Anthropology*, 1963, *4*, 235–295.

Friedman, N. Point of view in fiction: The development of a critical concept. *PMLA*, 1955, *70*, 1160–1184.

Höhlig, M. Speaker orientation in Syuwa (Kagate). In J. E. Grimes (Ed.), *Papers on discourse*. Dallas: Summer Institute of Linguistics, 1978.

Hunt, G. F. Paragraphing, identification, and discourse types in Hanga. In J. E. Grimes (Ed.), *Papers on discourse*. Dallas: Summer Institute of Linguistics, 1978.

Jacobs, M. *The content and style of an oral literature: Clackamas Chinook myths and tales*. Chicago: University of Chicago Press, 1959.

Pattern in cultural anthropology. Homewood, Ill.: Dorsey, 1964.

Jaffe, A. H., & Scott, V. *Studies in the short story* (rev. ed.). New York: Holt, Rinehart and Winston, 1960.

Johnson, N. S., & Mandler, J. M. A tale of two structures: Underlying and surface forms in stories. *Poetics*, 1980, *9*, 51–86.

Jose, P. E., & Brewer, W. F. The development of story liking: Character identification, suspense, and outcome resolution. *Development Psychology*, in press.

Kintsch, W., & Greene, E. The role of culture-specific schemata in the comprehension and recall of stories. *Discourse Processes*, 1978, *1*, 1–13.

Labov, W. *Language in the inner city*. Philadelphia: University of Pennsylvania Press, 1972.

Lichtenstein, E. H., & Brewer, W. F. Memory for goal-directed events. *Cognitive Psychology*, 1980, *12*, 412–445.

An evaluation of four classes of story theories. In preparation.

Mandler, J. M. A code in the node: The use of a story schema in retrieval. *Discourse Processes*, 1978, *1*, 14–35.

Mandler, J. M., & Johnson, N. S. Remembrance of things parsed: Story structure and recall. *Cognitive Psychology*, 1977, *9*, 111–151.

Mandler, J. M., Scribner, S., Cole, M., & DeForest, M. Cross-cultural invariance in story recall. *Child Development*, 1980, *51*, 19–26.

Newman, J. F. Participant orientation on Longuda folk tales. In J. E. Grimes (Ed.), *Papers on discourse*. Dallas: Summer Institute of Linguistics, 1978.

O'Faolain, S. On convention. In H. Summers (Ed.), *Discussions of the short story*. Boston: Heath, 1963.

Olrik, A. Epic laws of folk narrative. In A. Dundes (Ed.), *The study of folklore*. Englewood Cliffs, N.J.: Prentice-Hall, 1965. (Originally published in German, 1909)

Perrine, L. *Story and structure* (3rd ed.). New York: Harcourt, Brace & World, 1970.

Rattray, R. S. *Akan-Ashanti folk-tales*. Oxford: Clarendon Press, 1969.

Rumelhart, D. E. Understanding and summarizing brief stories. In D. LaBerge and J. Samuels (Eds.), *Basic processes in reading and comprehension*. Hillsdale, N. J.: Erlbaum, 1977.

Schank, R. C., & Abelson, R. P. *Scripts, plans, goals, and understanding*. Hillsdale, N.J.: Erlbaum, 1977.

Schmidt, C. F., Sridharan, N. S., & Goodson, J. L. The plan recognition problem: An intersection of psychology and artificial intelligence. *Artificial Intelligence*, 1978, *11*, 45–83.

Scholes, R., & Kellogg, R. *The nature of narrative*. London: Oxford University Press, 1966.

Schöttelndreyer, B. Narrative discourse in Sherpa. In J. E. Grimes (Ed.), *Papers on discourse*. Dallas: Summer Institute of Linguistics, 1978.

Shimkin, D. B. Wind River Shoshone literary forms: An introduction. *Journal of the Washington Academy of Science*, 1947, *37*, 329–352.

Smith, E. W. The function of folk-tales. *Journal of the Royal African Society*, 1940, *39*, 64–83.

Steffensen, M. S., & Colker, L. Intercultural misunderstandings about health care: Recall of descriptions of illness and treatments. *Social Science and Medicine*, 1982, *16*, 1949–1954.

Stein, N. L., & Nezworski, T. The effect of organization and instructional set on story memory. *Discourse Processes*, 1978, *1*, 177–193.

Sternberg, M. *Expositional modes and temporal ordering in fiction*. Baltimore: Johns Hopkins University Press, 1978.

Stross, B. Serial order in Nez Percé myths. In A. Paredes & R. Bauman (Eds.), *Toward new perspectives in folklore*. Austin: University of Texas Press, 1972.

Tannen, D. A comparative analysis of oral narrative strategies: Athenian Greek and American English. In W. L. Chafe (Ed.), *The pear stories.* Norwood, N.J.: Ablex, 1980.

Tedlock, D. On the translation of style in oral narrative. In A. Paredes & R. Bauman (Eds.), *Toward new perspectives in folklore.* Austin: University of Texas Press, 1972.

Thompson, S. *The folktale.* Berkeley: University of California Press, 1977.

Thorndyke, P. W. Cognitive structures in comprehension and memory of narrative discourse. *Cognitive Psychology*, 1977, *9*, 77–110.

Toba, S. Participant focus in Khaling narratives. In J. E. Grimes (Ed.), *Papers on discourse.* Dallas: Summer Institute of Linguistics, 1978.

Toelken, B. The "Pretty languages" of Yellowman: Genre, mode, and texture in Navaho coyote narratives. In D. Ben-Amos (Ed.), *Folklore genres.* Austin: University of Texas Press, 1981.

van Dijk, T. A. Action, action description, and narrative. *New Literary History*, 1975, *6*, 273–294.

Watters, D. Speaker-hearer involvement in Kham. In J. E. Grimes (Ed.), *Papers on discourse.* Dallas: Summer Institute of Linguistics, 1978.

10

A metaphor for literacy: creating worlds or shunting information?

FRANK SMITH

Metaphors are the legs of language on which thought steadily advances or makes its more daring leaps. Without metaphor thought is inert, and with the wrong metaphor it is hobbled.

Metaphors are inescapable. Language cannot address reality directly (whatever "reality" might be without metaphor). Metaphors are the analogies by which one thing is explored or discussed in terms of another, the familiar used as a fulcrum to reveal the unknown.

Thought can be entirely contained within metaphorical frameworks that define present and future understanding in an entire realm of enquiry, just as a map summarizes but also constrains travel throughout a geographic region. Such metaphorical structures are known as *models* (or by the more elegant synonym *paradigms*). Models and paradigms are more than perspectives; they are all-encompassing, all-confining nets within which thought is organized and trammeled. Thus metaphor can limit what inquiry will consider.

The argument

My argument is that a change of metaphor is required for thinking about language. I shall propose that our perceptions of literacy are narrowed if not distorted by the pervasive tendency, in education as well as in language theory and research, to regard language solely as the means by which information is shunted from one person to another. The model from which I want to escape perceives language as synonymous with communication and communication as the transmission of information, the exchanging of messages like sums of money or bags of oranges. What you get is what you are given. It all seems to me wholly inappropriate and misleading.

It is not only with respect to language that I am concerned with the intellectual fallout from a mushrooming of the information metaphor. Science generally tends to derive its metaphors from contemporary technology. The world, society, individuals, and especially brains and bodies are widely perceived in terms of computers, as systems that feed off information. The current paradigm in cognitive psychology regards the brain as a repository of information, thought as "information processing," and learning as the mechanism by which new information is acquired.

On the other hand, I propose to argue that:

1. very little of what the brain contains can be appropriately thought of as information;
2. very little of the brain's commerce with the world (including other people) can be appropriately regarded as the exchange of information;
3. learning is rarely a matter of acquiring information;
4. the brain is not very good at acquiring information – it is not the most "natural" thing for the brain to do; and
5. language is not a particularly efficient means of transmitting information—it is not the most "natural" thing for language to do.

I shall also propose two paradoxes – that:

6. writing is less efficient than speech for the communication of information; but that, on the other hand,
7. writing is more "natural" than speech in some important respects; it is better suited to do those things that the brain is more likely to do and more effective in doing.

Finally I shall argue that the view in education that the function of writing is the communication of information must have suppressed many potential authors from an early age and also must have done a good deal to lower standards of spelling, punctuation, and other important aspects of the secretary's craft. In other words, the information-transmission metaphor has worked directly against the interests of literacy.

The alternative

At this point I should perhaps give some indication of what I am for, a flavor of the metaphor I favor, which I would like to substitute for information shunting as a way of thinking about language and the brain.

My alternative is that the primary, fundamental, and continual activity of the brain is nothing less than the creation of worlds. Thought in its broadest sense is the construction of worlds, both "real" and imaginary, learning is their elaboration and modification, and language – especially written language – is a particularly efficacious but by no means unique medium by which these worlds can be manifested, manipulated, and sometimes shared. My metaphor pictures the brain as an artist, as a creator of experience for itself and for others, rather than as a dealer in information.

It would not be difficult to elaborate upon my metaphor in various ways – to begin to dissect the internally consistent (and sometimes externally validated) systems of knowledge, belief, and possibility that the brain creates, explores, and occasionally communicates. The argument is basically constructivist, not in itself provocative or unusual in other areas of psychology or philosophy, especially with respect to perception and memory. I could analyze the imperatives of this creative process, looking more specifically at the way in which it organizes worlds – including the world we call the real one – in terms of imposed categories, attributes of categories, and category interrelationships (Smith, 1975). The metaphor itself could be examined more deeply, looking, for example, at how the term *create* literally means to cause to come into existence, to generate possibilities of experience. I could enlarge upon the doubly productive nature of creativeness in both art and cognition, first in the generation and selection of alternatives out of which an imaginative product or artifact can be shaped, and then as the artifact itself becomes a source of exploration and discovery for oneself and others, a new source of possibilities in the world, a new world.

But instead I want to put my metaphor to the test, to examine through use my contention that the creation of worlds is a more productive and appropriate metaphor for language, literacy, and learning than the shunting of information.

1. Very little of what the brain contains is information. Like most of the common and useful words of every language, the word *information* is ambiguous, gaining – or losing – specific meaning from the context in which it occurs. And like such words as *language, meaning, word,* and *communication,* it can be used very loosely indeed. For example, one can call everything found in a brain – or in a book – information. But such indiscriminate usage says nothing because it homogenizes the contents of the brain and leaves us to find another term for those aspects that are indeed informative (just as the assertion that life is but a dream leaves us to find a new term to distinguish the events within our lives that are dreams). The brain contains many aspects, affective and conative, feelings and values and intentions, that cannot be called information in any meaningful sense.

More specific definitions of information share the characteristic of facilitating decisions; information is what helps us make up our minds (and is therefore something different from "the mind"). The notion that information facilitates decision making by reducing uncertainty is one of the original and fundamental insights of information theory (Shannon & Weaver, 1949). Information is regarded as any kind of signal – any distinctive feature or significant difference – that reduces uncertainty by eliminating alternative choices. Thus traffic lights are informative, the red or the green light reducing uncertainty about whether to proceed through an intersection. Information is a difference that makes a difference (Bateson, 1979). Such a notion is inherent in distinctive-feature theories of speech production and recognition (Jakobson & Halle, 1956; Miller & Nicely, 1955) and of reading (Gibson, 1965; Smith & Holmes, 1971). In such a sense, anything in the world can be informative, since anything can be a signal – provided, of course, that it is properly interpreted. Signals that cannot be interpreted, that do not reduce uncertainty, are technically regarded as "noise." In such a sense, information can only exist in the world, not in the brain. What the brain must contain is the understanding that can interpret signals, that can tranform noise into information.

A second, more general meaning of the term *information* is *facts*, or representations of selected aspects of reality, that may exist in both the world and the brain. Facts come in a variety of forms, in formulas, in maps and diagrams, and in language. It is a fact that Paris is the capital of France, that two times two equals four, that water is wet, and that *h-o-r-s-e* is the spelling of the word *horse*, which is the name of a particular kind of animal. Facts exist objectively in what Popper (1972) calls "World 3," the world of human artifacts and ideas. And facts exist in the human brain when they have been memorized. Many people – beginning with Samuel Johnson – seem to believe that education is a matter of learning all the facts that one needs to know or learning where to find them. However, like the more specific form of information, facts reduce uncertainty only to the extent that they can be interpreted, even when they have been committed to memory.

A fact in the brain may be more accessible than a fact in a book, but it is still not informative in itself – it still has to be interpreted.

That Paris is the capital of France is a fact that is meaningful to me. I also know that Gaborone is the capital of Botswana, but this is less informative to me because I know little else about the city or the country. And the fact that $E = mc^2$ reduces no uncertainty for me at all because I have no idea of how to make use of it, even though I have succeeded in committing it to memory.

In other words, the information that we have in the brain in the form of memorized facts must (like the facts and signals also available in the world around us) be interpreted by something else in the brain, something that is not information but that enables us to make sense of information, which in itself must be far more extensive than the information in the world or in the brain.

What is it that we have in the brain that enables us to make sense of the world, to interpret signals and make sense of information? I have argued elsewhere (Smith, 1975) that the brain contains nothing less than a *theory of the world*, a theory that is an interpreted summary of all past experience – "a history of all the problems an individual has had to solve" (Popper, 1972) – that is the basis not only of our present understanding of the world but more importantly of our predictions of the future.

Such a theory contains all our knowledge, beliefs, and expectations about the objective world in which we find ourselves. We are confused whenever we encounter an occurrence in the world that we cannot relate to our theory and surprised when something occurs contrary to our expectations. Information may have gone into the construction of the theory, but it was constructed of far more than information. The theory was constructed of hypotheses, confirmed or disconfirmed partly on the basis of our experiences of the world around us, partly on the basis of our own internal tests, our thinking. Where did the hypotheses come from? From the theory itself. Nothing the theory cannot hypothesize can be part of the theory (nothing the theory cannot make sense of can be made sense of). What were the theory's original hypotheses? The learning possibilities that we were born with.

To catalog the theory of the world that we have in the head would be to describe the world as we know it, with all its complexities and interrelationships, an impossible Kantian task. A catalog of the theory that we are born with, the innate possibilities of real and imagined worlds, is only just beginning to be studied by developmental psychologists and psycholinguists.

Cognitive psychologists are, I think, referring to aspects of the theory of the world when they talk of the *schemata* of memory

(Bartlett, 1932) or of thought (Kintsch, 1974, 1977), of *scenarios* (Schank & Abelson, 1977), *plans* (Miller, Galanter, & Pribram, 1960), or *descriptions* (Norman & Bobrow, 1979). All of these are the possibilities that enable us to interact with the world, to make sense of its circumstances and to fulfill our own intentions. When our theory of the world fails, when we cannot use it to interpret what is happening to us, we are like a person stumbling through a dark and unfamiliar room, furnishing it with only what the imagination can bring.

Yet there is much more to the theory that we have in the head than all our understanding of what the world is like. We constantly manipulate the theory – or rather the theory constantly manipulates itself – to explore and experience what the world might be like, what we wish it could be like (or are afraid it could be like) or had been like. We can construct worlds that would never otherwise exist, in every art form, in language, and in our own heads.

The world in the head is dynamic, constantly changing, both in the course of its own enterprises and in its interactions with the world around. The objective world itself is rarely static. That cars and buses exist may be a relatively permanent part of my theory of the world, but their particular concurrence as I drive along the road is something my theory must continually predict, modify, and erase.

Anticipation leads all our interactions with the world, which is another way of saying that imagination structures reality. Fantasy is not reality manipulated; reality is a fantasy constrained by the objective world. As David Olson has commented, reality is fantasy that works.

The brain is not a repository of information like a library or the memory banks of a computer. Estes (1980) is only the most recent experimental cognitive psychologist to remark that the brain does not store anything at all; it is an interactive organ with a life of its own, constantly changing its state on the basis of its own operations as well as of "information" from the world around. The perceived world is a vast and dynamic canvas that the brain creates, explores, and changes according to its own criteria of logic, intention, and aesthetic preference, with only the minimum necessary regard for the demands of reality, just as a painter will check if a picture is congruent with a particular landscape, but still give priority to the artistic intent.

2. *Very little of the brain's commerce with the world is the exchange of information.* Reading is frequently defined as the acquisition of infor-

mation from print, and reading is frequently taught and tested as if information shunting were its sole purpose. Rosenblatt (1980) satirizes the educational perspective in an article entitled "What Facts Does This Poem Teach You?" She distinguishes two purposes for reading – *efferent*, when the object is to acquire information, and *aesthetic*, when the intention is fulfilled within the act of reading itself. Her complaint is that schools transform what should be aesthetic reading, performed for the sheer pleasure and satisfaction of doing it, into the drab and disenchanting routine of assimilating and regurgitating information.

It is easy to distinguish Rosenblatt's two functions of reading. Efferent reading is occurring when we would just as soon not be reading at all – for example, if someone else would tell us the sports scores, consult the catalog, review the small ads, or summarize the day's news. We are rarely held in thrall by the huge cast of characters, each uniquely identified, in the telephone directory. With aesthetic reading, on the other hand, we are reluctant to have the experience end. We are not reading to acquire information, but to explore a world of sensations or ideas. What we bring to the text is as important as the text itself. We are annoyed if someone tries to deprive us of the reading by telling us how the story ends. We slow as we reach the concluding pages of the book in order to extend the experience.

Extending the experience is the basis of most normal discussions (as opposed to the stilted classroom travesties) about books, movies, plays, television programs, works of art, and events in everyday life. These are not exchanges of information; no one may say anything that is not known already, but each helps in the reconstruction and continuation of aspects of the original experience.

Conversations are frequently the same. The participants do not exchange messages; they weave a fabric, woof and warp, sometimes creating a tapestry of shared ideas that is indeed a work of art. A conversation can be like a walk through the woods, an unmapped meander with no goal beyond the activity itself, certainly not undertaken for the purpose of coming out on the other side. The only thing predictable about the ground to be covered is that the participants will stay within arm's reach of each other.

Conversations, walks, car journeys, entire days . . . all can be undertaken for the sake of the experience itself rather than for reaching a particular destination or achieving a particular end, a creative rather than a passive enterprise. Even when new "facts" about the world are assimilated, they become part of the theory of the world because the theory has reached out and selected them,

they become part of the constructive endeavor. The human brain is
not a vacuum cleaner, mindlessly sucking up every particle of
information in its way. The information routinely gathered by the
brain may often be acquired without awareness or effort, a by-
product of the experience in which we are engaged, but it is always
relevant to what is known already.

Much of the time the world with which we interact is the world in
the head, even when we are ostensibly interacting with the world
around. We reflect upon what might be going on, upon what might
have been going on, and upon what might be going to go on. The
brain does not remain supinely content to take and interpret life as
it comes; it creates its experiences. All this is related to aspects of
human mental life that I feel have never been satisfactorily explained,
such as the apparently universal fascination with panoramas and
dioramas, with models and miniatures and scenes from great heights,
with intricate constructions and subtle mechanisms. Curiosity and
exploration are not explained by being called "drives." Play is
essentially creative behavior; it has no apparent purpose beyond the
activity itself – and Sutton-Smith (1979) has noted that children's
language in play is richer than their language in more mundane
activities. Perhaps dreams are the purest instances of the brain
constructing worlds, of experience without information.

The brain has difficulty in distinguishing "reality" from fantasy,
and not only in children. The "willing suspension of disbelief" that
is supposed to constitute the theatrical experience seems to me to
have the matter backwards; it is belief that is difficult to suspend. A
film, or even a book, can move us irresistibly to tears, laughter, or
fear, no matter how hard we try to tell ourselves "it isn't real." Can
we always distinguish what actually happened, what we have read,
and what we only imagined in the past? Is reality a fantasy with a
tag attached, a tag that can easily be detached?

3. *Learning is rarely a matter of acquiring information.* We learn without
knowing what we learn. A moment's reflection and we can recall –
we can construct – what we were wearing yesterday and the day
before, details of the meals we had, the people we talked with, the
newspapers we read, the television that we watched. If we cannot
remember the specific days, newspapers, or television programs
before that, it is not because they have been forgotten but because
what we have learned from them has been integrated more generally
into our theory of the world; they have become part of everything
that we know. Our memory for certain kinds of events of the past is

truly remarkable; we recognize faces, spoken and written words, and late-night movies that we have not encountered for years, and the recognition brings with it a broader tissue of recollections.

We learn so easily that learning of the kind I have just illustrated is often not considered to be learning at all, or its pervasiveness is overlooked. This is because the relative difficulty of learning in the structured, deliberate, information-gathering manner of school and formal study is often so conspicuous.

The learning that is easy and continual is the learning that is accomplished as part of our daily interaction with the world – and with the world in our head. It is not the cramming of new information, but the elaboration and modification of the theory of the world in the head. "Facts" are often learned consciously, but understanding grows inconspicuously with the development of the theory in the head, in the extension of experience, just as the muscles develop inconspicuously in the practice of an athletic activity.

Learning and experience are inseparable, however the experience occurs. Psychologists have argued that our memory for an event is the way in which we made sense of the event (Tulving & Thomson, 1973), just as Popper (1972) asserted that any individual's knowledge was a history of the problems that the individual had had to solve. The word *experience* comes from the same root as *experiment*; it is more than something that happens, it is a test. The brain learns the way an artist learns, not by accumulating facts, but by exploring possibilities, by testing its own creations.

4. The brain is not very good at acquiring information. As I have just indicated, learning is often unfairly characterized as a difficult and arduous activity because of the conspicuous effort that it so often seems to entail in an educational context. The brain is a highly efficient learning device, but only when it is actively making sense of something, not when it is consciously striving to assimilate facts. Rote learning – the deliberate effort to memorize unrelated items of information – is so difficult and inefficient as to be clearly unnatural, the brain's least preferred way of learning.

Consider the 100-year history of the "scientific" study of verbal learning in experimental psychology, beginning with the invention of the nonsense syllable by Ebbinghaus (Boring, 1957). Nonsense was required because experimental results were "lawful" and replicable only when subjects could make no sense of the stimuli, when everyone had an equivalent task of striving to memorize by rote a sequence of unrelated facts. But the history has been one of constant struggle, between experimenters trying to contrive better and better nonsense and subjects trying to make sense of it (Smith, 1975). Because sense destroys experiments. The only predictable thing about learning when individuals manage to make it meaningful in some way is that it takes place very much quicker than nonsense learning and lasts a good deal longer. The brain learns best when it is most creative.

The acquisition of information by rote might not in itself be unnatural, since the brain does seem capable of accomplishing it to some degree. But such an effort is so inefficient that any tendency in psychology and in education to regard learning primarily as a matter of difficulty and deliberate intention in preference to something more meaningful and creative would appear to be most unnatural indeed.

5. *Language is not a particularly efficient means of communicating information.* The relative inadequacy of language in matters affective is widely recognized, in poetry, in science, and in everyday life. No flood of words can take the place of a look, a sigh, or a touch of the hand in communicating friendship or sympathy. The more subtle the intent, the more impotent language seems to be to express it.

For more general information, however, language is widely regarded not just as an effective medium but often as the exclusive one. In a few summary pages, Popper (1976) pithily disposes of this view. He argues that increased precision can only be achieved in language at the cost of clarity (p. 24), that speakers and writers can never protect themselves completely from being misunderstood (p. 30) because they can never anticipate every context in which their remarks might be interpreted, and that in fact we never really know what we are talking about (p. 27), because we can never understand all the implications of what we say.

There are two fundamental and related problems for language with respect to information transmission, both connected to its strength from other points of view. The first lies in its ambiguity; words and sentences can be interpreted in a variety of ways, not idiosyncratically but with respect to context. The imperative "Fire" means one thing at a conflagration and another at an execution. The commonest English nouns can also be verbs or adjectives, or both, often with a variety of senses for each syntactic function. Normally we are not aware of this inherent ambiguity, but only because listeners and readers are able to bring sense to utterances through context – not only the linguistic context but also their own prior knowledge and their understanding of the utterer's specific intentions. The second problem is that the surface structures of language do not represent meaning directly in any case, but rather require interpretation based on the syntactic and semantic intuitions of the recipient.

More precise languages do exist – the languages of logic and mathematics, for example, of knitting patterns and computer programs. Such languages are not as rich and productive as natural language; their applications are limited to the specific contexts in which they occur. What they gain in precision they lose in power. But in any case, such languages do not reflect the way the brain works. None of the world's 3,000 or more natural languages function in the unambiguous information-shunting modes of computers, and all seem much easier to learn (since infants universally have very little difficulty with them).

Natural languages are productive and creative systems, flourishing on inventiveness and initiative in interpretation. What they achieve is limited – or extended – by what the people who share them can mutually bring to their language exchanges. Language creates a whole new realm of possible experiences for human beings, but it does this by reflecting more the personal characteristics of the individuals who use it on any particular occasion rather than the "information" that passes between them.

There are more efficient ways of communicating information – in formulas, diagrams, and photographs. It is perhaps significant that none of these media is one in which creative artists typically work, in contrast to natural language, painting, and music, unless the artists go beyond the literal bounds of the medium to impose their own personal vision. It would be foolish to argue that language cannot be used for the transmission of information, but it is far from the sole function of language, and it is not one for which language is particularly suited. That is why we have traffic lights and road maps.

6. *Speech is better than writing for communication.* The question is essentially one of resources. Since language is basically fallible as a means of information transmission, it needs to draw on everything it can to achieve communication effectively. In particular, every possibility must be exploited to capitalize upon the contribution that the recipient must make to understand messages. And language that is spoken has more resources than language that is written.

There is one advantage that every speaker has over writers, the possibility of using intonation for subtlety and for emphasis. Punctuation, italicizing, capitalizing, and underlining offer only a shadow of the modulating powers of the human voice. And in face-to-face situations the speaker's repertoire is enlarged enormously, not only because a wide range of conventional facial and other physical gestures exist but because the speaker can respond from moment to moment to the listener's understanding and uncertainty. When speech can be seen carrying the listener like a surfer upon a wave, the speaker can accelerate, abbreviate, whisper, even become careless without going beyond what the listener will tolerate. When difficulties occur, the speaker can revise, repeat, recall, foreshadow, reemphasize, elaborate, illustrate, and summarize, all in tune with the needs of the listener. None of these resources is available to the writer, deprived of the principal source of the speaker's strength: a close interaction with the recipient. A great deal of communication can take place in the absence of words, in the absence of a common language even, when the two participants can see each other; speech serves to cement shared understandings. But writers and readers must usually interact without appeal to each other's sensitivity (personal letters excepted). They are kept apart by a text that is supposed to unite them but that like a two-sided mirror can only reflect back upon them their own images.

Writing is widely supposed to be better than speech for communication because it is relatively durable and easily transportable. In addition, writing can often be scrutinized at the recipient's pleasure; entire passages can be reread or skipped; readers can proceed at their own pace, can move ahead as well as back, without concern for the speed or sequence in which the text was produced. But these aspects of written language do little to enhance communication. If anything they serve only to dissipate understanding. A text, like any work of art or artifice, serves primarily as a vehicle by which the perceiver's own world constructions are promoted rather than the producer's.

Writing is not good for communicating information; it is good only for codifying it. Writing freezes language and carries it to new contexts beyond the reach or understanding of the producer, who has no control over how the text will be interpreted. It is truly the language of the blind. This is why writing is always subject to exegesis, why there is interminable haggling over the meaning of testaments, constitutions, laws, contracts, even newspaper articles.

Olson (1977) argues that a strength of written language is that it has to mean what it says. In my view the great weakness of written language is that it can never be sure of saying what is meant. Writers are always tempted to think that their text is transparent, because they are the ones who know what they wanted to say. They are not only denied the recipient's perspective, they lose control of the text the moment it is read. My earlier quotations from Popper about the limitations of language for anyone who hopes to communicate apply particularly to writing. Written language invites contention, and then by its persistence through time and space offers every facility for the contention to expand and persist.

7. *Writing is better than speech for the creation of worlds.* Writing may not be superior to speech for the communication of information, which I have argued neither speech nor the brain itself are very good at in any case. But writing is infinitely more efficacious than speech in another respect. It is superbly more potent in creating worlds. And since I also argue that creating worlds is the brain's primary concern, then I am forced to the conclusion that writing might in some ways be considered more natural than speech; it does better than speech what the brain does best.

Writing is typically regarded as more permanent than speech, for the superficial reason that its manifest form endures longer. But from a more meaningful point of view, speech is permanent and writing provisional, because anything spoken can never be altered or erased (unless we are talking to ourselves). One slip of the tongue and we can argue for an hour that we did not intend what we said and still fail to persuade a listener. Writing, on the other hand, is malleable. It is a plastic art. In writing we not only can create worlds, we can change them at will. Writing enables us to explore and change the worlds of ideas and experience that the brain creates. This is the enormous power and attraction of writing, I feel, especially for children – until something happens to persuade them that writing does not have this power at all.

The power of writing is not initially lost upon many children. A child writes "The dog died" and is astounded at what has been accomplished. The child has put a dog into the world that did not exist before – created a world that would not otherwise have existed – and then has killed the dog. None of this can be done in any other way. And if the child is contrite, a stroke of the pen is all that is required to bring the dog to life again, something else again that would be difficult to accomplish in any other way.

It may be argued that the child who has killed the dog will be anxious to show this drama to other people, thus demonstrating a desire to communicate information. Children also like to share what they enjoy reading. But children do not generally have a passion for conveying information to adults (as opposed to making a good impression on them or manipulating their behavior). Children do not normally expect to be in possession of information that adults do not already have and are likely to be interested in. There are two reasons why children might enjoy having adults read their first brief literary productions: one is to share the wonder of the creation itself and the second is to show how clever they are. Such motivations are not absent from more adult texts one sometimes finds published in professional journals or pinned on staffroom notice boards.

I can anticipate at least two objections to my suggestion that writing might be considered more natural than speech in some important ways. While spoken language is universal, cultures still exist that do not have writing, which appears to be a relatively recent arrival on the human scene. And while just about every child can learn to speak at an early age and rapid rate in the absence of any formal instruction, writing generally has to be taught, often with considerable difficulty and limited success.

My response to the two objections is the same – that writing requires an external technology. *Language* appears to be part of the inherited potential of every child, and in the case of speech it is fortunate that just about every child is also born with a vocal apparatus capable of expressing this potential in audible form. The problem with language from a visual point of view is that it requires tools. When supplied with a convenient instrument, like an electric type-writer, children can learn to write at the age of two (Doman, 1975), and there is an extensive literature on children who have learned to read at the age of two or three. To assert that writing is unnatural because it does not occur in many cultures is like arguing that swimming is unnatural because it may not be often or easily learned by people who do not have access to water, such as desert dwellers. One does not become a writer if the tools do not lie conveniently to hand, so to speak.

The difficulty that many children encounter in learning to write may also be inseparable from the instruction they receive, a topic to which I shall return in due course when we renew acquaintance with our young dramatist and the saga of the dog that died.

The principal disadvantage of speech is that we usually have very little time to organize it and scarcely any chance at all to reflect upon it or to accommodate intrusive thoughts, either as speakers or listeners. It is therefore not well suited for the kind of creative activity that the brain performs best. It may indeed only be because of its relative utility for communication, in conjunction with the other expressive resources that human beings have available, as well as because a suitable audible-language-productive instrument is built in, that speech has persisted as a universal and perhaps somewhat overrated human talent.

Some practical implications

My aim is to change a prevailing metaphor. I am not against "communication," nor would I deny its importance or even argue that one should not learn to use language as best one can to accomplish communicative ends. But I feel that the limitations of language as a medium of communication and the limitations of communication as a metaphor for language should both be recognized.

This is not simply a matter of playing with words. As I said at the beginning, the metaphors we choose structure the way we perceive the world. In cognitive psychology, for example, I fear that the tendency to perceive the brain primarily as an information-processing device ignores the most central and most interesting aspects of learning and thought, just as the earlier associative model in the study of verbal learning led to a distorted perception of the nature of memory. Indeed, some of the more extreme applications of an information-processing approach seem to me to have been a reversion to a rigid stimulus–response psychology (e.g., Anderson & Bower, 1973), where comprehension is regarded simply as an ability to respond with a sentence identical to the stimulus. Computer simulations of "language processing" have evaluated models of human understanding in terms of how well they could be translated into computer programs. More recently, schema theories have tended to look at language comprehension in terms of the prior knowledge and expectations of the individual (e.g., Rumelhart, 1975) – still often characterized as the "receiver," however. Psychologists are still a long way from studying how individuals construct their personal models of the world, the genesis of their knowledge and expectations.

Something that mildly surprises me is the general drabness of the metaphors that psychology does employ, the unimaginativeness of the theories to which it is inclined. The physicalist model of billiard ball causality that to many psychologists has always seemed the epitome of scientific control and aspiration is many years out of date, abandoned by physicists themselves. To find exciting and imaginative theories today, throbbing with color and with marvel, one has to turn to astronomy, nuclear physics, or genetic biology. To try to comprehend what is dimly perceived through powerful electron microscopes and telescopes seems to require the mind of a poet. Why, then, should that most remarkable universe of all, the human brain, be approached in such a grey and mechanistic way?

Particularly regrettable is the drab and mechanistic approach that the communication metaphor often introduces into classrooms. Paradoxically, the desire to produce effective communicators may actually help to destroy the ability of many children to write. The danger is that the information-transmission emphasis can lead to an almost exclusive perception of writing from the perspective of a reader, rather than from the writer's point of view.

Let me return to the young author of the "The dog died." When this story is read by a teacher who adopts a reader's point of view (and parents are also very good at this) the child will be told something like, "It isn't very long, is it? Can't you tell me the dog's name or what color it is?" As if these facts fall into the same existential category as the birth and death of a living creature in three short words. As if it is the length of a piece of writing that matters. Worse, the adult comment might have something to do with two spelling mistakes and a punctuation error in those three short words – scarcely likely to encourage the child to write longer fragments in the future, certainly not with words whose spelling is in doubt.

The consequence of premature and exclusive concern with the reader's point of view, I have argued elsewhere (Smith, 1982), is that schools attempt to produce secretaries instead of authors. Children are expected to learn to spell and punctuate as their admission fee to the privilege of writing, and such a procedure not only inhibits potential authors, denying to many children both the pleasure and the learning opportunities of spontaneous personal writing, but it produces awful secretaries as well. I am not arguing that spelling and punctuation are not important, but that instruction that gets in the way of a child's writing will just not succeed in its aims.

And a consequence of such failures, reinforced by the general perceptions that literacy is both difficult and solely for communication, is that reading and writing are fatally trivialized. Children may not be exposed to reading as a compelling aesthetic experience. They may not have writing demonstrated to them as a means of creating worlds that they themselves can experience and explore (and that they may if they wish subsequently decide to share with others). They may be subjected to drills and homilies that teach them that literacy is work, punitive, and a bore. Even if they do "learn to write," what they will learn is that the purpose of reading and writing is the shunting of information.

Such is the lesson that seems well learned by many college students. They are reasonably good at writing if they are told what exactly to write, and when, and how much. They are very competent in quoting the views of others (with the references beautifully displayed) and even in providing summary statements. But they are most unconvincing in constructing their own point of view or in arguing for or against the views of others, because they have rarely had the experience of doing so.

Concluding constructions

I am not proposing a solipsistic point of view. I am not arguing that the brain as an artist actually creates the objective, physical world that the body as a whole inhabits. World creating is not an asocial activity; the brain's theory is constrained by its shareability (at least in those aspects of the theory that must be shared with other people). The closeness of two individuals' theory of the world doubtless reflects the closeness of their cultures and of their roles and stations in those cultures. The world that the brain creates is at the same time personal, social, and physical. Readers of the same book can share the same experience, to the extent that two people can ever share the same experience. Indeed, written language permits very special kinds of experience to be shared, from myth to science, from narrative to poetry.

I also do not wish to communicate or create pessimism and despair. The shelves of our libraries may buckle under compendiums of information, but they can also be replete with good stories, insightful observations, and interesting ideas. I hear of many individuals, in educational institutions and out, who have difficulty coping with all the information to which they are exposed (let alone that which they do not understand), but I rarely hear anyone complain of the wealth of reward and pleasure that written language so prodigiously provides, the possibilities of a broader experience of the world around and of the public and private worlds that we ourselves construct.

Finally, I do not want to suggest that my proposed change of metaphor will be easy. A considerable difficulty with perceiving the brain as an artist is that it does not facilitate control or "accountability" in educational contexts or replication in psychological experiments. Creativeness is not easily quantified. The contents of the human brain are so vast that sheer description is out of the question. If the value of a model is determined by the rigor with which it can be evaluated, then the brain as artist looks like getting as short shrift as

212   FRANK SMITH

any struggling artist in these days of "objective" economic decisions.
The relative value of metaphors cannot be assessed "objectively."
There is no statistical test that will decide which is "correct." The
question is which metaphor is the most productive, and the answer
will depend on what one's intention is in the first place – to measure
and control human behavior or to understand it.

REFERENCES

Anderson, J. R., & Bower, G. H. *Human associative memory*. Washington, D.C.:
    Winston, 1973.
Bartlett, F. C. *Remembering*. Cambridge: Cambridge University Press, 1932.
Bateson, G. *Mind and nature: a necessary unity*. New York: Macmillan, 1979.
Boring, E. G. *A history of experimental psychology*. New York: Appleton-Century-
    Crofts, 1957.
Doman, G. *How to teach your baby to read*. New York: Doubleday, 1975.
Estes, W. K. Is human memory obsolete? *American Scientist*, 1980, *68*, 62–69
Gibson, E. J. Learning to read. *Science*, 1965, *148*, 1066–1072.
Jakobson, R., & Halle, M. *Fundamentals of language*. The Hague: Mouton,
    1956.
Kintsch, W. *The representation of meaning in memory*. Hillsdale, N.J.: Erlbaum,
    1974.
    On comprehending stories. In M. A. Just & P. A. Carpenter (Eds.),
    Cognitive processes in comprehension. Hillsdale, N.J.: Erlbaum, 1977.
Miller, G. A., Galanter, E., & Pribram, K. H. *Plans and the structure of behavior*.
    New York: Holt, Rinehart & Winston, 1960.
Miller, G. A., & Nicely, P. E. An analysis of perceptual confusions among
    some English consonants. *Journal of the Acoustical Society of America*, 1955,
    27, 338–353.
Norman, D. A., & Bobrow, D. G. Descriptions: An intermediate stage in
    memory retrieval. *Cognitive Psychology*, 1979, *11*, 107–123.
Olson, D. R. From utterance to text: The bias of language in speech and
    writing. *Harvard Educational Review*, 1977, *3*, 257–281.
Popper, K. *Objective knowledge: An evolutionary approach*. Oxford: Clarendon,
    1972.
    Unended quest: An intellectual autobiography. London: Fontana Collins, 1976.
Rosenblatt, L. M. "What facts does this poem teach you?" *Language Arts*,
    1980, 57(4), 384–394.
Rumelhart, D. E. Notes on a scheme for stories. In D. Bobrow & A. Collins
    (Eds.), *Representation and understanding: Studies in cognitive science*. New
    York: Academic Press, 1975.
Schank R. C., & Abelson, R. P. *Scripts, plans, goals and understanding*. Hillsdale,
    N.J.: Erlbaum, 1977.

Shannon, C. E., & Weaver, W. *The mathematical theory of communication.* Urbana, Ill.: University of Chicago Press, 1949.

Smith, F. *Comprehension and learning.* New York: Holt, Rinehart & Winston, 1975.

Writing and the writer. New York: Holt, Rinehart & Winston, 1982.

Smith, F., & Holmes, D. L. The independence of letter, word, and meaning identification in reading. *Reading Research Quarterly,* 1971, 6(3), 394–415.

Sutton-Smith, B. (Ed.). *Play and learning.* New York: Gardner, 1979.

Tulving, E., & Thomson, D. M. Encoding specificity and retrieval processes in episodic memory. *Psychological Review,* 1973, 80, 352–373.

PART III

Literacy and competence

11

Literacy development: a psychogenetic perspective

EMILIA FERREIRO

In this chapter I will discuss the relevance of Piaget's theory for the understanding of literacy development. My task is not an easy one, because Piaget never focused his work on literacy as such. The central core of Piaget's contribution to both epistemology and psychology is a general theory of the processes of acquisition of knowledge. As far as my own research activity is concerned, both with reference to the approach to the problem and to the kind of interpretation offered, Piaget's theory serves as an assimilatory schema that enables the construction of "observables" (that is, the organization and assignment of meaning to seemingly chaotic masses of data) as well as the comprehension of their interrelationships. I will argue that, as a general theory of the acquisition of knowledge, Piaget's theory is entirely applicable to literacy knowledge, that is, to the processes of the building up of the writing system as an object of knowledge.

My presentation will be necessarily rather abstract. I will take as the starting point what is the culmination and synthesis of the main tenets of Piaget's theory on the equilibration of cognitive structures (Piaget, 1975) and try to show on the basis of available data how it works on literacy development. As the starting point is epistemological in nature, it is worth mentioning that the term *object* means "object of knowledge," and the term *subject* means "knowing subject."

Consider a few general remarks that characterize some of Piaget's fundamental ideas about cognitive development. (They will be presented rather dogmatically, because it would take an entire course to develop the kind of argumentation and the type of facts that are behind each one of them.)

1. Action is the origin of all knowledge, including logicomathe-matical knowledge. The term *action* applies not only to "physical action" (just as the term *object* does not apply only to "physical

object"). Depending on the type of object and on the level of development of the subject, the term *action* refers to social inter-actions or inner-actions as well; but in any case, action involves (a) a transformation of the object (sometimes a physical trans-formation, but more important, a conceptual transformation); (b) a transformation of the subject (a widening of the domain of application of the schema or a modification of the schema).

2. Action is the unit of analysis of behavior, where *behavior* does not mean the same as in the behaviorist tradition. It includes not only the action that is performed, but also the meaning of the action, and of the objects of the action, for the subject. This implies the idea of an organized and organizing totality: Action is organized into schemata, and the schemata organize the world of objects. It is the coordination and reciprocal assimilation of schemata that lead to different levels of organization of the knowing subject.

3. Cognitive development is an *interactive process*. The construction of knowledge always implies a part that is contributed by the object (with its physical, social, and cultural properties) and a part that is contributed by the subject (with his or her assimilation schemata). Facts are *not* directly *given*. In order to be able to identify facts out of a mass of raw data, the subject, whatever his or her level of development, has to organize them. This is what is called, in epistemological theory, the construction of observables by interaction between the object and the subject.

4. Cognitive development is a *constructive process*. It is characterized by the reconstruction of already acquired knowledge at new levels and by the effective construction of novelties.

5. Cognitive development is a *dialectical process*. It is characterized by continuous construction of interdependencies between pre-viously uncoordinated systems and it leads to new totalities, the properties of which are not reducible to the properties of the uncoordinated systems. Piaget speaks of this as *dépassements*, that is, a new synthesis, a "going beyond." It is also characterized by the coordination of affirmations with negations, by the relativi-zation of concepts, by a spiral construction, by a continuous interaction between what is considered possible and what be-comes necessary, by an endless process in which each new solution to a problem introduces new problems.

Now let us apply these key ideas from Piaget's theory to the experimental and observational data on literacy development that my collaborators and I have collected.

Cognitive problems that are common to other well-known domains of development also arise when children try to understand the writing system. For instance, it seems evident that children face *classification problems.* Consider first the difficulties inherent in the classification of the graphic material as such. All our non-iconic symbols are constituted of combinations of two types of lines: straight and curved ones. But some of them are called "letters" and some of them are called "numbers." The same combination (for instance, a vertical line with a contiguous circle) is called a letter – as in *b* or *d* – or a number – as in *9*. There is not a clear perceptual basis for such a distinction. Later on, once this distinction has been established, new classification problems arise: Many different graphic forms are called by the same name and considered equivalent – but not interchangeable (since capital letters are not expected to be mixed indiscriminately with lowercase letters in the same piece of writing). There are also classification problems involved in the distinction of the objects that are the carriers of different types of meaningful texts, such as directories, story books, picture books, shopping lists, and so on.

Because of space limitations I will be able to consider only one example from the large variety of cognitive problems connected with writing development: *the relationship between the whole and its constituent parts.* Even this single example can be examined here across a relatively short period of literacy development. From the very moment when a piece of writing is considered to be a compound of various parts, that is, when the child first entertains "the hypothesis of minimum quantity" (Ferreiro & Teberosky, 1982), the coordination of these parts with the constituted totality becomes a problem. At first, graphic elements are no more than the pieces needed to constitute a "readable" totality. Properties attributed to the whole do not differ from properties of the parts: A name attributed to the entire piece of writing may also be read in each one of the graphic constituent elements, in spite of the fact that once any one of these elements is taken out of the totality it loses the property of being a signifier – as children say, "with only one letter you cannot read . . ."

Later on, when children start controlling systematically the variations in the quantity of characters that compose each piece of writing they have produced, some privileged situations will allow them some initial attempts of coordination. For instance, in order to write *cats* as the word that goes with the picture of three little cats, children count the cats and write as many letters as there are cats. They do the same with cards that are supposed to refer to the names of sets

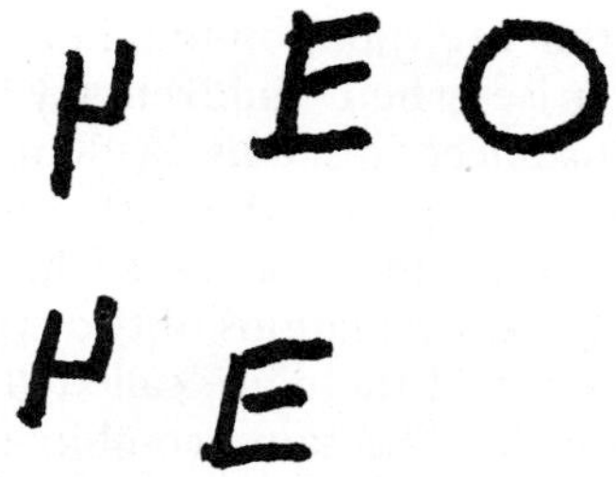

$$\mu\,E\,O$$

$$\mu\,E$$

Figure 11.1. *Paola* (4 years, 11 months): *"Manzanas"* (apples). She explains: "Five numbers so it could be five apples" (*"Cinco números para que sean cinco manzanas"*).

of real objects: six letters for six apples, four letters for four tomatoes, and so on (Figure 11.1). In these cases, each letter stands for a single object, and the whole – the "readable" string – stands for the plural name. The relationship between the parts and the whole, in a given piece of writing, is understood as an analogic relation with the objects referred to: The whole – that is, the written string – is a representation of the set of objects, and each one of its parts – that is, each letter or equivalent grapheme – represents one of the elements of the set. The properties of the parts and the properties of the totality are not the same, but they are related. This is a satisfactory solution, but it is not a stable one, because it turns out to be in contradiction with another important and very powerful hypothesis, that of the minimum quantity. When the name of a single object is written, a single letter is not enough and, in all these cases, the relationship of each letter to the written name remains a problem.

At the same level of development we may obtain two different written representations for a plural name: When children are asked to write the name for a set of objects (that is, a plural name), they may adjust the number of letters to the number of objects (with the restriction that the quantity of objects must be equal to or greater than the required minimum quantity). But when children start with a singular name and move then to a plural one (from *cat* to *cats*, for instance), the result looks very different. However, on further analysis we realize that the same principle is being applied. If three letters were utilized to write *cat*, the plural is obtained by repeating the same initial string as many times as there are cats to be represented (depending on the number of cats you are dealing with) (Figure 11.2). The reason behind this kind of a solution seems to be quite clear: When children *start* by writing a plural name directly, one

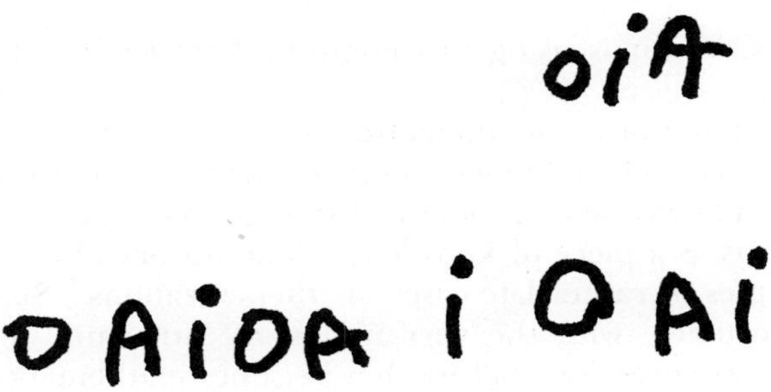

oiA

ᗡAiOA i O Ai

Figure 11.2. *Javier* (5 years, 5 months): *Top row* – "*Gatito*" (little cat). *Bottom row* – "*Gatitos*" (three little cats in the picture). He explains as he is writing: "One little cat" (the first three letters), "the little cats here" (six letters), "another cat" (the three remaining letters).

letter is enough for them to refer to one object. However, when they start by writing a singular name and *then* have to write the plural, they need more than one letter for a single object. Hence, we see that the principle of minimum quantity is being applied in both cases, but the conditions under which the principle is applied have in fact varied. Such cases make clear why those initial attempts of coordination are so unstable and why they require such a great cognitive effort.

Another kind of attempt to establish a coordination between the parts and the totalities is shown in the following example: Victor (5 years, 2 months) needs at least three letters in order to obtain "a readable string"; we are trying, together with him, to form a good written representation of the word *barco* (boat). Only one letter is not enough – it says only "ba" – and with two letters it is the same – it still says only "ba," as he explains. But with three letters it says "bar-co." What happens is very interesting. To a string judged as "noncompleted" he attributes a "noncompleted" word. But it is not that each letter represents a syllabic part of the word – with either one or with two letters, he insists that it says "ba." His reasoning is that with one letter missing it is "an incomplete boat"; a "bar-co" without "co" is not a real barco. But instead of saying that some essential part of the boat is not still there (as could be the case with an iconic representation – saying, for instance, that the sails are missing), the child refers to a linguistic form, making use, without being aware of it, of the known fact that these linguistic forms – that is, the words – are also made up by the combination of elements or parts. Thus, Victor is using this linguistic knowledge without "thematizing" it.

The Piagetian notion of "thematization" is essential to understanding the child's problem. Something that is first used as an instrument of thought may become an object of thought, changing at the same time its status as a piece of knowledge. The history of science shows clear examples of rather late cases of "thematizations." Such was the case, for instance, with the very notion of "structure" in algebra. Structures were used long before they became "mathematical objects" as such, that is, as objects, the properties of which become an object of thought.[1]

Thematization implies then a certain degree of awareness. While the role of thematization in literacy development would be a subject in itself, I will indicate only a few relevant considerations. At the purely linguistic level, we have shown four clear stages of the psychological status of the syllable (Bellefroid & Ferreiro, 1979). We asked children to search for a name within a particular semantic field given one or more syllables of this name, as well as the reverse problem – namely, that they pose a similar task to us. At first, the syllable is used occasionally, in certain circumstances, without taking advantage of this "knowing how." Later, the syllable begins to act as a useful cue for searching for the completion of the name, but it remains impossible to coordinate it with others of the same nature. For example, if the child is given two syllables of the name, instead of coordinating them in the search for only one name each syllable triggers off an individual exploration. At a third stage the syllable becomes a real part of the name, but an unordered part. Finally, the child understands that a syllable of a name is not only a part of it, but an ordered part, that any name is a composite of parts in a given invariant order. Only then information about the order of the parts with reference to the whole, such as "it starts by . . ." and "it ends by . . . ," are processed simultaneously taking into account the part-to-whole relationship and the serial position. At this point the child is capable of producing the same kind of information for other people. All this developmental process is foreign to the thematization of the syllable as such, that is, of a "knowing about" this particular object. But all this development takes place at more or less the same period as that during which the child constitutes the writing system as a cognitive object. My intention is not to defend the idea that a cognitive awareness of certain linguistic unities is a prerequisite for literacy development, but rather to show that the transition from the "knowing how" to the "knowing about" is not a direct one: It may involve an undetermined series of steps (how many and which ones are matters of empirical research, guided but not a priori determined by purely speculative arguments). To become aware of certain "knowhow" always implies a reconstruction of this knowledge at new level, and each reconstruction takes time and requires much cognitive effort to overcome the perturbations that have to be compensated for (see Piaget, 1975, p. 136).

Let us now go back to the problem of the coordination of a totality and its constituent parts. Children face this problem not only when they produce a piece of writing, but also when they try to interpret a piece of writing done by someone else. In both cases children face this problem not only at the level of the letters of a word, but also at the level of the different strings of letters that compose a larger text (a sentence, for instance). I have shown elsewhere (Ferreiro, 1978; Ferreiro & Teberosky, 1982) the unexpected results that appear when children try to understand the meaning of the constituent parts of a written sentence. Even when they accept that a given sentence is written, children cannot conclude that each one of the spoken words is written in the same order in which they are spoken. The same initial difficulties that we have observed at the level of the written word appear at the level of the written sentence: The lack of differentiation between the properties of the totality and the properties of the constituent parts leads children to say that each written word "says" the entire sentence. From then on, a laborious process begins, developing simultaneously in two opposite but inter-dependent directions: The differentiation of the properties of the parts from the properties of the totality *and* integration of the properties of the parts into the properties of a totality.

In their attempt at this coordination, children start to look differ-ently at written texts. Perhaps the initial consideration between "completion" and "incompletion" to which we have already referred leads to the idea that each part of a written name may correspond to a part of the spoken word – not only may an incomplete part of the spoken word stand for an incomplete part of the written word, but, in addition, one part of the spoken word may stand for one part of the written word. At this time, a new coordination takes place: The relationship between the parts and the totality, with reference to the written text, is not resolved until a new kind of equilibrium occurs. Now it is the consideration of the relationship between two different totalities: on the one hand, the parts of the spoken word – its syllables – and the word itself; on the other hand, the parts of the written word – its letters – and the string of letters as a whole.

The search for a one-to-one correspondence in the domain of literacy has, therefore, exactly the same properties as are found in the domain of numerical equivalence.

Once again, we need to be cautious in our conclusions. I am not suggesting that children need to be able to establish numerical equivalences in order to arrive at the "syllabic hypothesis." Cognitive operations are the answers to real problems. As Piaget and Inhelder have stated, "Logic is in no way foreign to life: Logic is only the expression of operational coordinations that are necessary for action" (Piaget & Inhelder, 1955, p. 304). Particular occasions calling for operational procedures are variable; they depend on changing circumstances that may vary from one child to another. In our longitudinal studies, some children clearly applied the operational procedure of the one-to-one correspondence that had already been developed in the numerical domain to the domain of the writing system. But others seemed to discover this operational solution in order to solve the writing problem first.

In either case, the development of the one-to-one correspondence proceeds through exactly the same steps in the case of the written text as in the case of counting a series of objects. At first, children allow themselves to repeat syllables, to jump letters, or to take more than one letter at a time in order to reach the end of the text just as they allow themselves, when they are counting objects, to repeat number names, to jump objects, or to disregard some of them in order to reach the final number.

Little by little, children come to apply the procedure more rigorously: Each letter stands for only one syllable, without repeating syllables and without omitting letters. When the syllabic hypothesis becomes well established, it begins to fulfill another function: It serves as an anticipatory schema and begins to control performance. Whereas in the beginning of the syllabic period the syllabic hypothesis serves only to justify a piece of writing already done, later it begins to gain control over the execution of the action. Finally, as an anticipatory schema, it can control the project of action beforehand; in order to know how many letters are needed, it is necessary only to count the syllables of the word.

Note that children's behavior in the domain of writing is the same as in purely numerical domains. In fact, they are solving the problem of *how many* letters there are in a given word; they are not solving another related but different problem – namely, *which* letters are required for a given word. One of the interesting and intriguing problems specific to literacy development is that children must cope with problems of both quantitative and qualitative correspondence.

The principle of minimum quantity implies that a piece of writing is always a composite of parts. But at the same time, another internal principle copes with the qualitative distinctions: This principle holds that a piece of writing may not use the same graphic character more than twice. It means that with only one letter, one cannot obtain anything readable; neither with a string composed of the same letter repeated three or more times can one obtain anything readable. This is the principle of "internal variation" that goes hand in hand with the principle of "minimum quantity." Thus, the parts of a given totality are initially differentiated by the requirement of "internal variation," that helps to differentiate the parts from each other. But this principle does not solve the problem of the function of these parts with relation to the totality. As the parts are different, they may have different values, but exactly which values?

The principle of "internal variation" applies at two different levels: At the level of a given piece of writing it limits the repetition of the same letter or graphic character, and at the level of pieces of writing it prevents the repetition of a particular string. In this last case, the requirement is not to use the same string of letters in different words because an objective differentiation is needed in order to give different interpretations. A very important qualitative change in literacy development takes place when children start thinking that they are not allowed to read different things if they see the same series of graphic elements. This has a tremendous importance, because the means to differentiate related strings of letters are sometimes very limited, and yet the children's search for internal coherence is so strong that they go well beyond what we can expect them to do in order to solve this problem.

I will give an example of this. Some children, at a given moment in their development, write any name with the same number of letters. This seems to be one of the procedures they adopt to counteract a disturbance: If you do not find any general principle to control the variations of quantity, you can try to counteract this perturbation by fixing the number of characters, once and for all. Some of these children have a very limited stock of letters at their disposal. Figure 11.3 shows the productions of a child who has a stock of only four letters, needs four characters for a piece of writing, and tries to apply the requirement of "internal variation," not only at the level of a given piece of writing, but also at the level of a

Figure 11.3.   Romina (4 years).

related set of pieces of writing. The first piece of writing is easily
done: She put down the four different letters of her stock, and that's
all. The next piece of writing poses a problem: She is not allowed to
use less than four letters, and she cannot repeat the same letters in
the same order. The only way to obtain a differentiation between
the pieces of writing, in this very constrained case, is to discover that
by changing the relative position of each one of the letters, different
totalities are obtained. This is a great cognitive accomplishment for
the 4- or 5-year-old, because it is the beginning of combinatoria
(which, as we know, is one of the acquisitions that characterizes the
formal operations period, that is, something that will take place, on
the average, 7 or 8 years later).

When the syllabic hypothesis is at its peak, children need different
letters for different written names, as they need different letters for
a given meaningful string. However, it does not mean that the same
letter will always represent the same syllable. An *A*, for instance, may
function as the first syllable of one name, as the last syllable for
another, and so on. It is its *positional* value that determines the
interpretation given. Children require one letter for each syllable,
but very often it is any letter for any syllable. Letters ought to be
different from each other, but it is not their intrinsic difference that
determines their subsequent interpretation. It is only a letter's

positional value that is taken into account. That is why we are speaking of a pure one-to-one correspondence. It is not the case that a letter − *A*, for instance − will receive only related syllabic values within a limited set of sound values. Any letter may stand for any syllable, just as any number may stand for any object in a set when one is counting − any one of the objects may be the "fourth" in one set and the "first" in another set, depending only on its position in the series and not on its intrinsic properties.[2]

These children have found a very satisfactory way to solve the problem of the relationship between the parts and the totality: In order to know how to write a given name, you start by counting the syllables, and then you put as many different letters as syllables; each letter represents one syllable; the ordered letters represent the ordered syllables of the word. However, this excellent solution will be refuted time after time by subsequent experience.

The writing system the child finds in his surrounding world does not accommodate itself to this assimilatory schema. The child understands what he does, but he cannot understand what the others are doing. Neither can he understand the kind of information he receives. All information provided by the environment is now highly perturbing (although earlier it was not). Now, in the face of perturbation, only three kinds of reactions are possible: You may leave it out, you may counteract it locally, or you may accommodate to it − that is, you may counteract it entirely by modifying the assimilatory schema and thereby attaining a new equilibration level. Once they are able to do the latter, the children abandon the syllabic hypothesis on their way to reconstructing the writing system on an alphabetic basis. But one thing is certain: Before they do it children will struggle obstinately to keep the assimilation schemata they had so laboriously built up.

The kind of analysis we have described with reference to the relationship between the whole and its parts may also be made with reference to many other problems that are involved in literacy development, problems such as those involving identity, conservation, construction of observables, and so on.

It is clear that we cannot simply invoke the spontaneity of the subject nor his or her creativity to account for these achievements. Spontaneity and creativity do exist, but they do not develop in a random direction. Our task is precisely to try to explain such directionality. Likewise, it is not the case that we may simply invoke social influences or social models. No doubt those social influences and social models do exist in the writing system and could not exist without the users. However, it is also clear that such social models do not perform the same function at all moments in development. Sometimes they have a positive role in the disequilibriation processes insofar as they function as perturbations; sometimes they play the equally positive role of being observables that are easy to assimilate. But sometimes they play a negative inhibitory role in the process of children's conceptualizations of the written language.

What therefore remains as our important task is to understand the precise mechanisms of such an interaction, the results of which can hardly be characterized as a reproduction, at the individual level, of a social reality. In literacy development one finds an effective construction of organizational principles that go against observations, against systematic schoolteaching, and against nonsystematic information.

A comprehensive theory of literacy development cannot leave these questions out. I have tried to show that such questions acquire a quite clear meaning within the framework of Piaget's theory.

NOTES

1. The first algebraic structure that was thematized was the group. Gauss and Ruffini, among others, had made use of the notion of group without being aware of it. The thematization arrives only with Galois (see Piaget & Garcia, 1982).
2. I shall not consider here the extremely interesting development, from an epistemological point of view, that takes place when the letters begin to have a certain stability within the range of sound values that may be attributed to them.

REFERENCES

Bellefroid, B., & Ferreiro, E. La segmentation des mots chez l'enfant. *Archives de Psychologie*, 1979, 47(180), 1–35.

Ferreiro, E. What is written in a written sentence? A developmental answer. *Journal of Education*, 1978, 4(160), 25–39.

Ferreiro, E., & Teberosky, A. *Literacy before schooling.* New York: Heinemann, 1982.

Piaget, J. *L' équilibration des structures cognitives.* Paris: PUF, 1975.

Piaget, J., & García, R. *Psicogénesis y historia de la ciencia.* Mexico City: Siglo XXI, 1982. (French version: *Psychogenèse et histoire des sciences.* Paris: Flammarion, 1983.)

Piaget, J., & Inhelder, B. *De la logique de l'enfant à la logique de l'adolescent.* Paris: PUF, 1955.

12

Preschool literacy-related activities and success in school

GORDON WELLS

The route that has led me to a concern with the relationship between spoken and written language has been a long and indirect one as, carrying out a longitudinal study of language development over the last decade, I have attempted to discover whether differential educational attainment does indeed have specifically linguistic antecedents, as was argued by many writers in the 1960s and 1970s from such different perspectives as those of, for example, Deutsch (1965), Labov (1970), and Bernstein (1971). Over this 10-year period we have collected data from a representative sample of 128 children, of whom 32 have been the subjects of a systematic investigation of the relationship between home and school uses of language.

The first phase of the research charted the course of these children's oral language development, tracing the emergence of the various linguistic systems and investigating the relationship between rate of development and differences in the children's environment.[1] Although variation in rate of development was found to be considerable, it was still the case that, by the time they entered school at 5 years of age, all the children studied had achieved a basic command of English and all communicated freely and effectively with the people in their home environment. Investigation of the speech addressed to these children in the early stages of development showed that rapidly developing children tended to participate more in conversations and to receive a larger number of utterances that were contingently related to their own meanings and activities (Barnes et al., 1983), but neither differences between children nor those between parents were strongly related to the children's class of family background (Wells, 1979).

As soon as the children started going to school, however, a very different picture emerged. Tests administered during the first term showed some of the children to be much more "ready for school" than others and, from the assessments carried out by the teachers, it was clear that some children were perceived as much more likely to succeed than others. What is more, both tests and teachers' assessments showed a highly significant relationship between rated ability and class of family background ($r = .5$ to $.6$, $p < .01$, $n = 32$). Tests carried out 2 years later showed that the initial assessment had predicted quite accurately; the correlation between the two assessments was $r = .8$ ($p < .001$) (Wells, 1981b).

Why were some children rated as so much less successful than others? The sample had been picked to exclude children with known handicaps and those who did not come from English-speaking families, so two of the most obvious causes of difficulty were not at issue. And why was there such a strong relationship between class of family background and ability, including teachers' assessments of oral language ability, when no such strong relationship had been found in the preschool years? As already stated, there were no grounds for considering any of these children to be "nonverbal," or even lacking sufficient resources for normal everyday interaction – as observations of them in the playground confirmed. Nor was there any evidence that nonstandardness of dialect or accent was providing an impediment to communication.

Yet there were certain contexts – and they were ones that were found to occur with considerable frequency in the classroom – in which the less successful children did seem to have particular difficulty. These were sequences of interaction organized around question–answer exchanges in which the child was required to demonstrate his knowledge of some piece of information or his understanding of some principle. Because the answers to such questions are already known by the questioner, we refer to them as *requests for display*. The following is an example.

A small group of children are looking at color slides of India. The teacher has selected a slide, looked at it through the viewer, and passed it to Rosie.

T: They're Indian ladies, and what else?

R: [*Looks through viewer*] I can see something.

T: What can you see?

R: And they're going in the sand.

T: [*Fails to understand*] Mm?

R: You have a look.

T: Well, you have a look and tell me. I've seen it already. I want to see if you can see. [*6-second pause*]

R: [*Looks through viewer*] Oh, they're going in the sand. They're going in the sand. [*20-second pause; T doesn't hear as she is attending to other children*]

T: What's behind the men? Can you see men in the red coats? [*2-second pause; R still looking*] Can you see the men in the red coats? What is behind those men? [*4-second pause*] Can you see?

R: [*Nods*]

T: What is it?

R: They're walking in . . .

T: Pardon?

R: They're walking.

T: They're walking, yes. But what's walking behind them? Something very big.

R: A horse.

T: It's much bigger than a horse. It's much bigger than a horse. It's big and grey and it's got a long nose that we call a trunk. [*Mimes a long trunk*]

R: Trunk. [*Imitates*]

T: Can you see what it is? What is it?

R: [*Nods*]

C: [*Unintelligible*]

T: No, that's what his nose is. It's nose is called a trunk. Can you see what the animal is?

R: N—no [= "*I can't guess*"]

T: It's much bigger than a horse. Let's give it to Darren and see if Darren knows. [*20-second pause; D looks. R puts her thumb in her mouth; T looks for more pictures in books*] There's a picture of the animal behind the men — with the red coats on. What's that?

R: The soldiers.

T: Mm?

R: Soldiers. ⎱ [*Simultaneously*]
D: Elephant ⎰

T: What's that? [*Points to the elephant*]

R: An elephant. [*As if knowing all the time*]

Although perhaps not entirely typical, episodes of this unsatisfactory kind are all too frequent in the classrooms we have observed: teachers trying hard to elicit answers that are self-evident and straightforward from their own point of view, but succeeding only in securing responses that they judge to be wrong or irrelevant or, in some cases, failing to secure any response at all. Elsewhere I have argued that this sort of impasse can only be avoided if teachers

become more aware of the *interactive* nature of conversation and
hence of the need for them to adopt a more negotiatory attitude in
their talk with pupils (Wells & Nicholls, forthcoming). However, my
purpose here is not so much to comment on teachers' use of display
questions as to consider such sequences from the perspective of the
difficulties experienced by the pupils.

Obviously some of the problems that face children like Rosie are
due to lack of specific experiences and of the vocabulary that encodes
those experiences. Some children, for example, have never seen an
elephant or even a picture of one, and many more have no knowledge
of elephants in any context other than a zoo. Such specific gaps in
knowledge are to be expected, and if they are considered important,
they can be remedied by various means. But even when the topic is
not outside such children's experience, they may still be unable or
unwilling to provide an answer that is acceptable. It seems, therefore,
that it is not so much the specific content of such questions that
makes them difficult to answer as the particular context in which
they are posed.

One explanation that has been offered (Mehan, 1978) is that the
display question sequence itself is a pattern of discourse that is outside
the children's experience, and in some cultures this may indeed be
the case (Heath, 1980; Scollon & Scollon, 1980). However, this was
not true for any of the children we studied; all of them had engaged
in what Bruner (Ninio & Bruner, 1978) calls "ritual naming," either
in relation to familiar objects or to representations of them in picture
books. For most of them there was also evidence that they had been
quizzed about familiar events and activities and understood what was
expected of them in such situations when they occurred in contexts
of meaningful and purposeful activity.

In the classroom, by contrast, the topics that children are asked to
attend to are most frequently selected by the teacher in terms of a
curricular framework that is known to him or her but not to the
children, and talk about them tends to concentrate on the naming
of objects, actions, and attributes in isolation from the particular
experience in which they are rooted in the children's individual
biographies. Information is elicited for its own sake rather than for
its relevance to some immediate practical activity to which the child
is already committed.

Some children have little difficulty in participating in such "decontextualized" talk, but others clearly find it bewildering. For although
the objects or events that the teacher asks about may be well known
to them as part of their out-of-school experience, that experience is

not easily accessible to them when the familiar context in which it is normally embedded is absent and has to be recalled or manipulated through the medium of language alone.

Literacy and the development of context-independent thinking

The distinction between context dependence and context independence in relation to problem solving and information exchange is now a familiar one. Bruner (1971) contrasts the cognitive abilities of members of traditional societies, such as the Wolof of Senegal, with members of Western societies in these terms, and Bernstein (1971) has used them to distinguish between the language codes available to members of working- and middle-class groups within Western societies. Both writers are, of course, concerned with relative rather than absolute differences: Lower-class members of Western societies can be expected to cope with context-independent task demands more effectively than members of more traditional societies. But there is also considerable within-group variation.

The same dimension of context dependence–independence has proved of importance for attempts to characterize the difference between spoken and written language (though here too, of course, we are concerned with a continuum rather than a dichotomy). And it is, I believe, significant that the availability of a writing system is one of the more important cultural differences between traditional and technologically advanced societies and further that differences in the kind and amount of writing actually carried out also tend to distinguish middle- from working-class members of societies that possess such a system (Griffiths & Wells, 1983).

Learning to read and write typically takes place at school, where it is just one part of the more general curriculum. It is not surprising, therefore, that it is schooling, rather than literacy in particular, that has been considered responsible for the cultural differences that have been found on the sort of problem-solving tasks referred to above. However, since schooling is compulsory for all children for 10 years or so in all technologically advanced societies, it cannot account for the class-associated differences found within those societies, nor can it account directly for the sort of differences that are found between the children in our study, since they were all still in their first term at school. On the other hand, even before children come to school, some may well have already learned quite a lot about written language, even though they have not yet learned to read and write, and this knowledge may enable them to cope better with the relatively context-independent display questions on which we observed such differences in ability.

This is indeed the interpretation we have put on the test and questionnaire data we have collected. Of all the tests that we administered on entry to school, the one that had the highest correlation with overall attainment 2 years later was Knowledge of Literacy ($r = .79$, $p < .001$), and this, in turn, was correlated with a cluster of variables derived from the questionnaire administered to the parents a few months earlier: Number of Books Owned by the Child ($r = .38$, $p < .05$), the Child's Interest in Literacy ($r = .45$, $p < .02$), and his or her Concentration in Activities Associated with Literacy ($r = .57$, $p < .001$). These test and questionnaire variables were also significantly associated with the children's class of family background ($r = .6$ to $.7$, $p < .001$).

Differential attainment in school, at least in the early years, we argued, was in large part due to differences between children in their experiences of written language in the preschool years and in their knowledge of the functions and mechanics of reading and writing. That such differences are class-related is a predictable consequence of the importance that level of achievement in literacy plays in the attainment and performance of jobs with different socioeconomic status; parents for whom literacy is an essential and satisfying part of everyday life will be more likely to transmit these practices and values to their children than those who have never achieved a high level of literacy themselves and for whom reading and writing are of much less importance either for work or for leisure activities. Thus, although we recognized that there were other contributory factors, at least as far as language was concerned, it was through the place and value given to literacy in the everyday activities of the family that we considered social and educational inequality to be transmitted from one generation to the next, rather than through the differential use of one particular code or dialect (Wells, 1981a, 1981b).

Preschool literacy-related activities and their effects on school attainment

The present study attempts to take the investigation one step further. The data discussed above were derived from parents' responses to questions asked in a structured interview. They were thus based on reports rather than on direct observation; they also lumped together activities that may contribute rather differently to children's under-standing of literacy. In the present study the data are derived from the transcripts of the recordings that were made at regular intervals in the children's homes. These samples of entirely spontaneous interaction, with no observer present, allow a more objective estimate to be formed of the types and frequencies of activity that the children actually engaged in in relation to reading and writing.

Four different kinds of activity were coded: looking at books or other printed material; listening to a story being read or told from a book; drawing and coloring; and writing (this last being defined as an activity so labeled by either the child or the parent). All these activities involve a visual representation of meaning and either the decoding of that information from a permanent source (book or magazine) or the attempt to encode it graphically in a form that is at least potentially permanent. They differ, however, in whether the visual representation that the child attends to is predominantly pictorial or involves linguistic symbolization. Looking at books con-taining pictures and drawing or coloring involve the child in recog-nizing or attempting to produce representations that are pictorial in form. In listening to a story being read or attempting to write a message her- or himself, on the other hand, the child is beginning to come to grips with a particular form and function of written language: its power to represent experience in symbols that bear only a conventional relationship to that which is symbolized and which can be interpreted in contexts other than those in which the experience occurred.

These distinctions are, of course, not always as clear-cut as this idealized account suggests. Stories read from books are not always very far removed in content and form from oral recountings of events that have actually been experienced; indeed, many of the books written for children, influenced by the "language experience" approach to the teaching of reading, deliberately attempt to reduce this gap to a minimum. Occasionally, too, looking at a picture in a book or magazine may give rise to sustained discussion very similar to that which may follow or be interspersed in the reading of a story. Writing also may begin as an extension of the attempt to represent meaning graphically through drawing (see Ferreiro, Chapter 11). Certainly both drawing and writing involve the attempt to represent concepts and not just percepts. However, there is an important difference between them in that, in his or her first attempts at writing, the child is not simply concerned with the representation of concepts but is also attempting to find a way of representing the language in which his or her conceptualization has been encoded (Vygotsky, 1978). Nevertheless, although the boundaries between these four types of activity may be blurred in theory, the distinctions are usually sufficiently clear-cut in practice for coding to be undertaken with considerable confidence.

Before proceeding, however, it is important to say a little more about the observations from which the data on the four activities were derived. Each of the 32 children was observed at 3-month intervals between the ages of $1\frac{1}{4}$ and $3\frac{1}{2}$ years. Recordings were made in the children's homes using a radiomicrophone worn by the child. The recording equipment was programmed to record 24 90-second samples at approximately 20-minute intervals between 9:00 a.m. and 6:00 p.m.[2] No observer was present during the recordings, contextual details being obtained later the same day by playing back the recording, sample by sample, and asking the parents to recall in as much detail as possible the location, activity, and participants for each sample.

The strength of this method of data collection is its naturalness. Activities and talk that were observed can be confidently accepted as typical of the experience of the children concerned. The method also has its limitations, however. The total amount of recorded time transcribed and analyzed from 18 of the observations (27 minutes) is a relatively small sample of the total day. The fact that a particular activity or type of talk was not observed does not allow us to conclude that it never occurred. On the other hand, if child A was observed to engage in a particular activity three times in a certain unit of time, for example, and child B not at all, it seems reasonable to infer that, for the period of time from which the samples were drawn, child A engaged in the activity more often than child B.

About activities that typically took place in the evening, such as the bedtime story, our observations can tell us nothing at all. Some children were probably read to at bedtime but never had a story read to them during the day; on the other hand, it seems rather less likely that children who were read to during the day did not also enjoy a story at bedtime. It must be stressed, therefore, that the frequency data obtained from the observations can only give a very rough estimate of the differences between children in the relative frequency with which they engaged in the four activities under investigation. At the same time, they have the merit of being derived from naturalistic observations rather than from questionnaire responses.

Two main questions were to be investigated: (1) Which of these activities is most strongly associated with progress in the early stages of learning to read in school? (2) Do any of these activities help the child to cope with the oral language demands of the classroom – in particular, the request for display of knowledge or competence?

If one emphasizes the decoding–encoding conventions that are involved in learning to read and write – left-to-right and top-to-bottom progression, letter identification and formation – there is no strong reason to expect any of these activities to be more helpful than the others, since none is specifically concerned with the transmission of these conventions. However, since all are in one way or another related to aspects of the literacy curriculum, to engage in any of them might be expected to be more beneficial than not to engage in them. On the other hand, if one stresses those features of written language that most strongly distinguish it from the spoken language typical of casual conversation – the relative self-sufficiency of the text as the basis for interpretation (i.e., context independence), the greater integration of its linguistic organization (Chafe, 1982), and the emphasis on the symbolic representation of experience – one would predict that listening to a story read aloud or attempting to write would provide a more helpful introduction to literacy than the activities of looking at and naming the pictures in a book or drawing and coloring.

With respect to the second question, it might appear that both looking at books and listening to stories, together with the sort of talk that typically accompanies these activities, would provide a useful preparation for the display question sequences that figure so prominently in teacher–pupil talk. Certainly there is a strong affinity between the naming of objects and the identification of attributes that typically occur when parents and children look at picture books together and the requests for display that occur in the classroom. Since two-dimensional representations of objects in books are both more "abstract" and more decontextualized than the particular three-dimensional objects that they represent and that the child encounters in the real world, the experience of looking at books may also lead the child some way toward coping with these same characteristics of teachers' requests for display.

However, simply looking at pictures in books or magazines does not require the child to contend with the representation of information in linguistic symbols in the way that listening to a story does. Stories also differ from pictures in being "self-contextualizing": The language of the story creates the context for its own interpretation, whereas in the majority of cases the pictures that young children look at have to be provided with a context from outside. Furthermore, with its plot and characterization, a story is likely to provide a richer basis for sustained discussion than the static stimulus of a picture. For all these reasons, although both activities may prepare a child for the oral language demands of the classroom, it is hypothesized that it is listening to stories that will be the more beneficial.

A third and subsidiary question concerned the relationship between the frequency with which these activities were observed to occur and the extent of the parents' own education.

Results

Learning to read

Of the four activities, looking at books was by far the most common. All children were observed to engage in this activity on at least one occasion. On the other hand, attempting to write was hardly observed at all: Only two children engaged in this activity, and on one occasion only. Writing was therefore not included in the subsequent analysis. Listening to a story and drawing both fell somewhere between the two extremes: 53% were observed to listen to a story on at least one occasion and 78% to engage in drawing or coloring.

The effect of these activities on subsequent progress in literacy was examined by treating each activity in turn as the independent variable and determining its relationship with the two dependent variables, Knowledge of Literacy at 5 years and Reading Comprehension at 7 years. Knowledge of Literacy scores were calculated by combining the scores on Concepts about Print and Letter Identification (Clay, 1972). Reading Comprehension was measured using the comprehension subscore from the Neale Analysis of Reading (Neale, 1969). Scores for each of the three activities (Looking at Books, Drawing and Coloring, and Listening to a Story) were arrived at by counting the number of observations during which the child engaged at least once in that activity. Scores on each of the independent variables were then dichotomized and the Mann–Whitney U test used to compare the higher- and lower-frequency groups' scores on the dependent variables.[3]

The results, which are given in Table 12.1, show that neither Looking at Books nor Drawing and Coloring was significantly associated with either of the measures of progress in literacy. Listening

Table 12.1 *Some effects of preschool literacy-related activities*

Activity	Knowledge of literacy (5 years)	Reading comprehension (7 years)	Teacher assessment of oral language (5 years)	Mother's education	Both parents' education
Looking at books	$U = 115$ $n_1 = 14$ n.s.	$U = 91.5$ $n_1 = 14$ n.s.	$U = 88.5$ $n_1 = 14$ n.s.	$U' = 117$ $n_1 = 14$ n.s.	$U' = 124$ $n_1 = 14$ n.s.
Drawing and coloring	$U' = 123$ $n_1 = 15$ n.s.	$U = 96.5$ $n_1 = 15$ n.s.	$U = 95.5$ $n_1 = 15$ n.s.	$U = 93.5$ $n_1 = 15$ n.s.	$U = 100.5$ $n_1 = 15$ n.s.
Listening to stories	$U = 74$ $n_1 = 15$ $p < .025$	$U = 76.5$ $n_1 = 15$ $p < .05$	$U = 60.5$ $n_1 = 15$ $p < .01$	$U = 72$ $n_1 = 15$ $p < .025$	$U = 52.5$ $n_1 = 15$ $p < .01$

Note: $n_1 + n_2 = 32$.

to a story read or told from a book, on the other hand, was significantly associated both with Knowledge of Literacy ($p < .025$, one-tailed) and with Reading Comprehension at age 7 ($p < .05$). These results thus provide some support for the hypothesis that facilitation of the early stages of learning to read is more likely to result from being given opportunities to become aware of the more symbolic and sustained context-independent properties of written language than from merely engaging in talking about and producing pictorial representations.

However, merely to report the number of occasions on which the children were observed to engage in the different activities gives no idea of the qualitative differences in the activities that occurred. These were most varied in relation to the ways in which children engaged with "booklike" objects. The use of this term is deliberate because the first difference noted was in the actual objects. While a few children possessed or borrowed a wide range of books written for young children from a library, and quite a large number possessed collections of nursery rhymes and alphabet books, there were a sizable minority who looked only at mail-order catalogs and magazines. Being read or told a story from a book was only possible for the first group and possibly the second. Even within the group that had access to storybooks, however, there was a considerable difference between parents in how they presented the story: Some merely read it from beginning to end, others would pause to discuss new or difficult concepts as they were encountered, and a few would engage in extended discussion of particular episodes either at the time or on some later occasion. Significantly, this last behavior was more common in parents who read stories more frequently.

Looking at books showed somewhat less variation, as for almost all children this typically took the form of "ritual naming" (Ninio & Bruner, 1978). In the early stages of language development, when vocabulary is expanding very rapidly, this activity is probably helpful in matching words and referents and delimiting the extension of class labels. Beyond a certain stage, however, it has diminishing value and indeed may become counterproductive if the child comes to believe that the main purpose of books is to provide material for the provision of labeling responses to display questions. While in a few cases looking at picture material did lead to more open-ended discussion of possibilities, motives, and consequences, this was far more likely to occur in relation to the illustrations encountered in the context of listening to a story or when the story was recalled in relation to some picture seen on a later occasion.

Some flavor of the difference between homes in this respect can be obtained by comparing the ways in which two children in our study, Sean and Gerald, spent the day on which we recorded them when they were 2¾ years old. In both cases, the day is represented by 18 samples obtained in the manner described above. The events occurring in these samples are presented in Tables 12.2 (Sean) and 12.3 (Gerald).

In Sean's day, one sample was spent looking at a picture book (Sample 3). The talk that took place between him and his mother is very representative of the many episodes of this kind in our recordings:

M: What's that? [*Points to a picture*]
S: House.
M: House. That's right: house.
S: Bump. [*S always says this when he sees a car*]
M: That's a car. Where's the telephone?
S: There . . . look.
M: That's right.
S: Um.
M: There's another one there.
S: What's that? [*Points to another picture*]
M: Cash register.
S: . . . [*Attempts to repeat*]
M: Cash register.
S: . . . [*Another attempt*] That dolly there.
M: Mm, dolly . . . like L's. [*Sister L has dolly*] Where's Sooty? Can you see Sooty?
S: [ā . . . ā . . . ā . . .] (= *eye*)
M: What's that?⎫
S: [ā . . . ā] ⎬ [*Spoken simultaneously*]
M: Eye. That's his eye.
S: [ā]
M: And that's another eye. That's right. Eye.
S: Uh. [*Laughs loudly — sees Mickey Mouse, always a cue for laughter*]
M: [*Laughs*] Mickey Mouse. Is that Mickey Mouse?
S: Uh.

In many ways Gerald's day is very similar to Sean's: He eats meals, is washed and dressed, and spends periods playing alone. But in certain important ways it is rather different, particularly with respect

Table 12.2. *A day in the life of Sean (2 years, 9 months)*

Sample	Time	Activity
1	9:14 a.m.	Sean asks Mother for some chocolate, which he can see on a kitchen shelf. When Mother leaves the room he pushes a chair over and climbs up to get the chocolate.
2	9:29	Sean eats a biscuit he has been given. He asks to have the record player on; Mother refuses.
3	10:21	Sean and Mother are looking at a picture book.
4	10:43	Sean is playing with bricks in lounge. Mother is present but not involved.
5	11:09	"Playschool" is on TV. Sean is playing alone with a toy truck.
6	11:51	Sean is playing with toys in lounge. Mother is present but not involved.
7	12:29 p.m.	Sean and Mother are eating midday meal. No talk.
8	12:57	Sean is playing alone in a bowl of water in kitchen sink.
9	1:13	Sean has got his sleeves wet. Mother is changing his jumper.
10	1:59	Sean is playing alone with large truck and bricks.
11	2:23	Mother gives Sean a biscuit and a drink of milk.
12	2:47	Sean is having a rest, sitting on Mother's lap.
13	3:37	Sean is playing with truck and bricks in lounge. Father is present but is reading a newspaper.
14	4:03	Elder sister L (age 5) has returned from school and is watching a TV program about conkers (horse chestnuts) and is talking to Father about how to play with them. Sean is half-listening, half-playing with toys.
15	4:21	Whole family is watching "Huckleberry Hound" on TV.
16	5:14	Sean is fighting amicably with L.
17	5:29	Sean is watching a TV commercial for chocolate and drawing Mother's attention to it.
18	5:45	Sean and L are eating their tea.

Table 12.3. *A day in the life of Gerald (2 years, 9 months)*

Sample	Time	Activity
1	9:15 a.m.	Gerald is objecting to having to clean his teeth.
2	9:37	Gerald is playing with sticklebricks (construction blocks). Mother is watching while she feeds Gerald's baby sister.
3	9:55	Gerald is talking to one of his toys about how he feels about his sister. Then he empties the laundry basket.
4	10:31	Mother is helping Gerald make a collage by sticking twigs in plasticine.
5	11:31	Mother is reading Gerald a story.
6	11:57	Gerald is listening to records, waiting for one that has a bell on it. He has his bell ready to play.
7	12:33 p.m.	Gerald and Mother are talking about postmen while they eat their midday meal.
8	1:03	Gerald is playing with a large sheet of paper. Mother makes suggestions as to how he can dress up in it.
9	1:19	Gerald is playing on the floor with baby. Mother is not present.
10	1:49	Gerald playing with sticklebricks. Mother is feeding baby.
11	2:27	Gerald has brought his Mother *Winnie the Pooh*. He wants her to read it to him.
12	2:45	Gerald and Mother are listening to radio: "Listen with Mother." Gerald joins in by making the noises called for by the program presenter.
13	3:13	Gerald is crayoning in kitchen. Mother is washing dishes.
14	3:25	Gerald has threaded beads on a string and is making the string into different shapes. Mother watches and comments.
15	3:39	Gerald is playing alone with his cars.
16	4:37	Gerald is playing with toy frog in kitchen sink and is talking to himself about his play. Mother is arranging some flowers and talking to Father.
17	5:27	Father is undressing Gerald in preparation for a bath.
18	5:57	Gerald is cleaning his teeth. Father is grumbling about having to remove all the toys from the bath.

to the part that books play in the activities he engages in with his mother. The first sample in Gerald's day that involves a book is Sample 5, when Mother reads him a story. As he listens, he looks at the pictures and interrupts:

G: Can I see the fairy? [*Sees the picture in the book*]

M: What's the fairy doing? What's he looking at?

G: Looking at what's up there.

M: Yes, oh dear. Isn't he naughty? He'll get into trouble if it isn't mended. [*Continues reading*]

Later in the day (Sample 11), Gerald asks for another story.

G: And I want that story. [*Turns over the pages of "Winnie the Pooh"*]

M: What's that story?

G: I know.

M: I don't know. [*Short pause; compares two books*] That one's just the same one as this. As the house for Eeyore. Don't you think?

G: No.

M: No? I think it is. It's the same pictures. There's Eeyore. What's happened to him?

G: I don't know.

M: What do you think's happening to him?

G: He's getting cold.

M: He's getting cold. Why is he getting cold?

G: I don't know.

M: I think it's the snow all over him – don't you think? [*Short pause*] "One day . . ." [*Starts to read story*]

In Sample 7, as they talk about postmen while they are eating, the influence of a previously read story can also be detected:

M: He unlocks the door of the postbox. He takes out the letters and puts them in his big bag.

G: And he takes them – takes them to Gerald's house.

M: Well, yes, if you're sending one he might take it to Grandma's house. If you're posting one perhaps he'll deliver one to Grandma. And then he'll take it on a train. And the letter will go all the way to Grandma's house. [*Short pause*] Won't it?

G: But the – but the – the controller takes them to Gerald's house. [*G has a book in which a postman is referred to as a "controller"*]

M: The controller?

G: Yes, he does.

As a result of the stories that are read to him, Gerald's world stretches beyond the present actuality into the world of imaginary characters whose actions and feelings he is invited to try to understand in terms of his own experience. Equally importantly, stories read are drawn upon as a means of making sense of the objects, people, and events in his day-to-day environment. Not surprisingly, Gerald is ranked 4th in Knowledge of Literacy on entry to school and 2nd in oral language ability; Sean's position in the rank order is 28th on both measures. For reading comprehension at age 7, their ranks are 15th and 29th, respectively.

Parental education

Differences between parents, such as those we have just been examining, in the ways in which they interact with their children in relation to books seem likely to be strongly influenced by their own attitudes to reading and writing, acquired during their education in school and, for some, also in college and modified by the uses they have subsequently made of the skills of literacy. Of prime importance is the parents' own enjoyment of reading: If they do not enjoy reading themselves, they are unlikely to spend time reading to their children. Furthermore, the habit of looking for explanations of particular events in general principles and of making such connections explicit is also one that is encouraged by the experience of reading, and even more by that of writing (Wells, 1981a).

There is also the so easily taken-for-granted matter of reading aloud. For some parents, reading a story is an unrewarding chore, which they perform with difficulty. Their rendering is halting and without expression − not such as to enthrall a young listener. Not surprisingly, those parents who reported that they did not enjoy reading stories to their children were very likely also to report that their children did not enjoy being read to. For other parents it is a pleasure that they perform with considerable skill. Since both they and their children enjoy the experience, it is likely to be frequently repeated − even to the point where the parent may have to refuse further demands in order to get on with other, equally important household tasks.

There are strong reasons, then, for expecting the relative emphasis that parents give to the sort of literacy-related activities discussed above to be strongly influenced by their own level of education. This was empirically investigated using information about the parents' level of education obtained in an interview with them just before their children started going to school. A 7-point scale was used, on which the two extremes were the following:

    1: Left school at minimal leaving age with no qualifications
    7: Received at least 3 years higher education at college or university
       and successfully completed the course

More than two-thirds of the mothers had left school at the minimal age, and half had also failed to obtain any qualifications. The figures for the fathers were similar: More than half of them had left school at the minimal age, and two-fifths had failed to obtain any qualifications then or later. Since mothers tend to spend much more time at home with preschool children than do fathers, two tests were made of the relationship between parental education and frequency of engaging the child in the different literacy-related activities, one for the mothers alone and one for both parents together. The Mann–Whitney U test was used in both cases. The results are set out in Table 12.1, columns 4 and 5.

The results show a striking parallel with those already reported for the relationship between the frequency of the three activities and scores on the later tests of Knowledge of Literacy and Reading Comprehension. Looking at books and the child's engagement in drawing and coloring were not significantly associated with either measure of parental education. Reading stories, on the other hand, was significantly associated with both mothers' education ($p < .025$) and both parents' education combined ($p < .01$). Relatively well-educated parents differ significantly from the less-well-educated in their tendency to engage in precisely that activity that we have found to be associated with their children's early success in reading.

Oral language ability in the classroom

It is not only success in reading that, we have argued, is facilitated by the reading and discussion of stories. Exploration of the symbolic, relatively context-independent potential of language, which is particularly characteristic of the written language of stories, it has been suggested, also prepares the child to cope with the style of teaching and assessing that is so frequently observed in schools. As already noted, it is not the request for a display of knowledge or competence in relation to an object or event that, of itself, seems to be a major cause of difficulty for children, but rather the context – or lack of a familiar, action-oriented context – in which the request is made. If this conjecture is correct, the frequency with which the children engaged in display question sequences while looking at books will not be expected to be strongly associated with their success in coping with the teachers' oral language demands in the classroom. Listening to stories, by contrast, will be expected to give children a significant advantage in this respect.

To test this hypothesis, an estimate of the children's ability to meet the oral language demands of the classroom was obtained from the assessment that was made of each child by his or her teacher during the first term in school. The assessment consisted of a number of sections covering social adjustment, oral language ability, other academic abilities, and physical development. Items took the form of alternative behavioral descriptions of increasing maturity. The teacher was asked to pick the description that most accurately described the typical behavior of the child being assessed. Only each child's total score for the section on language ability was used in the present instance, and, with the Mann–Whitney U test, the relationship between these scores and frequency of engaging in the three literacy-related activities was determined. The results are shown in column 3 of Table 12.1.

Once again it is the experience of listening to stories that stands out as the distinguishing characteristic of the children judged to be competent in oral language in the classroom context ($p < .01$). Nonetheless, this does not mean that the sort of talk that occurs while looking at books is entirely without value in relation to school. The results indicate a trend in the direction of a positive relationship (the value of $U = 88.5$ almost reaches a level of statistical significance), which suggests that the earlier experience of answering questions about names and attributes does to some extent prepare children for similar experiences in school. However, while all the children had at least some experience of this kind, only a minority were read to with any frequency, and, as was seen in the comparison between Sean and Gerald, the sort of talk that arises from stories provides the child with a far richer experience on which to draw in meeting the oral language demands of the classroom. It was this additional experience, therefore, that was significantly more likely to characterize the children whom the teachers assessed as more competent.

An independent replication

The classification of literacy-related activities used in the study just reported was originally suggested by Moon (1976). In a secondary analysis of the data reported from the longitudinal study *Children Learning to Read* (Wells & Raban, 1978), Moon examined the preschool

Table 12.4. *Preschool literacy-related activities: a replication*

Activity	Knowledge of literacy (5 years)	Reading comprehension (7 years)	Mother's education	Both parent's education
Looking at books[a]	$U = 32.5$ $n_1 = 9$ n.s.	$U = 35$ $n_1 = 9$ n.s.	$U = 36.5$ $n_1 = 9$ n.s.	$U = 34$ $n_1 = 9$ n.s.
Drawing and coloring	$U = 25$ $n_1 = 10$ $p < .05$	$U = 28$ $n_1 = 10$ n.s.	$U = 41.5$ $n_1 = 10$ n.s.	$U = 36$ $n_1 = 10$ n.s.
Listening to stories	$U = 19.5$ $n_1 = 10$ $p < .025$	$U = 17$ $n_1 = 10$ $p < .01$	$U = 16.5$ $n_1 = 10$ $p < .01$	$U = 10$ $n_1 = 10$ $p < .001$

Note: $n_1 + n_2 = 20$.
[a] With acknowledgements to Cliff Moon (1976), whose data were used for this replication.

experiences of 20 children in detail. He examined the transcripts made when these children were between 39 and 60 months for a variety of activities that might be associated with early progress in literacy in school. These variables were then grouped into three summary variables: Child Interest in Literacy, Parental Interest in Literacy, and Child's Metalinguistic Awareness. As was anticipated, both the former variables significantly predicted scores at 5 years on the test of Knowledge of Literacy and at 7 years on the Neale Analysis of Reading (Moon & Wells, 1979).

In the context of the present investigation, it was decided to reexamine Moon's original data, in which reading stories, looking at books, and drawing and coloring were tallied separately. Scores for each of these activities were derived as described above and compared with the dependent variables Knowledge of Literacy at 5 years, Reading Comprehension at 7 years, and Parental Education[4] using the Mann–Whitney U test. The results, which are given in Table 12.4, show that listening to stories is strongly associated with all the dependent variables ($p < .025$ to $p < .001$), but drawing and coloring only with knowledge of literacy ($p < .05$). Looking at Books failed to achieve a level of statistical significance in relation to any of the dependent variables. These results can be taken as providing substantial support for the particularly beneficial effect of reading stories to preschool children.

The importance of stories

Supported by evidence drawn from longitudinal observations of a socially representative sample of children in the two contexts of home and school, the central argument of this chapter has been that success in school is intimately related to the early acquisition of literacy. This argument has of course been stated many times before and, put in such general terms, it is almost self-evidently true. Since so much of the school curriculum depends on being able to read and write, the acquisition of these skills is obviously necessary for success.

In seeking to foster the acquisition of literacy, however, teachers have tended to emphasize the "mechanics" of reading and writing: the recognition and naming of letters, the decoding of words according to "phonic principles," the motor skills of handwriting, and the rules of spelling and punctuation. Because these are the skills that are regularly tested, with scores being used in some institutions to regulate promotion, they have come to be seen as the essence of literacy, and prereading activities designed to ensure rapid mastery of these skills have found their way into the homes of some educationally conscious parents. The result is that children in many classrooms – and even in some homes – spend long hours in repetitive and routine activities involving simple pictorial representations and geometrical shapes, almost meaningless basic reading texts, and worksheets, in order to practice the many subskills that this approach to reading has managed to generate.

Now I do not wish to claim that being able to decode new words or to spell conventionally are unimportant abilities. They clearly are necessary components of effective reading and writing. But to focus on them to the near-exclusion of the content and purpose of written communications, and of the mode of thinking that these characteristically involve, is to stunt the development of literacy rather than to promote it.

In claiming that success in school depends on the acquisition of literacy, then, I am concerned less with the "mechanics" of literacy and more with the development of familiarity with the ways in which language is used in characteristically written as opposed to spoken communication.

There are many features with respect to which written language differs from spoken language, but these can be grouped together under a number of general oppositions that arise from the contexts of typical use. Chafe (Chapter 6), for example, proposes that they can be subsumed under two very broad oppositions: integration versus fragmentation and detachment versus involvement, the former contrast arising from the differing time constraints under which writers and speakers typically operate and the latter from the different stances that they typically adopt vis-à-vis their audience. Emphasizing the different relationships that hold between message, meaning, and experience in written and spoken language, Olson (1977) focuses on the contrast in "locus of meaning": In typical conversational speech he sees meaning as residing in an interaction between the participants, their shared experience and commonsense knowledge, and the situation in which the communication takes place; in formal written language, on the other hand, the meaning is to a much greater extent "in the text." These oppositions are of course based on the most extreme contrast between casual conversation and formal, expository writing; they should therefore be understood as the poles of a continuum rather than as sharp dichotomies.

Discussions of these differences are usually concerned with the speech and writing of adults. In the language experienced by young children the contrasts are not so marked, but the same tendencies are still at work. Blank (1980), for example, in a recent consideration of the essential characteristics of reading with which the learner has to come to terms, lists the following:

1. The disembedded quality of reading
2. The sustained sequential aspect of written discourse
3. The implicit connectedness of ideas
4. The conventions of written language
5. The receptiveness of reading (p. 5)

These are remarkably similar to the distinguishing features of written language just discussed, and it is significant that, in ordering them, Blank gives the greatest importance to the disembedded and sustained characteristics of texts.

Of even greater importance for the argument of this chapter, however, is the fact that, with the exception of point 4, above, these characteristics apply equally to the spoken language used in many curricular tasks. As already suggested, it is not so much the frequency of requests for display that causes the difficulty experienced by the less successful pupils, but the disembedded nature of the problems that are posed in these questions and in the other speech acts that occur in implementing the school curriculum. For what is required is that, in order to understand and respond appropriately, the child should treat the verbal formulation of the message as the chief locus of meaning, disregarding if necessary the immediate context and the personal associations triggered by some detail of the total situation. Donaldson (1978), who first used the term *disembedded* in this context to refer to thinking that moves beyond the context of familiar events and situations – "beyond the bounds of human sense" (p. 76) – makes the same point more broadly when she summarizes the task that faces the child as follows:

What is going to be required for success in our educational system is that [the student] should learn to turn language and thought in upon themselves. He must become able to direct his own thought processes in a thoughtful manner. He must become able not just to talk but to choose what he will say, not just to interpret but to weigh possible interpretations. His conceptual system must expand in the direction of increasing ability to represent itself. He must become capable of manipulating symbols. (Pp. 88–89)

And for the reasons outlined above, she too sees this development as being intimately related to experience with written language. If both learning to read and write and successful participation in curriculum-related talk at school are dependent on developing familiarity with the characteristically written uses and forms of language, we should expect children to be at an advantage on entry to school if they have already had experience of this kind. Hence the importance attached to introducing children to books at an early age. The study reported here has confirmed that expectation, but has made a further distinction between looking at picture books and listening to stories read aloud and shown that it is the latter that is of greater importance.

The activity of looking at and talking about picture books is, nevertheless, not without value. New vocabulary may be learned, and the child will gain practice in answering display questions. He will be trained, as Heath (1980) puts it, to be a questioner–answerer in relation to books. However, while the ability to answer questions about names and attributes, which is what is fostered by this activity, may give the child an initial advantage in classrooms that emphasize these skills, it is of limited long-term value. More importantly, the activity of looking at books does little to introduce the child to actual written language.

Through listening to a story read aloud, by contrast, the child has experience of the sustained organization of written language and of its characteristic rhythms and structures. He is also introduced to a form of language functioning in which the language alone is used to create experiences. For even when accompanied by illustrations, stories require no other context than themselves for their interpretation. They thus provide the child with the opportunity to discover the power that language has to create and explore alternative possible worlds with their own inner coherence and logic.

The child's experience of story is not, of course, restricted to what is read aloud from written texts. From a very early age all of us engage in "storying," creating fictions in which we replay and recombine actual experiences and construct imaginary extensions and alternatives to them. In young children's imaginary play, alone or with other children, we can see this storying in action and we can note how here, as in the world of story presented through books, it is language that creates the context against which the action takes place: "Pretend this is a giant's castle. I'm a giant and you're a witch." It is language, too, that transmutes cardboard boxes into dungeons, pumpkins into glass coaches, and provides the narrative thread that gives coherence to the sequence of events. Even when it is not rendered observable through play, however, we can be sure that the storying continues, for, as Gregory (1974) argues: "By neither being tied to fact nor quite separate, fiction is a tool necessary for thought and intelligence and for considering and planning possibilities. Fiction is vitally important – indeed we may live more by fiction than by fact" (p. 439).

To be fully effective, though, the private fictions of the individual must come to intersect with those of other members of the culture, both in principles of organization and evaluation and, to a considerable extent, in content. This may happen through the sort of imaginative play referred to above and through other types of talk in what has been called the "spectator role" (Britton, 1970). But it is particularly likely to happen, I would argue, as the child listens to and talks about stories that are told in traditional form or, in a literate culture, read from a written book. Such stories provide a validation of the child's own inner storying (Spencer, 1976) and offer models for its further development.

At first the stories that children hear will be of most value to them by extending experience and by encouraging the "fictionalizing of . . . experience" (Scollon & Scollon, 1980); but gradually, if they are of such a quality as to stir the imagination, stories will lead them to reflect on their experience and to consider alternative interpretations. And since, as Britton (1983) points out, the world of story and the real world are not sharply divided but interpenetrate each other, children may eventually learn to utilize the strategies developed in relation to the understanding and creation of stories, both factual and fictional, for the kinds of reading, writing, and thinking that characterize the full range of subjects of academic study.

It is this development taking place, in embryonic form, that we get glimpses of in the discussions that Gerald has with his mother about the stories that she reads to him: Mother inviting Gerald to consider the way in which the characters in the stories experience their fictional world; Gerald drawing upon the framework provided by a story previously read to interpret his own experience of letters and postmen.

As these extracts show, it is not the reading of stories on its own that leads children toward the reflective, disembedded thinking that is so necessary for success in school, but the total interaction in which the story is embedded. At first they need a competent adult to mediate, as reader and writer, between themselves and the text; but even when they can perform the decoding and encoding for themselves, they continue to need help in interpreting the stories they hear and read and in shaping those that they create for themselves.

The manner in which the adult — first parent and later teacher — fulfills this latter role is almost as important as the story itself. If stories are simply read as part of a daily routine, without being further discussed, they are likely to remain inert and without much impact on the rest of the child's experience. If they are used chiefly as the basis for display question sequences that focus on the meanings of particular words or on isolated items, such as the names of the characters or the details of particular events, again they are unlikely to provide encouragement for the exploratory but controlled thinking that written language facilitates.

However where, through discussion, stories are related to children's own experiences and they are encouraged to reflect upon and ask questions about the events that occur, their causes, consequences, and significance, not only are their inner representations of the world enriched, but also their awareness of the ways in which language can be used in operating on these representations is enhanced.

In summary, because stories are self-contextualizing, sustained symbolic representations of possible worlds, they provide the child with the opportunity to learn some of the essential characteristics of written language. Reading and discussing these stories helps the child to cope with the more disembedded uses of spoken language that the school curriculum demands.

ACKNOWLEDGMENTS

The research reported in this chapter was funded by grants from the Social Science Research Council (U.K.) and from the Nuffield Foundation, whose support is gratefully acknowledged.

NOTES

1. A summary of the aims and methods employed in the various phases of the research can be found in Wells (1981a).
2. To allow for the possibility of short periods when the child was out of range of the recorder as a result of a visit to the store or to fetch a sibling from school, only 18 of the 24 samples were selected for analysis. Where all 24 samples were in range, 1 out of each sequential set of 4 was excluded at random.
3. The distribution of scores for the three literacy-related activities was as follows: looking at books, 0–7, median 3; drawing and coloring, 0–4, median 1; listening to a story, 0–7, median 1. The median score was used in each case in determining the dichotomization.
4. No data on oral language ability in the classroom were available for this sample of children.

REFERENCES

Barnes, S. B., Gutfreund, M. D., Satterly, D., & Wells, C. G. Characteristics of adult speech which predict children's language development. *Journal of Child Language*, 1983, *10*, 65–84.

Bernstein, B. *Class, codes, and control* (Vol. 1). London: Routledge & Kegan Paul, 1971.

Blank, M. Language and school failure: Some speculations about oral and written language relationships. Typescript, Rutgers Medical School, 1980.

Britton, J. *Language and education*. Allen Lane: Penguin, 1970.
  Writing and the story world. In B. Kroll & C. G. Wells (Eds.), *Explorations in the development of writing*. Chichester: Wiley, 1983.

Bruner, J. S. *The relevance of education*. New York: Norton, 1971.

Chafe, W. L. Integration and involvement in speaking, writing, and oral literature. In D. Tanner (Ed.), *Spoken and written language*. Norwood, N.J.: Ablex, 1982.

Clay, M. M. *The early detection of reading difficulties: A diagnostic survey*. London: Heinemann Educational, 1972.

Deutsch, M. The role of social class in language development and cognition. *American Journal of Orthopsychiatry*, 1965, *35*(1), 78–88.

Donaldson, M. *Children's minds*. London: Fontana, 1978.

Gregory, R. L. Psychology: Towards a science of fiction. *New Society*, 23 May 1974, 439–441.

Griffiths, M., & Wells, C. G. Adults' uses of writing. In B. Kroll & C. G. Wells (Eds.), *Explorations in the development of writing*. Chichester: Wiley, 1983.

Heath, S. B. What no bedtime story means: Narrative skills at home and school. *Language in society*, 1982, *11*, 49–76.

Labov, W. The logic of non-standard English. In F. Williams (Ed.), *Language and poverty*. Chicago: Markham, 1970.

Mehan, H. Structuring school structure. *Harvard Educational Review*, 1978, *48*, 32–64.

Moon, B. C. *Pre-school reading experience and learning to read*. M.Ed. Thesis, University of Bristol, School of Education, 1976.

Moon, B. C., & Wells, C. G. The influence of home on learning to read. *Journal of Research in Reading*, 1979, 2, 53–62.

Neale, M. D. *Neale Analysis of Reading Ability* (2nd ed.). Basingstoke: Macmillan Education, 1969.

Ninio, A. Z., & Bruner, J. S. The achievement and antecedents of labelling. *Journal of Child Language*, 1978, 5, 1–16.

Olson, D. From utterance to text: The bias of language in speech and writing. *Harvard Educational Review*, 1977, 47(3), 257–281.

Scollon, R., & Scollon, S. B. K. The literate two-year old: The fictionalization of self. Typescript, Centre for Cross-Cultural Studies, University of Alaska, 1980.

Spencer, M. Stories are for telling. *English in Education*, 1976, *10*(1), 16–23.

Vygotsky, L. S. *Mind in society*. Cambridge: Harvard University Press, 1978.

Wells, C. G. *Influences of the home on language development* (Bristol Working Papers in Language I). University of Bristol, 1979.
 Learning through interaction: The study of language development. Cambridge: Cambridge University Press, 1981a.
 Some antecedents of early educational attainment. *British Journal of Sociology of Education*, 1981b, 2, 181–200.

Wells, C. G., & Nicholls, J. C. The negotiation of meaning: Talking and learning in the early years. In J. C. Nicholls (Ed.), *Talk at home*. Forthcoming.

Wells, C. G., & Raban, E. B. *Children learning to read* (Final Report to the Social Science Research Council). Centre for the Study of Language and Communication, University of Bristol, 1978.

13

Oral and literate competencies in the early school years

NANCY TORRANCE and DAVID R. OLSON

Introduction

A central problem for educational theory is the differential effects of schooling on children – why some children are better able than others to master the forms of competence taught in the schools. The explanation examined here is the relationship that holds between the child's competence with the "mother tongue" – the ordinary oral language of the home – and the more formal, decontextualized, and explicit language that makes up a part of the language of school.

Two descriptions of the relation between the language of the home and the language of the school have been advanced. Bernstein (1971) attempted to explain school failure by linguistic "code" differences between social classes. Because the language of the school is thought to be identical to "middle-class" language, middle-class children have less difficulty in school than do lower-class children. A second explanation is that the language of the home is essentially continuous with the language of the school but that some children are more sophisticated in their uses of ordinary language and hence are better prepared to deal with the language of the school. Wells (1981), for example, has found a relation between some oral language activities and progress in learning to read.

Our concerns in this project fall between these alternatives. We have attempted to determine children's competence with a variety of aspects of language, ranging from lexical and syntactic structures to more communicative discourse structures, in an attempt to determine which aspects of oral competence are relevant to the acquisition of the literate skills of reading and writing. Hence we have attempted to identify the major dimensions of oral language use, to construct scales for measuring these dimensions, and then to relate these dimensions to the children's progress in learning to read and write. We have examined these issues by sampling children's language during the first three years of schooling, from kindergarten to grade 2, as the child is prepared for and eased into early reading. By examining the relationship between measures of oral performance in these years and some other measures of cognitive, linguistic, and finally reading performance, we hope to uncover the ways in which the structure and uses of oral language competence – the "mother tongue" – are related to the development of literacy skills.

However, there is no straightforward means to assess competence with oral language. Standardized tests can measure vocabulary, some aspects of the knowledge of grammar, and some aspects of reading and reading comprehension. However, the major aspect of oral language competence is not captured simply in measures of vocabulary or syntax, although these are very important, but rather in the pragmatic aspects of language, namely, the extent to which children manage to "hold up their end" in conversation by taking their turns, acknowledging the contribution of their conversational partners, and contributing to the dialogue. They can also hold up their end of the conversation by staying on the topic, introducing new topics appropriately, introducing remote topics, and by making their conversational contributions clear, grammatical, and to the point. Our strategy was to examine these various aspects of structure beginning at the discourse level. Hence, the basic unit of analysis selected has been that of a functioning, contextually appropriate utterance – that is, a speech act.

The choice of speech act as the basic unit of analysis permits analysis in either of two directions – downward to the clause and word level at which we may examine children's competence with linguistic forms or upward to the text level at which we may examine children's competence with discourse forms. In this chapter we shall examine both children's competence with the higher-order discourse structures and their competence with lower-order syntactic and lexical structures and conclude with some analysis of the relations between the two and of both to the acquisition of literacy skills.

Speech act theory is an attempt to relate sentences to situations of their use through analyzing the relation between sentences and utterances, *utterance meaning* being the intended meaning of a sentence in a particular context. An *intended meaning*, or an *utterance meaning* or a *speaker's meaning*, depending on whose terminology you prefer, is treated as a combination of a sentence meaning and a context (Searle, 1969; Olson & Hildyard, 1983). In other words, sentences are means for mapping contexts into intentions (Bierwisch, 1979). To give some simple examples:

Sentence	Context	Intended meaning
"You're standing on my toes"	(You really are)	Move your foot
"You're standing on my toes"	(You really aren't)	You're invading my space
"I hear talking"	(in a classroom)	Be quiet

In order to capture what utterances are doing pragmatically, in addition to what they mean semantically, Austin (1962) proposed that utterances be treated as speech acts composed of both a propositional content and an illocutionary force. The propositional content in turn is made up of predicates and referring expressions, whereas illocutionary force describes the use of sentences to make assertions, to make promises, to issue commands, and so on. Both propositional content and illocutionary force are relevant to the construction of discourse (Dore, 1977; Dore & McDermott, 1982). Just as the propositional content of two utterances may be related through, say, lexical repetition, so the illocutionary force of two utterances may be related through question–answer pairs, assertion–acknowledgment pairs, or command–compliance pairs. Whereas illocutionary force cohesion tends to operate primarily between adjacent pairs of utterances, semantic or propositional cohesion may operate not only between adjacent pairs but also over longer stretches of discourse to make up what we refer to as discourse topics and discourse episodes. We have attempted to state the relations between turns, topics, and episodes in a conversation by means of the set of rewrite rules shown in Figure 13.1.

A conversational discourse may be seen as consisting of a sequence of episodes. Such episodes, while following one another in time, are semantically – that is, propositionally – discrete. Any particular episode, in turn, is made up of a series of semantically related (r) topics. A change in episode is marked by a change to a semantically unrelated topic and is often introduced with a conversational device (Dore, 1980) that appears to signal the change. A conversational topic is a series of adjacent and semantically related turns that contribute to a single propositional focus or theme, the semantic relations between turns generally being marked by one of the cohesive

Discourse   ⟶ $\text{episode}_1 + \text{episode}_2 + \cdots + \text{episode}_n$

Episode   ⟶ $r(\text{topic}_1 + \text{topic}_2 + \cdots + \text{topic}_n)$

Topic   ⟶ $r(\text{turn}_1 + \text{turn}_2 + \cdots + \text{turn}_n)$

Turn   ⟶ $r(\text{speech act}_1 + \text{speech act}_2 + \cdots + \text{speech act}_n)$

Speech act   ⟶   illocutionary force + propositional content

^{r}Illocutionary force   ⟶   comments, directives, turnabouts

^{r}Propositional content   ⟶   conjunction, reference, substitution, lexical cohesion, ellipsis, phonological associations

Comments   ⟶   assertions, acknowledgments, responses, rhetorical questions

Directives   ⟶   genuine questions, indirect questions, clarification questions, requests for action, suggestions

Turnabouts   ⟶   comment + directive

Figure 13.1

devices described by Halliday and Hasan (1976). A change in topic within an episode occurs when the new topic is semantically related but the propositions expressed have a different focus or theme and therefore contribute to the construction of a different semantic structure. The relation between topics within an episode may therefore also be marked by cohesive devices, although, as we shall try to demonstrate, not as strongly as nor by means of the same devices that generally mark cohesion within a topic. Turns are the discrete contributions of different speakers to the construction of a topic. Related turns, like topics, tend to be marked by some semantic cohesive devices. A turn consists of one or more speech acts that may be cohesively linked to previous speech acts. Speech acts are therefore the basic units of analysis of a conversation.

Propositional content cohesion has to do with the semantic relations between propositions and may be examined in terms of the textual cohesive devices of Halliday and Hasan (1976) including reference, lexical cohesion (repetition and collocation), substitution, ellipsis, and conjunction. To this list we have added phonological associations, such as rhyming and word play.

As we mentioned, speech acts are utterances composed of an illocutionary force as well as a propositional content. As our primary concern is with the construction of discourse rather than with syntax or semantics per se, we have singled out those aspects of illocutionary force and propositional content that are used for cohesive purposes (see Figure 13.1). Illocutionary force cohesion consists of the pragmatic relations between speech acts in a conversational discourse; questions call for answers, comments for acknowledgments, commands for compliance, and so on. Within a topic, for instance, illocutionary force may vary; that is, expectations may be set up more or less forcefully in the course of turn taking, and related turns within a topic will generally be marked by some illocutionary force cohesion in addition to semantic or propositional cohesion.

Reviewing the embedded structures of Figure 13.1 from the other direction, we may say that the illocutionary and propositional aspects of speech acts in a conversational turn are related to those of an adjacent turn through illocutionary force and propositional cohesive devices. Such related turns make up topics. Topics are maintained as long as the field of discourse as marked by semantic relations remains the same, while the illocutionary force relations may vary. A series of topics that bear some general semantic relations make up an episode. Finally, a conversation consists of one or more episodes.

The procedures for applying an analysis of illocutionary force and semantic cohesion to our transcripts have been developed and pilot-tested. Details of the analysis and preliminary findings will be summarized in a later section of this chapter. (See also Olson, Bell, & Torrance, 1983). These forms of analyses are similar to those developed by Dore (1978) and Brown (1980). In particular, Kaye and Charney's (1980) notion of a turnabout, namely an utterance that simultaneously links backwards and forward in the discourse, has been useful in the analysis. Similarly the discourse analyses of Gregory and Malcolm (1982) and Benson and Greaves (1981) have influenced our descriptions of the discourse rules.

As part of our analysis of competence with oral language, we have also examined lexical and syntactic features of our children's conversations. Hence, below the level of speech acts, utterances were analyzed in terms of clause structures. The basic clausal unit was a matrix sentence consisting of a main clause plus subordinate clauses. Utterances were scored in terms of their grammatical well-formedness, their length and complexity, their degree of embedding, their use of modifiers and qualifiers, and the like.

We are in the process of applying this account of the structure of conversation to part of the data collected in the longitudinal study mentioned above. The purpose of that analysis is to examine just how children go about engaging in conversation – how they create discourse, episodes, topics, turns, how they respond to the turns of others, how they construct episodes, how they change topics, what locutionary and illocutionary devices they use, and so on. Once we have determined how children participate in conversational discourse we will be in a position to examine how their relative competence with these devices is related to the more formal requirements of school language, particularly reading and writing. Our analysis of the conversations of 6-year-old peer dyads will, we hope, contribute to the development of these tools.

The longitudinal study

The data described are part of the data collected in a three-year longitudinal study designed to assess the relationship between oral language competence and early reading skill. We have collected language samples from a group of children in a variety of formal and informal tasks when the children were in kindergarten, grade 1, and grade 2. We have also measured performance in a variety of cognitive tasks and reading and writing tasks in order to relate oral language performance to aspects of schooled performance.

Subjects

Twenty-nine children from primarily English-speaking homes participated in this study. They were drawn from two Toronto public schools, one in a primarily working-class neighborhood and the other in a primarily professional neighborhood. The subjects were tested midway through each of the three years over which the study extended.

Method

Our battery of tasks include tests of reading (Durrell Analysis of Reading Difficulty), verbal and nonverbal IQ tests (WPPSI and WISC Block Design and Vocabulary subtests), some formal language tasks like story retelling and block description, writing tasks (structured and unstructured), and tasks designed to elicit free speech in a cooperative play setting. It is the language samples resulting from the last of these, cooperative play, that shall be our focus in this chapter. In order to obtain these samples, we paired the children and left each pair sitting by themselves in a room for 5 minutes, ostensibly to wait for "game" materials to be brought to the room. They were encouraged to talk to each other while waiting. After 5 minutes, the experimenter returned with a set of Lego blocks and asked the children to build one toy between them out of the blocks. They were instructed to discuss what they would build and encouraged by the experimenter to talk. These 20-minute sessions were tape-recorded and videotaped for later transcription.

Language samples are currently being analyzed along with scores obtained on reading, block design, and vocabulary tasks. We have so far confined our analyses to the second-year data collected when the children were midway through grade 1 and were approximately $6\frac{1}{2}$ years old.

Analyses of language samples

In our analyses of speech samples, we have attempted to find indices of the quality of various aspects of the children's oral language, and to this end several different analytic devices have been developed. First, analyses were performed on the lexical and grammatical structure of the utterances themselves, and second, analyses were made of the ways in which these utterances were organized into discourse.

Analyses performed on the structure of the utterances include the semantic and syntactic properties of clauses that make up speech acts following methods employed by Wells (1980) and Quirk et al. (1972). Transcribed samples of the children's language have been analyzed for grammatical well-formedness, clause embedding, length and complexity, use of modifiers and qualifiers, verb inflection and complexity, types of grammatical errors, and lexical choices in some semantic domains, particularly psychological verbs. A pronominal analysis was devised to examine how children use pronouns in various tasks and situations and in the presence or absence of available referents.

The analyses of discourse features examined over the entire sample of 29 children include various aspects of conversational skill, such as how topics are constructed and maintained, and the devices used for maintaining topics and for turn taking. To obtain some validity for these measures as aspects of conversational skill we obtained independent judgments by two raters of each child's effectiveness in controlling and maintaining the conversation ($r = .76$). The analysis of the relations between and within conversational turns in terms of both illocutionary force cohesion and semantic cohesion is currently being applied to the conversational data. We shall describe this latter analysis and the preliminary findings it has yielded for 12 children in a later section of the chapter. First, however, we shall consider the structural and discourse analyses completed for the entire sample and our conclusions regarding the relation of oral language competence and early literacy.

Structural and conversational features of discourse and their relationship to reading

To date we have carried out extensive structural and discourse analyses of the speech samples of 29 children for two of the oral language tasks from the second-year data. These two samples are free speech with a peer and cooperative play with a peer. These two tasks have been combined to make one sample of conversation for each pair of children. Structural and discourse measures have been applied to this conversation to yield separate scores for each child that could then be compared to their scores on the vocabulary and block design tests and to the results of the standardized reading test (Durrell) administered in March of the second year of the project.

The statistical analyses to date have been mainly correlational. These results may require more complex statistical procedures, since these data require taking into account the lack of independence between partners in our conversational samples. We are currently exploring ways of circumventing this problem. Correlational analyses on data of this kind are therefore reported as preliminary.

Those measures entered into the correlational analyses include the following:

1. *General skill and ability measures:* The Vocabulary subtest of the WISC (VOCAB); the Block Design subtest of the WISC (BLDES); and a measure of oral reading obtained on the Durrell Analysis of Reading Difficulty (READ).
2. *Lexical knowledge:* Psychological verbs such as *think, know, wonder, like, hate,* and so on were divided into four categories: linguistic, perceptual, affective, and cognitive. Only types of affective (AFFTY) and cognitive verbs (COGTY) were used differentially

by our children and so are included in the analysis. We also scored each child on the range of subordinate conjunctions in their conversations (SUBTY).

3. *Structural features of clauses:* The mean length of independent clauses (MLU); the ratio of independent clauses containing modifiers and qualifiers to the total number of such clauses (MQRAT); the ratio of subordinate clauses to the total number of clauses (SCRAT); the number of cognitive verbs taking complex infinitive, gerund, or clause complements (COGCX); and finally the number of coordinate conjunctions used to relate clauses within a speaker's turn (CCJ/C).

4. *Conversational measures:* In addition to the combined conversational rating that each child received from the two independent judges (CONV), verbal fluency was measured by the number of turns each child contributed (TURNS) and conversational cohesion was measured by the proportion of turns that were turnabouts (PRO-T). We also considered the number of coordinate conjunctions at the beginning of a turn used to link the speaker's turn with a preceding turn (CLD/T); the number of topics each speaker introduced (N-TOP); the proportion of topics raised in turnabout structures (T-OP); and the number of remote or abstract topics introduced (RTO).

The correlations among these variables are shown in Table 13.1. Only those correlations that are significant ($p < .05$) are entered. Several interesting patterns have emerged.

First, measures of verbal and nonverbal IQ are related to each other and, as we expected, to reading. What is unexpected is that block design is a better correlate of reading than is vocabulary. This may be an indication that the early stages of reading acquisition are somewhat mechanical, perhaps more related to the recognition of letters and words than to language competence more generally. It remains to be seen if reading scores obtained in later school years, when the children are in grade 2 and then in grade 3, come to be more closely related to vocabulary and less related to block design. This may occur for two reasons: First, as the children pass through the early mechanical stage of reading, their oral reading scores may better reflect reading for comprehension; and second, the nature of the reading test itself will be altered in grade 3 so that comprehension rather than oral decoding will be measured.

Next, consider the lexical and structural features of children's oral language. The variety of cognitive verbs used by the children in our sample correlates more strongly with their reading score than with either measure of IQ and is, in fact, the strongest correlate of reading

Table 13.1. *Structural and conversational aspects of language competence in 29 6-year olds: relation to reading, verbal, and nonverbal measures*

				Lexical			Structural					Conversational					
	VOCAB	BLDES	READ	COGTY	AFFTY	SUBTY	MLU	MQRAT	SCRAT	COGCX	CCJ/C	CONV	CLD/T	TURNS	PRO-T	N-TOP	T-OP
BLDES	.53	—	—	—	—	—	—	—	—	—	—	—	—	—	—	—	—
READ	.33	.57	—	—	—	—	—	—	—	—	—	—	—	—	—	—	—
Lexical																	
COGTY	.39	.44	.59	—	—	—	—	—	—	—	—	—	—	—	—	—	—
AFFTY	—	—	—	—	—	—	—	—	—	—	—	—	—	—	—	—	—
SUBTY	—	—	—	.34	—	—	—	—	—	—	—	—	—	—	—	—	—
Structural																	
MLU	—	—	.33	—	—	—	—	—	—	—	—	—	—	—	—	—	—
MQRAT	—	—	(.30)	—	-.39	—	—	—	—	—	—	—	—	—	—	—	—
SCRAT	—	—	(.30)	.49	—	.49	—	-.35	—	—	—	—	—	—	—	—	—
COGCX	—	—	—	.64	—	.59	—	—	.79	—	—	—	—	—	—	—	—
CCJ/C	—	—	.34	—	—	.46	—	—	.36	.31	—	—	—	—	—	—	—
Conversational																	
CONV	.40	—	—	—	.39	.32	.41	—	—	.35	.58	—	—	—	—	—	—
CLD/T	.33	—	—	—	—	—	—	—	—	—	.58	.53	—	—	—	—	—
TURNS	—	—	—	—	—	—	—	—	—	—	.31	.33	—	—	—	—	—
PRO-T	—	—	—	—	—	—	—	—	—	—	—	.41	.49	—	—	—	—
N-TOP	—	—	—	—	.35	—	—	—	—	—	—	.35	—	.48	—	—	—
T-OP	—	—	—	—	.33	—	—	—	—	—	.39	.43	.37	—	.41	.46	—
RTO	—	—	—	—	—	.41	—	-.42	—	(.30)	—	.43	—	.33	—	.65	.42

that we obtained. Our better readers use more psychological verbs reflecting cognitive processes (*think, know, decide, wonder,* etc.) than do poorer readers. They do not, however, use a greater variety of affective verbs (*like, hate, love, care,* etc.), nor indeed do good readers use a greater variety of psychological verbs overall when preliminary analyses were performed on the data. Further, although reading scores are not directly related to the variety of subordinate conjunctions used, the variety of cognitive verbs a child used and the number of cognitive verbs taking complex complements were both related to reading scores. It may be that utterances containing a cognitive verb like *think* or *know* are complex constructions in which the complement of the cognitive verb is a subordinate clause introduced by a subordinate conjunction. We shall return to this point presently.

The analysis of structural variables indicates that better readers construct longer independent clauses (MLU) than less-skilled readers, presumably in part because they pack more modifiers and qualifiers into these independent clause structures (MQRAT). However, preliminary analyses indicate no difference between better and poorer readers on the overall number of modifiers and qualifiers used. Better readers also tended to use more subordinate clause structures (SCRAT) and used more complex complements (infinitive, gerund, or clause structures) with cognitive verbs (COGCX). Finally, many of these lexical and structural variables, as expected, tend to be interrelated. Indeed, many of the variables reflect slightly different measures of the same structures: subordination, coordination, and modification. Because of the interrelations between variables, multiple regressions were run to predict reading scores. Two factors, the variety of cognitive verbs and mean length of independent clauses, accounted for 39% of the variance in reading scores ($F_{2,26} = 8.17, p < .01$).

These are some indications that at least some structural aspects of children's oral language competence are related to children's learning to read. As mentioned, the child's use of cognitive verbs – those verbs that indicate how the propositional content of the sentence is to be taken – is the highest correlate of reading scores. We analyzed them primarily because we were interested in the possibility that literacy – that is, learning to read and write – encouraged the differentiation of *form* from *meaning*, and hence accentuated the difference between what was *said* and what was *meant*. We have also noted how children use these verbs differentially to mark literal from intended meaning, as in cases of sarcasm and metaphor. We know, for instance, that children from homes in which the distinction between *said* and *meant* is lexically marked in fact tend to differentiate between production errors and comprehension errors; that is, as listeners they know when the speaker did not say what he or she meant (Robinson, Goelman, & Olson, 1983). But we are surprised that their use is more closely related to reading than is any other measure of structural complexity. Clearly, they require more careful examination.

While these relations among reading, cognitive verbs, and complex linguistic structures are interesting, it remains unclear just why the relations occur. The early reading tests that discriminate better from poorer readers tend to be simple paragraphs – these paragraphs do not contain any complex verbs, they contain no complex clause complements, and yet the children who handle these devices orally tend to be the better readers. We can offer three hypotheses for this relationship, hypotheses that we are in the process of empirically examining.

The first is that good readers use more cognitive verbs because these verbs can occur in complex syntactic environments and it is that complex syntax, as a general indication of a high level of structural competence, that predicts reading. It may be recalled that we find that good readers tend overall to use more subordinate constructions than poor readers. Further, we may recall that Kalmár (Chapter 8) finds that these clause complements do not occur in a nonliterate language, and Chafe (Chapter 6) finds they occur more frequently in writing then in speech. These cognitive verbs, then, may play directly into those subordinate constructions to permit the expression of complex ideas. Hence, a child with this complex syntax and these cognitive verbs could express his or her stance to a proposition (John expects that *X*, John wonders if *X*, John decided that *X*, and so on) or interrogate his listener's stance toward propositions – and, further, can do so in a single utterance. The poor readers in our study were less likely to do so – and perhaps were less able to do so. Instead of saying, "Did you know that *X*," the poor reader typically says, "You know what? *X*." As examples of this, consider the following utterances generated by two children discussing the task they are involved in:

GOOD READER: What game do you think we're gonna play?
POOR READER: What are we gonna do?

Similarly, two children interrogate their listeners' memories in different ways:

GOOD READER: Remember when we brang things to the teacher and I fell down?

POOR READER: We done this last year too in the same time. Didn't we? Remember?

While these are important differences in oral language competence, they do not directly explain why children who use these devices can read simple paragraphs better than children who do not.

A second possible explanation for the high correlation between reading and the use of these cognitive verbs is that cognitive verbs reflect the child's knowledge of vocabulary generally. It is well known that vocabulary development is highly correlated with reading skill. In fact, our cognitive verbs, including *decide, remember, doubt* and *expect,* tend to be used by our good readers but not our poor readers. Again, while these are important differences in oral language competence, they do not directly explain why children who use such verbs can read simple paragraphs lacking these verbs better than children who do not.

The third hypothesis, and the one we favor, is that these cognitive verbs are part of a system of concepts for decontextualizing language and thought. Basic to this system are the verbs that mark an understanding of the relation between speaker's meaning and sentence meaning (Olson, 1977), that is, between what a word or sentence means rather than what *one* means by it. It is this differentiation, we believe, that a child must master in learning that not only do people mean things by what they say but that the words and sentences per se "mean" something. This is a basic move in coming to recognize "words" as constituents of utterances, and it is a move that may be prerequisite to "reading" any words at all.

Why the other cognitive verbs also relate to reading is not so clear, but it is possible that it is only when a speaker can clearly recognize that what was said was not equivalent to what was meant, and that some sayings are better representations of what was meant than others, that he or she is in a position to choose correctly between the psychological commitment to what was said in terms of such verbs as *know, think, believe, guess, doubt,* and so on. Indeed, Vendler (1970) and Searle (1979) have argued that there is an intimate relation between the verbs of saying and the verbs of meaning; for each speech act verb such as asserting or promising, there is a corresponding psychological verb such as believing and intending. Hence the metalinguistic verbs of saying and the metacognitive verbs of meaning may be closely related in acquisition as well as in structure. And it may be that these differentiations are much more relevant to written texts than to ordinary oral discourse.

We have designed a series of tasks to help us choose among the hypotheses explaining why these cognitive verbs relate to the acquisition of literacy. Although these tasks were administered as part of the third-year test battery, the analyses have not yet been completed. Preliminary analysis indicates that good and poor readers differ in their competence with these verbs. It remains to be seen if the good reader's competence with these verbs is a byproduct of being exposed to the literate language of written texts.

With regard to the measures of conversational skill shown in the lower half of Table 13.1, we find that the conversational measures tend to be interrelated and also relate to the subjective ratings of conversational skill. The strongest correlate of global conversational skill is the use of coordinate conjunctions to link a speaker's utterance with the preceding speaker's turn. Significant yet decreasing correlations were obtained between global conversational skill and the number of topics opened by turns that are turnabouts (that is, turns that both respond to the listener and make demands on the listener), the number of remote topics opened, the proportion of turns that are turnabouts, the number of topics raised by each speaker, and the number of turns each speaker contributes. Given the high expected intercorrelations among these conversational measures, a multiple regression was carried out to determine the best predictors of conversational ratings. Results of this analysis yielded two predictors of conversational skill, coordinate conjunction links to previous turns and the number of turns each speaker contributes ($F_{2,26}$ due to regression = 8.55, $p < .01$). These two factors accounted for 40% of the variance in conversational ratings, and no further factor contributed significantly to the prediction. This suggests, then, that our measures of conversational skill do tap at least some of the ways in which good conversationalists manage discourse. Conversely, it appears that our judges of conversational skill base their judgments largely on the smoothness of turn taking and the productive fluency of the speakers. Specifically, judges take into account the contingencies between turns (via turnabouts and conversational links) and verbal fluency (the number of turns taken in a fixed interval of time).

As for the relationship between these measures and our other variables, we see a slight tendency for conversational rankings to reflect verbal IQ but not to be related to reading test or block design scores. Note also the relationship between the range of affective verbs used and aspects of topic openings. Good conversationalists seem to raise concrete or immediate topics by interrogating their listener's feelings about a shared event. For example:

> Do you like the house or hate it?

was offered as a change in topic by a good conversationalist. In raising remote or abstract topics, though, these children use cognitive verbs and complete sentence structures:

> Remember when we brang things to the teacher and I fell down and mine got broke?

Finally, we see a relation between the uses of coordination within a turn to link clauses and between turns to link conversational contributions.

The pattern that emerges is that of a good conversationalist who keeps the conversation moving smoothly in the transfer of turn taking, who manages to be responsive and to make demands within a single turn, and who readily offers up new topics for conversation when required.

Discourse cohesion: building higher-order discourse structures

In the conversational analyses described to this point, we have noted particularly the relations at the lowest levels of discourse, the structure of speech acts making up a turn, and the relations between them. One of the purposes of our analyses, however, was to attempt to capture not simply the relations between adjacent utterances, but the structure of an entire conversational discourse. This involves, as mentioned, the attempt to see how topics are raised, maintained, and dropped, how they are combined to make up episodes, and how the episodes make up a discourse. These analyses are still at an early stage and we have not, to date, assigned a score to every child for every utterance in terms of these scoring schemes. However, we have looked at the conversational structures for 12 children, 6 of whom were judged as good conversationalists and 6 as poorer by our raters. In order to consider how good or poor conversationalists differ in their use of illocutionary force cohesion and semantic cohesion when constructing turns, topics, and episodes, we will briefly describe the analysis of conversational cohesion devised in our laboratory by Barbara Bell.

Illocutionary force cohesion

If we consider the individual speech acts possible in conversation, we note three categories. *Comments* consist of Austin's class of assertions, responses, and acknowledgments, as well as rhetorical questions, all utterances that are ordinarily in the indicative mood. *Directives* are the class of questions and requests that include genuine questions, indirect questions, clarification questions, requests for action, and suggestions. *Turnabouts* are the class of speech acts that incorporate aspects of both comments and directives; they acknowledge the prior turn of the interlocutor and incorporate a directive into a single speech act.

In terms of conversation management, comments, directives, and turnabouts vary in the strength of the contribution each makes to the building of discourse. Assertions and rhetorical questions are not direct responses to the preceding turn and are therefore minimally linked backward. Further, because assertions and rhetorical questions do not demand a response from the listener, they set up minimal expectations for the next speaker to comply with. They do, however, *maintain* the discourse, albeit somewhat weakly. Acknowledgments and responsives, on the other hand, are direct responses to the preceding turn, and are therefore maximally linked backward. They set up minimal expectations for the listener to comply with, however, calling for only an on-topic turn. Directives usually require a response from the listener and therefore set up greater expectations for the listener to comply with than do comments; they are therefore discourse-*facilitating*. Directives are not necessarily linked to preceding utterances, however, and are therefore minimally linked backward to discourse. Turnabouts, as well as responding or acknowledging preceding turns, require a response from the listener. They fulfill the obligations required by the previous utterance, while simultaneously setting up expectations for the listener to comply with, and are therefore stronger conversation-*building* devices than are either comments or directives. Thus, an analysis of illocutionary force cohesion indicates how a speaker maintains and builds conversations by fulfilling his or her obligations as a hearer and by making demands on his or her listener. A summary of this analysis is shown in Table 13.2.

Semantic cohesion

Propositional or semantic cohesion is present when "the interpretation of some element in the discourse is dependent on that of

Table 13.2. *Speech Acts as Illocutionary Cohesive Devices in Conversation*

Speech acts	Degree of effectiveness	Links to discourse	
		Backward	Forward
Comments			
Assertions	Discourse-	Minimal:	Minimal: expects
Rhetorical	maintaining	continues the	an on-topic
questions		discourse	turn
Acknowledgments	Discourse-	Maximal:	Minimal: expects
Responsives	facilitating	responds	an on-topic
		directly to	turn
		discourse	
Compound comments			
Responsive +	Discourse-	Maximal:	Minimal: expects
assertion	facilitating	responds	an on-topic
Acknowledgment		directly to	turn
+ assertion		discourse	
Directives			
Questions	Discourse-	Minimal:	Maximal: expects
	facilitating	continues the	a specific
		discourse	response
Turnabout			
One of responsive,	Discourse-	Maximal:	Maximal: expects
or acknowledg-	building	responds	a specific
ment + one of		directly to	response
question, re-		discourse	
quest for action,			
or suggestion			

Source: Bell (1982).

another" (Halliday & Hasan, 1976, p. 4). An analysis of semantic cohesion therefore investigates the meaning relations between utterances that contribute to the maintenance of a topic.

For this analysis, all utterances are classified as either linked to discourse, linked to the environment, or, where the information is entirely new, unlinked. Utterances are linked to the environment generally by means of exophoric reference, frequently accompanied by a pointing gesture. Utterances are linked to a discourse topic if they express some "given" information, that is, information that has been mentioned at an earlier point in the discourse. These discourse links are classified in terms of Halliday and Hasan's (1976) rules for semantic cohesion, including the use of reference, substitution, ellipsis, conjunction, or lexical cohesion. As we have mentioned, we also treated as cohesive those utterances that were phonologically related to previous utterances.

Through the application of Halliday and Hasan's rules it was also possible to determine to which utterance in the preceding conversation a given utterance was linked. Sentences to which utterances were linked were classified as either immediately or remotely preceding and as generated by self or by other.

In sum, this analysis describes the propositional or semantic cohesive devices that our children use to maintain conversations. While illocutionary force cohesion serves not only to maintain but also to build and facilitate conversations through making demands on the listener, propositional or semantic cohesion serves to maintain conversations through the cohesive ties of the speaker's contribution to those of the speaker's partner. The major devices for maintaining propositional or semantic cohesion are exemplified in Table 13.3. They include pronominal references – exophora and anaphora, conjunctions between and within turns, ellipsis, lexical cohesion, and substitution.

Conversational devices

Conversational devices are linguistic devices that stand halfway between illocutionary-force cohesive devices and semantic cohesive devices. They serve primarily either to introduce a speech act or to respond to a speech act and are composed of illocutionary force without propositional content. We have classified three types: exclamative conversational devices that express attitudes nonpropositionally, such as swearing and other expletives ("Oh, boy"; "Oh, my God"); directive conversational devices that are nonpropositional particles that call for an attentional response from the listener ("*Oh*, there's a square"; "*Hey*, not that"; "*See*, it's a sleeping bag"); and other devices that are politeness markers, such as "please" and "thank you."

We will now describe briefly our preliminary findings on the use of these devices by good and poor conversationalists at the turn, topic, and episode levels.

Turns. As we noted earlier, illocutionary force cohesion tends to operate at the lower levels of discourse structure, namely across and within turns. A detailed inspection of illocutionary force cohesion

Table 13.3. *Example of semantic cohesion analysis*

Conversation	Semantic relation	Relating device
E: You're gonna play a game together . . . and I'm going to go and get the *pieces* . . . so while I'm gone you two can talk to each other . . .	—	—
J: I wonder what *that's* for.	Linked to environment	Exophoric reference – *that*
C: *She's* gonna take a movie.	Linked to environment and linked to discourse (adjacent)	Exophoric reference – *she* Ellipsis – *(with that)*
J: How could *she* take a *movie* with *that* little thing?	Linked to discourse (adjacent)	Anaphoric reference – *she* Lexical repetition – *movie* Anaphoric reference – *that*
C: *It's* a movie camera.	Linked to discourse (adjacent)	Anaphoric reference – *it* Lexical collocation – *movie camera*
J: *Then* where's the *movie script*?	Linked to discourse (adjacent)	Linking conjunction – *then* Lexical collocation – *movie script*
C: I don't know. :	Linked to discourse (adjacent)	Ellipsis – *(if it's a movie camera)* Ellipsis *(where the movie script is)*
J: I wonder what *the pieces* are . . . *ah*, do we have to check our eyes or something?	Linked to discourse (remote) Unlinked (new topic)	Lexical repetition – *the pieces* No relating device (Conversational device – *ah*)
E: Do you know what you wanna build?	—	—
J: A house. :	Linked to discourse (adjacent)	Ellipsis – *(I want to build)*
J: I'll make the *door* . . . this will be the *front* . . . you make the back *one*.	Linked to discourse (remote) Linked to discourse (adjacent) Linked to discourse (adjacent)	Lexical collocation – *(house–door)* Ellipsis – *(front door)* Nominal substitution – *one*

for six good and six poor conversationalists in our subject sample suggests that good conversationalists tend to respond more often to the illocutionary force of the previous utterance, fulfilling expectations somewhat more often (95%) than do poor conversationalists (89%). Further, our good conversationalists used a higher proportion of turnabouts (25%) than did our poor conversationalists (11%). Consider L's utterance in the following example, which is typical of a good conversationalist:

K: Does your mother have blue eyes?
L: Yeah . . . does yours?

Thus L not only fulfills the expectations set up by K, but also sets up new expectations for K. An example typical of one of our poor conversationalists:

G: Is he your friend?
J: Yeah, course he is.

J fulfills G's expectations but does not set up any new ones. This finding confirms the observed correlation between turnabouts and conversational skill reported in the analysis on the full sample of 29 children.

In addition to using more turnabouts, our good conversationalists made greater demands on their partners through the use of simple directives (9.5%) than did our poor conversationalists (1.6%). Again, good conversationalists seem more likely to set up expectations that make demands of the listener and thereby control the conversation. Poor conversationalists, on the other hand, produced more utterances that were simple acknowledgments (23.1%) than did good conversationalists (16.3%). Thus, poor conversationalists seem to fail, not at meeting the demands set up by their conversational partners, but at setting up expectations for following turns. Our good conversationalists, then, appear to take control of their conversations through utterances that are turnabouts and simple directives.

With regard to semantic cohesive devices, we have so far been able systematically to investigate only the use of conjunctions as cohesive elements. We find that our six good conversationalists use more coordinate conjunctions both within turns – that is, as clause links – and at the beginning of turns – that is, as turn links. Hence, utterances like the following are typical of good conversationalists:

P: . . . *but* we need people in it *or* else it will look ugly.
S: . . . *and* we're not going to put Granny . . . like that's one house *but* no Granny.

The structural device of using coordinate conjunctions is thus important for stating the logical relationship not only between clauses within a turn but also between clauses across turns. Across turns, conjunctions mark an on-topic contribution of a speaker. Further, they specify the logical relationship to the preceding utterance.

In addition to these cohesive links, we find that good conversationalists also use more psychological verbs in their utterances than do poor conversationalists. One reason that psychological verbs may be used in conversation is that, as polite forms, they are a means of increasing listener options. Consider the following examples:

G: Wonder what they're doing.
A: Remember, she said, "Nothing silly."

These apparent assertions are in fact polite ways of making demands on the listener. But this indirectness has an interesting conversational effect. When stated indirectly, these requests have a weaker illocutionary force; they do not require an answer or a response in the same direct way that simple directives do. And so we find that they are less likely to elicit responses from poor conversationalists than would a direct question or request. Consider G's unsuccessful attempts to elicit a response from J:

G: Know what they're gonna do?
J: [11-second pause]
G: I wonder what they're gonna do.
J: [25-second pause]

J, one of our poorer conversationalists, does not respond until G resorts to a more direct request:

G: Say "talk out nice and loud."
J: Talk out nice and loud.

So while these polite forms allow more freedom to the listener, such freedom may frequently result in no response at all, particularly from poor conversationalists. We shall return to the use of psychological verbs in the raising of topics.

Our preliminary investigation of cohesion at the level of the turn has, we believe, revealed some of the devices good conversationalists use in building and maintaining a discourse. We now consider how such devices may be used at the next level of structure, namely, the establishment and maintenance of topics.

Topics. Topics in our conversational samples are of three major types: those that refer to immediate objects in the environment, those that are based on events stored in memory, and those that are based on created events generated by either or both of the interlocutors. In this section, we will describe differences between our six good and six poor conversationalists in the introduction and maintenance of topics.

First, good conversationalists attempted to find common topics. Once raised, good conversationalists also tended to sustain them over several turns. On the other hand, poor conversationalists raised fewer topics, sustained them for fewer turns, and had more and longer temporal delays when the attempts to raise topics failed. Not only were good conversationalists more likely to introduce new topics without delay, they were also more likely to interrupt their partners or begin simultaneously with their partners when introducing new topics. This situation can be construed as a struggle for the right to determine the topic; it is as if good conversationalists had more to say than the time allowed.

Further, when good conversationalists changed topics they more often used directives that are suggestions ("Let's do X"), directives that are indirect questions ("I wonder X"), and comments that are assertions preceded by a psychological verb ("I know X"; "I think X"). All these forms seem to function as polite forms; they invite a response but give the listener greater options in how to respond. This may be a particularly effective device for engaging the listener in conversation at the point of a topic change. The listener is invited to respond but has the greatest options available, from an on-topic response to a response that changes the topic altogether.

Finally, in the early free speech segment better conversationalists raised more concrete topics but not more remote topics. This strategy may be an attempt quickly to find a common theme where communication could be readily established. In the later, Lego portion of the transcripts, good conversationalists raised more remote topics than did poor conversationalists. So our good conversationalists introduced more remote topics overall, but a higher proportion of these were raised later in the discourse. This tendency may reflect some sensitivity on the part of good conversationalists to the establishment of a stronger intersubjective base over time.

Episodes. In his analysis of the interactions between 2-year-olds and adults, Roger Brown (1980) reports that episodes break down when the child makes an irrelevant response. At these points, the continuity of the conversation is broken. Our episodes were not defined by a failure to respond: In our conversational data, episodes changed when a new topic, semantically unrelated to the preceding one, was launched by one of the participants and responded to by the other. If the attempt to change topic was ignored – that is, if the listener continued the preceding topic – we considered the utterance an interruption of the episode. If the attempt was followed by a pause of 10 seconds or more, we considered the utterance an attempt that failed. Hence, if a child failed to respond to a direct question or direct request, the conversation would break down. However, where speaker expectations were less strong, episodes could change without a real breakdown in communication. Consider the following example:

s: I knew he's out of breath he like heh-heh out of breath.
p: (He-he-he-he) . . . he puff up and down.
   [Episode break]
s: *Hey*, how do you like the house so far?
p: Yes . . . we need a back door, too.

This transition occurred smoothly and without any breakdown in the conversational exchange.

That episode boundaries were conspicuous not only to the analysts but also to the participants is reflected in the fact that requests for repair occurred most often at episode boundaries. When the topic was introduced in the form of an assertion, essentially out of the blue, it was more likely to be followed by a "What?" or some other request for repair. This was particularly true when the assertion was not introduced with a signaling device such as "Hey" in the above example. When such attention-getting devices were employed, calls for repair were less frequent. Typically, any request for clarification was fulfilled and communication between partners then continued.

In some cases, the end of an episode was marked by extended silence that clearly marked discrete episodes in the conversation. As with topics, good conversationalists tended to launch new episodes with a minimum delay, as in the example above. Consider the following series of unsuccessful attempts to launch an episode:

g: You know what they're gonna do . . . they're gonna take pictures of us with that thing. . . .
   [11-second silence] [Episode break]
g: I wonder what they're gonna do.
   [36-second silence] [Episode break]
g: It's almost recess.
   [5-second silence] [Episode break]

G: They're gonna take pictures of us . . . look.
[Episode break]
E: No whispering – I can't hear you . . . talk up nice and loud.
J: OK.
G: [Laugh] Say, "Talk out nice and loud."
J: Talk out nice and loud.
[Episode break]

Although the first few utterances illustrate G's attempts to elicit a response on a semantically related topic, because J fails to respond within a reasonable length of time G advances alternative topics. Note again the form of utterance that finally elicited a response from J. His first turn, consisting of a rhetorical question and an assertion, failed to get a response. The second turn, consisting of an indirect question, also fails, as do the two following assertions. G finally uses an utterance that has a more demanding illocutionary force, a direct request for action, "Say, '*X*,'" and it is with this speech act that he finally elicits a response from J. Consider the following successfully launched episode from the same pair of children:

TOPIC 1
G: Is Quinn your brother?
J: No.
G: Is he your friend, right?
J: Right.
G: Is he your friend?
J: Yeah, course he is.

TOPIC 2
G: He used to go to Beaver's with me . . . you used to be in Beaver's? Yeah, I think you used to, you . . .
J: He, I know he used to be in Beaver's.
G: I quitted Beaver's when I when I was six.

TOPIC 3
G: I'm still six.
J: I'm still six, too . . . before, before I was –
G: . . . when I – when I was four – } [simultaneously]
J: Before I was five, now I'm six.
G: I'm six, too.
[Episode break]

In this example, G's initial attempt at launching a topic utilizes a yes–no question and successfully elicits a resonse from J. Within this episode G introduces a continuous series of three topics with some aspects that are semantically related; the predicate of one becomes the subject of the next. "Quinn" is established as the subject of topic 1. The "he" in G's first utterance in topic 2 establishes a semantic link by anaphoric reference, to "Quinn," at the same time as it introduces a new predicate, "Beaver's," which becomes the new topic 2. The "six" in the first utterance of topic 3 links that utterance to the immediately preceding one through the use of lexical repetition. Note that G, a good conversationalist, failing in his more polite, indirect attempts to engage J in conversation, resorts to direct requests and yes–no questions and is thereby more successful at establishing a common topic. Once this is established, G is able to resort again to the conversationally weaker but more polite form of assertions with which he began. Note also that once a common topic is established, G, like many of our better conversationalists, keeps the conversation going by quickly launching new topics that are semantically related; hence, he shifts the topic rather than abruptly introducing one potentially unknown to the listener. Note finally that G, typically of good conversationalists, first attempts to launch the episode with two indirect questions introduced by the psychological verbs *know* and *wonder*. Not only does an expression like "I wonder what they're doing" give the listener more than one option for his reply – from no response at all to a lengthy exposition – it also invites a discussion about feelings or thoughts on the topic.

Conclusions

What can we say in general about children's conversations and about the features that make up successful oral conversation? Children, presumably like adults, generate speech acts that are linked to adjacent speech acts via illocutionary force cohesion – questions draw answers, commands draw responses, and comments draw acknowledgments and other comments. But in addition, adjacent pairs of utterances are linked via the propositional content to form and maintain topics. Often these adjacent pairs of utterances maintain the topic of the preceding utterances for several turns. Alternatively, the precise topic is not preserved, but the topic slides or shifts moderately – from Quinn to Beaver's to birthdays – to make up a series of related topics within an episode. Alternatively, the episode may end and the children will fall silent or raise another topic to begin a new episode. These topics are drawn from a restricted set; most frequently they come from the immediate environment – eye charts, microphone, the Lego blocks, and so on. Or they come from some shared background knowledge – things that happened in school or are planned for after school, people they both know such as the teacher or, as we saw, Quinn. Finally, rather than recall a shared episode, they may construct a new episode through role playing, singing, or being "silly." Some of these playful episodes create the topic for talk, and sometimes all they require from the interlocutor is appreciation in the form of a laugh. By means of these immediate topics, remote topics, and created events, many of the children easily keep the conversational interaction moving.

Although all children used basically these same sets of structures, the good conversationalists tended to use some devices more than the less successful conversationalists. At the turn level they were more likely to generate speech acts that set up particular expectations in their listener, and ordinarily they complied with the expectancies set up for them. They semantically linked their contributions to those of their partner through a variety of cohesive devices. Exemplary was their use of conjunctions to link their utterance to that of the previous speaker – "but what if . . . ?" – and simultaneously to connect their own speech acts within a turn.

At the topic, episode, and discourse levels the good conversationalists put more turns into a topic and more topics into an episode, and they switched easily, usually via what we have called conversational devices, from one episode to the next. Indeed, many of the good conversationalists announced more topics than were picked up. There was considerable vying for establishment of topics; sometimes the other speaker was ignored while a child tried through a second or third turn to get their topics launched.

Thirdly, good conversationalists tended to use language more for the expression of thought than simply for requesting and commanding. Indeed, this is what seems to be most characteristic of development. If we consider a sample of conversational interaction reported by Brown (1980) between a 2-year-old and an adult, we find that adults keep the conversation going primarily through the use of what we have called directives and turnabouts. These devices, as we pointed out, have strong illocutionary force – they require responses. With our first-grade children, especially the more skilled conversationalists, we find fewer directives and more indirect requests, assertions, and comments. And as we noted, they introduced their indirect questions with such psychological verbs as *wonder, think, guess,* and the like, especially to introduce new topics. Earlier we mentioned that this indirectness may be in the service of politeness. But these devices may have a second, perhaps more important purpose; they take the emphasis off action and put it onto thought. Introducing topics by saying, "I wonder . . . ," as opposed to the direct question "What is . . ." invites the discussion of ideas and feelings as opposed to the simple reporting of facts. Good conversation, then, is not simply a matter of learning to control the discourse through strong illocutionary force devices such as direct questions and commands, as we had thought at the outset, but rather of exploring the possible semantic relations between ideas. It is through the development of such conversations that language becomes an important instrument of thought.

What, finally, is the relationship between oral language competence and early reading skill? First, we believe we measured two somewhat different aspects of oral language, the first having to do with the semantic and syntactic structures of the language and the second with the conversation or discourse aspects of language use. The first aspect may reflect the logical dimension of language use, that use of language presumably specialized in literacy. The second may reflect the more social or interactional dimension of language use, presumably that use of language of primary relevance to oral conversation. Our hypothesis about the relationship to reading has been borne out — namely, those children more skilled in handling the semantic and syntactic structures of language, particularly cognitive verbs and subordination, are indeed better able to cope with early reading. Skill in turn taking and holding up one's end of a conversation, on the other hand, does not relate to success in learning to read. Nonetheless, these conversational skills, while apparently not related to literacy, do vary greatly in children and make up an important part of oral competence.

These findings are based on a small set of data from a narrow range of oral tasks. Before our findings can be of general theoretical or practical value, they must be deepened and generalized. We will subsequently continue to examine the relationships that are beginning to emerge and to look for developmental changes in the oral language skills in our sample of children. By doing so, we hope to find the ways in which oral language competence changes in the early years of school and how it is related to the acquisition of literacy skills.

REFERENCES

Austin, J. O. *How to do things with words.* Ed. J. O. Urmson. New York: Oxford University Press, 1962.

Bell, B. Analysis of cohesion in the oral conversational discourse of primary school children. Typescript, Ontario Institute for Studies in Education, 1982.

Benson, J. D., & Greaves, W. Field of discourse: Theory and application. *Applied Linguistics*, 1981, 2(1), 45–55.

Bernstein, B. *Class, codes, and control.* (Vol. 1). London: Routledge & Kegan Paul, 1971.

Bierwisch, M. Utterance meaning and mental states. Typescript, Zentralinstitut für Sprachwissenschaft der Akademie der Wissenschaften der DDR, 1979.

Brown, R. The maintenance of conversation. In D. R. Olson (Ed.), *The social foundations of language: Essays in honor of Jerome S. Bruner.* New York: Norton, 1980.

Dore, J. Children's illocutionary acts. In R. O. Freedle (Ed.), *Discourse production and comprehension* (Vol. 1). Norwood, N.J.: Ablex, 1977.

Variation in preschool children's conversational performances. In K. E. Nelson (Ed.), *Children's Language* (Vol. 1). New York: Gardner Press, 1978.

The pragmatics of conversational competence: Two models, a method, and a radical hypothesis. Typescript, Baruch College and the Graduate Center, City University of New York, February 1980.

Dore, J., & McDermott, R. Linguistic indeterminacy and social context in utterance interpretation. *Language*, 1982, *58*, 374–398.

Gregory, M., & Malcolm, K. Generic situation and discourse phase: An approach to the analysis of children's talk. Typescript, York University, 1982.

Halliday, M. A. K., & Hasan, R. *Cohesion in English.* London: Longman, 1976.

Kaye, K., & Charney, R. How mothers maintain "dialogue" with two-year-olds. In D. R. Olson (Ed.), *The social foundations of language and thought: Essays in honor of Jerome S. Bruner.* New York: Norton, 1980.

Olson, D. R. From utterance to text: The bias of language in speech and writing. *Harvard Educational Review*, 1977, 47(3), 257–281.

Olson, D. R., Bell, B. J., & Torrance, N. G. Discourse cohesion in first grade children's conversations. In G. Ewing, S. Ehrlich, & S. Embleton (Eds.), *Focus on discourse: Papers in honor of H. A. Gleason.* Toronto: Department of Linguistics, University of Toronto, 1983.

Olson, D. R., & Hildyard, A. Writing and literal meaning. In M. Martlew (Ed.), *The psychology of written language.* New York: Wiley, 1983.

Quirk, R., Greenbaum, S., Leech, G., & Svartvik, J. *A grammar of contemporary English.* London: Longmans, 1972.

Robinson, E., Goelman, H., & Olson, D. R. Children's understanding of the relation between expressions (what was said) and intentions (what was meant). *British Journal of Developmental Psychology*, 1983, *1*, 75–86.

Searle, J. *Speech acts: An essay in the philosophy of language.* Cambridge: Cambridge University Press, 1969.

Intentionality and the use of language. In A. Margalit (Ed.), *Meaning and use*. Boston: Reidel, 1979.

Vendler, Z. Say what you think. In J. L. Cowan (Ed.), *Studies in thought and language*. Tucson: University of Arizona Press, 1970.

Wells, G. The language experience of five-year-old children at home and at school. Typescript, University of Bristol, 1980.

Some antecedents of early education attainment. *British Journal of Sociology of Education*, 1981, 2, 181–200.

14

Oral–written differences in the production and recall of narratives

ANGELA HILDYARD and SUZANNE HIDI

Possible differences between oral and written discourse have interested a wide range of researchers in educational, linguistic, philosophical, psychological, sociological, and developmental fields. This work has addressed the structural relationship between oral and written language (e.g., Chafe, 1982; Hildyard & Olson, 1982a; Tannen, 1980; Vachek, 1976), differences in the recall and recognition of spoken and written language (Hildyard & Olson, 1982b; Sachs, 1974), the production of written versus spoken language (Bereiter & Scardamalia, 1980; Chafe, Chapter 6; Hidi & Hildyard, 1983; Hildyard & Hidi, 1982), and the development of written and oral competencies (Ehri, Chapter 16; Olson & Torrance, 1981; Torrance & Olson, Chapter 13; Wells, Chapter 12).

The focus of the present chapter is on differences between the written and oral productions of children who are still acquiring literate competency. Essentially, we have asked two main questions: Are there structural differences between the written and oral productions of elementary school students? and Are there differences in what is stored mentally when one speaks as opposed to when one writes? To answer these and several related questions, we conducted a series of studies with children in grades 3, 5, and 6. However, before discussing these studies, we would like to present a brief analysis of the theoretical issues as we see them.

Structural differences between oral and written language

The idea that there are structural differences between oral and written language is not new and can be traced at le st to Locke (1690/ 1961) and Sprat (1667/1966), if not to the ancient Greeks (see Goody & Watt, 1968). In describing structural differences, Olson (1977) for example, has argued that "to preserve verbal statements in the absence of a writing system such statements would have to be biased both in form and content towards oral mnemonic devices. . . . language is thus shaped or biased to fit the requirements of oral communication" (p. 263). Goodman and Goodman (1977) have looked at written language, arguing that "written language can be polished and perfected before it is read: therefore it tends to be more formal, deliberate and constrained than oral language" (p. 322). However, these views differentiate language not only in terms of structure, but also in terms of the intended function of the discourse. That is, some of the clearest structural differences emerge when one compares oral conversations with written expository texts. Unless one keeps in mind that some genres are more appropriate for some kinds of communications than are other genres, then structural differences can be attributed to modality when they should, more rightly, be attributed to intent or function (cf. Tannen, Chapter 7).

Even allowing for differences in function, Chafe (1982, Chapter 6) has recently argued that written and spoken language have two basic structural differences. Firstly, spoken language tends to be fragmented, whereas written language has a more integrated quality. Secondly, spoken language always assumes a social context and social involvement, whereas written language may be more detached. Tannen (1980) has expanded these distinctions further by arguing that cohesion in written language is signaled primarily through lexical devices such as conjunctions, whereas in oral language cohesion is signaled by paralinguistic or nonverbal means.

Unfortunately, some recent studies in which discourse types have been constant did not support these distinctions. Gould (1980), for example, was unable to detect any structural differences between business letters written by adults and similar letters that they dictated. Bereiter, Scardamalia, and Goelman (1981) reported very similar data for children, namely, that when discourse type is kept constant, few qualitative differences existed in children's dictated and written productions. We shall return to the question of a possible interaction between discourse function, modality, and discourse structure in our final discussion.

Next, let us turn to the effect of modality not upon the product, but upon the stored representation of that product. In studies with adults and children, Hildyard and Olson (1982b), Horowitz (1968), and Sachs (1974) all reported that the recall of what children read is qualitatively different from the recall of language they hear. Hildyard and Olson (1982b), for example, found that 9- and 14-

year-olds who read a short narrative were able to recall more nonessential information than students who had heard the same narrative. Further, the readers were more accurate in differentiating what was stated explicitly in the narrative from what reasonably could be inferred. It would seem, then, that readers are able to capitalize upon such qualities of written language as permanence, self-pacing, visual imagery, and so on and thereby store more of the surface features of the text. However, Kintsch et al. (1975) have reported finding no differences in the recall of material read as opposed to heard. One question we examine in this series of studies is whether differences will emerge if the comparison is between a writer recalling what he or she has written and a speaker recalling what he or she has spoken. That is, to what extent does the modality of production influence what is stored in the memory of the producer?

The analysis of children's oral and written discourse

The studies that we report were conducted over a three-year period. An assumption on which these studies are grounded is that the production and recall of discourse is guided by schemata (cf. Schallert, 1982; Kintsch, 1982) some of which may be highly specialized toward a specific modality. For example, the schema we have for friendly conversations with a colleague presumably are biased toward including or relying upon oral properties of conversation such as the social setting, the opportunity to use nonverbal cues, and conversational maxims (Grice, 1975; Lakoff, 1977) that are primarily oral in nature. Correspondingly, some schemata are biased toward writing, a prime example being expository texts that necessitate an internally coherent, logical structure (Olson, 1977; Widdowson, 1978).

By the time children begin school, they are already fairly competent in producing oral forms of discourse that satisfy adult standards for communication in this modality (Ervin-Tripp & Mitchell-Kernan, 1977). We take this competence to show that school-aged children have well-developed schemata for oral production. However, these same students often cannot produce written discourse of the same standard. This suggests that some aspects of these schemata for written production are undeveloped. Some devices are specific devices for integrating texts, such as conjunctions and the like, as well as higher-order schemata for such genres as descriptions, instructions, and the like. Comparing the oral and written productions of a

Planning

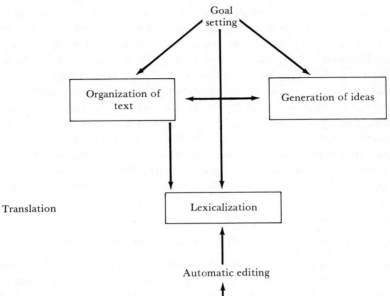

Figure 14.1. Model of discourse production. (Based on Flower & Hayes, 1979, and Kintsch, 1980.)

particular genre may help identify both common and unique facets of each of these partly overlapping schemata.

The particular model of general discourse production we have chosen to adopt was first developed by Flower and Hayes (1979) and subsequently expanded by Kintsch (1980). Essentially, the model has three major phases: planning, translating, and reviewing (see Figure 14.1). During the planning phase, the student/writer generates ideas and organizes the text. These operations, together with the phases of translation and reviewing, occur interactively and are under the control of a goal-setting component. The generation of ideas is constrained both by the topic of the discourse and by the intended audience. The effect of these constraints is to guide the search of the knowledge base, which is assumed by Kintsch to be some form of propositional network.

Constraints are also placed upon the organization process. One constraint derives from the content, that is, the set of ideas retrieved or developed by the generation process. Another constraint is due to the specialized rhetorical strategies associated with the particular discourse type. The output of the organization phase is a text structure "ready to be put into words by the translation process" (Kintsch, 1980, p. 19). The end product of the translation process, the discourse, is subjected to editing, of which there are assumed to be two forms: automatic editing, which takes place at any time and which interrupts other ongoing activities if necessary, and a more formal systematic review, which is normally done after the completion of a unit of discourse.

Given these stages in the development of a piece of discourse, our concern is with the effect of modality upon the various subprocesses. Flower and Hayes were mainly concerned with characterizing the writing process of the competent writer; similarly, Kintsch, in further developing the model, was concerned with writing. Thus, the model is assumed to represent the major stages in the production of written discourse. However, it seems plausible that many of the same operations are involved in producing oral monologues. In particular, regardless of modality, the person must generate ideas, organize the discourse, translate the product into actual words, and so on. However, the intended modality of the discourse may affect the implementation or the operation of these various components, and examination of oral and written productions could provide clues as to which, if any, of the major stages of production are modality-sensitive. For example, differences that occur in the content of written discourse as opposed to oral discourse may suggest that the generation of ideas is modality-sensitive; differences in logical structure could reflect a sensitivity of the organizational component to modality; and so on. In our first two studies we have looked at three specific components, namely, the generation of ideas, the organization of text, and lexicalization (or translation) to determine whether modality affects discourse production. We have not focused on editing since it has been well documented – for example, by Nold (1981) and Bracewell, Bereiter, and Scardamalia (1979) – that children rarely voluntarily engage in high-level revision. The first study was designed primarily to determine the nature and extent of qualitative differences in the oral and written narrative productions of children in grades 3 and 5. The second study looked at the difference between the oral and written narratives of a slightly older age group.

Study 1. "Once upon a time": the oral and written narratives of grade 3 and grade 5 students

Children in the elementary grades are usually quite willing to write narratives.[1] However, a visit to the average grade 3 or grade 4 class reveals a large variation in students' ability to generate topics as well as variation in the quality and content of their narratives. Since our primary concern was to compare oral and written forms, we controlled topic, content, and expected audience as far as possible. Thus, all students were given the following introduction: "Once upon a time, in a faraway place, there lived a king who was mean and greedy. One day a stranger knocked at the castle door." They were asked to complete the story in their own words. Twenty grade 3 and 23 grade 5 students produced narratives for us; 10 of the grade 3 and 12 of the grade 5 students spoke their narratives into a tape recorder, while the remainder wrote their narratives. All children were given as much time as they needed to complete their stories. The writers were encouraged to ask for assistance in spelling if necessary.

The protocols were compared on several dimensions:

(a) *Quantitative measure.* The number of words in each protocol were counted with the exception of straight repetition (for example, "the king . . . the king went") and fillers such as "um," all of which were excluded from the oral protocols.

(b) *Cohesion.* Each protocol was rated on a 5-point scale with respect to its overall grammatical and logical structure, on the assumption that cohesive discourse is syntactically correct and lexically appropriate and that ideas follow logically (see Halliday & Hasan, 1976; Widdowson, 1978). A rating of 1 indicated no evidence of cohesion, while a score of 5 indicated that the writer/speaker had an excellent grasp of the rules of cohesion. (It should be noted that we set criteria for cohesion appropriate for grade 3–5 students.)

(c) *Story structure.* It has been well documented by Stein and Glenn (1979), Mandler and Johnson (1977), Propp (1968), and others that it is possible to parse well-formed stories into structural components. Some of the components are thought to be necessary while others are considered to be optional. In reading our protocols, it became apparent that while children may be guided by story grammars/story structure in their comprehension and recall of narratives (Stein & Glenn, 1979; Mandler & Johnson, 1977), they do not necessarily use the same story grammars to guide their production of narratives. For example, we found many examples of narratives that contained only some of the essential components of traditional story grammars. In order to deal with this problem, the oral and written protocols were carefully reviewed, and those elements that were found to occur in more than one individual production were identified. Thus, we included such elements as the elaboration of the initiating event (Who opened the door? How did the stranger look? etc.), a description of states and/or feelings (Was the stranger hungry, poor, sad, etc.? Was the king happy, mad, indifferent?) and so on. All protocols were categorized in terms of these components.

(d) *Story quality.* Stories were rated in terms of a global assessment of their semantic structure. The structural measure identified in (c) above essentially looked at whether particular story components were included without regard for the nature of the interaction of the components in the narrative. However, it is the interaction of the components that enables us to differentiate a good story from a bad story, that is, to assess overall "storylike" quality. All protocols were therefore rated on a 5-point scale: The highest score (5) indicated that the child had included the necessary elements and integrated them into a unified whole.

Summaries of the length, cohesion, and story quality are shown in Table 14.1; a summary of story structure is shown in Table 14.2. As indicated, the written protocols were significantly shorter than the oral protocols. However, few qualitative differences emerged in terms of cohesion, story structure, and story quality. The written narratives were marginally more cohesive than oral productions, but this difference did not approach significance. Similarly, differences in story quality were also nonsignificant. Further, in comparing the proportion of subjects within each grade level who produced the specified narrative elements, the structural *similarities* across the written and oral productions were striking.

Since semantic and cohesive differences did not emerge but the oral protocols were significantly longer than the written protocols, it would seem that our subjects tended to organize their discourse similarly in both modalities but expressed themselves with more words when they spoke than when they wrote. In writing, then, perhaps economy can be achieved through focusing on essential core meaning and eliminating information that serves merely to elaborate upon that central meaning.

ANGELA HILDYARD AND SUZANNE HIDI

Table 14.1. *Comparisons of the oral and written narrative productions of students in grades 3 and 5*

	Grade 3		Grade 5	
	Oral	Written	Oral	Written
Length (number of words)[a]	83	65	164	125
Cohesion[b] (5-point scale: 1 = low 5 = high)	3.2	3.3	3.4	3.9
Semantic well-formedness[c] (5-point scale: 1 = low 5 = high)	2.7	2.6	3.1	3.5

[a] An analysis of variance resulted in significant main effects for grade level ($p < .01$) and for oral vs. written production modes ($p < .01$).
[b] An analysis of variance revealed no significant effects of grade or mode of production.
[c] An analysis of variance revealed a significant main effect for grade level ($p < .05$).

Table 14.2. *Comparison of the proportion of grade 3 and grade 5 students who include specific structural components in their oral and written narratives*

	Grade 3		Grade 5	
	Oral	Written	Oral	Written
Elaboration of initiating event	.5	.6	.5	.3
Description of the states and feelings of the main characters	.4	.3	.6	.6
Central plot	.8	.9	1.0	.9
Consequence of actions and ending	.8	.8	.6	1.0

In terms of the characterization of the discourse production process we presented in Figure 14.1, these data do not provide support for generation and organizational mechanisms that are modality-specific. That the length of the productions differed across the two modalities may indicate either that the translation process is influenced by modality or that the automatic editing process is modality-specific. For this latter case, the writer may institute on-the-spot revisions to the discourse that serve to economize in terms of lexicalization. Our second study was designed to pursue these questions further.

Study 2. "Once upon a time revisited": the oral and written narratives of grade 6 students

Our comparison of the oral and written protocols in Study 1 centred around rather general measures of cohesion and structure.[2] One intent of the second study was to compare protocols with respect to some of the cohesive links such as conjunctions that, Chafe (Chapter 6) and Tannen (1980) have suggested, differentiate written from spoken language. In addition, since Study 1 led us to conclude that writers tend to express similar content as speakers but with fewer words, we decided to conduct more precise analyses of the number of idea units expressed in the productions as well as the range and frequency of occurrence of different lexical units. Finally, we wished to determine if we could replicate our earlier results using a different population of subjects and different story content (brought about by using different story openings).

The subjects in Study 2 were 36 grade 6 students randomly selected from two grade 6 classrooms. As one of the cohesive links we wished to assess was the use of conjunctions, we chose grade 6 children rather than younger ones on the assumption that by age 12 children would have reasonably large repertoires of conjunctions from which to draw (Geva & Hildyard, 1981).

As in our earlier study, each student was given an introduction and asked to continue the story in his or her own words. Half wrote their narratives and half spoke them into the tape recorder. We used five different introductions, which were randomly assigned across children and condition. Each introduction included a central character, a specific quality of that character, and a potential initiating event, all of which were placed into a storylike frame, as follows:

> Once upon a time there was a king who was so greedy that no one really liked him. Very early one morning the king heard someone knocking at his door.

> A long time ago there was a boy who was very selfish. One morning while he was out for a walk he saw something lying by the side of the road.

> Once upon a time there was a fox who was so bad-tempered that he had no friends. One sunny morning the fox heard something tapping on his window.

> There was once a boy who was so friendly that he always had lots of friends coming to visit him. One day the boy opened his door and found someone there crying.

> Many years ago there lived a princess who was so shy that she never spoke to anyone. One day while out in the forest she heard someone making a strange sound.

Several qualitative and quantitative analyses were carried out on the protocols, as follows:

(a) *Number of words.* The number of words in each protocol was tabulated, again excluding straight repetitions and fillers such as "um," "OK," and so on from the oral transcripts.

(b) *Number of idea units.* Each protocol was parsed into idea units, an *idea* being defined as a clause containing a main verb, subject, and object plus modifiers. Our definition of an *idea unit* is very similar to Chafe's (Chapter 6), who also defines it as a clause containing "all the information a speaker can handle in a single focus of consciousness."

(c) *Conjunctions.* Following the scheme of Halliday and Hasan (1976), all conjunctions were categorized as additive, adversative, temporal, or causal. The number of conjunctions within each of these categories was tabulated.

(d) *Lexical units.* We found in Study 1 that while essentially the same structural components were included in both the oral and written protocols, the written protocols were much shorter. We therefore decided to look more carefully at the types of words used in the narratives to see whether certain lexical forms were more prevalent in one modality than in the other. Accordingly, type-token ratios were calculated for all protocols for the categories of noun, pronoun, adjective, verb, and adverb.

(e) *Structural components.* Due to the fact that we used five different story introductions or topics, it was not practical to conduct the same type of structural analysis as was done for Study 1. As an alternative we awarded points for the inclusion of particular story categories. The two categories of the "elaboration of the initiating event" and "description of states and feelings" were collapsed into one, and up to 2 points were awarded for the inclusion of these components. A

Table 14.3. *Comparison of the oral and written transcripts of grade 6 children*

	Oral (N = 18)	Written (N = 18)
Average number of words	151	149
Average number of idea units	19	18
Average number of conjunctions		
Additive	8	5*
Adversative	1.7	.8
Temporal	.5	.3
Causal	1	2.
Total:	11.2	8.1**
Average number of lexical units (number of tokens in parentheses)		
Nouns	17(27)	15(30)
Pronouns	9(27)	10(22)
Adjectives	4(6)	7(10)
Verbs	16(30)	20(33)
Adverbs	3(4)	6(7)
Structural components (maximum score = 8)	5.1	6.8**

*$p < .05$.   **$p < .01$.

further 2 points were awarded for the provision of a central plot or conflict, and another 2 if the child provided a satisfactory consequence or resolution. Finally, up to 2 additional points were awarded to those students whose narratives tied together the structural components – for example, taking account of the fact that the king was greedy, the princess was shy, and so on. Thus, this measure combined the story quality and story structure measures of Study 1.

A summary of the analyses is shown in Table 14.3. As is apparent, we found no significant differences between the 18 oral and 18 written protocols in terms of length, number of idea units, or nature and frequency of the various lexical units. Indeed, the measures are almost identical across the two modalities. Unlike the first study, then, we find that the narrators are expressing themselves in almost the identical number of words and number of idea units as are the writers. Further, the selection of particular word types (e.g., adjectives, nouns) is equivalent across the two modalities.

Our analyses of conjunctions indicated that, contrary to what we expected, there was a greater incidence of the use of conjunctions in the oral protocols than in the written ones. Not surprisingly, the most commonly occurring conjunction was *and*. As has been reported by Ervin-Tripp (1977) *and* is a very common cohesive device in oral language and is often used, together with intonation, as a substitute for the other conjunctive forms. If we delete all occurrences of *and* from the tabulation, we are left with an average of four conjunctions per oral protocol and three conjunctions per written protocol. It would seem, then, that our grade 6 writers were not drawing more frequently upon conjunctions as a substitute for oral language cohesive devices. Rather, we find a significantly higher frequency of conjunctions in the oral protocols.

Interestingly, one measure that did result in significant differences between the two sets of protocols was the analysis of the structural components. Contrary to our earlier findings with younger children, we found that the written narratives received higher structural scores. These data may indicate that it is only by grade 6 that students are becoming sufficiently skilled in writing that they start to be able to capitalize upon features of written language in order to improve the internal structure of their productions. As Chafe (1982; Chapter 6) and others have pointed out, the process of writing is less time-constrained and permits slower, more conscious decision making as well as repeated scanning. These features should facilitate the efficient implementation of the planning and review phases of the writing process. With respect to time constraints, we did permit both our writers and our narrators to take as much time as they needed to complete their narratives. However, the narrators were required to produce the narrative in the presence of an experimenter. Just as long "planning" pauses are not commonly acceptable in conversations, so too we may expect that the children were reluctant to indulge in extensive planning in their oral productions. Of course, some children did engage in long pauses, and in future studies we may look at the relationship between pauses and structure.

With respect to the effect of repeated scanning in writing, contrary to our expectations, we did observe that several children appeared to read through their narratives at frequent points during the production process and often erased parts of what they had written. We did not permit our narrators to listen to what they had recorded.

Another interesting difference between these data and our earlier data concerns the length of the oral and written productions. Recall that in our first study, the oral protocols were significantly longer than the written protocols. In this second study we find that the oral and written protocols are equivalent in length. As Frank Smith (personal communication) has suggested, this may indicate that by grade 6 students are beginning to develop a sense of the amount of information that should be included in a narrative.

In sum, then, this second study indicates that while most of our measures do not show any significant effects of modality, we do find evidence that the organization of the narrative may be affected by modality. Whether this is due to an organization process that is modality-sensitive, to a later editing component that is modality-sensitive, or to a combination of the two is not clear at this point. We shall investigate these issues further in future studies.

So far we have focused on the effects of modality on the production of a narrative. We turn now to the cognitive consequences of these production differences. Specifically, we looked at children's recall of their own productions. Most studies of the effect of modality upon recall have first required subjects to read/listen to some discourse and subsequently retrieve it for free recall, probed recall, or recognition. The findings have tended to indicate that while subjects retain the gist of a piece of discourse after reading or listening to it, readers are better able to recall specific surface features than are listeners. Our third study was intended to determine whether qualitative differences in recall will also emerge in the recall of oral versus written productions. That is, rather than look at differences between reading and listening, we have looked at differences between speaking and writing.

Study 3. Remembering what one has written versus remembering what one has said

Regardless of the effect of modality upon the actual output in the production of discourse, it is the case that writing both permits a slower rate of production and makes available the potential for repeated scanning.[3] To what extent do these two unique features affect subsequent recall? Are written productions recalled more accurately than oral productions? Is the written recall of a written original more accurate than the oral recall of that written original? If one's original production was oral but then one is required to recall it in a written form, does the act of writing down what was said require one to focus more precisely on the original meaning? Such questions permit us to assess differences in the processes involved more precisely than is possible from a simple comparison of the outputs.

Table 14.4. *Percentage of idea units recalled in verbatim and paraphrase forms, together with the percentage omitted plus intrusions*

	WO/WR (N = 9)	WO/OR (N = 9)	OO/WR (N = 9)	OO/OR (N = 9)
Verbatim	36%	18%	21%	14%
Partial verbatim	28	28	20	28
Paraphrase	16	21	21	20
Total recalled	80	57	62	62
Omissions	20	32	40	39
Intrusions	6	11	5	19

Key: WO = written original; WR = written recall; OO = oral original; OR = oral recall.

In order to answer these questions, the 36 grade 6 children from Study 2 were asked to recall their narratives four days after they had originally produced them. Half the writers recalled in a written format and half in an oral form; half the oral narrators recalled orally and half wrote their protocols. All the children were given the appropriate introduction as their only retrieval cue and were asked to recall their story, using the same words as far as possible.

Our analysis of the recall protocols focused essentially on the relationship between the idea units incorporated in the original productions and those in the recall. Using as a basis the analysis of the original protocols into idea units, we looked for the occurrence of these same idea units in the recall. The nature of the relationship was categorized as follows:

Verbatim: The surface form of the idea unit was retained.

Partial verbatim: Some minor nonsemantic differences occurred between the original and the recall.

Paraphrase: The gist of the idea unit was retained but its surface form was modified.

Omission: An idea unit in the original was not retained in the recall.

Intrusion: An idea unit in the recall did not occur in the original.

Table 14.4 shows the frequency of occurrence of each of the categories across the four conditions (written original/written recall; written original/oral recall; oral original/written recall; oral original/oral recall). These figures indicate that, first of all, the children were surprisingly accurate in their recall of the story content four days after the original productions. For all groups, over 60% of the idea units originally produced were recalled. This is in marked contrast to children's recall, over a similar four-day period, of school-type texts that they are asked to read and remember (Hidi, Baird, & Hildyard, 1982). Also shown in Table 14.4 is that the children who both produced and recalled in a written form recalled *significantly more* than the other three groups. Moreover, it is especially interesting to note that the major difference occurred with the verbatim recall. That is, those who wrote both productions were better able to retain the original surface form in their recall. It would seem, then, that the act of writing enhances recall perhaps by enabling students to pay closer attention to surface form.

The data also show that the number of idea units omitted depended on the modality of the original production: Those children whose original productions were oral omitted more idea units than did those children whose original productions were written. What kinds of omissions were the children making? Approximately one-quarter to one-third of the omissions were classed as central omissions; that is, the idea unit that was left out of the recall was considered to be essential to the coherence of the original story (cf. Hildyard & Olson, 1978). The remaining omissions tended to be elaborative in nature; that is, an idea unit that contained elaborative detail would be omitted from the recall. To illustrate, one child's original oral production contained the following: "The King got some gold things. He got a pin, a bowl, a dish, and some jewelry. Later he. . . ." The recall was as follows: "The king got some gold things. Later he. . . ." In other words, the child left out the list of items, which, for this story, simply provided nonessential detail.

Both types of omissions occurred significantly less when recall followed a written original production. This provides support for the suggestion that writing permits one to focus more carefully upon the content and form of the narrative. Not only were the written originals structurally more complete, as shown in Study 2, but the children were better able to recall the idea units contained in them. It would seem, then, that the effect of modality upon initial production and subsequent recall is additive: The written originals are superior, and recall in the written modality is more accurate.

Our final analysis concerned those idea units that were included in the recall but that had not appeared in the original production. Here we found the modality of recall to be important: *More intrusions* occurred for oral recall (on average, 2.7 additional idea units per protocol) than for written recall (on average, 1.0 additional idea unit). In other words, those children required to recall in a spoken form tended to include more new information within their stories.

Table 14.5. *Example of a written original and the child's written recall of that narrative*

Original

Once upon a time there was a fox who was so bad-tempered that he had no friends. One sunny morning the fox heard something tapping on his window. He went to see what it was and no one was there. So he opened the door and saw that there was some bushes rustling. He went over to the bushes parted them and pssst he was got. He stank. He parted the bushes again and saw a skunk with glasses and a briefcase. He said "I am very sorry every time I bend down that happens and I had dropped my pen in the bushes". "Okay". "Now by the way I am an air freshener salesman, would you like to buy some"? "Sorry I already have some". "Well I think you should use it because it smells pretty bad around here. Goodbye sir".

Recall

Once upon a time there was a fox who was so bad-tempered that he had no friends. One sunny morning the fox heard something tapping on his window. He looked out the window and didn't see anything so he opened the door and saw the bushes rustling. He went and parted the bushes and pssst he was got. He ducked then came and parted the bushes again and saw a skunk with glasses and a briefcase and he said, "I am very sorry that always happens when I bend and I had dropped my eraser in the bushes". Fox, "It's all right". "Oh by the way I am a salesman and I am selling air freshener would you like to buy some"? "No I already have some". "That's good because you really need it"!

It is interesting, however, to note that the number of intrusions was greater when the original had also been in the oral form, again suggesting that the act of writing an initial narrative focused students' attention upon the specific content and not simply the gist of the story.

It may be useful to look at examples of the protocols to illustrate some of the points we have been making. Table 14.5 shows examples of written protocols, and it is apparent that very little of the original production has been altered over the four-day period. In Table 14.6, on the other hand, is a narrative from the oral original and oral recall condition. Here we do see some quite substantial modifications. Note, for example, that the child confuses the role of the central character. In the original, the fox is always assumed to be the central character – the one doing the cooking and eating. In the recall the child first starts by having the fox as the central character, then changes to the hare, and halfway through the narrative realizes that it was the fox who cooked the hare and not vice versa. This third

Table 14.6. *Example of an oral original and the child's oral recall of that narrative*

Original

Once upon a time there was a fox who was so bad-tempered that he had no friends. One sunny morning the fox heard something tapping on his window. He jumped up from bed, all of a sudden when he heard, this fox because he was very hungry. He had had a restless night and was eager for something to eat. When he got to the window he found that it was a hare. So he went to the door and invited the hare in for some tea. As soon as the hare reached the door he grabbed and held it with all his might. He put it in the box and kept it there and put some water on to boil. He skinned the hare and then put it in the pot and cut up some vegetables and put them in with the hare and set it into the oven. He let it cook for about an hour, pulled it out, checked it, and it still wasn't done so he put it in again. Finally when he thought it was done he took it out and realized then, (um) that it was a fake, it was a decoy. So by that time he was very mad and ran out of the house and into the woods quickly killed a nearby owl and gobbled it up.

Recall

Once upon a time there was fox who was so bad-tempered that he had no friends. One sunny morning the fox heard something tapping on his window. The fox was hungry after a good night's sleep and he jumped up from his bed to see who was at the door. He found a hare at the door and thinking very smart he invited the hare in for some tea. The hare got in the house [pause] and was invited to sit down, and instead of getting the fox some tea, he prepared a pot with potatoes and vegetables and then When he went to give him the tea, he grabbed at the fox – grabbed at the hare, and put him in the oven. And he let it cook for about an hour and took it out and checked it, and then put it back in – it wasn't cooked. After two more hours, he took it out and found no hare. The fox was very angry by this time and he had been deceived. And it was just a decoy. And he ran outside and seeing yet another hare and quickly killed it and ate it.

study, then, suggests that writing permits a closer attention to structural components and surface form. It is not clear whether the effects of modality are due to a deeper, more detailed, or more precise encoding of the written form or to differential retrieval mechanisms. In order to examine these possibilities, it is necessary to control for either the encoding or the retrieval mechanisms. One way of achieving this control is to develop a recognition task, since such a task provides retrieval cues against which the original productions have to be assessed. Oral/written differences in recognition would therefore indicate encoding that is sensitive to modality. This was the purpose of the final study.

Study 4. Recognizing one's own production

In Study 4, children were asked to differentiate what they themselves had produced from paraphrases, inferences, or compatible propositions derived from their original productions. Our subjects were 20 grade 6 students, 10 of whom were assigned to an oral group and 10 to a written group. The children were given the same five introductions as were used for Studies 2 and 3 and asked either to write or to tell the rest of the story. This part of the procedure was carried out early in the morning. The oral protocols were immediately transcribed, and a team of experimenters then prepared individual student questionnaires. Each unique questionnaire included six questions: Two were of a forced-choice nature, two of the choices being exact statements from the protocol while the other two were paraphrases of those statements; the remaining four questions were presented in a yes–no format, two of them being statements that the child had actually produced while the remaining two sentences were written by us to be compatible with the child's own production. For example, we created inferential statements and summary statements.

The questionnaires were given to the students in the afternoon of the same day. They were simply asked to indicate which of the statements they had actually produced themselves.

Our writers were significantly better (mean score of 5.4 out of a possible maximum of 6) at recognizing their own productions than were the speakers (mean score of 4.4 out of a maximum of 6). More striking are the numbers of children by condition who were completely accurate in recognizing statements they themselves wrote approximately two to three hours previously and rejecting those we had created: Seven of the writers obtained the maximum score of 6, while only two of the children in the oral production group were completely accurate.

It would thus seem that, even controlling for retrieval through the provision of cues, we are still left with oral–written differences. This suggests that the source of the differences may indeed be traced to modality-sensitive encoding. We should point out one caveat in our interpretation, however: Due to practical problems, we required all the children to undergo a written recognition task. Obviously, one control lacking in our study (and one that we do intend to carry out) is an analysis of the effect of asking students to recognize things they said when the choice is presented to them in an oral format.

Summary

One of the main purposes of the series of studies we have outlined in this chapter has been to attempt to delineate and describe in more detail some features of those processes adopted by elementary school-aged children in their production of written discourse. In particular, we have attempted to determine which features of the key production stages of idea generation, organization, translation, and editing—reviewing are unique to the written as opposed to the oral modality.

Essentially, we have found that with 8- to 11-year-olds, that is, children who are still mastering the basics of writing, few differences are apparent between their oral and their written narratives: They write as well as they narrate (or, alternatively, they write as poorly as they narrate). However by age 12, the age at which, perhaps not coincidently, they begin to master formal operations in the Piagetian sense, we begin to notice some structural superiority of written procedures. We have taken these data to mean that during the early grades the processes involved in both oral and written production are generally common to both modalities. The only exception, according to our interpretation of the data, occurs with respect to the editing process: Written language permits more careful and/or more frequent editing than does oral language. However, as children become more competent in written productions, we have argued, they begin to capitalize upon some of the unique features of that modality, with the result that written protocols appear to be better structured than do oral protocols.

We have found that this ability to capitalize upon features of written language by grade 6 is also manifest in children's recall and recognition of what they themselves have produced. According to our data, it would seem that because writing permits closer attention to detail and makes repeated scanning possible, children who write are better able to recall their productions than are children who narrate. In spite of the fact that, in general, overt productions are similar in speaking and writing, the processes appear to be dissimilar, as our recall data show.

We therefore suggest that our subjects' increased sensitivity to what in fact was said (written) in the course of writing as opposed to speaking is one of the major cognitive effects capitalized upon in writing. It appears that in writing, children learn to notice the wording and to develop the ability to examine, vary, and edit their wording in order to make the discourse or text a more precise reflection of the intended meaning.

Each of our four studies involved the production or recall of one particular genre – namely, narratives where, as we indicated in the introduction to this chapter, there is clearly a relationship between genre and modality and between modality and intent. One task facing students is to become aware of which genres are better suited to which modality. More important, however, is the task facing the teacher – namely, to determine whether the skills that result in improved narratives will also result in improved expository prose. We look forward to conducting studies that address this problem.

ACKNOWLEDGMENTS

The research reported in this chapter was funded by a grant from the Spencer Foundation to D. R. Olson, A. Hildyard, and N. Torrance; a grant from the Sloan Foundation to C. Bereiter; and a grant from the Ontario Institute for Studies in Education to A. Hildyard and S. Hidi. We would like to thank David Olson, Carl Bereiter, and Marlene Scardamalia for their continued support and helpful criticism. We would also like to thank Phil Winne for his extensive review of an earlier version of this chapter.

NOTES

1. A more detailed summary of this study can be found in Hidi and Hildyard (1983).
2. A summary of this study can be found in Hildyard and Hidi (1982).
3. A summary of this study can be found in Hildyard and Hidi (1982).

REFERENCES

Bereiter, C., & Scardamalia, M. From conversation to composition: The role of instruction in a developmental process. In R. Glaser (Ed.), *Advances in instructional psychology* (Vol. 2). Hillsdale, N.J.: 1980.

Bereiter, C., Scardamalia, M., & Goelman, H. The role of production factors in writing. In M. Nystrand (Ed.), *What writers know: The language and structure of written discourse*. New York: Academic Press, 1981.

Bracewell, R. J., Bereiter, C., & Scardamalia, M. A test of two myths about revision. Paper presented at the Annual Meeting of the American Educational Research Association, San Francisco, 1979.

Chafe, W. L. Integration and involvement in speaking. In D. Tannen (Ed.), *Cohesion in spoken and written language*. Norwood, N.J.: Ablex, 1982.

Ervin-Tripp, S. Wait for me, Roller-Skate! In S. Ervin-Tripp & C. Mitchell-Kernan (Eds.), *Child discourse*. New York: Academic Press, 1977.

Ervin-Tripp, S. & Mitchell-Kernan, C. Introduction. In S. Ervin-Tripp & C. Mitchell-Kernan (Eds.), *Child discourse*. New York: Academic Press, 1977.

Flower, L., & Hayes, J. A process model of composition (Tech. Rep. 1). Pittsburgh: Carnegie-Mellon University, Document Design Project, 1979.

Geva, E., & Hildyard, A. Children's comprehension and use of conjunctions. Paper presented at the Annual Meeting of the American Educational Research Association, Los Angeles, 1981.

Goodman, K. S., & Goodman, Y. M. Learning about psycholinguistic processes by analyzing oral reading. *Harvard Educational Review*, 1977, *47*(3), 317–333.

Goody, J., & Watt, I. The consequences of literacy. In J. Goody (Ed.), *Literacy in traditional societies*. Cambridge: Cambridge University Press, 1968.

Gould, J. P. Experiments on composing letters: Some facts, some myths, and some observations. In L. W. Gregg & E. R. Steinberg (Eds.), *Cognitive processes in writing*. Hillsdale, N.J.: Erlbaum, 1980.

Grice, H. P. 1975. Logic and conversation. In P. Cole & J. L. Morgan (Eds.), *Syntax and semantics*, Vol. 3, *Speech acts*. New York: Academic Press, 1975.

Halliday, M. A., & Hasan, R. *Cohesion in English*. London: Longman, 1976.

Hidi, S., Baird, W., & Hildyard, A. That is important but is it interesting? Two factors in text processing. In A. Flammer & W. Kintsch (Eds.), *Discourse processing*. Amsterdam: North Holland, 1982.

Hidi, S., & Hildyard, A. The comparison of oral and written productions in two discourse types. *Discourse Processes*, 1983, *6*, 91–105.

Hildyard, A., & Hidi, S. Remembering what you said versus remembering what you wrote: Children's recall of their own oral and written narratives. In A. Flammer & W. Kintsch (Eds.), *Discourse processing*. Amsterdam: North Holland, 1982.

Hildyard, A., & Olson, D. R. Memory and inferences in the comprehension of oral and written discourse. *Discourse Processes*, 1978, *1*, 91–117.

On the structure and meaning of prose texts. In W. Otto & S. White (Eds.), *Reading expository material*. New York: Academic Press, 1982a.

On the bias of oral and written language. In D. Tannen (Ed.), *Spoken and written language: Exploring orality and literacy*. Norwood, N.J.: Ablex, 1982b.

Horowitz, N. W. Organizational processes underlying differences between listening and reading as a function of complexity of material. *Journal of Communication*, 1968, *18*, 37–46.

Kintsch, W. Psychological processes in discourse production (Tech. Rep. 99). Boulder: Institute of Cognitive Science, University of Colorado, 1980.

Text representations. In W. Otto & S. White (Eds.), *Reading expository material*. New York: Academic Press, 1982.

Kintsch, W., Kozminsky, E., Streby, W. J., McKoon, G., & Keenan, J. J. Comprehension and recall of text as a function of content variables. *Journal of Verbal Learning and Verbal Behavior*, 1975, *14*, 196–214.

Lakoff, R. Language and society. In R. Wardaugh & H. Brown (Eds.), *A survey of applied linguistics*. Ann Arbor: University of Michigan Press, 1977.

Locke, J. *An essay concerning human understanding*. 1690. (Reprinted by Dent, London, ed. J. W. Yolton, 1961).

Mandler, J., & Johnson, N. S. Remembrance of things parsed: Story structure and recall. *Cognitive Psychology*, 1977, *9*, 111–151.

Nold, E. W. Revising. In C. H. Frederiksen, M. F. Whiteman, & J. F. Dominic (Eds.), *Writing: The nature, development, and teaching of written communication*. Hillsdale, N. J.: Erlbaum, 1981.

Olson, D. R. From utterance to text: The bias of language in speech and writing. *Harvard Educational Review*, 1977, *47*(3), 257–281.

Olson, D. R., & Torrance, N. G. Learning to meet the requirements of written text: Language development in the school years. In C. H. Frederiksen & J. F. Dominic (Eds.), *Writing: The nature, development, and teaching of written communication*. Hillsdale, N.J.: Erlbaum, 1981.

Propp, V. *Morphology of the folktale*. Austin: University of Texas Press, 1968.

Sachs, J. Memory in reading and listening to discourse. *Memory and Cognition*, 1974, *2*, 95–100.

Schallert, D. L. The significance of knowledge: A synthesis of research related to schema theory. In W. Otto & S. White (Eds.), *Reading expository material*. New York: Academic Press, 1982.

Sprat, T. *History of the Royal Society of London for the Improving of Natural Knowledge*. London, 1667. (Reprinted by Washington University Press, St. Louis, ed. J. I. Cope & H. W. Jones, 1966.)

Stein, N. L., & Glenn, C. G. An analysis of story comprehension in elementary school children. In R. O. Freedle (Ed.), *New directions in discourse processing* (Vol. 2). Norwood, N.J.: Ablex, 1979.

Tannen, D. Oral and literate strategies in spoken and written discourse. Paper presented at the conference Literacy in the 1980's, University of Michigan, Ann Arbor, June 24–27, 1980.

Vachek, J. *Selected writings in English and general linguistics*. The Hague: Mouton, 1976.

Widdowson, H. G. *Teaching language as communication*. Oxford: Oxford University Press, 1978.

15

Development of dialectical processes in composition

MARLENE SCARDAMALIA and CARL BEREITER

Writers often claim that the process of writing plays an important role in the development of their thought. A collection of testimonies to this effect may be found in a special issue of *Visible Language* (vol. 14, no. 4, 1980) devoted to the dynamics of language. In this chapter we want to enquire into the roots of that role and how writing comes to play it. We should make it clear from the beginning that we are not talking about how writing might make one in general a better thinker – through the effects of working with a visual symbol system (Vygotsky, 1978), for instance, or through the mental calisthenics involved. These general effects are probably unresearchable, given the difficulty of separating them from the effects of literacy per se and of living in a literate culture. Rather, we are talking about the direct effect of writing. How it is that thoughts and knowledge are enhanced by writing about them? What makes writing our thoughts different from simply mulling them over in the mind or talking about them with people?

The following points embrace most of the direct cognitive benefits we have found attributed to writing:

1. *The "emperor's new clothes" phenomenon.* Many ideas that we believe to be clear, well worked out, original, and profound are discovered not to possess these qualities as soon as we try putting the ideas down in coherent prose. Writing, more than conversation, seems to force a critical analysis of our own thoughts.

2. *Text organicity.* A developing text is sometimes said to take on a life of its own so that the writer does not quite know what it will end up saying and in fact does not have absolute control over the outcome. In this way thought may diverge creatively from its intended channels.

3. *Revision.* The reshaping of a text through successive drafts produces a corresponding rethinking and evolutionary development of thought.

4. *Sustained thought.* Writing encourages a more sustained and elaborated thought, partly because of the lack of interruption. Even in solitude, however, writing may be important to keep thought moving ahead. Without it, the mind may perseverate on a single point or go off woolgathering. An oral equivalent of the treatise is hard to imagine.

While these may be genuine benefits, none of them, we shall argue, is an automatic consequence of engaging in written composition. They are concomitants of a sophisticated approach to writing that is itself a significant intellectual attainment. When we look at student and novice writers, we are often struck by the opposite of the phenomena noted above:

1. Writing down ideas does not seem to make their inadequacies apparent to student writers. A recent national evaluation described analytical essays written by school-age students as "fragmentary, superficial and cryptic" (National Assessment of Educational Progress, 1981, p. 23).

2. Text organicity implies that certain unexpected turns in the writer's thought are caused, not by wandering off the point, but rather by the need to preserve the unity of the emerging text, with its stance, structure, layers of meaning, and so on. But student writing is frequently characterized by the lack of these qualities (National Assessment of Educational Progress, 1975). In a study by Bereiter, Scardamalia, and Cattani (1981), elementary school students showed only the beginnings of awareness of internal constraints of text that require certain information to preserve coherence while other information is optional. With specially written paragraphs in which the contrast between essential and optional was striking, they reliably selected the optional sentence for deletion, although they did not offer structural reasons for the choice. But in their own texts they showed only a chance level of selectivity in choosing deletable sentences. That this had to do with a lack of organicity in their texts is indicated by the fact that the one subgroup that did show above-chance selectivity consisted of older children whose texts were judged to be tightly knit and who had received explicit instruction in testing for the effects of deletion on coherence.

3. The benefits of reshaping through successive drafts are apparently seldom experienced because of the minimal amount of revision students carry out and because of its concentration on small proof-

reading types of changes (National Assessment of Educational Progress, 1977; Nold, 1981; Scardamalia & Bereiter, 1983).

4. Sustained thought in composition presupposes ability to sustain the composing process itself. This appears to be a serious problem in its own right, and the difficulty in sustaining composition appears in turn to depend to a considerable degree on difficulty in generating content (Bereiter & Scardamalia, 1982). Thought in writing for novice writers seems to be, if anything, prematurely curtailed rather than extended by the writing process (Scardamalia, Bereiter, & Goelman, 1982).

It is indeed worth contemplating the possibility that for most people writing is an impediment rather than an aid to thought. While we have no direct evidence of this, it has been suggested to us continually through comparing what students produce in writing and what they are able to come forth with in interviews and discussions. These oral interchanges reveal substantial pools of knowledge not drawn on in composition. Students appear able to see many possible objections to what they have written, although they do not deal with these objections in their texts (Scardamalia & Bereiter, 1983).

The contribution of writing to thought is quite possibly a contribution enjoyed only by the highly literate few (not even all who could be called skilled writers). In order to discover how the cognitive advantages of writing might be extended to a greater number we need, first, to understand more deeply the process by which these advantages are realized and, second, to understand better the development of these processes in the composing behavior of students. In the present chapter we draw on a number of developmental studies of writing in an effort to make contributions to these two kinds of understanding.

How writing influences or fails to influence thought

The process by which conversation promotes the growth of thought is called dialectic. It occurs when conversational partners holding different opinions strive to reach a mutually agreeable position and in the process advance beyond the level of understanding that either partner possessed at the beginning. Is there an analogous process in writing?

The essential role of give and take in conversation has led a number of people to speculate that thought in writing depends upon an internalized dialogue (Gray, 1977; Widdowson, 1983). The writer, according to this view, plays a dual role, alternately taking the part of each partner in a conversational pair. Through such interchange the benefits of a dialectical process might be achieved by the solitary writer.

Although this internal dialogue theory of the composing process has much intuitive appeal, available evidence does not support it. If internal dialogue were a regular and essential part of thoughtful composition, one would expect to see much evidence of it in the thinking-aloud protocols of expert writers. Expert writers do indeed evidence considerable thought about audience reaction when it is appropriate (Flower & Hayes, 1980), but they seem to approach audience-related problems in the same way that they approach other text problems. That is, they approach them through the normal kind of monologue and not through an internal dialogue.

It seems to us that the dialectical character of composition does not arise from any clear-cut dialogue-like process. Rather, it arises from the conflict between requirements of text and requirements of belief. In trying to resolve such conflicts, both the text and the writer's beliefs are subject to change. In the fortunate case, the change is in the nature of a synthesis, the hallmark of dialectic.

We may think of composition as taking place within a problem space (Newell & Simon, 1972). This psychological problem space may be further thought of as divided into two areas, a rhetorical space and a substantive space. Within the substantive space are worked out problems having to do with the writer's beliefs and knowledge. In the rhetorical space are worked out problems related to the composition itself. If one is asked to write an essay on capital punishment, for instance, and one has not thought very much about this topic, a great deal of the problem-solving effort will be concentrated within the substantive space. It will be concerned with working out one's own views on the topic and bringing in relevant knowledge, experience, emotional reactions, relations to other values one holds, and so on. Apart from these substantive problems, however, there is also the problem of producing a successful essay, an essay that accomplishes one's purpose of convincing readers of the validity of one's position or possibly of inducing the reader to share one's doubts and perplexities about the issue.

One way to compose, a way often recommended in composition textbooks, is to keep the two problem spaces separated. First work out the substantive problems, the result being possession of a set of assertions or facts that are to be communicated, then shift to the rhetorical space and devise the means for expressing them. Such a method of composing, if rigidly adhered to, would effectively exclude the dialectical process described above. Writing would not influence thinking in an immediate way. A dialectical process arises, however, when there is interaction between the two problem spaces. This occurs when rhetorical problems are solved through means that involve changes in substance and where substantive changes – that is, alterations in belief or knowledge – are perceived as creating significant problems in the rhetorical space.

This somewhat esoteric formulation of the dialectical process in composition may be brought down to earth with a variety of familiar examples.

1. Considering why readers might object to, misunderstand, or have no interest in what we are trying to say leads us to discover inadequacies in the substance of our message.

2. Demands of the genre influence content. This is obvious in the example of the research report, where the need to find citations, to state purpose and method, to deal with qualifications in the conclusion, and so forth frequently force substantive changes and developments on us. Less formal genre requirements may also influence content. For instance, the expectation that a business letter will end with some kind of closure may force the writer to think out a next step or a proposed resolution of the issue raised in the letter.

3. Searching for text elements – transitions, examples, definitions, additional reasons, and so on – often drives the writer back into the substantive problem space to develop content further.

4. Problems of word choice, initially motivated by the desire to achieve a certain rhetorical effect, often lead the writer to consider alternate shades of intended meaning, thus altering or sharpening the writer's own understanding of what was intended. Abstract thought may be significantly influenced – sometimes for the worse – by the need, for purposes of convenient reference, to devise brief labels for complex concepts.

5. The mere need to achieve sufficient quantity – to say enough about a major point, for instance, to establish its importance in the mind of the reader – may lead the writer to further development and elaboration of ideas. On the other hand, the rhetorically motivated need to delete or rearrange material may force a substantive reconsideration of priorities.

6. There is a more fundamental way in which rhetorical choices impinge on problems of substance, but it is one that does not lend itself to simple examples. This is through the buildup of internal constraints in text. Explicit statements, definitions, and the like have

entailments that accumulate and increasingly constrain the content of subsequent statements. It is through this buildup of internal constraints, it would appear, that a text is said to take on a life of its own and to develop in unforeseen directions.

The dialectical process implies a real tension between rhetorical and substantive concerns. If one concern predominates wholly, there will not be sufficient tension to lead to a new synthesis. The writer wholly concerned with rhetorical demands and willing to alter substance in any way to meet them becomes the stereotypic Madison Avenue lost soul, producing carefully calculated vacuities. With student and novice writers, however, the imbalance seems to be in the other direction. Belief tends to predominate, and problems of rhetoric are either not recognized or are solved through ploys that leave the substance unchanged.

In a variety of studies we have questioned students about their writing, listened to them composing aloud, or presented them with special rhetorical problems to wrestle with. From these observations we have gleaned a rather formidable list of ways in which student writers manage *not* to come to grips with rhetorical problems. It should not be thought that all student writers display all of the following attitudes or strategies, nor should it be thought that any of these are deliberately intended to avoid problem confrontation. They undoubtedly have a variety of causes and justifications.

1. *A take-it-or-leave-it attitude toward audience.* Students can frequently anticipate audience objections, but they do not recognize it as their responsibility to do anything about them. As one student cogently put it, "Some people won't agree with you no matter what you say."

2. *Willingness to put up with recognized weaknesses in structure or content.* In pilot research carried out by Clare Cattani-Brett, subjects had to compose a story based on a picture showing a man up in a tree and a bear on the ground below standing in the remains of a picnic. The typical story, of course, was of a picnic interrupted by a foraging bear. Subjects were then asked to revise their stories to conform to a second picture that was like the first except that in place of the bear was a harmless looking rabbit. The typical strategy was to keep the original story intact, substituting rabbit for bear and adding some explanation such as that the rabbit had rabies or that the person in the tree was allergic to rabbits. On subsequent questioning, subjects would readily admit that the second story was quite feeble and implausible, but until questioned it did not seem to occur to them that they had any choice but to allow it to be feeble. The story's inadequacies, in other words, were accepted as a natural consequence

of the nature of the task. One may argue, of course, that this is a reasonable attitude to take toward such a task, as it might be to other school writing tasks that students often do in a perfunctory manner (Britton et al., 1975). Reasonable or not, this "low road" approach (Bereiter & Scardamalia, 1983) avoids rhetorical problems that could lead to substantive reformulation if taken seriously.

3. *Poor and vague diagnoses.* Recent studies have shown that while students can frequently detect that something is wrong with a composition, they cannot clearly identify the problem and thus they have difficulty in applying problem-solving strategies to it (Bartlett, 1980; Scardamalia & Bereiter, 1983; Cattani, Scardamalia, & Bereiter, 1981).

4. *Satisfaction with superficial connections.* The search for substantive connection between one idea and another that the writer wants to get to is often a powerful incentive to deeper analysis of content. Novices, however, tend to rely on additive conjunctions (Hildyard & Geva, 1981), juxtaposition (Goldstein & Perfetti, 1979), and superficial linkages that involve little semantic constraint (Paris, Scardamalia, & Bereiter, 1982).

5. *Use of conversational ploys for sidestepping difficulties.* Because of the need to keep up a certain pace in social speech, people develop a variety of devices for quick solution of rhetorical difficulties. When carried over into written composition these conversational ploys have the effect of neutralizing rather than solving the problems and thus avoiding a dialectical process. A common ploy is to treat a counter-example as an exception, without considering its implications. The handy expression for doing this is "well, anyway." Another ploy is the "nod" to opposing viewpoints ("Some people may think . . . but they are wrong") with no further explanation. Perhaps the most common ploy, however, is the topic shift. Whenever a rhetorical difficulty or blind alley is encountered, the topic is shifted. If this is done according to the rules of topic shift in conversation (Schank, 1977) the discourse will remain coherent according to standards of small talk, though generally not according to the standards of prose composition.

6. *Use of the knowledge telling strategy* (Bereiter & Scardamalia, 1983, in press). This strategy, which we find pervasive in student writing, amounts really to a reporting of thoughts. Rhetorical problems are few and typically confined to low level problems of style.

For the most immature writers it seems that the only rhetorical problem that has an impact on substantive problem solving is the problem of quantity. The effort to fill up the page while staying on topic forces an extended search of the writer's knowledge and beliefs on a topic. This is no doubt helpful to writers in the beginning stages of literacy. Donald Graves (personal communication) has noted, in fact, that essays on the theme "Everything I know about . . . " constitute a genre that competes in popularity with the personal experience narrative in the writing of primary grade children. For writing to influence thought beyond this rudimentary level, however, it seems necessary for an internal dialectical process to be set in motion, and for this to occur students must somehow be brought into confrontation with and must persist in attempting to solve rhetorical problems of kinds that have substantive implications.

Inducing thought in writing

Existing school procedures for improving writing tacitly acknowledge that writing does not spontaneously promote thought. One large class of educational procedures goes by the name of prewriting activities. These activities may be quite various, involving discussion, films, readings, drawings or constructions, and the like. Their common function, however, is to provide some sort of stimulus to thought, usually social, so that the student writer need not rely on the composing process itself to provide stimulus to thinking. Other procedures serve to facilitate thinking during the composing process or between drafts of compositions. These include conferencing (Graves, 1978) and peer response (Elbow, 1973). In these cases a definite dialectic process is invoked, but it is a social, conversational one, not an internal dialectical process.

Structured procedures have been developed for working out content in advance of writing – procedures that lead to more extended or analytical thought (Young, Becker, & Pike, 1970; Robinson, Ross, & White, in press; Jones & Amiran, 1980). Through the use of matrices, tree diagrams, or question sequences, constraints and demands are put upon the student's thinking that are presumably not forced upon it by the looser structure of the composition task. Thus, curiously, instead of relying on composition as a means of promoting thought, other devices are introduced to promote thinking, composition itself becoming a straightforward matter of expression. In terms of our earlier formulation of problem spaces, these devices and prewriting activities promote problem solving and constructive thought within the substantive space rather than promoting an interaction between the two problem spaces.

Consequently, the existing school approaches may be seen as external aids that compensate for the lack of a dialectical process in composition. This does not seem to be their intent, however. Rather, the intent is to educate students to become better writers, and this implies that the external procedures will eventually become internalized, that is, incorporated into the student's thought while composing. Such internalization has not yet been demonstrated. Before we can be optimistic about internalization we need to know how the mental processes involved in prewriting activities correspond to those of expert writers. Practicing writers, we assume, seldom actually fill out matrices, ask themselves fixed series of questions, or do anything else of such a formal nature. The question is, however, whether formal prewriting activities are sufficiently analogous to the mental processes of expert writers that they can serve as a means of internalizing dialectical processes. If not, they may serve as a substitute for dialectical processes, but probably only a partial substitute.

A different type of facilitation has been developed recently, which uses external aids explicitly designed to support a simplified version of the processes used by experts, thus providing a basis for internalization. Procedural facilitation, as it is called (Bereiter & Scardamalia, 1982; Scardamalia & Bereiter, in press), is based on research into the composing process that seeks to identify executive procedures used in composition and their main points of difficulty. The simplification and aids that are introduced to help beginners surmount these identified difficulties are ones that can later be deleted and leave intact the executive procedure that has been set in motion.

Two procedural facilitations will be reported. These facilitations aim to boost the level of reflective thought or critical thought that goes on in composition, but to do so without stimuli or aids to thought that stand outside the composing process. Rather, the effort has been to introduce procedures that students can incorporate into their composing processes. These facilitations are of both educational and scientific interest. The educational interest lies in investigating ways of improving thought in writing that have promise of eventual internalization into the writer's own strategic repertoire. The scientific interest lies in the light that is thrown on the composing process through interventions that affect it in certain ways and leave it unaffected in others. The first study deals with aspects of revision. The second study deals with advance planning of compositions.

An attempt to boost problem recognition in revision

Revision is a useful point of focus for research on thought in writing because it can be carried out at a range of levels, from a deep level that involves reconsideration of the whole form and content of a composition up to a superficial level that involves only cosmetic changes (Nold, 1981). Students tend toward the latter end of the continuum (National Assessment of Educational Progress, 1975; Bracewell, Bereiter, & Scardamalia, 1979). With the help of peer feedback, however, students have shown themselves able to carry out quite substantial revisions and rewritings of text (Graves, 1979). Such dependence on external feedback has made it seem that novices may lack ability to view their own compositions from the reader's standpoint (Barritt & Kroll, 1974). A study by Scardamalia and Bereiter (1983), however, suggests that this is not the source of the problem. When elementary school children were given procedural support and finite lists of possible evaluations, they detected inadequacies in their compositions that agreed very closely with the evaluations by an expert of the same compositions. Students were much less able than the expert, however, to diagnose – that is, to identify the cause or locus of these inadequacies. Frequently they detected an inadequacy but elected to do nothing about it.

Such failure to confront problems could be due either to (a) lack of motivation, (b) lack of means for dealing with the problem, or (c) not knowing what the problem was. The last factor rests on the distinction between evaluation and diagnosis. This is the difference between "I feel weak" and "I have a vitamin deficiency." Students demonstrated themselves competent at making the former kind of judgment, but the latter, more analytical judgment escaped them. Bartlett (1980) observed a similar phenomenon with respect to pronoun reference. Students could recognize when something was wrong, but they were unable to pin down the difficulty to an unreferenced pronoun, for instance, and consequently they were unable to produce appropriate remedies. For generations, teachers have tried to circumvent this weakness of students in recognizing what the problems are with the composition through the use of the red pencil, pointing out difficulties, suggesting things needing alteration. But what would happen if students, without being told what the problems are in a text, were assisted with a routine to broaden and intensify their effort to define problems? This question was the focus of a study by Cattani, Scardamalia, and Bereiter (1981).

This study applied the CDO (COMPARE–DIAGNOSE–OPERATE) model of Scardamalia and Bereiter (1983). The three main components of this model are the ones indicated in its name. The COMPARE phase involves detecting mismatch between the mental representation of the actual composition and of the intended composition. This component was facilitated by having the subject read

Table 15.1. *Thirteen phrases on diagnostic cards used to aid experimental subjects in text analysis*

Choppy – ideas aren't connected to each other very well.
Hard to tell what the main point is.
Too much space given to an unimportant point.
The writer ignores the obvious point someone would bring up against what they are saying.
Doesn't give the reader reason to take the idea seriously.
Part of the essay doesn't belong with the rest.
Incomplete idea.
Says something that's not believable.
Says the idea in a clumsy way.
The reader will have already thought of this.
Weak reason.
Too few ideas.
Example doesn't help to explain the idea.

---

through the essay to be evaluated, placing down markers wherever some inadequacy was detected. Subjects placed a green marker if they were sure what the problem was and a red marker if they were not. The focus of the study was on the DIAGNOSE component of the process. Experimental subjects were provided with the 13 cards listed in Table 15.1. Subjects were asked to consider each of these diagnostic cards in turn and to judge whether it applied to the composition and, if so, where – whether to the text as a whole or to a specific part. For practical reasons, the OPERATE phase was reduced to having subjects suggest revisions without actually carrying them out.

The study was run individually on 20 students from grade 6 and on 16 from grade 12, each group evenly divided between experimental and control subjects. The control treatment was the same as that described above, including the placement of markers during the COMPARE phase. But during the DIAGNOSE phase control subjects were simply asked to identify and explain all of the problems they had detected. Each subject diagnosed five essays and suggested revisions for two of them. One of these was an essay previously written by the subject. The other four essays were drawn from a pool of nine grade 6 and 8 essays selected for the number, variety, and representativeness of the inadequacies they contained. Of these four essays, one was the same for all subjects and was presented last. The others were selected randomly and presented in counterbalanced

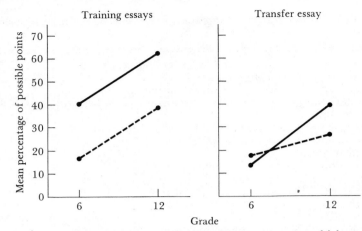

Figure 15.1. Quality of diagnoses, based on extent to which subject's diagnoses agreed with those of professional editor. Solid lines = experimental; dashed lines = control.

orders, along with the self-written essay, which was placed in either the second or fourth position. Subjects suggested revisions for their own essay and also for the final essay. This final essay furthermore served as a transfer test, in that experimental subjects and control subjects alike performed their diagnoses without benefit of the diagnostic cue cards.

Findings

Each of the essays was diagnosed by a professional editor, who generated for each one a list of diagnostic statements. Two independent raters then evaluated the degree of correspondence between diagnoses made by subjects and each item on the expert's list. A score of 3 for a given item on the expert's list indicated that the subject had identified that identical problem, whereas a score of 0 indicated that the subject had failed entirely to mention that particular problem diagnosed by the editor. Figure 15.1 shows quality of diagnosis scores expressed as a percentage of possible points. Thus, 100% would indicate that the subject had identified accurately and thus obtained a score of 3 for each diagnostic statement made by the editor. The combined scores for all four training essays show a significant treatment effect that is common to both grades 6 and 12 ($F_{1,34} = 12.05$, $p < .05$). Quality of diagnoses on the transfer essay,

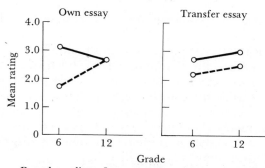

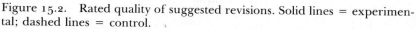

Figure 15.2. Rated quality of suggested revisions. Solid lines = experimental; dashed lines = control.

however, shows an advantage for the experimental group only at grade 12 (F for the treatment effect is 5.59, $p < .05$; F for grade-by-treatment interaction $= 7.97$, $p < .01$). Thus it appears that students at both grade levels made superior diagnoses when assisted by the diagnostic cards, but only the grade 12 students showed transfer to diagnosis without cards.

Quality of suggested revisions was rated by two independent raters using a 5-point scale, with the top rating indicating a revision that the rater would actually have chosen to make and the lowest rating indicating revision that would be expected to make the composition worse. Subjects suggested revisions for only two of the five essays, it will be recalled, their own essay and the transfer essay. Mean quality of suggested revision scores for these two essays are shown in Figure 15.2. In suggesting revisions for their essays, experimental subjects at grade 6 greatly exceed the controls, whereas at grade 12 there is no difference. On the transfer essay there is a difference favoring the experimental group at both grade levels.

There were indications that the experimental treatment served to direct attention to higher-level text units. Among experimental subjects approximately 79% of diagnoses were directed toward sentence, paragraph, or whole text levels, whereas this was true of only 55% of diagnoses among control subjects. Even the latter percentage seems fairly high, however, in view of findings such as those of the National Assessment of Educational Progress (1977). It is quite possible, therefore, that the process of placing markers in the margin wherever difficulties or inadequacies are detected – a process common to both experimental and control groups – may have been effective in raising attention to a higher level of text features.

This study indicates that students can detect and discover solutions for rhetorical problems, given support in the form of a procedure as well as in the form of cues suggesting possible problem specifications. Performance on the transfer task indicates that by grade 12, at least, there is clearly some internalization of the facilitative procedures, which influences both diagnosis and the selection of problem solutions. The improvement at grade 6 in students' ability to suggest revisions to their own essays suggests that there may even have been some internalization at this grade level, even though it was not revealed in an ability to make superior explicit diagnoses without external aids.

An attempt to facilitate reflective thought in composition planning

The following studies dealt with advance planning, that is, with planning before writing of the first sentence begins. Although planning carried out in the actual course of writing should, in principle, be a more promising arena for stimulating dialectical processes, we focused on advance planning instead because prior experience with other procedural facilitations had made it clear to us that when young writers are in the process of writing, almost everything they think of or that is brought to their attention tends to be assimilated directly into the text. The dialectical process, furthermore, is clearly possible in advance planning because the important tension is not that between thinking and writing but rather that between belief and rhetorical concerns, and this can occur apart from the physical production of text.

The facilitative procedure used in the two studies to be reported here required students to think aloud while carrying out the advance planning of compositions. Students took no written notes, and so as much as possible all of their thought in advance of writing was captured in the oral protocol. The facilitative intervention consisted of periodically providing the student with cues in the form of sentence openers that the student was to incorporate into the oral planning protocol (not into the text later to be written). A typical planning cue is "An important point I haven't considered yet is. . . ." In one version of the procedure, the experimenter sat with the student as the student planned aloud and at opportune moments handed the student a card with a sentence opener that the experimenter had chosen as particularly appropriate for inducing the student at that moment to look in a different way at the immediate problem, to branch off in a different direction, to consider a possible audience reaction, or to examine the writer's own feelings more closely.

Obviously, such a procedure has properties of dialogue; yet we would argue that it is more properly thought of as assisted monologue. In fact, the experimenters actively discouraged a dialogue response as would occur if the student reacted to the proffered card as if it were a conversational input from the experimenter. Instead, the student was urged to incorporate the sentence opener into his or her own discourse, if at all possible, and if not, simply to reject the card. The difference between dialogue and assisted monologue is crucial because in the case of dialogue, removal of the assistance means the destruction of the dialogue, whereas in the case of assisted monologue, removal of the assistance leaves the student with normal think-aloud planning intact.

Two studies were carried out investigating the effects of variations in the manner of administering the planning cues. The first study investigated the variable of who selects the planning cues – the experimenter, a peer, or the writer. A second study used randomly sequenced cues comparing the effectiveness of cues compatible with a go-on strategy of composing (Bereiter & Scardamalia, 1981) to the effect of cues that encourage reflection, reconsideration, and self-criticism. The primary motive of these studies was practical – to assess the overall educational promise of the approach and to discover workable means of implementing it. However, the procedural variations are of some interest in cognitive developmental terms also in that they involve a range of amounts of external judgmental input, and thus the results give an indication of the extent to which students are able to function independently in the planning of compositions.

In Study 1 subjects wrote under three conditions:

1. *Experimenter-administered.* This is the condition described above in which the experimenter selected and gave the subject planning cues chosen with a view to raising the level of the subject's reflective thinking about content and purpose. The set of cues is listed in Table 15.2.
2. *Peer-administered.* The same procedure was followed, except that another student selected and administered the cards for the student who was planning a composition.
3. *Self-administered.* Subjects planned aloud without help. Half the subjects were provided with planning cue cards and were

encouraged to use them; half were urged to do the best they could without cards.

Four opinion essay topics were employed in a balanced design, so that a subject never wrote on the same topic twice, nor on a topic that he or she had helped a partner with. The experimenter-administered condition always came first, with the order of subsequent conditions systematically varied. In advance of any of the experimental conditions, however, students were oriented to use of the planning cue cards through a role reversal technique that had been found in pilot investigations to be useful in giving students the idea of what the use of planning cues could do. In the orientation session the experimenter planned an essay, and the student selected and handed the cue cards, being urged to select ones that would help the experimenter to plan a better essay. In this way, students had a chance both to see how the sentence openers could be incorporated into the planning monologue, as this was demonstrated by the experimenter, and to gain an appreciation of the motive behind the whole procedure, as this was experienced through their efforts helping the experimenter.

In the second study, each subject first planned aloud and wrote an essay without any assistance, except for a 15-minute videotape shown in advance that demonstrated the process of planning a composition aloud. Then each subject was oriented to the use of planning cue cards, as in Study 1 and subsequently planned and wrote two essays using experimenter-administered cards. Different sets of cards were used in the two essays, however.

The two sets of cards are shown in Table 15.2. It will be seen that in addition to cards common to both conditions, the "go-on" set contained cues that direct the writer's attention ahead to additional ideas, to elaborations, and so on. It was thought that these kinds of cards would support the common strategy of school-age writers of using inputs as cues for ideas to use in extending their texts (Bereiter & Scardamalia, 1982, in press). The reflective set, on the other hand, contained cues that direct attention backward to what has already been planned, to possible objections and alternatives, and to ways of putting ideas together.

In both cases the cue cards were administered by the experimenter in a prearranged random order. (Half the subjects composed first with "go-on" cards, then with reflective cards; half the subjects used the opposite order, with topics counterbalanced across conditions.) A cue was administered when there was a pause in planning, but without thought to the appropriateness of the cue to what the subject

Table 15.2. *Sentence openers used to facilitate planning under experimental conditions*

Cards: Studies 1 and 2	Study 1 All conditions	Study 2 "Go-on" condition	Study 2 "Reflective" condition
An example of this . . .	X	X	X
I could develop this idea by adding . . .	X	X	X
I could make my main point clearer if . . .	X	X	X
The reason I think so . . .	X	X	X
The way to make readers pay a bit more attention is . . .	X	X	X
My next point . . .	X	X	X
My own feelings about all this are . . .	X	X	X
This reminds me . . .	X	X	X
An even better idea is . . .	X	X	X
My main idea is . . .	X	X	X
A whole new way to think of this topic is . . .	X		X
But many readers won't agree that . . .	X		X
A topic sentence that would show I'm a serious thinker is . . .	X		X
No one will have thought of . . .	X		X
This isn't very convincing because . . .	X		X
An important point I haven't considered yet is . . .	X		X
A good point on the other side of the argument is . . .	X		X
If I want to start off with my strongest idea . . .	X		X
A criticism I should deal with in my paper is . . .	X		X

Table 15.2. (*cont.*)

Cards: Studies 1 and 2	Study 1 All conditions	Study 2 "Go-on" condition	"Reflective" condition
I need some facts to support my argument so . . .	X		
This will lead to . . .		X	
Another idea that's good is . . .		X	
I could explain this better by . . .		X	
What I like . . .		X	
Not only that, but . . .		X	
This could make readers . . .		X	
I'll change that a little by . . .		X	
Readers would like . . .		X	
I don't have enough ideas so . . .		X	

was planning at the time. The main justification for a random presentation was that it permitted isolating the effect of cue content from other variables in the facilitating situation. A resourceful experimenter, given almost any set of cue cards, could probably achieve some beneficial effect by selecting the best possible card at just the right moment. As for the possible disruptive effect of random presentation, subjects were encouraged simply to reject any card that seemed inappropriate at the moment. Given the tendency of normal thought during composition to leap hither and thither (Hayes & Flower, 1980), we did not think it was obvious in advance that a random presentation would be disruptive or useless, and it seemed important for practical reasons to find out whether such a simple and economical procedure could have beneficial results on thought in planning.

Both studies were carried out on randomly selected children from the sixth grade of a single university area elementary school. Sixteen experimental subjects were used in Study 1 and 8 in Study 2. In addition, 20 subjects from the same pool provided control essays on one of the topics used in the experimental studies.

Table 15.3. *Ratings of essays in two studies using planning cues*

Condition	Amount of reflective thought[a]	Overall quality[b]	Quality of individual ideas[c]
Study 1 (*N* = 12)			
Experimenter-administered	1.56	6.81	2.04
Peer-administered	.94	6.06	1.62
Self-administered	.81	5.75	1.79
Study 2 (*N* = 8)			
Unassisted	.94	6.13	2.33
"Go-on" cards	1.56	5.75	2.25
Reflective cards	1.31	6.63	3.00
Control essay comparison			
Classroom control (*N* = 20)	.35	3.98	—
Combined experimental (*N* = 18)	1.19	4.02	—

[a] Scale ranging from −3 to +3.
[b] For Study 1 and Study 2, essays were scored ipsatively; 3 points given to middle essay and 1 to 5 points given to other two essays; average of two independent ratings. For control essay comparison, essays rated on a scale of 1 to 7 points. Scores are therefore only comparable within studies.
[c] Number of high-quality ideas.

Findings

Let us first consider the comparison of essays written by the 20 control subjects, who wrote under normal classroom conditions, with those of 18 of the experimental subjects drawn from the two studies who wrote on the same topic. We have here, then, a comparison of essays produced in a variety of thinking-aloud planning conditions with those produced under normal classroom conditions. Each essay was rated blind by two raters on a scale of −3 to +3, indicating the amount of reflection on ideas demonstrated in the essay. The estimated reliability of the combined ratings was .86 (Spearman–Brown). As is shown at the bottom of Table 15.3, essays by the experimental subjects obtained significantly higher ratings (M = 1.19 vs. .35, t_{36} = 2.07, $p < .05$). Although there were too few essays from each experimental condition to permit a comparison of the separate conditions with control, the fact is that each of the six experimental conditions had a higher mean rating than the control essays.

The same kinds of ratings were also used for within-subject comparisons of experimental treatments, as shown in the upper part of Table 15.3. In Study 1 there was a significant treatment effect ($F_{2,30} = 4.74$, $p < .05$). Newman–Keuls tests revealed that the experimenter-administered condition significantly exceeded the peer-administered and the self-administered conditions, while the latter two conditions did not differ significantly from each other. No significant treatment effect was found in Study 2 ($F < 1$) although the tendency was for the baseline essays to be scored lower than those of the two conditions using cue cards. There was no advantage in reflectiveness ratings favoring the condition using reflective cards, however; in fact, as Table 15.3 shows, the difference, though small, was in the contary direction, favoring the "go-on" cards.

Two other assessments were carried out, the results of which are also shown in Table 15.3. One involved global ratings of the quality of the essays and the other involved ratings of the quality of individual ideas in essays. Neither of these showed any significant differences among conditions or between experimental and control essays. Thus, the effect of experimental treatments and of the experimenter-administered planning cues in particular is apparently to produce essays that show more *evidence of reflective thought* but not superior compositions resulting from this thought.

Our impression, although it remains to be documented, is that for the young writers studied in these experiments there is a trade-off between reflectivity and coherence. Maximum coherence and quality of presentation are achieved by taking a single idea and developing it. Thinking about implications, alternatives, problems, and the like leads these young writers into a more discursive mode of presentation that appears rambling, sometimes even scatterbrained. This is not bad, of course, given that what students are producing as texts are first drafts that could be cleaned up and organized later; but as texts judged in their own right they appear on balance to be not superior to those of children who have gotten along with less preplanning.

Much of the potential interest of these studies lies in the thinking-aloud protocols rather than in the texts themselves. At this writing, however, that work remains to be done. Judging from the evidence of the compositions produced, the use of planning cues does seem to have promoted greater thought in writing and to have done so through means that are potentially internalizable. The superiority of the experimenter-administered intervention indicates that full internalization is not likely to be rapid. It will depend on growth of the knowledge needed for self-monitoring as well as growth of ability for on-line problem recognition.

Conclusion

From both the testimony of sophisticated writers and what they reveal through thinking-aloud protocols (Flower & Hayes, 1980), we know that writing can be intellectually very demanding, requiring attention to both rhetorical and substantive issues. Our contention in this chapter has been that it is the tension between these two kinds of problems that leads to the deepening of reflective thought through writing. On the other hand, most of the problems of writing can be avoided without disaster. Readers tend to be tolerant and resourceful and can go to great lengths to make up for the inadequacies of the writer. Minimally adequate writing has a low processing demand (Bereiter & Scardamalia, 1984).

When writing is simply a process of assembling knowledge, there is no dialectical process involved, and there is consequently minimal development of knowledge and understanding in the process of composition. The main point of our chapter has accordingly been that the dialectical process in writing that leads to the deepening of reflective thought is not an automatic consequence of experience in writing. It is an achievement. The achievement of dialectical processing in writing, furthermore, would appear to be not only a cause of, but also the result of, reflective thought during composition.

Reflectivity accordingly is both means and goal in learning to become a writer. Nature has ways of solving such chicken-and-egg problems, but in the case of writing it appears that for far too many students, novices, and ordinary people the solution is not achieved and that writing does not serve as a dialectical process for the growth of knowledge and understanding. The experiments reported here offer some encouragement to the view that nature can be assisted in developing the processes that lead to reflection.

ACKNOWLEDGMENTS

We are indebted to the Social Sciences and Humanities Research Council of Canada for making the work presented in this chapter possible. Support for related work has come from the Ontario Institute for Studies in Education and the Alfred P. Sloan Foundation. We wish to thank Rosanne Steinbach in particular, as well as Leslie McIlroy, for data collection and analysis.

REFERENCES

Barritt, L. S., & Kroll, B. M. Some implications of cognitive-developmental psychology for research in composing. In C. R. Cooper & L. Odell (Eds.), *Research on composing: Points of departure*. Urbana, Ill.: National Council of Teachers of English, 1974.

Bartlett, E. Development of referencing skills in good and poor elementary and junior high school writers. Paper presented at National Institute of Education/FIPSE Joint Conference, Los Alamitos, Calif., September 1980.

Bereiter, C., & Scardamalia, M. From conversation to composition: The role of instruction in a developmental process. In R. Glaser (Ed.), *Advances in instructional psychology* (Vol. 2). Hillsdale, N.J.: Erlbaum, 1982.

Does learning to write have to be so difficult? In A. Freedman, I. Pringle, & J. Yalden (Eds.), *Learning to write: First language, second language*. New York: Longman, 1983.

Information-processing demand of text composition. In H. Mandl, N. L. Stein & T. Trabasso (Eds.), *Learning and comprehension of text*. Hillsdale, N.J.: Erlbaum, 1984.

Cognitive coping strategies and the problem of "inert knowledge." In S. S. Chipman, J. W. Segal, & R. Glaser (Eds.), *Thinking and learning skills: Current research and open questions* (Vol. 2). Hillsdale, N.J.: Erlbaum, in press.

Bereiter, C., Scardamalia, M., & Cattani, C. Recognition of constraints in children's reading and writing. Paper presented at the annual meeting of the American Educational Research Association, Los Angeles, April 1981.

Bracewell, R. J., Bereiter, C., & Scardamalia, M. A test of two myths about revision. Paper presented at the annual meeting of the American Educational Research Association, San Francisco, 1979.

Britton, J., Burgess, T., Martin, N., McLeod, A., & Rosen, H. *The development of writing abilities (11 – 18)*. London: Macmillan Education, 1975.

Cattani, C., Scardamalia, M., & Bereiter, C. Facilitating diagnosis in student writing. Typescript, Ontario Institute for Studies in Education, 1981.

Elbow, P. *Writing without teachers*. London: Oxford University Press, 1973.

Flower, L., & Hayes, J. R. The cognition of discovery: Defining a rhetorical problem. *College Composition and Communication*, 1980, *31*(2), 21–32.

Goldstein, E., & Perfetti, C. Psycholinguistic processers in writing: Preliminary studies of memory and text structure. Paper presented at conference of Canadian Council of Teachers of English, Ottawa, May 1979.

Graves, D. H. *Balance the basics: Let them write*. New York: Ford Foundation, 1978.

What children show us about revision. *Language Arts*, 1979, *56*(3), 312–319.

Gray, B. *The grammatical foundations of rhetoric*. The Hague: Mouton, 1977.

Hayes, J. R., & Flower, L. Identifying the organization of writing processes. In L. W. Gregg & E. R. Steinberg (Eds.), *Cognitive processes in writing*. Hillsdale, N.J.: Erlbaum, 1980.

Hildyard, A., & Geva, E. Understanding and using conjunctions. Paper presented at the annual meeting of the American Educational Research Association, Los Angeles, April 1981.

Jones, B. F., & Amiran, M. Applying structure of text and learning strategies research to develop programs of instruction for low achieving students. Paper presented at the National Institute of Education – Learning Research and Development Center Conference on Thinking and Learning Skills, Pittsburgh, October 1980.

National Assessment of Educational Progress. *Writing mechanics, 1969–1974: A capsule description of changes in writing mechanics* (Rep. 05-W-01). Denver, 1975.

Write/rewrite: An assessment of revision skills; selected results from the second national assessment of writing (ERIC Document Reproduction Service ED 141 826). Washington, D.C.: U.S. Government Printing Office, 1977.

Reading, thinking, and writing: Results from the 1979–80 National Assessment of Reading and Literature, (ERIC Document Reproduction Service ED 209 641). Washington, D.C.: U.S. Government Printing Office, 1981.

Newell, A., & Simon, H. A. *Human problem solving.* Englewood Cliffs, N.J.: Prentice-Hall, 1972.

Nold, E. W. Revising. In C. H. Frederiksen & J. F. Dominic (Eds.), *Writing: The nature, development, and teaching of written communication.* Hillsdale, N.J.: Erlbaum, 1981.

Paris, P., Scardamalia, M., & Bereiter, C. *Synthesis through analysis: Facilitating theme development in children's writing.* Paper presented at the annual meeting of the American Educational Research Association, 1982.

Robinson, F., Ross, J., & White, F. *Curriculum development for effective instruction.* Toronto: OISE Press, in press.

Scardamalia, M., & Bereiter, C. The development of evaluative, diagnostic, and remedial capabilities in children's composing. In M. Martlew (Ed.), *The psychology of written language: A developmental approach.* London: Wiley, 1983.

Fostering the development of self-regulation in children's knowledge processing. In S. S. Chipman, J. W. Segal, & R. Glaser (Eds.), *Thinking and learning skills: Current research and open questions* (Vol. 2). Hillsdale, N.J.: Erlbaum, in press.

Scardamalia, M., Bereiter, C., & Goelman, H. The role of production factors in writing ability. In M. Nystrand (Ed.), *What writers know: The language, process, and structure of written discourse.* New York: Academic Press, 1982.

Schank, R. C. Rules and topics in conversation. *Cognitive Science,* 1977, *1,* 421–441.

Vygotsky, L. S. *Mind in society: The development of higher psychological processes.* Cambridge: Harvard University Press, 1978.

Widdowson, H. G. New starts and different kinds of failure. In A. Freedman, I. Pringle & J. Yalden (Eds.), *Learning to Write: First language, second language.* New York: Longman, 1983.

Young, R. E., Becker, A. L., & Pike, K. E. *Rhetoric: Discovery and change.* New York: Harcourt, Brace and World, 1970.

PART IV

Literacy and reading

16

Effects of printed language acquisition on speech

LINNEA C. EHRI

Introduction

Pictures that allow the mind to behold invisible aspects of reality may be worth much more than the 1,000 words proclaimed in the adage. When children learn to read printed language, they become capable of visualizing what they are saying and hearing. When children learn to read clocks and calendars, they acquire a visual means of representing the passage of time. When children learn to read music, they become able to visualize what is sung or played on an instrument. In each case, a visual–spatial representational system is acquired by the mind for perceiving and thinking about experiences that cannot be seen and that have temporal duration rather than physical extent as a basic property. Acquisition of a spatial model offers several potential advantages. It enables the possessor to hold onto and keep track of phenomena that themselves leave no trace or have no permanence. It imposes organization upon the phenomena by specifying units, subunits, and interrelationships that might otherwise be difficult to detect or discriminate. However, some degree of distortion or inaccuracy may also result because properties of space may not be completely isomorphic with properties of the nonspatial modality and because the spatial system, being a cultural invention, carries no guarantee that it is perfectly conceived.

The purpose of this chapter is to consider the acquisition of one type of "picture," printed language, and to develop and present evidence for two ideas: (1) that a visual representational system for speech is acquired when children learn to read and spell, and (2) that because print gets established in memory by being built onto the learner's knowledge of spoken language, acquisition may work various changes in children's competencies with speech.

First it is important to review what aspects of speech are made visible in print. Written English includes two basic types of spatial symbols, one nested within the other. Horizontal sequences of letters separated by empty spaces symbolize words. Letters within words symbolize phonetic segments that are blended together in pronunciations.[1] In the present chapter, spellings and letters will be referred to as *symbols,* while the aspects in speech being represented will be termed their *referents.* In the case of spellings, the referent is a composite that includes the word's pronunciation, its syntactic function, and meaning. In the case of letters, the referent is the phonetic subunit. Sentences are another aspect of speech represented in print as sequences of words initiated by a capital letter and ending in a period. Less attention will be paid to sentences than to words and letters, since the latter are regarded as the primary units of the visual representational system to be established in memory.

Print maps speech systematically at both the lexical and the phonetic levels. Lexical symbols are in one sense more reliable than phonetic symbols, since spellings represent the same word referents consistently whereas letters represent either a single phonetic element, combinations of such elements, or sometimes no element at all. However, although there is greater phonetic variability across word spellings, there is no phonetic variability within specific words since spellings are fixed by convention in English. In this respect, phonetic symbolization and lexical symbolization are equally reliable.

The possibility that printed language aids in the perception and analysis of speech is suggested by several facts about spoken language. At the lexical level, speakers experience most words in the context of other words, and their attention is centered upon meanings, not upon linguistic structure. Moreover, there are no auditory signals segmenting fluent speech into word units. Hence, words as components of speech are neither salient nor clearly marked. Also, many words such as auxiliaries, past tense verbs, prepositions, and conjunctions depend for their meaning upon the presence of other words. If heard as isolated sounds without contexts, these words may not be recognized because they evoke no independent meaning. The pronunciations of some words may even change when they are lifted out of context and pronounced separately (e.g., "of" versus "gimme a piece *a* candy"), and this may make recognition harder. The fact that linguists cannot agree about how to define words as units of speech testifies that there is substantial ambiguity to lexical segmentation. At the phonological level, the problem of segmenting pronunciations into phonetic units is even more formidable, since sounds are folded into each other and in some instances coarticulated (Liberman et al., 1967). Also, many sounds, especially those in consonant clusters, are very brief in duration, making detection difficult. Gelb (1952) claims that alphabetic orthography has been invented only once. This suggests that conceptualization of such a system is far from straightforward and thus has much to gain from a visual representational system.

Although printed language may provide the clearest view of speech, there may be other ways to gain awareness as well. At the lexical level, words have a syllabic structure that supplies a possible basis for identifying boundaries between monosyllabic words, or at least between vocalic nuclei of such words. Also, since words can be substituted for each other and combined and recombined in different orders across sentences, and since stress assignment within sentences operates on words, speakers may gain some awareness of words as separate units by manipulating and monitoring these features of spoken sentences. At the phonetic level, the speaker may gain some awareness of sound units by monitoring articulatory and acoustic cues associated with mouth movements as speech is produced slowly or carefully. In fact, the Auditory Discrimination Program designed by Lindamood and Lindamood (1975) to remediate reading and spelling difficulties teaches students to discriminate and label the articulatory movements of their mouths (e.g., /p/ is a lip popper, /th/ is a tongue cooler). This serves as a reminder that structures in speech may not be inaccessible but may merely be harder to penetrate without print. However, in the absence of print, there may be little reason to undertake such an analysis.

Among linguists, there appears to be consensus that printed language has little formative influence on speech. Most linguists are not much interested in writing. In fact, many do not consider it a topic of study in linguistics since it is not language but only a reflection. Bloomfield (1933) describes print as "merely a way of recording language by means of visible marks." Further on, he says, "In order to study writing, we must know something about language, but the reverse is not true" (p. 21). There are some exceptions among linguists, however. Gleason (1961) portrays the relationship between speech and writing as intimate and possibly interdependent. Although he pays more attention to the dependence of written language structure on spoken language, he acknowledges that the influence may run in the opposite direction in the form of spelling pronunciations and a literary form of speech. "One effect of a well established standard written language is the creation of a speech form which approximates an oral rendition of the literary language" (p. 438). The idea of spelling pronunciations is developed more extensively by Kerek (1976), who proposes that word spellings provide an alternative, psychologically compelling model for sound that competes with and may replace spoken pronunciations when the two differ. He proposes the iconic principle of "one graphic form – one phonetic form" (p. 326). According to this principle, when orthography is discrepant with speech, there is pressure to change pronunciations so as to maximize the iconic relationship. Kerek cites several examples of historical shifts in pronunciation that conform to orthographic patterns – for example, *victuals,* which used to be pronounced "vittels." Householder (1971) is perhaps the most extreme in that he argues for the primacy of writing over speech. Among other things, he points out that historically there are many more instances where spellings have changed the pronunciations of words than where pronunciations have altered spellings. Also, the law is on the side of spellings. It cares little if people decide to pronounce their names differently, but court action is required to make an altered spelling legitimate.

In contrast to linguists, psychologists, particularly those interested in how children learn to read, have paid much attention to the relationship between print and speech. Their interest has centered not on spelling pronunciations or literary forms of speech, however, but rather on children's developing knowledge of structural units in speech. Opinion differs about whether print shapes or merely reflects what develops in speech. This is evident in alternative explanations for the large positive correlations between reading acquisition and children's ability to segment sentences into word units and words into phonetic units. One interpretation is that structural knowledge of speech is a prerequisite or readiness skill that matures between the ages of 5 and 7, making a child ready to learn to read (Mattingly, 1972). Other interpretations are that linguistic segmentation skill is a consequence of learning to read or that the two interact during the acquisition process (Ehri, 1979). Print would be assigned a passive role in the first case, an active formative role in the latter cases.

The strict prerequisite (passive) view appears to be incorrect based on evidence presented by Morais et al. (1979). They administered a phonetic analytic task to Portuguese literate and illiterate adults who were thought to be similar in other respects (origin, childhood history, employment). Whereas illiterates were unable to add or delete phones at the beginnings of nonwords, literates performed the tasks easily. That these differences were detected in adults indicates that awareness of phonetic units in speech does not develop spontaneously during childhood but rather requires special experiences such as learning to read an alphabetic system.

There is also disagreement among psychologists about the role of print as a representational system in memory. This is apparent in alternative theories about how children learn to read. Also, these theories differ in whether and how print is regarded as influencing speech during reading acquisition. One view is that readers learn associations between visual forms of words and their semantic referents. This is termed a whole or sight word strategy, where words are stored in memory as visual gestalts (Smith, 1972). The representational system in this theory is strictly lexical. Although reading experiences might be expected to improve learners' awareness of words as units of speech, they would have little impact on learners' awareness of phonetic units or their pronunciations of words, since letters are not thought to be analyzed for their associations with sound. Any phonetic benefits of printed language might be attributed not to reading experiences but to spelling experience, which is regarded as quite a different process.

Another view is that children learn to read by converting letters into sounds, blending the sounds, and then recognizing the word from its pronunciation (Liberman et al., 1977). This is the decoding view of word recognition, thought to be fostered by phonics instruction. The visual representational system suggested by this view is a limited one in which only letters are stored in memory as symbols for sounds. Printed words remain outside the mind on the page, always to be converted to a pronunciation before accessing meanings in memory. Proponents of this view might be expected to regard experiences with printed language as making learners highly sophisticated about the phonetic structure of words. Printed language might even be seen as changing the way learners pronounce words if there is a discrepancy between spellings and pronunciations and if the words are read frequently enough. However, in actuality, proponents of this view have not drawn these conclusions. This is perhaps because they have declared speech primary and print as "parasitic on speech" (Liberman et al., 1980). They prefer to regard knowledge of the phonetic structure of speech as a prerequisite, not a consequence, of print experiences.

From this cursory review, it is apparent that traditional approaches to reading acquisition have paid only partial attention to the possibility that printed language might become established in memory as a visual representational system for speech. Furthermore, these views have attributed little if any formative powers to print. Assumptions about the primacy of speech have precluded recognition of the possible impact of print among proponents of a phonetic view. Also, commitment to one level of analysis in print, either lexical or phonetic, and exclusion of the other has limited the scope of these views. Another limiting factor may be their exclusive concern with reading and not spelling skill.

Theory of printed language acquisition and evidence

An alternative view, one that has been guiding our research on how children learn to read and spell (Ehri, 1978, 1980a, 1980b), is that the full representational system offered by printed language is acquired and stored in memory during acquisition. Lexical representations in the form of alphabetic images are stored in memory. Also, letters are learned as symbols for sounds, both within specific word spellings and as general rules. As will be evident, this view carries several implications regarding the consequences of literacy for linguistic and cognitive processing, since print itself is viewed as a tool of memory.

According to the theory, beginners' knowledge of language includes a lexicon of words acquired from their experience with speech. The lexicon is comprised of word units having several identities. Each word has a phonological identity, that is, how the word sounds and is articulated. Each word has a syntactic identity, how the word functions in sentences. Each has a semantic identity, what the word might mean in various contexts. In the course of learning to read, another identity is added to the lexicon: an alphabetic image of the word. This image is integrated with the other identities to form a unit in lexical memory. La Berge and Samuels (1974) refer to this process as unitization. Alphabetic and phonological identities are unitized when letters are processed as symbols for sounds. Alphabetic, syntactic, and semantic identities are unitized when printed words are read and given meaningful interpretations in sentence contexts. As a result, alphabetic representations come to function as symbols for meanings as well as sounds.

Spellings are thought to enter memory not as unanalyzed visual figures but as sequences of letters bearing systematic relationships to acoustic and/or articulatory segments detected in the word's pronunciation. The first few times a printed word is seen, its component letters either singly or in combination are processed as symbols for component phonetic segments, the letter sequence enters memory, and it becomes a visual symbol for the sound structure of the word. The process by which letters enter memory as symbols for sound is called *phonetic symbolization*. To store images, the reader must be able to analyze words into the relevant phonetic segments suggested by letters seen in the spelling. Likewise, he or she must be familiar enough with the sound-symbolizing function of the letters to recognize how each matches up with sounds in the pronunciation. To the extent that letters are grounded in sound, clear alphabetic representations are formed that can be used for reading printed words accurately and rapidly as well as for producing approximately correct spellings.

Various studies have been interpreted as providing evidence that word spellings are stored in memory and that letters enter memory by being processed as symbols for sounds in pronunciations. (Fuller descriptions of this research can be found elsewhere: Ehri, 1980a, 1980b; Ehri & Wilce, 1979, 1980b, 1982). The purpose of the next section is to review this evidence and its implications for the impact of print on speech.

Spellings to shape conceptualization of sounds

One series of studies was undertaken to show that the storage of spellings in memory affects the way learners conceptualize the sound structure of words (Ehri & Wilce, 1980b). We reasoned that if, when printed words are stored, letters are interpreted as symbols for sounds, then we ought to see some *variations* in learners' conceptualization of the phonemic structure of words depending upon how the words are spelled and which sounds are represented by letters. For example, the spelling of *pitch* may cause readers to think it has four phonemes, whereas the spelling of *rich* may indicate only three phonemes. In both words, a phonetic element corresponding to the extra letter *t* is present in articulation. Whether or not readers think of /t/ as a separate phoneme may depend upon the presence of a letter symbol in the spelling.

Experiment 1 was designed to test the relationship between spelling knowledge and phonemic segmentation. Seven pairs of words were selected so that each pair shared the same target phoneme, yet the spelling of one member symbolized an extra phonetic element adjacent to the phoneme while the spelling of the other member symbolized only the phoneme. These word pairs, their shared phonemes, and the extra phonetic elements are listed in Table 16.1. A phonemic segmentation task was used to reveal how fourth graders

Table 16.1. *Extra-letter and control word pairs, phonetic description, frequency that extra phonemes were detected (phonetic segmentation task), and frequency of correct word spellings (maximum = 24 subjects per word)*

Word pairs		Sound structure			Phoneme detection		Spellings	
Extra-letter	Control	Shared phoneme	Extra phonetic element		Extra-letter	Control	Extra-letter	Control
catch	much	/č/	t	alveolar tap	15	1	19	24
pitch	rich	/č/	t	alveolar tap	13	3	18	24
badge	page	/ǰ/	d	alveolar tap	13	0	17	24
can you	menu	/u/	y	glide	19	0	24	20
new	do	/u/	w	glide	18	0	24	24
own	old	/o/	w	glide	12	0	19	24
comb	home	/m/	b	bilabial stop	6	0	20	24
				Means:	13.7	.6	20.1	23.4

conceptualized the phonological structure of these words. Children positioned counters in a row, one for each sound as it was pronounced. A spelling task was employed to determine whether children knew all the letters in the words.

Based upon our theory, it was expected that among children who knew the spellings, extra segments would be detected in words whose orthographic identities included letters symbolizing those segments but would be omitted in words lacking extra letter symbols. This is what we found. As evidenced in Table 16.1, sounds were discovered frequently in words whose spellings included a letter for that sound but were almost never detected in words whose pronunciations were parallel but whose spellings lacked the letter.

Children were able to spell most of the target words. However, there were some misspellings. To determine whether subjects were less likely to detect an extra segment if they did not know the word's spelling, the number of these cases was counted. There were 21 misspellings in which the extra letter was omitted. In 90% of these, the extra sound was also not detected in the segmentation task. This suggests that it is when children acquire orthographic symbols that they become aware of additional phonemes in the pronunciations of words.

It was evident from subjects' comments that spellings were influencing their segmentations. Some children remarked about their uncertainty whether you could really hear the *b* in *comb* or the *t* in *pitch*. This was in spite of the facts that the experimenter never mentioned spellings and that subjects' attention was focused upon sounds in words, not letters. However, spellings were not the sole basis for segmentations. Only two subjects allocated chips for silent *e* and only three subjects did so for *c* and *h* separately. Most children ignored truly silent letters, and they created only one sound in segmenting words spelled with consonant digraphs such as *ch*. This suggests that spellings interact with pronunciations to determine how the sound structures of words are conceptualized. Letters do not dictate sound structure. Neither are they ignored.

A second experiment was conducted to investigate whether phoneme conceptualization can be shaped by experiences with the printed forms of words – specifically whether, for identically pronounced words, the way readers conceptualize their sound structure depends upon which sounds they see symbolized in the words' spellings. Fourth graders practiced reading five pseudowords assigned as names of animals. Half the subjects read spellings with extra letters, half saw control spellings. The pairs of words (extra letters underlined) were: *banyu–banu; drowl–drol; simpty–simty; tadge–taj; zitch–zich*. A phonetic segmentation task and a spelling task followed.

Results supported the hypothesis. Phonetic elements symbolized by extra letters were distinguished as separate phonemes almost exclusively by subjects who learned these spellings. Whereas every extra-letter subject included between two and five extra-letter sounds in his or her segmentations, all but two control subjects found no extra sounds, the two exceptions finding only one apiece. These findings indicate that the visual forms of words acquired from reading experiences serve to shape learner's conceptualizations of the phoneme segments in those words.

Spellings to shape pronunciations

Not only extra phonetic segments but also extra syllabic segments may be acquired when children learn the spellings of words. Evidence for this was collected in a syllable segmentation task. The words presented were ones whose spellings contain one more syllable than their typical pronunciations – words such as *different, comfortable, interesting,* and *temperature*. Of interest was whether knowledge of the spellings of these words might cause subjects to regard them as having the extra syllable in their pronunciations. When children were asked to segment the words into syllables, they tended to identify syllables with letter groups – *in/ter/est/ing*. Further, extra syllable segments were detected more frequently by subjects who knew spellings than by subjects who did not for 10 of the 11 words presented. These results were corroborated in a study by Barton and Hamilton (1980), who found that literate adults were much more apt to segment multisyllabic words as they were spelled than were borderline literates. Both studies offer evidence for the formative influence of print over speech, specifically over the pronunciations of words.

What happens to silent letters?

English word spellings sometimes include letters lacking any referent in sound, usually no more than one letter per spelling. There are various ways that learners might handle this discrepancy between print and pronunciations. One possibility suggested by Kerek's (1976) iconic principle as well as by results of the segmentation studies is that silent letters are incorporated into the pronunciations of words.

Alternatively, silent letters may be realized in special spelling pronunciations of words stored in memory but never used in normal speech (e.g., "lis-ten" for *listen*).[2] A third possibility is that when spellings are stored in memory, silent letters get tagged as exceptions.

We undertook a series of experiments to study how silent letters are stored in memory and whether they differ from pronounced letters In a letter judgment task, we ruled out the possibility that silent letters are incorporated into normal pronunciations of words. Most seventh graders judged pronounced letters to be pronounced and silent letters to lack a referent in speech. Then we conducted five experiments to compare children's memory for silent and pronounced letters in words whose spellings were familiar (Ehri & Wilce, 1982). The task had three parts. First, subjects were shown a list of words to read. This indicated which target words were already familiar. Next, subjects were told to imagine the spelling of each word in their mind's eye. When they could see it, they were shown a single letter and asked to decide whether or not the letter was present in the spelling. For example, they imagined the word *kind* and were asked, "Does it have an *n*?" Third, they were surprised with a recall task. Each letter was shown, and children identified the word they had imagined for that letter. Pairs of words having the same or similar target letters and comparable spellings were selected. In one word, the target letter was pronounced. In the other word, it was silent. Examples are *s* − *island* vs. *n* − *insect*; *w* − *wrong* vs. *world*; *t* − *whistle* vs. *k* − *freckle*. The subjects in one or another study were second, third, and fourth graders.

Results revealed that subjects were quite accurate in judging silent and pronounced letters in the words being imagined. Although performance was close to perfect, children were significantly more accurate in detecting pronounced than silent letters. This indicates that letters are more easily stored in memory when they symbolize sounds. However, it is not the case that silent letters are kept out of memory. They are retained almost as well. Furthermore, in the recall task, silent letters prompted better recall of the words previously judged than the pronounced letters did.

From these findings, we conclude that silent letters do have a different status from pronounced letters in memory. Silent letters are harder to remember. However, once learned, their distinctive relation to the words makes them better recall prompts than their pronounced forms.

To summarize this section, we have proposed that printed language is acquired as a representational system when children learn to read and spell. Various findings indicate that spellings of words are retained in memory by functioning as symbols for sounds and that as a result spellings may influence the way readers conceptualize the sound structure of words and possibly even the way they pronounce words under certain circumstances. The purpose of the next section is to extend consideration of the various ways that acquisition of a visual–spatial system might affect spoken language.

Evidence for the impact of print on speech

Conceptualization of phonetic segments

Results of the phonemic segmentation study with words such as *pitch* and *rich* showed that one effect of experience with alphabetic orthography is to teach children how to conceptualize spoken words as sequences of phonemes. Phonemic awareness is not the same as phonemic perception. Even infants have been observed to respond differentially to phonemic contrasts. Phonemic awareness refers rather to the ability to attend to, conceptualize, and consciously manipulate phoneme-size units in speech. The capability appears to emerge in children around the ages 5 to 7. Lewkowicz (1980), Golinkoff (1978), Ehri (1979), and Liberman et al. (1977) among others have reviewed numerous studies indicating that there are strong positive correlations between phonetic analytic skills and success in learning to read. Results of the study by Morais et al. (1979) comparing literate and nonliterate Portuguese adults (see above) indicate that these skills do not develop in the *absence* of experience with print. This suggests that the bulk of this knowledge emerges when children begin interacting with print and learning how letters in spellings map sounds in pronunciations. Although beginners may bring some phonemic insights from their experience with speech, the view to be developed here is that orthography helps them stabilize and organize their phonetic knowledge and teaches them the full system – that is, which phones are to be considered as separate segments in speech and which phones are to be ignored.

One source of information revealing how naïve spellers conceptualize the phonetic structure of speech and how these perceptions change as a result of experience with print can be found in studies of children's spellings. Read (1971, 1975), Chomsky (1977), and Beers and Henderson (1977) among others have analyzed the spellings of prereaders and beginning readers and have identified various ways that children's representations of speech shift from naïve to more conventional conceptualizations. Also, we have collected, analyzed, and compared the spellings of more and less mature beginning readers. Of interest here are the changes in spellings that reflect the acquisition of new insights about the structure of speech.

Comparison of novice and mature spellings confirms that novices do not detect and represent as many phonetic segments as mature spellers. Segments are overlooked not because the children lack knowledge of letter–sound relations. This is indicated by the fact that spellers symbolize the sounds correctly when they occur in uncomplicated phonetic environments. Rather, sounds are overlooked because spellers have not had sufficient experience with conventional print to learn how to divide the sound stream appropriately. When the entire sound of a consonant letter name is detected in a pronunciation, the letter may be selected to stand for both the vowel and the consonant. Table 16.2 presents some examples. The immature pattern appears on the left, the more mature pattern on the right. Children's spellings are italicized; the word being spelled is in parentheses. Correction of these letter name errors involves learning to attend consistently to phonetic rather than syllabic units.

One type of phonetic unit proving illusive to novices are schwa vowels, which are commonly omitted in spellings when they occur before the vocalic consonants /l/ and /r/ and in unstressed syllables. Examples of misspellings are given in Table 16.2. Interestingly, in learning to detect and represent these phones, some beginning spellers appear to go overboard in their analyses; that is, they find extra segments not symbolized in the conventional system. The right-hand column in Table 16.2 provides some examples of this, where spellers separated the vocalic phone from the consonantal phone in /l/ and /r/ and symbolized each with a separate letter. (This process of overanalysis is called *epenthesis* by linguists.) We also saw this happen with some pseudoword spellings written by beginning readers: *shangcke* (shenk), *trayulse* (trels). These examples illustrate that experience with conventional spellings also teaches children the limits of phonetic analysis.

Not only vowels but also consonants are sometimes omitted in novices' spellings. One of the most interesting is the preconsonantal nasal (i.e., the occurrence of /m/ or /n/ between a vowel and a consonant, as in *bumpy*). Examples of children's misspellings are given in Table 16.2. Omission appears to occur because the nasal lacks its own place of articulation. Rather, it combines with the vowel to form a single phonetic segment, a nasalized vowel. This is an instance where conventional orthography actually misleads the reader into

Table 16.2. *Characteristics of children's invented spellings*

1. Separating vowels from consonants (spellings capitalized)

a. Letter name errors

Vowel omitted	Vowel represented
yl (while)	*wil, woil, wiel* (while)
prd, prit (pretty)	*prede* (pretty)
dsid, (decide)	
hlte, hlde (helped)	*helpt, hilpt* (helped)
twlv (twelve)	
yrde (yard)	*yared* (yard)
bcoz (because)	*becoz* (because)
kt (Kate)	

b. Schwa vowels

Omitted	Represented	Overrepresented
chikn (chicken)	*chicin, chikon* (chicken)	*ferend* (friend)
kitn (kitten)		*peridiee* (pretty)
opn (open)		*balaosis* (blouses)
wotd (wanted)	*woted, wontid* (wanted)	*daragan* (dragon)
petd (painted)		*teracder* (tractor)
traktr (tractor)	*trackder, trater* (tractor)	
spidr (spider)		
wotr (water)		
brd (bird)		
grl (girl)		
tabl (table)	*tabal, tabul* (table)	
pesl (pencil)		
tmoro (tomorrow)		
blazs (blouses)		

c. Preconsonantal nasals

Omitted	Represented
bope, bupee (bumpy)	*bumpe, bompy* (bumpy)
mostr, mosdr (monster)	*manstr, monstr* (monster)
wus (once)	*wans* (once)
fred (friend)	*ferend, frend* (friend)
kide (kind)	*kinde, cinde* (kind)
thek (think)	*tink* (think)
pesl (pencil)	
blaket (blanket)	
whedo (window)	
thaq (thank you)	

Table 16.2.   *(cont.)*

2. Segmenting and classifying phonetic segments
a. Affricatives

Nonconventional	Conventional
hikn (chicken)	_chikn_ (chicken)
nahr (nature)	_nacher, neatcher, natuer_ (nature)
hagr, hratr (tractor)	_tradr, traktr_ (tractor)
hek, chrac (truck)	_troc, truk_ (truck)
gagn, jagn, jragan (dragon)	_dragen_ (dragon)
kolah (college)	

Phonetic	b. Inervocalic alveolar flaps With *t*
wadr (water)	_wotr_ (water)
pride (pretty)	_prite_ (pretty)
tradr (tractor)	_tratr_ (tractor)
drde (dirty)	_drte_ (dirty)
ladr (letter)	_nobute_ (nobody)
bodom (bottom)	_mitl_ (middle)
bedr (better)	_patr_ (powder)
adem (atom)	_rety_ (ready)

believing that the vowel and consonant are two separate sounds even though they are one sound phonetically.

To verify that spellings of novices and experts reflect differing conceptualizations of the sound structure of preconsonantal nasals in words, with novices ignoring the nasal and experts regarding it as a separate sound, we compared the phonetic segmentations and spellings of first graders and fourth graders on words containing preconsonantal nasals.[3] Results confirmed this difference. Although first graders represented most of the other sounds in their segmentations and spellings, they omitted the nasal in all but one spelling, and they never segmented it as a separate sound. In contrast, fourth graders included the nasal in all spellings, and varying proportions of subjects marked it as a separate sound segment in different words: *bank* – *81%, beyond* – 69%, *king* – 44%. Identification of a separate nasal segment in the final case is interesting since linguists regard /ŋ/ as one phonetic segment. Apparently, spellings persuade some learners that there are two sounds.

Another type of shift occurring when novices gain more experience
with print is in the classification of sounds. Invented spellings reveal
some nonconventional classifications. Affricative sounds are those
produced by a stop closure followed immediately by a slow release
of the closure. Examples are /č/ in church, /ǰ/ in judge. Affrication
turns out to be a salient feature for beginners. In their spellings,
they may regard the affricates in words such as *truck* and *chicken* as
the same sound and symbolize these sounds with the letter *h*, which
contains affrication in its name. Some examples are given in Table
16.2. In contrast, children more knowledgeable about print distinguish between *tr* and *ch* sounds and recognize whether one or two
phonetic segments are involved. Very likely, it is familiarity with
orthographic conventions that corrects this deviant analysis. Evidence
for this is provided by Barton, Miller, and Macken (1980). In this
study, they taught preschoolers to segment the first sound in words
such as /m/ in *mouse* and /b/ in *bear*. Then they examined how these
children analyzed the initial consonant cluster /tr/ as in *truck*. They
found that whereas nonreaders regarded the clusters as single sounds,
children having some reading ability segmented the clusters into two
phonemes.

Another case where novices differ from experienced spellers in
their classification of sounds involves the alveolar flap falling in a
stressed syllable between two vowels (e.g., *letter, middle*). In American
English dialects, the sound produced is closer acoustically to a /d/
than a /t/. However, the sound may be symbolized by either *d* or *t* in
conventional spellings. Examples of children's misspellings are given
in Table 16.2. Whereas novices hear the flap as /d/ and spell it *d*,
children more experienced with print recognize that the sound could
be /t/ and sometimes use *t* in their spellings.

The shifts in spelling patterns reviewed above are thought to occur
as beginners gain experience with print. We collected additional data
to determine whether each type of shift correlates with reading and
spelling acquisition and distinguishes more from less mature reader/
spellers. One inadequacy of invented spelling data is that the words
spelled are real. When more mature patterns are exhibited, it is not
clear whether this arises because children have acquired the general
pattern or because they remember those particular word spellings.
To minimize the influence of this factor, we made up nine pseudowords for first and second graders ($N = 68$) to spell. Their knowledge
of several patterns was tested, including schwa vowels (*gurb, nacher*),
preconsonantal nasals (*shenk*), affricates (*nacher, trels*), and alveolar
flaps (*jutty*). The children's ability to read and spell real words was

also measured to assess their maturity with print. Nonsense spellings were scored for the features of interest, and scores were correlated with reading and spelling measures.

Results were positive in the case of schwa vowel spellings ($r = .57$, $.62, p < .01$). Better reader/spellers symbolized schwa with a separate letter, whereas less mature readers omitted the letter. Also, results were positive for preconsonantal nasals ($r = .52, .58, p < .01$). Better readers represented the nasal, whereas less mature readers did not. Correlations were low and nonsignificant for affricative spellings, primarily because most subjects correctly represented /č/ as *ch* and /tr/ as *tr*. Use of immature forms may be limited to children who have received less formal reading instruction than our subjects. Analysis of flap spellings revealed that most subjects used the letter *d*, which is more accurate acoustically. However, there were some differences according to maturity level: 87% of the poorest spellers and 85% of the best spellers selected *d*, whereas only 59% of the moderately good spellers used *d*, the remainder selecting *t*. This suggests that a shift toward *t* may emerge temporarily among children once they gain some experience with print.

In this same study, we also determined whether better reader/spellers were the ones most likely to analyze words into all their phonetic segments. The measure of phonetic segmentation skill was the number of pseudoword spellings that included a letter for each phonetic segment. (Schwa vowels and preconsonantal nasals were ignored since these were tapped in other measures.) Liberal scoring criteria were used in accepting letters as sound symbols. Calculation of the correlations between this measure and subjects' reading and spelling scores revealed significant values ($r = .43$ to $.49, p < .01$). This indicates that more experienced readers were more likely to perform complete phonetic analyses of pronunciations.

An additional study of children's conceptualization of alveolar flaps was conducted to determine whether experiences with print might shape children's perception of flap sounds in words. According to the theory developed above, since flaps are ambiguous, spellings might influence how they are perceived in speech, as /d/ or /t/. Children unfamiliar with spellings should analyze flaps acoustically as /d/. Once they acquire some experience with print and learn that flaps are sometimes symbolized by *t* in spellings, they may shift and perceive them as /t/ in sound. The ambiguity should be resolved for particular words as these spellings are stored in memory and as letters are interpreted as defining which sounds are supposed to be there in pronunciations.

In this study, first, second and fourth graders listened to a tape recording of 30 familiar words containing flaps. In some of the words, flaps were created by adding inflections (i.e., *hottest, saddest*). In other words, flaps were present in root forms (i.e., *little, ladder*). Each word was included in a defining sentence. The speaker was careful to articulate a flap when the words and sentences were tape recorded. Children listened, repeated each word, then judged whether they heard a /d/ or a /t/ in the middle of the word. They responded by naming the letter (*d* or *t*) containing the sound heard. We expected that older subjects' judgments would correspond to spellings more than younger subjects since older subjects had learned more of the spellings. We expected accuracy to be greater for *d*-spelled flaps than *t*-spelled flaps since unfamiliar spellings should be judged acoustically.

Results confirmed these expectations. Older subjects' judgments matched spellings more than younger subjects'. Analysis of the errors of subjects who misjudged at least four words ($N = 35$) revealed a strong bias to say *d* rather than *t*, indicating that acoustic cues were being monitored by subjects and used when spellings were unfamiliar. This is one reason why judgments for *d*-spelled flaps were more accurate than judgments for *t*-spelled flaps. Also, it indicates that correct /t/ judgments were not random guesses. Five subjects exhibited a bias to say *t*, and four of these were first graders. This provides some evidence that beginners may shift temporarily to exclusive use of *t* when this becomes learned as a symbol for flaps. Only one of the subjects (a first grader) exhibited no bias favoring *d* or *t* in his errors, indicating that subjects were not naming letters randomly.

Interestingly, flaps spelled with *t* in inflected words were not judged more accurately than *t*-spelled flaps in nonderived words (e.g., *smarter* vs. *party*). This was surprising since we expected subjects, young and old, to think of morpheme roots and to recognize the correct underlying sounds in the derived words. The results suggest that lexical derivational sources did not have much impact upon performance in this task. This contrasts with the strong effects of spellings on performance.

Although the above findings are suggestive, they are not conclusive. We presumed but did not verify that subjects judging sounds correctly were familiar with the words' spellings. We presumed that in our subjects' dialect the pronunciations of our words did include a flap rather than a distant /t/ or /d/. We presumed that older subjects' pronunciations were not different from younger subjects' as a consequence of experiences specific to speech. Furthermore, we did not manipulate subjects' experiences with print to show its influence directly. These factors await investigation.

Findings of this alveolar flap study are consistent with results of the phonetic segmentation (*pitch–rich*) study, both supplying evidence that print may exert a formative influence on speech when speech contains ambiguity resolved in the spelling.

Pronunciations of words

If spellings alter the way speakers conceptualize the phonetic structure of words, they might also be expected to influence how learners pronounce words when letters in the spellings symbolize somewhat different sounds from those in pronunciations. Evidence for this was found in the syllable segmentation study described above involving words such as *interesting, different,* and *comfortable.* Subjects who were familiar with the spellings of these words divided their pronunciations into the syllables symbolized in spellings much more frequently than subjects who did not know the spellings. This suggests that unpronounced letters may get incorporated into pronunciations. However, our work on silent letters reported above was interpreted to indicate that whether or not this happens depends upon how the unpronounced letters are processed when the spellings are stored in memory. Letters that are clearly absent in spoken pronunciations (e.g., the *s* in *island*) may be tagged as silent during the acquisition process, and this may eliminate pressure to pronounce these letters.

Other factors no doubt also influence whether the presence of a discrepancy between spellings and sound will cause pronunciations to change in the direction of spellings. Some factors may inhibit change, whereas other may promote change. For example, if speakers hear the spoken version of the word frequently, change may be unlikely. However, if they hear pronunciations different from their own and more like spelling pronunciations, change may be very probable. Change may also depend upon whether learners pay close attention to letter–sound relations when the spellings are learned. Another factor may be whether speakers possess single or multiple pronunciations for words stored in memory. If the latter is the case, then spellings might not alter any existing pronunciation but might simply add a new pronunciation. Although little evidence is available to choose from among these possibilities, what evidence there is provides some clues.

In our study of children's word spellings, we noticed that children sometimes subtly mispronounced words as they spelled them. The deviancy in speech might not have been detected except that the misspelling caused us to listen more carefully. One type of error involved mixups between closely articulated lax (short) vowels, especially /I/ (short *i*) and /ɛ/ (short *e*). We observed that 18% to 20% of the short-vowel spellings produced by a group of immature first-grade spellers exhibited *i–e* substitutions. Examples are: *gist* (guessed), *ind* (end), *git* (get), *melk* (milk), *niks* (necks), *levd* (lived), *cech* (catch). The final example shows confusion between /ɛ/ and /æ/ (short *a*). In listening to children pronounce the words, sometimes it was hard to tell which of the vowels was being articulated. The sound produced appeared to be somewhere in between the two categories. Data presented by Lieberman (1980) confirm that in some children's speech there is substantial overlap in the formant frequencies of these two vowels. Such observations open the possibility that pre-readers' vowel pronunciations may exhibit more deviancy or variability before than after they learn letter symbols for the vowel system and word spellings for particular pronunciations. Having to distinguish among the lax sounds in *i, e,* and *a* spellings may strengthen these as discrete categories of sounds. Having to learn vowel letters in the spellings of particular words may clarify the correct or "ideal" pronunciations and eliminate mispronunciations or variability in pronunciations.

There is some evidence that learning the spelling system for vowels influences how people perceive vowel relations and organize them into pairs. Jaeger (1979) conducted a concept formation experiment. Adults learned to distinguish positive from negative instances of vowel shift alternations for pairs of words. Positive instances were consistent with Chomsky and Halle's (1968) rules and with spelling rules for short and long vowels (e.g., *profane–profanity, deceive–deception*). Negative instances were not (*detain–detention, false–fallacy*). Then subjects were given test cases to determine whether they were responding on the basis of vowel shift rules or spelling rules. It was reasoned that if Chomsky and Halle's phonological system governed performance, subjects should consider *abound–abundant* a positive instance and *presume–presumption* a negative instance.[4] If spelling rules governed performance, however, the opposite judgments should predominate. Results supported the latter. That learning the orthographic system causes subjects to group vowel sounds into short and long pairs was further supported by some of Jaeger's subjects who acknowledged this as the basis for their judgments. Moskowitz (1973) and Templeton (1979) interpret their evidence similarly to suggest that when children learn to read they come to organize information about vowels according to orthographic rather than phonological criteria.

Returning to our spelling study, other subtle mispronunciations of words were also revealed in the spellings of novice readers. Phonemes were deleted: *gro* (girl), *bisaco* (bicycle), *god* (gold), *sogr* (soldier), *owese* (always), *sothing* (something), *sucas, soikas, suokays* (suitcase), *inportin* (important). Syllables were deleted: *crans* (crayons), *sigret* (cigarette), *ambluce* (ambulance), *sprise* (surprise). Sounds were substituted: /f/ for /θ/ as in *bof* (both); /r/ for /w/ as in *tref* (twelve), *mord* (mowed); /w/ for /r/ as in *wang* (wrong), *wemeabr* (remember), *thewe* (there); /n/ for /m/ as in *inportetn* (important). The progressive inflection (-*ing*) was often misspelled and mispronounced as -*een*, -*ene*, -*in*, -*en*. Since mispronunciations of words appear to drop out as children learn to read, it may be that print is the instigator of correction.

It is perhaps not surprising to find deviant or variable word pronunciations in children's speech, since this is what they often hear. Research reviewed by Reddy (1976) shows that in connected speech words may differ markedly from their pronunciations in isolation. Acoustic and phonetic properties exhibit much greater variability, and boundaries between words may be obliterated. Cole and Jakimik (1978) cite several processes that undermine the phonological clarity and stability of words in fluent speech: geminate reduction, where two consonants are reduced to one across word boundaries, as in "sumore" (some more), "they wave flags," where the voiced–voiceless distinction is eliminated; vowel reduction or deletion, where unstressed vowels are pronounced schwa or omitted entirely, as in "go 'n see" (go and see), "choc'late" (chocolate); alveolar flapping, in which the /t/–/d/ distinction is obscured, as in "fat Albert"; stop consonant deletion, when the stop occurs between a nasal and another consonant, as in "frien's" (friends), "kin'ness" (kindness), "twen'y" (twenty), or when the following word begins with a stop consonant, as in "jus great" (just great); palatalization, where the sounds /d/, /t/, /s/, and /z/ are palatalized when followed by a palatal and an optional intervening boundary, such as in /dIjyu/ (did you), /hIsuz/ (his shoes). These examples make it clear that word pronunciations are neither unitary nor stable in fluent speech. Even in isolation, some words may have alternative forms, a casual pronunciation in which some sounds are reduced or deleted and a careful pronunciation that includes all the sounds and is truer to spellings (e.g., *chocolate, twenty*).

Another cause of variable or nonliterate pronunciations of words is dialect. Pronunciations are more discrepant with spellings in some dialects than in others. Compared to standard English (SE), black English (BE) word pronunciations differ markedly from spellings. In BE, vowel contrasts are lost in certain consonant contexts (e.g., before /n/ as in *pin–pen*). Final *th* is pronounced like either /f/ or /v/ (e.g., "wiv" for *with*, "bof" for *both*). Consonants are weakened or deleted in many contexts – for example, /t/ and /d/ at the end of consonant clusters (e.g., "pas" for *past* or *passed*, "tol" for *told*), /l/ and /r/ before consonants or at the ends of words ("hep" for *help*, "so" for *sore*); /n/ may be lost except for an echo as a nasal vowel; /z/ and /s/ may be lost, but usually only from blends (Burling, 1973). Kligman, Cronnell, and Verna (1972) collected spellings from black dialect-speaking second graders. They report several inventions illustrating the dialect features described above: *mouf* (mouth), *dese* (these), *fas* (fast), *plan* (plant), *move* (moved), *walk* (walks), *nest, nesses* (nests), *hode, hole* (hold), *wam* (warm), *tin* (ten), *bat, bot* (bite), *steel* (still), *bause* (boys). Sound substitutions, consonant delections, and vowel variations were all observed. Groff (1978) looked for the same dialect-based errors in older children (fourth to sixth graders) and found many fewer instances. One explanation for the reduction in errors is that experience with print teaches dialect speakers the spellings of words as well as their literary pronunciations. Some correlational evidence for this is offered by Desberg, Elliott, and Marsh (1980), who examined the relationship among reading, spelling, and math achievement scores and dialect radicalism in a group of black elementary school children. Those who had better command of SE forms were better readers and spellers than those who did not. In contrast, achievement in math was not related to dialect. Although this evidence falls short of indicating a causal relationship, it does suggest that dialect speakers may acquire knowledge of SE word pronunciations by learning to read and spell words.

The impact of print upon pronunciations may not be limited to nonstandard dialect speakers or to prereaders with deviant pronunciations. It may be that the process of learning to read and spell words teaches all readers a literary English dialect reflecting the visible phonology represented in spellings. According to the theory developed above, this literary pronunciation is not necessarily one that renders all the letters pronounced. Rather, it is the pronunciation that reflects how the letters in spellings were analyzed as sound symbols when the spelling was stored in memory. It is held in memory as an "ideal" context-free pronunciation for the word. Its attachment to spellings gives it stability and makes it resistant to further change. Although the pronunciation may not be used in casual speech, it nevertheless tells its possessor how that word is "supposed" to be pronounced, or how it is pronounced slowly or carefully, or how it is pronounced by an educated person.

The possibility that learning to read equips the speaker with literary pronunciations explains a curious phenomenon described by Goodman and Buck (1973), who listened to several BE-speaking children read a text aloud and then retell the story from memory. Whereas the readers showed no dialect miscues in the reading task, they displayed much dialect involvement during their retelling immediately afterward. The reason why speakers may be able to read text without their spoken dialects is that print activates its own set of pronunciations, those that were established by spellings when they were stored in memory and unitized with pronunciations.

The acquisition of literary pronunciations founded upon and stabilized by spellings stored in memory also explains how writing serves to constrain changes in speech in communities of speakers over time. According to Gelb (1952), English has changed relatively little over the last 400 or 500 years as a result of its writing system. This contrasts with strong shifts occurring before that time. Also it contrasts with rapid linguistic changes evident in modern times among primitive societies that lack a phonetic written language. Gelb points out that some American Indian languages are changing so fast that people of the present generation have difficulty conversing with people three to four generations older.

Bright (1960) presents evidence from a comparison of South Asian Indian dialects to indicate that printed language, by freezing phonology, serves to limit changes occurring in speech (Bright & Ramanujan, 1962). He observed that in one geographical area where the Brahmin dialect contrasted with the non-Brahmin dialect in having a written form, phonemic changes were less apparent in Brahmin than non-Brahmin speech. However, in another geographical area where neither dialect had a written form, both Brahmin and non-Brahmin speech exhibited phonemic change in approximately equal degree. It may be that pronunciations are more subject to change in the absence of print, since they exist only in the minds and memories of speakers. Print, by casting pronunciations in fixed phonetic forms, gives them permanence outside the minds of speakers and thus frees them from total dependence.

One might expect the impact of spellings on pronunciations to be greatest in languages where the orthography maps speech phonetically, where single spellings of words are prescribed, and where the majority of the speakers are literate.[5] English orthography conforms to these criteria perhaps more than some other orthographies. Reder (1981) studied the pronunciations of Vai speaking adults in Liberia. Vai orthography differs from English orthography in that it is syllabic rather than alphabetic and it includes alternate spellings of words to match variable pronunciations. Furthermore, only some people learn to read and write Vai, since it is not taught in schools and has limited use in the culture. Reder compared literate and nonliterate adults' pronunciations of words that were undergoing change in speech and that had variable spellings in print. These were polysyllabic words pronounced either with or without a medial /l/ – for example, /kalo/ or /kao/, meaning "moon," and written either with or without the /l/ symbolized. Reder compared the frequency of medial /l/ word pronunciations to determine whether having an internal written representation that included the /l/ symbol might cause literates to pronounce the word with /l/ more often than nonliterates. This is what he found. However, the frequency of occurrence of /l/ in speech was not terribly high even among literates. Whereas they included the /l/ symbol in spellings about half the time, they included it in speech less than a quarter of the time. These findings indicate that experience with print influences speech by increasing the frequency of a less common pronunciation. Perhaps this occurs because the two printed forms exist side by side in memory, reminding literate speakers of both options. (Equal awareness is suggested by the fact that both spellings were written equally often). However, the less common pronunciation remains less common in speech of literates, perhaps because it does not have the status of a literary pronunciation, since spellings exist for both spoken forms. The fact that /l/ forms are used at all in Vai speech may be noteworthy. This may be a case where orthography has preserved a less common pronunciation from extinction.

Perception of lexical segments

Whereas the spatial model of speech embodied in print may actually create in the speaker's mind the idea that speech is comprised of sequences of discrete phonetic units, it is less likely that print implants a completely novel idea about segments at the lexical level, since children are familiar with many content words (nouns and adjectives), since syllabic divisions in speech provide some clues to word bound-aries, and since words are combined and recombined unconsciously in forming sentences. Nevertheless, results of several studies make it clear that some types of words are not obvious units of speech to children unfamiliar with print. Prereaders have substantial difficulty in lexical analytic tasks that require dividing meaningful sentences into words or picking single words out of sentences. In contrast, beginning readers can perform these tasks quite easily (Ehri, 1975, 1976, 1979). At the lexical level, the function of print may be to establish clear entries for words in memory in the form of spellings unitized with pronunciations and meanings so that when the words are heard in speech, their separate identities are recognized.

One of the most difficult word types for prereaders to recognize is context-dependent words, which evoke little meaning if unaccompanied by other words. Examples are function words such as *might, could,* and *from* and past-tense forms of irregular verbs such as *gave.* Holden and MacGinitie (1972) observed that prereaders had difficulty isolating these words from adjacent words in a sentence segmentation task. We found that prereaders had trouble recognizing these as real words when the words were presented as isolated spoken forms (Ehri, 1979). Since speech does not make children aware of these as separate words, we reasoned that print might teach this lesson.

We conducted a study to explore the effect of two different kinds of reading experiences with function words (Ehri and Wilce, 1980a). Half the first graders practiced reading the words in meaningful printed sentences. The other half read words in unorganized lists of words. After reading each list, the latter group then heard the words rearranged into the same sentences read by the other group. One of the posttests given after word training measured subjects' ability to detect the presence of the function words in spoken sentences played on a tape recorder. The sentences were different from those read or heard during training. The target words received minimal stress and pitch in these sentences. Furthermore, in half the sentences, the word was "buried" by overlapping sounds from other words flanking it (e.g., if the target word was *gave*: "The green frog gave vegetables to the hungry rabbit."). In the other half, adjacent sounds were distinctive (e.g., "The rich grandfather gave dollar bills to the needy children."). For each sentence, subjects were shown four function words that they had read, they listened to the sentence, and reported whether they heard any of the four words. It was expected that subjects who had learned the printed words in sentences would outperform list readers, since the experience of associating spellings with sentence meanings as well as pronunciations was expected to establish the function words as more complete entries in lexical memory.

Results confirmed our expectations. Subjects who had read the words in contexts detected significantly more of these words in the spoken sentences than list readers (means = 15.5 vs. 13.2 correct out of 20 maximum). Interestingly, burying words in sentences did not make detection any more difficult. This indicates that processing was not conducted on an acoustic or phonetic basis but involved a deeper lexical level of analysis. From these results we conclude that printed language experiences that integrate spellings with meanings and pronunciations set up word units in the lexicon that are superior for distinguishing these units in speech. Although we showed that the way function words are read influences lexical awareness, we did not test the claim, proposed above, that learning printed symbols for function words is critical for setting these words up as accessible units in the lexicon. This hypothesis awaits investigation.

Once spellings are unitized with the other identities of words, one would expect all this information to be mobilized in memory when words are encountered. Even in strictly auditory tasks requiring listeners to process and respond to spoken words, spellings stored in memory should be activated and influence performance. Various studies have indicated this is true. Seidenberg and Tanenhaus (1979) had adults listen to several words on a tape recorder and decide whether each rhymed with a cue word. Some of the rhyming words on the list were orthographically similar to the cue word (e.g., *clue–glue*), some were different (e.g., *clue–shoe*). They found that subjects detected orthographically similar rhymes faster than orthographically dissimilar rhymes. In another experiment, they had subjects judge whether two aurally presented words rhymed. Included among the nonrhyming pairs were words with similar spellings (e.g., *bomb–tomb*) and words with different spellings (e.g., *bomb–room*). Here, it took subjects longer to reject words with similar spellings. These results show that the spellings of words influence the perception of rhyme. Similar spellings facilitate detection of positive instances but interfere with the detection of negative instances.

Jakimik, Cole, and Rudnicky (1980) studied the impact of spellings in a lexical decision task. They had adult subjects listen to a list of spoken words and nonwords and indicate whether each was a real word by pressing a buzzer. The words were arranged so that in some cases successive words shared the same first syllable and spelling (e.g., *barber, bar; napkin, nap*). In other cases, successive words shared the same first syllable but were spelled differently (e.g., *laundry, lawn*;

record, wreck). Also included were control words that differed in sound and spelling. Other studies of lexical decision performance have shown that when words are related, facilitation occurs in judging the second word. Of interest here was whether similarities in spelling and/or sound might enable subjects to recognize the lexical status of the second word faster. Results revealed that reaction times were improved, but only when the words had similar spellings, not when they were similar phonologically but different orthographically. Additional experiments were performed that replicated these findings. These results provide further evidence that orthographic representations of words are activated in spoken-language tasks. Findings also suggest that orthographic organization of words in the mental lexicon may be more central or salient than phonemic organization, perhaps because orthography was the factor that helped to establish clear stable word entries in memory when the spellings of the words were learned.

There is another study indicating that orthography may impair the perception of speech when orthographic knowledge creates expectations that conflict with what is actually heard. Valtin (1980) describes this study performed by the German linguist Jung (1977). He constructed pairs of sentences containing verbs that were pronounced identically except that the vowel was long in one case and short in the other. Also, the spellings of the words were distinct, with the difference in vowel length marked orthographically (e.g., *fliegt* vs. *flickt*). Pronunciations of verbs were interchanged in some of the sentences recorded on tape. Children with poor and normal spelling skills listened to each sentence and then judged whether its verb contained a long or a short vowel sound. Jung found that the poor spellers perceived the vowel sounds correctly whereas the good spellers judged the sounds according to their knowledge of the words' spellings.

Memory for words

Evidence presented above indicates that when words are heard, spellings may be activated in listeners' minds. This may influence not only their perception of the words in speech but also their memory for the words. Our study indicating that orthography has mnemonic value (Ehri & Wilce, 1979) revealed that first and second graders who knew letter–sound relations were able to learn meaningless consonant–vowel–consonant (CVC) sounds faster when they saw spellings of the sounds during study periods than when they heard and rehearsed the sounds, or heard oral spellings for the sounds, or heard the sounds segmented phonetically, or saw misspellings. Another experiment was conducted to compare two additional conditions for remembering sounds. In one case, children heard letter names for the CVC sounds and they were told to imagine what the spellings looked like. In the control condition, subjects rehearsed the CVC sounds orally several times. As expected, spellings still facilitated memory for the sounds. These results indicated that orthography can function to preserve sounds in memory when spellings symbolize the sounds to be remembered. Spellings do not even have to be seen to have this effect on memory.

The mnemonic advantage provided by spellings in a word memory task was demonstrated directly by Sales, Haber, and Cole (1969). They required adults to remember six words displaying vowel variations (e.g., *hick, heck, hack, hook, hoak, hawk*). Subjects either saw or heard the words presented in 48 different sequences. After each, they repeated them back in the order presented. Recall was better when the words were seen than when they were heard, presumably because spellings helped to preserve the words in memory.

Readers' ability to use spellings to enhance memory for speech may explain results of a study by Olson (1982) in which second graders were more accurate in processing and remembering the exact words in sentences than kindergarteners. It may be that older subjects, being readers, remembered the surface structure of sentences better because they had access to clear entries of the words in their lexicons and could use spellings to preserve the sequence of words in memory.

Metalinguistic skills

Another consequence of having a concrete picture of language in one's mind is to facilitate metalinguistic processes. Certainly it is much easier to detach language from its communicative function, treat it as an object, and study its form when one has fixed visual–spatial symbols to see and manipulate. Without such symbols, in fact, speech cannot be viewed but only heard, which makes it much less amenable to examination. When speakers can see or imagine the exact words, they can pay attention to what was said rather than what was meant if the two are discrepant. Torrance and Olson (Chapter 13) present evidence that differentiation between the wording and the meaning of sentences distinguishes beginning readers from prereaders. Skousen (1979) uses differences in phonemic analyses that distinguish preliterate children from literate adults as evidence that some of the phonemic metalinguistic analyses of speech performed by linguists arise solely from orthographic considerations – for example, their analysis of alveolar flaps in words such as *ladder, latter, pedal, petal, pretty,* and *powder* as /t/ or /d/, or their analysis of preconsonatal nasals as separate phonemes rather than nasalized vowels, as in *sink* and *bank.*

Metalinguistic skills benefit from print not only when children learn what speech looks like but also when they learn terminology for describing its form. Francis (1973) presents evidence that the meanings children possess for terms such as *word* and *sentence* are dominated by their experiences with print. In explaining what words and sentences are used for, children were observed to refer to reading and writing in their replies, but few if any mentioned the use of words or sentences in spoken language. When the topic of words in speech was raised, some children claimed that they "thought a pause occurred between all spoken words because there were spaces between words in writing." This comment illustrates how printed language symbols and terminology provide children with the schema for conceptualizing and analyzing the structure of speech.

In their study comparing high- and low-level literate adults, Barton and Hamilton (1980) report that the most striking difference between the two groups' answers to various analytic questions about language was that in contrast to the lows, the high-level literates had available two sources of information to consult. They could analyze the spoken form or the written form, and depending on the situation, they might use either one.

Concluding comments

To summarize, it is suggested that written language supplies a visual–spatial model for speech and that when children learn to read and spell, this model and its symbols are internalized as a representational system in memory. The process of acquiring this system works various changes on spoken language, particularly at the phonetic and lexical levels. Learning spellings as symbols for pronunciations teaches children that words consist of sequences of discrete phonetic units. For sounds that are nonobvious or overlapping or ambiguous in speech, letters may clarify how to conceptualize them as separate sounds. If children's pronunciations are nonstandard and if spellings symbolize standard pronunciations, print may teach children how to say these words. Also, spellings may teach speakers ideal or literary pronunciations for words, particularly if learners speak a nonliterary dialect and if they hear literary pronounciations from other speakers. If spellings include unpronounced letters and if learners do not hear these letters pronounced, then when spellings are acquired the letters may be marked as silent and this may eliminate pressure to pronounce these letters. Alternatively, speakers may store special spelling pronunciations when sound-discrepant spellings are learned. Another influence at the lexical level worked by print may be to clarify words as separate units of speech with distinctive pronunciations and meanings. The process of learning spellings as they symbolize meanings in print may help to establish words as clear, accessible lexical entries in memory. This may be particularly true for context-dependent words, whose properties may be harder to distinguish in fluent speech. Once spellings are established in the lexicon, they may influence the perception of spoken words by being activated in memory when the words are encountered. Spellings may facilitate thinking about similarly pronounced words when the spellings are also similar but may inhibit thinking when the spellings are different. Activation of spellings for pronounced words may also improve listeners' memory for the words. Having a visual–spatial model for speech may facilitate performance in various metalinguistic tasks requiring speakers to detach language from its communicative function and inspect its form. Printed language may exert an impact not only upon individual speakers but also upon groups of speakers by fixing their pronunciations of words and thus inhibiting change over time. These are some of the effects that appear to result from experiences with printed language.

ACKNOWLEDGMENTS

Research reported in this chapter was supported by grants from the National Institute of Child Health and Human Development and the National Institute of Education. Gratitude is expressed to Lee Wilce, who assisted in the conduct of this work. A revised version of this chapter appeared as "How Orthography Alters Spoken Language Competencies in Children Learning to Read and Spell," chap. 7 of John Downing (Ed.), *Language Awareness and Learning to Read* (New York: Springer-Verlag, 1984), pp. 119–147.

NOTES

1. Although linguists differentiate between phones and phonemes and consider only the former appropriate for describing actual sounds,

psychologists often treat the two terms synonymously. In this chapter the latter convention will be adopted, and the terms *phone, phoneme, phonetic segment*, and *sound* will be used interchangeably. This is not intended to imply that there are no differences or that the differences are unimportant, but only to indicate that a basis for choosing among them is lacking and awaits clarification.

2. Readers have been observed to create spelling pronunciations in their attempts to remember word spellings (Blumberg & Block, 1975; Ehri, 1980a). A friend of mine who claimed to use this strategy regularly told me that he even creates correlates in sound for double consonant letters – for example, as in *DIFFERENT* – by making the middle sound last longer in the pronunciation.

3. These data were taken from segmentation and spelling tasks administered as part of other studies with first and fourth graders. The tasks included preconsonantal nasal words mixed in with other words. Subjects' responses on these words were pulled and analyzed. There were four first-term first graders who each segmented and spelled five pseudowords: *ling, ponk, bund, gant, wimp*. There were 37 fourth graders who segmented and spelled the three real words reported in the text. It is unlikely that in the segmentation task subjects were simply marking letters they knew in word spellings, since they had to pronounce the sound segments corresponding to each token as they positioned it in a row.

4. The shift illustrated in *abound–abundant* is the only one out of the five long–short vowel spelling patterns where Chomsky and Halle's rules yield a different alternation from that yielded by spelling rules. The two systems specify the same alternations for long-to-short *a, e, i,* and *o,* but not long-to-short *u*. According to spelling rules, the shift is from [u] to [Λ] (e.g., *rude* to *rut*). According to Chomsky and Halle's system, it is [aw] to [Λ]. This is why Jaeger picked this as her test case.

5. It is interesting to wonder whether the presence of a single prescribed spelling for each word in an orthography misleads speakers into believing that each word also has only one pronunciation, and furthermore, whether if an orthography allowed variable spellings for words, the pronunciations of words would also become more variable among speakers.

REFERENCES

Barton, D., & Hamilton, M. E. *Awareness of the segmental structure of English in adults of various literacy levels.* Typescript, Department of Linguistics, Stanford University, 1980.

Barton, D., Miller, R., & Macken, M. A. Do children treat clusters as one unit or two? *Stanford University Department of Linguistics Papers and Reports on Child Language Development*, 1980, *18*, 105–137.

Beers, J. W., & Henderson, E. H. A study of developing orthographic concepts among first graders. *Research in the Teaching of English*, 1977, *11*, 133–148.

Bloomfield, L. *Language*. New York: Holt, Rinehart and Winston, 1933.

Blumberg, P., & Block, K. K. The effects of attempting spelling before feedback on spelling acquisition and retention. Paper presented at the annual meeting of the American Educational Research Association, Washington, D.C., 1975.

Bright, W. Linguistic change in some Indian caste dialects. In C. A. Ferguson & J. J. Gumperz (Eds). *Linguistic diversity in South Asia. International Journal of American Linguistics*, 1960, *26*, 19–26.

Bright, W., & Ramanujan, A. K. Sociolinguistic variation and language change. In H. G. Lunt (Ed.), *Proceedings of the Ninth International Congress of Linguists*. Cambridge, Mass: Mouton, 1962.

Burling, R. *English in black and white*. New York: Holt, Rinehart, and Winston, 1973.

Chomsky, C. Approaching reading through invented spelling. In L. B. Resnick & P. A. Weaver (Eds.), *Theory and practice of early reading* (Vol. 2). Hillsdale, N.J.: Erlbaum, 1977.

Chomsky, N., & Halle, M. *The sound pattern of English*. New York: Harper & Row, 1968.

Cole, R. A. & Jakimik, J. Understanding speech: How words are heard. In G. Underwood (Ed.), *Strategies of information processing*. London: Academic Press, 1978.

Desberg, P., Elliott, D., & Marsh, G. American Black English and spelling. In U. Frith (Ed.) *Cognitive processes in spelling*. London: Academic Press, 1980.

Ehri, L. C. Word consciousness in readers and prereaders. *Journal of Educational Psychology*, 1975, *67*(2), 204–212.

Word learning in beginning readers and prereaders: Effects of form class and defining contexts. *Journal of Educational Psychology*, 1976, *68*, 832–842.

Beginning reading from a psycholinguistic perspective: Amalgamation of word identities. In F. B. Murray (Ed.), *The development of the reading process* (Monograph 3). Newark, Del: International Reading Association, 1978.

Linguistic insight: Threshold of reading acquisition. In T. G. Waller & G. E. MacKinnon (Eds.) *Reading research: Advances in theory and practice* (Vol. 1). New York: Academic Press, 1979.

The development of orthographic images. In U. Frith (Ed.), *Cognitive processes in spelling*. London: Academic Press, 1980a.

The role of orthographic images in learning printed words. In J. F. Kavanagh & R. Venezky (Eds.), *Orthography, reading, and dyslexia*. Baltimore: University Park Press, 1980b.

Ehri, L. C., & Wilce, L. S. The mnemonic value of orthography among beginning readers. *Journal of Educational Psychology*, 1979, *71*, 26–40.

Do beginners learn to read function words better in sentences or in lists? *Reading Research Quarterly*, 1980a, *15*, 451–476.

The influence of orthography on readers' conceptualization of the phonemic structure of words. *Applied Psycholinguistics*, 1980b, *1*, 371–385.

The salience of silent letters in children's memory for word spellings. *Memory and Cognition*, 1982, *10*, 155–166.

Francis, H. Children's experience of reading and notions of units in language. *British Journal of Educational Psychology*, 1973, *43*, 17–23.

Gelb, I. J. *A study of writing*. Chicago: University of Chicago Press, 1952.

Gleason, H. A. *An introduction to descriptive linguistics*. New York: Holt, Rinehart and Winston, 1961.

Golinkoff, R. M. Critique: Phonemic awareness skills and reading achievement. In F. B. Murray & J. J. Pikulski (Eds.), *The acquisition of reading: Cognitive, linguistic, and perceptual prerequisites*. Baltimore: University Park Press, 1978.

Goodman, K. S., & Buck, C. Dialect barriers to reading comprehension revisited. *Reading Teacher*, 1973, *27*, 6–12.

Groff, P. Children's spelling of features of Black English. *Research in the Teaching of English*, 1978, *12*, 21–28.

Holden, M. H., & MacGinitie, W. H. Children's conceptions of word boundaries in speech and print. *Journal of Educational Psychology*, 1972, *63*, 551–557.

Householder, F. *Linguistic speculation*. Cambridge: Cambridge University Press, 1971.

Jaeger, J. J. Vowel shift rule vs. spelling rules: Which is psychologically real? Paper presented at the annual meeting of the Linguistic Society of America, Los Angeles, 1979.

Jakimik, J., Cole, R. A., & Rudnicky, A. I. The influence of spelling on speech perception. Paper presented at the annual meeting of the Psychonomic Society, St. Louis, November 1980.

Jung, U. O. H. Zur auditiven Diskrimination legasthener und normaler Schüler. *Linguistik und Didaktik*, 1977, *31*, 210–218.

Kerek, A. The phonological relevance of spelling pronunciation. *Visible Language*, 1976, *10*, 323–338.

Kligman, D. S., Cronnell, B. A., & Verna, G. B. Black English pronunciation and spelling performance. *Elementary English*, 1972, *49*, 1247–1253.

LaBerge, D., & Samuels, S. J. Toward a theory of automatic information processing in reading. *Cognitive Psychology*, 1974, *6*, 293–323.

Lewkowicz, N. K. Phonemic awareness training: What to teach and how to teach it. *Journal of Educational Psychology*, 1980, *72*, 686–700.

Liberman, A. M., Cooper, F. S., Shankweiler, D., & Studdert-Kennedy, M. Perception of the speech code. *Psychological Review*, 1967, *74*, 431–461.

Liberman, I., Liberman, A. M., Mattlingly, I., & Shankweiler, D. Orthography and the beginning reader. In J. F. Kavanagh & R. L. Venezky (Eds.),

Orthography, reading, and dyslexia. Baltimore: University Park Press, 1980.

Liberman, I. Y., & Shankweiler, D. Speech, the alphabet, and teaching to read. In L. B. Resnick & P. A. Weaver (Eds.), *Theory and practice of early reading*. Hillsdale, N.J.: Erlbaum, 1977.

Liberman, I. Y., Shankweiler, D., Liberman, A. M., Fowler, C., & Fischer, F. W. Phonetic segmentation and recoding in the beginning reader. In A. S. Reber & D. L. Scarbrough (Eds.), *Toward a psychology of reading*. Hillsdale, N.J.: Erlbaum, 1977.

Lieberman, P. On the development of vowel production in young children. In G. H. Yeni-Komshian, J. F. Kavanagh, & C. A. Ferguson (Eds.), *Child phonology*, Vol. 1, *Production*. New York: Academic Press, 1980.

Lindamood, C. H., & Lindamood, P. C. *The auditory discrimination in depth program*. Boston: Teaching Resources Corporation, 1975.

Mattingly, I. G. Reading, the linguistic process, and linguistic awareness. In J. F. Kavanagh & I. G. Mattingly (Eds.), *Language by ear and by eye*. Cambridge: MIT Press, 1972.

Morais, J., Cary, L., Alegria, J., & Bertelson, P. Does awareness of speech as a sequence of phones arise spontaneously? *Cognition*, 1979, *7*, 323–331.

Moskowitz, B. A. On the status of vowel shift in English. In T. E. Moore (Ed.), *Cognitive development and the acquisition of language*. New York: Academic Press, 1973.

Olson, D. What is said and what is meant in speech and writing. *Visible Language*, 1982, *16*, 151–161.

Read, C. Pre-school children's knowledge of English phonology. *Harvard Educational Review*, 1971, *41*, 1–34.

Children's categorization of speech sounds in English, (Res. Rep. 17). Urbana, Ill.: National Council of Teachers of English, 1975.

Reddy, R. Speech recognition by machine: A review. *Proceedings of the IEEE*, 1976, *64*, 501–531.

Reder, S. The written and the spoken word: Influence of Vai literacy on Vai speech. In S. Scribner & M. Cole (Eds.), *The psychology of literacy*. Cambridge: Harvard University Press, 1981.

Sales, B. D., Haber, R. N., & Cole, R. A. Mechanisms of aural encoding. IV: Hear–see, say–write interactions for vowels. *Perception and Psychophysics*, 1969, *6*, 385–390.

Seidenberg, M. S., & Tanenhaus, M. K. Orthographic effects on rhyme monitoring. *Journal of Experimental Psychology: Human Learning and Memory*, 1979, *5*, 546–554.

Skousen, R. English spelling and phonological representation. Paper presented at the annual meeting of the Linguistic Society of America, Los Angeles, December 1979.

Smith, F. Phonology and orthography: Reading and writing. *Elementary English*, 1972, *49*, 1075–1088.

Templeton, S. Spelling first, sound later: The relationship between orthography and higher order phonological knowledge in older students. *Research in the Teaching of English*, 1979, *13*, 225–264.

Valtin, R. Deficiencies in research on reading deficiencies. In J. F. Kavanagh & R. L. Venezky (Eds.), *Orthography, reading, and dyslexia*. Baltimore: University Park Press, 1980.

17

Interactions between spelling and sound in literacy

RODERICK W. BARRON

Historical–linguistic influences on the development of English orthography

Prior to acquiring literacy, knowledge of individual words can be characterized in terms of semantic, syntactic, and phonological information. The auditory–temporal organization of spoken language provides a medium for obtaining access to this lexical knowledge in perception and for representing it in production. The acquisition of literacy, however, allows lexical knowledge to be accessed and produced through the visual–spatial medium of written language. Orthography can be regarded as providing a visual–spatial organization for written words that parallels the auditory–temporal organization for spoken words provided by phonology. In addition, orthography and phonology can be regarded as providing an interface in the lexicon between the information conveyed by their respective physical mediums and the syntactic and semantic aspects of lexical knowledge.

The purpose of this chapter is to examine some interactions between the visual–orthographic (spelling) representations of words and their phonological (sound) counterparts in the lexicon during the process of acquiring and using the skills of literacy. Although most of the chapter will be devoted to examining orthographic–phonological interactions involved in the processes of reading and spelling, it will begin with a historical–linguistic perspective on the relationships between orthography and phonology.

Several different relationships are possible between spelling and sound in alphabetic writing systems. One possibility is that orthography is merely a transcription of phonology, with the ideal relationship involving a one-to-one correspondence between individual graphemes and phonemes. Some current orthographies, such as Spanish, Finnish, Serbo-Croatian, and Czech (e.g., Bolinger, 1975; Katz &

Feldman, 1981; Lukatela & Turvey, 1980; Vachek, 1959/1973), come fairly close to this ideal, and they can be regarded as being optimal in the sense that they have a relatively simple and invariant relationship between spelling and sound. English orthography fails miserably when evaluated against this notion of optimality, as there are a number of deviations from the one-grapheme-to-one-phoneme ideal; in fact, none of the vowel letters and only a few consonant letters (e.g., *r* and *q*) are limited to just one corresponding phoneme. The divergence of English orthography from the goal of being essentially a transcription of speech is due, at least in part, to some historical influences upon the development of written English.

Modern English orthography is the product of almost a thousand years of modifications in Old and Middle English. These modifications were brought about by factors as diverse as military invasions, religious conversions, scribal practices, and printers' errors (Scragg, 1974). Apparently, very early English orthography conformed rather closely to a one-to-one relationship between graphemes and phonemes (e.g., Vachek, 1959/1973). The Norman conquest and the accompanying influence of the Catholic church produced an important change in the orthography by making French, and the Latin on which it was based, the standard for both secular and religious written communication. Gradually, French and Latin spellings, as well as Greek and other languages, were incorporated into English orthography. This process was particularly active during the Renaissance, when there was a revival of interest in Greek and Roman culture and knowledge of Greek and Latin etymology was an indication of social as well as literate accomplishment. For a time, the spellings were relatively unstable and varied from text to text, no doubt encouraged by such factors as the tendency to pay legal scribes by the inch for their writing (Latin-based spellings were longer and thus generated higher fees) and the practice of adding and subtracting letters from words in order to produce even margins in early printed texts (e.g., *pity* might be spelled *pyty, pytie, pittie,* or *pyttye* depending upon the spacing requirements involved in setting a text) (Scragg, 1974).

Discrepancies began to develop between spelling and sound as modifications of early English phonemic spellings began to stabilize and written material became more widely available. The actual pronunciations associated with many written words were not consistent with the pronunciations that would be produced by applying a small set of simple rules, where those rules were generally consistent with the ideal of a one-grapheme-to-one-phoneme relationship between spelling and sound. Some of these discrepancies have been retained in the form of exception words (e.g., Baron & Strawson, 1976; Glushko, 1979) that violate current spelling-to-sound and sound-to-spelling rules. The deviant characteristics of many of these words can be traced to certain scribal practices and etymological influences. The exception words *debt* and *subtle,* for example, appear to have borrowed their spellings, including the "silent" letter *b,* from the Latin words *debitum* and *subtilis,* respectively. Nevertheless, they have retained the pronunciation corresponding to their earlier, more phonemic Middle English spellings (*det* or *dette* and *sutil*) (Onions, 1966). Occasionally, exception words originated from errors in etymology. The *sc* digraph in *scissors* (spelled *sisoures* in Middle English), for example, appears to have been borrowed from the Latin word *scindere,* "to cut," rather than from the more accurate Latin word *cisorium,* meaning a cutting instrument (Scragg, 1974). Some very frequent exception words (e.g., *done, love, have*) originated from the sixteenth-century tendency to add the letter *e* to many words ending in a consonant. The spellings of these particular words have survived despite the later orthographic convention of having the final letter *e* signal that a word should be pronounced with a long vowel (e.g., *bone, cove,* and *pave*). Finally, Venezky (1976) has pointed out that exception words such as *above, come,* and *honey* were spelled in Old English with the letter *u* rather than the letter *o.* Apparently, the *o* was introduced by scribes in order to avoid the visual confusions that were produced when a sequence of downstrokes was used in writing letter pairs such as *uv, um, un* and *uw.*

Although many of the exceptions to strict grapheme–phoneme correspondences in spelling can be rationalized on linguistic and historical grounds, individuals concerned with making the skills of literacy more widely available in the population began calling for some reform in English spelling. Even though spelling reform met with some successes, and is still advocated (e.g., Haas, 1969; Pitman & St. John, 1969), English orthography has been very resistant to change in the last few hundred years despite changes in phonology during that period of time. In fact, several investigators (e.g., Bolinger, 1975; Householder, 1971; Kerek, 1976; Samuels, 1972; Scragg, 1974) have suggested that orthography may exert a substantial influence upon phonology. This influence appears to come about through the tendency to pronounce certain words, such as *often, postman, palm,* and *balm* as they are spelled (e.g., by pronouncing the previously unsounded *t* and *l* in the examples above) rather than by using the pronunciations conventionally associated with them. Householder (1971) has argued that there are a large number of these spelling-pronunciations, apparently involving many more words than pronunciation-spellings (words whose spellings have been modified to conform to current pronunciations – e.g., *nite* for *night*). Kerek (1976) has pointed out several ways that spelling-pronunciations might influence phonology. One involves an analogical process (see also Bolinger, 1975) in which the tendency to pronounce an orthographic form as it is spelled in one word (e.g., pronouncing the digraph *th* as /θ/ rather than /t/ in the word theater) is extended in other words with similar spellings (e.g., *thyme, Thames*). Apparently, this process can strengthen the status of an element (e.g., *h*) in the phonology by "desilencing" it. Kerek (1976) also suggests that spelling-pronunciations may weaken general phonological rules (e.g., the rule that unstressed lax vowels are reduced to a schwa) by providing a large number of counterexamples (e.g., the second *o* in *Oregon* is pronounced with a stressed /a/ by individuals who are acquainted with the word only in print). In general, spelling-pronunciations are a relatively conservative force in the English language as they tend to reverse or at least slow the historical divergence between orthography and phonology.

English orthography may also be resistant to change because the orthographic system has evolved to specify more than just information about individual sound values. Smith (1980a, 1980b), for example, has shown that basic features of English orthographic structure, such as the "silent" final letter *e* (Smith, 1980a) and doubled consonants (Smith, 1980b), provide readers and spellers with morphemic, lexical, semantic and etymological information as well as information about sound. Lexical information, for example, is indicated by silent *e*'s when they distinguish plurals from nonplurals (e.g., *raise–rays*) and by doubled consonants when they distinguish homophones (e.g., *canvass–canvas*). Etymological information is indicated, with reasonable reliability, by the tendency for Latin or French words of early origin to have silent final *e*'s (e.g., the affixes *-able, -age, -ance, -ate*), while Latin or Greek words of later origin tend not to double the final letter *s* (e.g., *focus, ethos*).

Another reason for the resistance of English orthography to change is that it appears to exhibit a great deal of regularity at linguistic levels other than those specifically concerned with one-grapheme-to-one-phoneme mappings. For example, a number of investigators (e.g., Bolinger, 1946, 1975; Chomsky & Halle, 1968; Haas, 1970; Householder, 1971; Vachek, 1959/1973, 1973; Venezky, 1970) have argued that English orthography tends to preserve similarity in morphemic information at the expense of similarity in sound. This idea is expressed by Vachek (1959/1973, p. 410) in a comparison of traditional writing systems (e.g., English) to phonetic transcription:

While any system of phonetic transcription provides means for an optical recording of the purely acoustic make-up of spoken utterances, the traditional writing system increasingly tends to refer to the meaning directly without necessarily taking a detour via the corresponding spoken utterances.

Word pairs such as *profane–profanity, critical–criticize, grade–gradual, expedite–expeditious, fact–factual, revise–revision, sign–resign,* and *divine– divinity* preserve their morphemic similarity even though their phonetic representations are not closely related (e.g., the letter *a* is a "long" *a* in *profane* and a "short" *a* in *profanity*). Drawing upon these examples, Chomsky and Halle (1968) proposed that English orthography is almost an optimal system. It is optimal, however, in a very different sense than mentioned earlier, as the orthography is viewed as corresponding more closely to underlying systematic lexical representations of individual items rather than to the surface phonetic representations of those items. The phonetic differences between *profane* and *profanity* are not acknowledged in their underlying lexical representations (e.g., profæn) or in their spelling (e.g., profan-), and as a result the morphemic similarity between the two words is preserved. Instead, the phonetic differences between the words are expressed through the application of general phonological rules (e.g., diphthongization, vowel shift, laxing) that generate surface phonetic forms.

Relationships between written and spoken English

This historical–linguistic analysis of English orthography may have some implications for how the relationship between written and spoken English should be regarded. Clearly, written English should not be considered as a simple, grapheme–phoneme transcription of spoken English. It is not systematic at that level of linguistic analysis, and this may be one of the reasons that it is regarded as being relatively difficult to learn, at least by novices in the language. Instead, written English should be regarded as a partially independent system (Bolinger, 1975; Vachek, 1959/1973, 1973) that provides a visual–spatial representation of language that is distinct from the auditory–temporal representation provided by spoken language and that supplies information that would not be available if the orthography were merely a phonetic transcription of spoken language (e.g., Smith, 1980b).

Regarding written and spoken English as partially independent from each other suggests the possibility that the acquisition of literacy may give individuals the opportunity to use several different strategies in processing written English. At one extreme, literate individuals can use the correspondences between orthography and phonology to translate written words into phonological representations in the process of accessing semantic and syntactic information in the lexicon. At the other extreme, they can access semantic and syntactic information directly on the basis of visual–spatial information, avoiding the use of phonological information altogether. Relying solely upon phonological information would allow the majority of words in English to be read and spelled, as well as many nonwords (e.g., *dorch*). One way this might be accomplished is through the application of a small set of spelling-to-sound or sound-to-spelling rules (e.g., Venezky, 1970; Wijk, 1966). There are, however, a sufficiently large number of words where the application of these rules would produce inconsistencies between spelling and sound. The separate meanings of homophones (e.g., *sail, sale*), for example, are lost when they are translated from spelling to sound (unless contextual information is available to disambiguate them). By definition, exception words (e.g., *have, sword, broad*) cannot be accurately translated into sound by applying spelling rules as they deviate from those rules. These considerations suggest that always using phonological information in reading and spelling has its limitations, at least when translation by rule is involved, and that it may be necessary to use visual information alone for homophones and exception words, as well as for acronyms (e.g., FBI, RCMP, CIA) and ideographs (e.g., &, @, $, %).

On theoretical grounds, there is nothing to prevent complete reliance upon visual information for all reading and spelling. Such a strategy would eliminate the inconsistencies between spelling and sound in English orthography by eliminating the need to translate written language into spoken language. In fact, Edgar Rice Burrough's character Tarzan (1912) learned to read and write by abstracting the patterns of statistical redundancy in English orthography (e.g., see Henderson, 1982, and Venezky & Massaro, 1979, for a description of English orthography from this perspective), even though he could neither perceive nor produce spoken language. Apparently, acquisition of literacy was very long and difficult for Tarzan, suggesting that there might be some advantage to learning spoken English prior to learning written English. This possibility is consistent with the difficulty most hearing-impaired individuals have in achieving the same level of literacy as their normal-hearing

counterparts (e.g., Conrad, 1979). The advantage of learning spelling-to-sound and sound-to-spelling correspondences is consistent
with the relatively greater success of phonics methods in reading
instruction (e.g., Chall, 1967).

This analysis of the difficulties that can arise from relying solely
upon phonological or solely upon visual information in processing
written English suggests the possibility that the acquisition and use
of literate skills in English may involve the ability to use both types
of information. Visual and phonological information may also be
involved in processing orthographies that have a more direct relationship (e.g., Serbo-Croatian) or a less direct relationship (e.g.,
Chinese) between spelling and sound than English. As previously
discussed, however, historical–linguistic influences upon English
orthography have produced a divergence between spelling and
sound. This divergence may require that fully literate individuals
exhibit a good deal of flexibility in using both visual and phonological
information, whereas it is possible that other orthographies may
encourage the use of one particular processing strategy over the
other. In fact, recent evidence suggests that subjects may be more
likely to use a phonological strategy with Serbo-Croatian than with
English (Katz & Feldman, 1983) and a visual strategy with Chinese
than with English (Hung & Tzeng, 1981).

Interactions between orthography and phonology will be discussed
by examining some models of how visual and phonological information might be used in reading and spelling by both fluent and
disabled readers. Evidence will be presented indicating that fluent
readers can exercise some strategic control over their use of these
two sources of information in recognizing printed words. This will
be followed by evidence indicating that good readers are characterized
by their ability to use visual and phonological information in both
reading and spelling, while poor readers are characterized by heavy
reliance upon visual information in reading and phonological information spelling.

Models and strategies for using visual and phonological information

Although there are a variety of ways of investigating the use of visual
and phonological information in reading, one of the most promising
involves comparing words that are regular in their conformity to
spelling-to-sound rules with the exception words that were discussed

earlier. Unlike specially constructed nonwords (e.g., *dorch, brane*), regular and exception words are part of everyday reading experience.

There are several ways of determining whether a word is a regular word or an exception word. Consider the words *wide* and *have*. According to spelling-to-sound rule criteria, *wide* is a regular word because it is consistent with the rule of lengthening the vowel when a word ends in the letter *e*. The word *have*, on the other hand, is an exception to that rule because various historical and linguistic factors have combined to result in the convention of pronouncing the letter *a* in *have* with a short rather than long vowel sound.

Another way of thinking about the differences between the words *wide* and *have* has recently been proposed by Glushko (1979, 1981). He argues that it is not rule conformity that distinguishes *wide* from *have*; rather it is the nature of the information that is activated when *wide* and *have* are read. He argues that the presentation of a word results in the activation of other words that share common spelling patterns. Glushko and others (see McClelland & Rumelhart, 1981; Rumelhart & McClelland, 1981, 1982) refer to these spelling patterns as orthographic neighbors. He defined *orthographic neighbors* as words that overlap in all but one letter with a to-be-recognized target word. According to Glushko, there are two levels of activation involved in reading words aloud. One level is visual and involves activating the visual representation of the target word (e.g., *have*) along with the visual representations of its corresponding orthographic neighbors (e.g., *cave, gave*, etc.). The other level is phonological and involves activating the phonological representation of the target word along with the phonological representations of the orthographic neighbors of the target word. Although activation of visual information begins before activation of phonological information, these two levels are likely to be operating simultaneously at some point during the process of recognizing a word. Presumably, either level of information can be used to activate semantic and syntactic information in the lexicon.

Glushko (1979, 1981) argued that regular and exception words can be distinguished at the phonological level of activation. The phonological neighbors of the word *wide* (e.g., *bide, hide, ride*, etc.) are regarded as being consistent in the sense that their overlapping letters (*i, d,* and *e*) have identical sound values. The phonological neighbors of the word *have* (e.g., *cave, gave, rave*), on the other hand, tend to be inconsistent in the sense that some of their overlapping letters, specifically the letter *a*, do not have identical sound values.

Glushko proposed that the inconsistency between the information activated by an exception word and its neighbors at the phonological

RODERICK W. BARRON

level would slow down the synthesis of a phonological representation for an exception word as compared to that of a regular word. His argument suggests that subjects would be slower at reading aloud exception than regular words, and he obtained that result. Other investigators have reported similar findings (e.g., Baron & Strawson, 1976; Gough & Cosky, 1977). The fact that subjects were slower on exception words indicates that both visual and phonological information was being used in reading aloud. If phonological information was not activated or activated very slowly, then there would be little opportunity for the conflicting phonological activations to arise in the exception words, and no differences in response times between regular and exception words would be expected.

It seems likely that the regular–exception word effect in reading aloud could also be accounted for by proposing that subjects are slower on exception words because they try, for example, to apply spelling-to-sound rules to words like *have* and are unsuccessful. As a result, they would then be required to access lexical memory on the basis of visual information and to retrieve the phonological representation of *have*. Such a model has been proposed by Baron and Strawson (1976) and Coltheart et al. (1979). Glushko, however, extended his activation–synthesis model to make a prediction that would not easily be made by a model that proposed that regular–exception word effects arise from unsuccessfully applying spelling rules to exception words. Glushko compared subjects' performance in reading aloud two types of regular words – for example, *wide* and *save*. Both these words can be pronounced correctly by applying spelling rules, in this case, the long-*e* rule. The only difference between *wide* and *save* is that *save* is a regular/inconsistent word. This word tends to activate a neighbor at the phonological level, specifically the word *have*, which has a nonidentical sound value in one of its overlapping letters (i.e., the letter *a*). Glushko found that subjects were slower on regular/inconsistent words than on regular/consistent words, such as *wide*, which has identical sound values for all of the overlapping letters making up its neighbors. Nonwords also activate neighbors, and Glushko predicted and found that nonwords (e.g., *bove*) that activate inconsistent phonological neighbors (e.g., *love*, *move*) are pronounced more slowly than nonwords (e.g., *bope*) that activate consistent phonological neighbors (e.g., *cope*, *dope*).

Glushko's results and model suggest that the recognition of individual words may be heavily influenced by the relationship between the target word and words that are related to it at the visual and phonological levels. They also tend to challenge the idea that subjects are slower on exception than on regular words solely because of unsuccessful application of spelling-to-sound rules. It seems likely, however, that some regular–exception word effects can be attributed to unsuccessful rule application (e.g., Parkin, 1982), particularly with words that have relatively few neighbors and one-of-a-kind pronunciations (e.g., *yacht*). Also, regular–exception word effects appear to be confined to relatively low-frequency words (Seidenberg et al., 1984). Despite these difficulties, however, Glushko's (1979, 1981) ideas, particularly the notion of lexical activation in the form of orthographic neighbors, appear to be useful in understanding how visual and phonological information is used in reading.

Although Glushko's results suggest that both visual and phonological information are involved in reading aloud, it is not clear whether phonological information plays any role in word recognition situations that do not explicitly require the production of a pronunciation. One way of examining this question is to see if a regular–exception word effect can be obtained in a lexical decision task. One advantage of this task is that subjects are only required to decide whether or not an item is a word; they are not required to read it aloud.

Evidence for a regular–exception word effect is mixed with a lexical decision task. In several experiments, Stanovich and Bauer (1978) found that lexical decisions in response to regular words were faster than to exception words. However, Coltheart et al. (1979) failed to obtain a difference between the two types of words in their lexical decision experiments. This negative finding, in particular, has lead Coltheart (1980) to question whether a phonological code is used in reading at all (see alternative interpretations of literature on this issue by Barron, 1978, and by McCusker, Hillinger, and Bias, 1981).

The Coltheart et al. (1979) lexical decision experiment does, however, appear to be vulnerable to several criticisms. One is raised by Bauer and Stanovich (1980), who found that about one-third of the regular words employed by Coltheart et al. were of the inconsistent variety identified by Glushko (1979). When Bauer and Stanovich (1980) removed the inconsistent words from Coltheart's list of regular words and reran the experiment, there was a trend indicating that consistent/regular words were about 30 msec (milliseconds) faster than the exception words, although the difference was not statistically significant. In two subsequent experiments, Bauer and Stanovich (1980) obtained a reliable regular–exception word effect when they used regular/consistent words.

Another reason why Coltheart et al. (1979) failed to obtain a regular–exception effect may lie with the characteristics of the nonwords they used. As Glushko (1979) has shown, nonwords can

activate orthographic neighbors and their corresponding phonological representations. It is possible that the neighbors of nonwords,
which are words, make it difficult for subjects to distinguish words
from nonwords in a lexical decision task. One way that subjects might
cope with this potential source of word–nonword confusion is to
reduce their use of phonological information. That strategy would,
at least, diminish word–nonword confusion at the phonological level.
One consequence of reducing the use of phonological information
is that the size of the regular–exception word effect might be reduced
or even eliminated. Accordingly, it is at least possible that the subjects
in the Coltheart et al. (1979) experiment reduced their use of
phonological information in order to diminish word–nonword confusion, and in doing so also reduced the size of the regular–exception
word effect. This possibility, plus the presence of a reasonably large
number of regular/inconsistent words, may have combined to eliminate the regular–exception word effect in their experiment.

In order to determine if word–nonword confusion and/or the use
of regular/inconsistent words had anything to do with why Coltheart
et al. (1979) failed to get a regular–exception word effect, a regular–
exception experiment was carried out in which consistent/regular
words were used and nonword neighbors were eliminated as a
potential source of word–nonword confusion (Barron, 1982).[1] The
latter was accomplished by using letter string nonwords that were
made up of consonants with one randomly placed vowel (e.g., *zxlfi*).
In order to determine if the letter string nonwords actually had any
orthographic neighbors, the nonwords were evaluated with a computer program that uses Kücera and Francis's (1967) word list as a
data base. The program was designed to generate all the words that
overlap with a target item in all but one letter, all but two letters,
and so forth. Very few of the letter string nonwords had orthographic
neighbors using the all-but-one-letter overlap criterion, and they did
not have many more neighbors with the all-but-two-letter overlap
criterion.

In addition to wanting to determine if a regular–exception word
effect could be obtained in a lexical decision task, there was interest
in knowing whether or not subjects could exercise some strategic
control over the use of phonological information. That they might
be able to do this is certainly implied by the interpretation offered
above of the effects of activating the phonological neighbors of
nonwords. In order to evaluate this possibility, a second group of
nonwords, referred to as *pseudohomophones,* was selected that had a
maximum likelihood of creating word–nonword confusion at the

phonological level. These items sound like but are not spelled like words (e.g., *baul*). Not only will pseudohomophones activate orthographic neighbors, but this type of nonword has the same phonological representation as a word (in fact, in this case, two words: *ball* and *bawl*). If subjects use phonological information in a lexical decision task and can control the activation of that information, then any regular–exception word effect obtained when the letter strings were nonwords should be reduced, if not eliminated, in the presence of pseudohomophone nonwords.

To summarize, the experiment involved two parts. Part 1 was designed to determine if a regular–exception word effect could be obtained with regular/consistent words and with nonwords that had few, if any, orthographic neighbors. Part 2 was designed to see if the size of the regular–exception word effect could be reduced by using pseudohomophone nonwords, which would produce a great deal of word–nonword confusion at the phonological level. The same adult subjects and the same set of regular and exception words were used in part 1 and part 2. The only factor that was changed between the two parts was the nonwords.

The results indicated that subjects used a phonological code in a lexical decision task, at least when the nonwords do not activate potentially confusing orthographic neighbors, as a significant regular–exception word effect (24 msec) was obtained when the nonwords were letter strings. They also indicated that subjects can exercise some strategic control over the use of phonological information as the regular–exception word effect was reduced to 5 msec (nonsignificant) when the words and nonwords were pseudohomophones and were very confusable at the phonological level.[2] These results are consistent with Davelaar et al. (1977), who showed that homophone effects are eliminated in lexical decision when the nonwords are pseudohomophones. The results are also consistent with the view of Spoehr (1978) and of Hawkins et al. (1976) that the use of phonological information is optional rather than obligatory in word recognition.[3] One of the questions that arises from these results is whether the use of phonological information in a reading-related task, like lexical decision, is related to skill differences in dealing with written language.

Reading skill and a dissociation between reading and spelling

There is considerable evidence suggesting that at least some poor readers may have difficulty using phonological information in reading. Poor readers are, for example, often slower and less accurate than good readers in reading aloud nonwords and words, unless the words are very-high-frequency (e.g., Perfetti & Hogaboam, 1975). Furthermore, Liberman, Shankweiler, and their colleagues (Liberman et al., 1977; Mann, Liberman, & Shankweiler, 1980; Mark et al., 1977) have shown that poor readers are relatively less impaired by phonologically confusable letters, words, and sentences in both recall and recognition tasks. These effects are obtained in listening as well as in reading (Shankweiler et al., 1979). Finally, Bradley and Bryant (1978) have shown that poor readers are less able to carry out phonemic analysis tasks than their good reader peers or younger readers who are reading at the same level. These and other results suggest that poor readers might show a smaller regular–exception word effect than good readers in a lexical decision task. They may, for example, activate phonological information more slowly than good readers, thus increasing the likelihood that response decisions will be based solely upon visual information. This possibility was investigated in an experiment (Barron, 1981, Exp. 1) involving good and poor readers in grades 5 and 6 who differed in reading comprehension skill but who were equated in nonverbal IQ.

In order to examine the ability to use visual as well as phonological information, regular and exception words were divided into items that had high summed single-letter positional frequency values and low summed single-letter positional frequency values (Mayzner & Tresselt, 1965). This is a measure of the frequency with which a single letter appears in a particular letter position in a word of a specific length. It can be regarded as an index of processing at the visual level in the sense that the letter identities of more frequently occurring letters may be activated more quickly than less frequently occurring letters. Mason (1975) and McClelland and Johnston (1977), for example, have shown that subjects are faster and more accurate at recognizing words made up of high (e.g., *pine, shoe*) than low-positional-frequency letters (e.g., *bluff, ocean*).[4] It was expected that the regular–exception effect might be smaller for high- than for low-positional-frequency words, as subjects might be more likely to arrive at a response decision about a high-positional-frequency item before phonological information was sufficiently activated. The results indicated that the regular–exception effect for the high-positional-frequency words was about the same size for good (39 msec) and poor (34 msec) readers, but the difference was only significant for the good readers. For the low-positional-frequency items, however, the size of the regular–exception word effect was significant for the good readers and much larger (94 msec) than for the poor readers (34 msec), where the effect was not significant.

These results suggest that the good readers were better able than the poor readers to use phonological information in reading, particularly when the items were low in single-letter positional frequency. These results are consistent with Barron (1980, Exp. 1), as good readers in that experiment produced a significant regular–exception word effect, whereas poor readers did not.

Considered together, these results on good and poor readers suggest that good readers are effective at using both visual and phonological information in reading. Some poor readers, on the other hand, seem to be relatively ineffective in using phonological information. This suggests that they may be particularly reliant upon visual information in reading. The option of using the redundancy provided by phonological information may not be as readily available to them as to the good readers.

Visual and phonological information also seem to be involved in spelling, and the use of these two sources of information can be illustrated by again comparing regular and exception words. Consider a simple spelling task in which subjects are presented with a word auditorily and asked to write it down. In this task many regular words can be spelled quite accurately by applying knowledge of sound-to-spelling rules and without any reference to the visual representation of the word. Many exception words, on the other hand, cannot be accurately spelled by applying rules. Instead, they seem to require the use of visual information. Some examples of exception words that are particularly difficult to spell without reference to visual information are *debt, sword,* and *yacht.* Spelling errors on these words tend to preserve the sound of the word. For example, *debt* is often spelled as *det, sword* as *sord,* and *yacht* as *yot.*

Good and poor readers were required to spell regular and exception words in an experiment reported in Barron (1980, Exp. 2). Grade 5 and 6 readers were again used. They were very similar in nonverbal IQ, but the poor readers were slower and less accurate than the good readers in reading aloud nonwords, which suggests they may have had relatively more difficulty in using phonological information.

The readers were presented with regular and exception words auditorily and required to write them down. Only words that the children could read aloud correctly were included in the data analyses, as the major concern was with how the children spelled words, particularly exception words, for which they had a visual representation. Only about 3% of the words could not be read aloud correctly, and the two groups of readers did not differ. Phonologically accurate spelling errors (e.g., *det* for *debt, sord* for *sword*) were of particular interest, as they provide an indication, at least with exception words, of the extent to which children attempt to spell words phonetically, without using visual information.

The two groups of readers did not differ on the regular words, but the percentage of phonologically accurate errors on the exception words was significantly higher for the poor readers (27.5%) than for the good readers (11.9%). These spelling data suggest that both groups of readers use phonological information in spelling, but that the good readers are better able also to use visual information to reduce the number of phonologically accurate errors they make on exception words. When compared with the reading results discussed earlier, these data suggest a dissociation for the poor readers between the information they use in reading and the information they use in spelling. Specifically, the poor readers appear to be heavily reliant on visual information in reading, possibly because they have difficulty using effectively phonological information. In spelling, however, they seem to be heavily reliant upon phonological information, possibly because they do not seem to use visual information effectively. Bryant and Bradley (1980) and Frith (1979, 1980) have reported similar dissociations between reading and spelling. Good readers, on the other hand, seem to use both visual and phonological information effectively in reading and in spelling.

There are several possible interpretations of the poor readers' reading–spelling dissociation. One is that poor readers are simply less likely to consult visual information when they are spelling, either internally or by using external cues, such as writing out several possible spellings. The major evidence against this possibility is that the readers did not appear to differ in the frequency of writing-out strategies or in attempts to correct their spellings.

Another and more speculative possibility is that the visual representations of words for the poor readers are not in a form that can be used effectively for spelling. Specifically, the poor readers may not have very good information about individual letter identities, which would appear to be critical in spelling exception words like *debt*. It is important to note that the poor readers' visual representations may be superficially adequate for reading, as it seems possible to recognize some words on the basis of partial visual cues such as initial and final letters and maybe even word shape, particularly when contextual cues are available (e.g., Haber & Haber, 1981; see also Henderson, 1980, 1982, for a critical review of wholism in word perception). It is possible, therefore, that the dissociation between reading and spelling for poor readers may have originated from the characteristics of the visual representations they have acquired for printed words. These representations may be more useful for reading than for spelling.

There is some indirect evidence that suggests that the visual representations of words for poor readers might be less suitable for spelling than those of good readers. One source of evidence is a study by Mitterer (1982), who identified a subgroup of poor readers who seemed to be specifically deficient in using phonological information in reading. He found that their reading performance was much more disrupted by case-alternated words (e.g., *wOrD*), which destroy word shape information, than was that of a group of poor readers who did not have as much difficulty using phonological information. Case alternation disruption was also relatively small for a group of normal readers in his study. Similarly, Guttentag (1981) found that poor readers show a larger case alternation effect than good readers in a word–picture Stroop task. These case alternation results suggest the possibility that some poor readers may have a somewhat more wholistic representation of printed words than good readers. It is possible that these wholistic representations, along with incomplete representations (e.g., containing only the first and last letters), are of limited usefulness in spelling, as each of the letter identities making up a word is not adequately specified.

Summary and some conclusions

Modern English orthography is the product of a variety of historical–linguistic influences upon the evolution of written English. The orthography appears to be relatively systematic, even optimal, at the morphemic level, but it is far from optimal in providing a transcription of the sounds of speech. The fact that the relationship between spelling and sound in English orthography tends to be unsystematic at the grapheme–phoneme level encourages the view that written English should be regarded as providing a visual–spatial representation of language that is partially independent of the auditory–temporal representation of spoken English.

Some models were discussed of how spelling (visual information) and sound (phonological information) might interact in the processing of written language. Evidence was presented indicating that subjects can exert some strategic control over the use of phonological information in simple word recognition tasks. Other evidence indicated that good readers were better able to use both visual and phonological information in reading and in spelling than poor readers, with some poor readers being especially reliant upon visual information for reading and upon phonological information for spelling. These results suggest that although spelling and sound diverge in English orthography, successful acquisition of the skills of literacy involves the ability to be flexible in using both the visual and the phonological characteristics of written language.

Finally, the fact that phonological information is more likely to be used by good than by poor readers suggests it is related to reading skill. It is possible, however, that the ability to use phonological information is merely part of the description of being a good reader and that phonological information has no real function in the reading process (e.g., Coltheart, 1980). Although this is difficult to rule out completely, there appear to be two possible roles for phonological information in reading. One, it may function as a backup code in the processes of accessing semantic and syntactic information. For example, it might be used when the identity of a word cannot be determined quickly by visual information alone. Second, it may have a role in retaining information during comprehension, particularly when combined with articulatory information. Finally, the process of acquiring phonological representations of printed words may have some secondary benefits for the acquisition of visual representations of printed words. Specifically, phonics-based approaches to learning to read may encourage children to attend to all of the letters in a word, rather than to superficial and unreliable cues such as the first and last letter and word shape. As a result, children may be more likely to acquire visual representations that include information about individual letter identities in a word. These visual representations may turn out to be advantageous for spelling as well as for reading.

ACKNOWLEDGMENTS

The research reported herein was supported by a grant from the Natural Sciences and Engineering Research Council of Canada (A9782). I wish to thank D. Besner, P. Bryant, P. Franklin, and J. Mitterer for their comments on an earlier version of this chapter. Portions of this chapter were presented in a talk at the 1981 meetings of the Lake Ontario Visionary Establishment (LOVE) in Niagara Falls, Ontario.

NOTES

1. The regular (40) and exception (40) words were equated in single-letter and bigram positional frequency (e.g., Mayzner & Tresselt, 1965), length, number of syllables, part of speech, and word frequency. They were also equated in number of orthographic neighbors (defined as a word that overlapped a target word in all but one letter) because of the possibility that the regular–exception word effect might be due to the number of neighbors activated by an item at the visual level and have nothing to do with the use of phonological information per se.
2. The error rates did not differ for the regular and exception words with either type of nonword, and there was no evidence of a speed–accuracy trade-off based upon correlations between the errors and response times.
3. One possible criticism of this experiment is that repeating the regular and exception words from the letter string to the pseudohomophone condition is sufficient to reduce the size of the regular–exception word effect. If that were the case, then it would be difficult to use the reduction in response time in part 2 as evidence for the strategic use of phonological information in judging a letter sequence to be a word. In order to test this possibility, a new group of subjects were recruited and the letter string condition (part 1) was simply run twice. Significant regular–exception effects were obtained both times the experiment was run (22 and 23 msec, respectively) that were of approximately the same magnitude. These results appear to rule out the repetition interpretation.
4. These words were also equated in word frequency, orthographic neighbor size, length, number of syllables, and part of speech. The nonwords were letter strings that did not have orthographic neighbors.

REFERENCES

Baron, J., & Strawson, C. Use of orthographic and word-specific knowledge in reading words aloud. *Journal of Experimental Psychology: Human Perception and Performance*, 1976, *4*, 207–214.

Barron, R. W. Access to the meanings of printed words: Some implications for reading and learning to read. In F. B. Murray (Ed.), *The recognition of words: IRA series on the development of the reading process.* Newark, Del.: International Reading Association, 1978.

Visual and phonological strategies in reading and spelling. In U. Frith (Ed.), *Cognitive processes in spelling.* London: Academic Press, 1980.

Reading skill and reading strategies. In A. M. Lesgold & C. A. Perfetti (Eds.), *Interactive processes in reading.* Hillsdale, N.J.: Erlbaum, 1981.

Reading skill and a dissociation between the information used in reading and spelling. Paper presented at the meeting of the Canadian Psychological Association, Montreal, June 1982.

Bauer, D., & Stanovich, K. E. Lexical access and the spelling-to-sound regularity effect. *Memory and Cognition,* 1980, *8,* 424–432.

Bolinger, D. L. Visual morphemes. *Language,* 1946, *22,* 333–340.

Aspects of language. (2nd ed.). New York: Harcourt Brace Jovanovich, 1975.

Bradley, L., & Bryant, P. E. Difficulties in auditory organization as a possible cause of reading backwardness. *Nature,* 1978, *271,* 746–747.

Bryant, P. E., & Bradley, L. Why children sometimes write words they do not read. In U. Frith (Ed.), *Cognitive processes in spelling.* London: Academic Press, 1980.

Burroughs, E. R. *Tarzan of the apes.* New York: Ballantine, 1912.

Chall, J. *Learning to read: The great debate.* New York: McGraw-Hill, 1967.

Chomsky, N., & Halle, M. *The sound pattern of English.* New York: Harper & Row, 1968.

Coltheart, M. Reading, phonological coding, and deep dyslexia. In M. Coltheart, K. Patterson, & J. C. Marshall (Eds.), *Deep dyslexia.* London: Routledge & Kegan Paul, 1980.

Coltheart, M., Besner, D., Jonasson, J. T., & Davelaar, E. Phonological recoding in the lexical decision task. *Quarterly Journal of Experimental Psychology,* 1979, *31,* 489–507.

Conrad, R. *The deaf schoolchild.* London: Harper & Row, 1979.

Davelaar, E., Coltheart, M., Besner, D., & Jonasson, J. T. Phonological recoding and lexical access. *Memory and Cognition,* 1978, *6,* 391–402.

Frith, U. Reading by eye and writing by ear. In P. A. Kolers, M. E. Wrolstad, and H. Bouma (Eds.), *Processing of visible language* (Vol. 1). New York: Plenum Press, 1979.

Unexpected spelling problems. In U. Frith (Ed.), *Cognitive processes in spelling.* London: Academic Press, 1980.

Glushko, R. J. The organization and activation of orthographic knowledge in reading aloud. *Journal of Experimental Psychology: Human Perception and Performance,* 1979, *5,* 674–691.

Principles for pronouncing print: The psychology of phonography. In A. M. Lesgold & C. A. Perfetti (Eds.), *Interactive processes in reading.* Hillsdale, N.J.: Erlbaum, 1981.

Gough, P., & Cosky, M. One second of reading again. In N. Castellan, D. Pisoni, & G. Potts (Eds.). *Cognitive Theory* (Vol. 2). Hillsdale, N.J.: Erlbaum, 1977.

Guttentag, R. E. The role of word shape as a recognition cue in children's automatic word processing. *Child Development,* 1981, *52,* 363–366.

Haas, W. (Ed.). *Alphabets for English.* Manchester: Manchester University Press, 1969.

Haas, W. *Phonographic translation.* Manchester: Manchester University Press, 1970.

Haber, R. N., & Haber, L. R. The shape of a word can specify its meaning. *Reading Research Quarterly,* 1981, *16,* 334–345.

Hawkins, H. L., Reicher, G., Rogers, M., & Peterson, L. Flexible coding in word recognition. *Journal of Experimental Psychology: Human Perception and Performance,* 1976, *2,* 380–385.

Henderson, L. Wholistic models of feature analysis in word perception: A critical examination. In P. A. Kolers (Ed.), *Processing of visible language* (Vol. 2). New York: Plenum Press, 1980.

Orthography and word recognition in reading. London: Academic Press, 1982.

Householder, F. W. The primacy of writing. In F. W. Householder (Ed.), *Linguistic speculations.* Cambridge: Cambridge University Press, 1971.

Hung, D., & Tzeng, O. Orthographic variations and visual information processing. *Psychological Bulletin*, 1981, *90*, 377–414.

Katz, L., & Feldman, L. B. Linguistic coding in word recognition: Comparisons between deep and shallow orthography. In A. M. Lesgold & C. A. Perfetti (Eds.), *Interactive processing in reading.* Hillsdale, N.J.: Erlbaum, 1981.

Relation between pronunciation and recognition of printed words in deep and shallow orthographies. *Journal of Experimental Psychology: Learning, Memory, and Cognition*, 1983, *9*, 157–166.

Kerek, A. The phonological relevance of spelling pronunciation. *Visible Language*, 1976, *10*, 323–338.

Kücera, H., & Francis, W. M. *Computational analysis of present-day American English.* Providence, R.I.: Brown University Press, 1967.

Liberman, I. Y., Shankweiler, D., Liberman, A. M., Fowler, C., & Fischer, W. F. Phonetic segmentation and recoding in the beginning reader. In A. S. Reber and D. L. Scarborough (Eds.), *Toward a psychology of reading.* Hillsdale, N.J.: Erlbaum, 1977.

Lukatela, G., & Turvey, M. T. Some experiments on Roman and Cyrillic alphabets of Serbo-Croatian. In J. F. Mattingly & R. L. Venezky (Eds.), *Orthography, reading, and dyslexia.* Baltimore: University Park Press, 1980.

McClelland, J. L., & Johnston, J. C. The role of familiar units in the perception of words and nonwords. *Perception and Psychophysics*, 1977, *22*, 249–261.

McClelland, J. L., & Rumelhart, D. E. An interactive activation model of context effects in letter perception. I: An account of basic findings. *Psychological Review*, 1981, *88*, 375–407.

McCusker, L. X., Hillinger, M. L., & Bias, R. G. Phonological recoding and reading. *Psychological Bulletin*, 1981, *89*, 217–245.

Mann, V. A., Liberman, I. Y., & Shankweiler, D. Children's memory for sentences and word strings in relationship to reading ability. *Memory and Cognition*, 1980, *8*, 329–335.

Mark, L. S., Shankweiler, D., Liberman, I. Y., & Fowler, C. A. Phonetic recoding and reading difficulty in beginning readers. *Memory and Cognition*, 1977, *5*, 529–539.

Mason, M. Reading ability and letter search time: Effects of orthographic structure defined by single letter positional frequency. *Journal of Experimental Psychology: General*, 1975, *104*, 146–166.

Mayzner, M. S., & Tresselt, M. E. Tables of single-letter and diagram frequency counts for various word length and letter position combinations. *Psychonomic Science Monograph Supplements*, 1965, *1*, 13–32.

Mitterer, J. O. There are at least two kinds of poor readers: Wholeword poor readers and recoding poor readers. *Canadian Journal of Psychology,* 1982, *36,* 445–461.

Onions, C. T. (Ed.). *The Oxford dictionary of English etymology.* New York: Oxford University Press, 1966.

Parkin, A. J. Phonological recoding in lexical decision: Effects of spelling-to-sound regularity depend upon how regularity is defined. *Memory and Cognition,* 1982, *10,* 43–53.

Perfetti, C. A., & Hogaboam, T. The relationship between single word decoding and reading comprehension skill. *Journal of Educational Psychology,* 1975, *67,* 461–469.

Pitman, J., & St. John, J. *Alphabets and reading.* New York: Pitman, 1969.

Rumelhart, D. E., & McClelland, J. L. Interactive processing through spreading activation. In A. M. Lesgold & C. A. Perfetti (Eds.), *Interactive processes in reading.* Hillsdale, N.J.: Erlbaum, 1981.

An interactive activation model of context effects in letter perception. II: The contextual enhancement effect and some tests and extensions of the model. *Psychological Review,* 1982, *89,* 60–94.

Samuels, M. L. *Linguistic evolution with special reference to English.* Cambridge: Cambridge University Press, 1972.

Scragg, D. G. *A history of English spelling.* New York: Barnes & Noble, 1974.

Seidenberg, M. S., Waters, G. S., Barnes, M. A., & Tanenhaus, M. K. When does irregular spelling or pronunciation influence word recognition? *Journal of Verbal Learning and Verbal Behavior,* 1984, *23,* 383–404.

Shankweiler, D., Liberman, I. Y., Mark, L. S., Fowler, C. A., & Fischer, F. W. The speech code and learning to read. *Journal of Experimental Psychology: Human Learning and Memory,* 1979, *5,* 531–545.

Smith, P. T. Linguistic information in spelling. In U. Frith (Ed.), *Cognitive processes in spelling.* London: Academic Press, 1980a.

In defense of conservatism in English orthography. *Visible Language,* 1980b, *14,* 122–136.

Spoehr, K. T. Phonological encoding in visual word recognition. *Journal of Verbal Learning and Verbal Behavior,* 1978, *17,* 461–469.

Stanovich, K., & Bauer, D. Experiments on the spelling-to-sound regularity effect in word recognition. *Memory and Cognition,* 1978, *6,* 410–415.

Vachek, J. Two chapters on written English. *Brno Studies in English I.* Prague, 1959. (Reprinted in J. Vachek, *Selected writings in English and general linguistics.* The Hague: Mouton, 1973.)

Written language. The Hague: Mouton, 1973.

Venezky, R. L. *The structure of English orthography.* The Hague: Mouton, 1970.

Notes on the history of English spelling. *Visible Language,* 1976, *10,* 351–365.

Venezky, R. L., & Massaro, D. W. The role of orthographic regularity in word recognition. In L. B. Resnick & P. A. Weaver (Eds.), *Theory and practice of early reading* (Vol. 1). Hillsdale, N.J.: Erlbaum, 1979.

Wijk, A. *Rules of pronunciation for the English language.* London: Oxford University Press, 1966.

18

Effects of phonology on beginning spelling: some cross-linguistic evidence

CHARLES READ

The chapters in this section examine literacy at its most detailed level: the relations between speech sounds and the characters that represent them. This level of analysis may seem essentially separate from the questions of society, textual structure, and meaning that are dealt with in other sections of this volume. But in fact these diverse levels of analysis have in common at least one property: structural complexity with potential cognitive consequences. Even at the orthographic level, the process of "bringing language into line with print" (McLuhan, 1964, p. 184) is not one of aligning spoken units with their written counterparts in a sequential manner. This chapter will examine one pattern in the beginning spelling of children who speak English, Dutch, and French. This pattern neatly illustrates the segmentation, categorization, and multiple levels of structure essential to orthography.

The spelling of nasal sounds

Children's beginning spelling includes some frequent nonstandard patterns that turn out to have surprising phonetic bases. One such pattern in English is the spelling of nasal consonants that immediately precede other consonants in the same syllable, as in *pump, bent,* and *sink.* Young children tend to omit these preconsonantal nasals in spelling, even though they do represent nasals at the beginnings and ends of syllables, as in *nap* or *pan* (Read, 1975, pp. 54–60, 105–116; Mayhew, 1977, pp. 42, 59). Thus children create spellings such as *bopy* (bumpy), *plat* (plant), and *agre* (angry).

In Read (1975) the tendency to omit nasals in just this preconsonantal position was observed with both preschoolers and first graders. In the sample of preschool spellings, preconsonantal nasals were omitted from 27% to 70% of the time, as shown in Table 18.1. The

Table 18.1. *Omission of preconsonantal nasals in sample of spellings by children less than 6 years old*

	Phoneme		
	/m/	/n/	/ŋ/
Percentage omitted	45	27	70
Examples	*bopy* (bumpy)	*plat* (plant)	*thekce* (thinks)
	nubrs (numbers)	*ad* (and)	*agre* (angry)

Source: Based on Read (1975).

same children omitted nasals in other positions about 1% of the time. In one spelling test in a first-grade classroom, 55% of the spellings of words like *pump* represented every segment except the nasal – for example, *pop*.

   The apparent explanation for this robust phenomenon in children's spelling is that preconsonantal nasals in English differ phonetically from what we regard as the same sounds in other positions. As Malécot showed in 1960, preconsonantal nasals are considerably shorter than others. In fact, the primary difference between *bet* and *bent* is that *bent* has a nasalized vowel. That vowel is usually followed by a nasal consonant, but it is little more than a trace: it may be only 30 msec (milliseconds) long, whereas the "same sound" in a syllable-final position may be 300 msec long. Thus a detailed phonetic representation of *bent* would be [bē(n)t] in which the parentheses mean that the [n] is very short. In fact, in some environments, such as two-syllable words with certain vowels, like *amble* and *anchor*, the nasal consonant may be absent altogether, with the nasalization being entirely in the vowel. It is thus not surprising that children frequently represent the /n/ of *Ben* and omit the /n/ of *bent*; the latter is often no more than one-tenth the length of the former. Given no special symbol for vowel nasalization, *bet* is a reasonable representation of *bent* in American English. To put it another way, the phonetic contrast between *bet* and *bent* is not the same as that between *bee* and *bean*, even though the difference in standard spelling is similar. Children's tendency to omit the nasal in *bent* (but not *bean*) reflects its phonetic form.

   In fact, it is characteristic of children's beginning spelling in English that nonstandard patterns reflect phonetic facts. Often these phonetic influences are not ones that parents and teachers recognize, however;

they are not merely spellings like *thru*. For instance, young children frequently represent certain pairs of vowels with the same letter; the vowels that they spell alike are phonetically similar. One result is that the vowel of *met* is often spelled *a* and that of *mitt* is often spelled *e* (Read, 1975, 1980).

That children's first spelling should be phonetic seems entirely plausible; their primary experience with their language has been with its spoken form. Moreover, they can be quite good mimics; by the time they enter school, they have adopted their native dialect in nearly every phonetic detail. Standard English spelling, however, reflects not only the phonemic form but also the history of the language, morphological relationships among words, and even the learned spelling reforms of the eighteenth and nineteenth centuries, all of which children are quite innocent of. The general conception of development in spelling that this contrast suggests, then, is that children begin spelling at the level of speech sounds, whereas the standard system they must master represents the language at the phonemic level and at higher levels as well.

The need to study other languages

Children's omission of preconsonantal nasals (and other early spelling patterns) have been well established for English, but for real understanding of beginning spelling we must study other languages as well. With its particular sound system and orthography, English requires children to make a phonetic, phonological, or morphological judgment at certain points in order to spell; these are the points at which we can gain insight into their approach to literacy. At other points, a representation, whether standard or not, may be chosen solely because of its relation to a letter name or its frequency in standard spelling. Such spellings show us little. By presenting children with different problems in beginning spelling, languages give us different windows on the process.

In the case of preconsonantal nasals, what might evidence from other languages tell us? First, it might simply confirm or disconfirm the generality of the omissions. If children in other languages also omit preconsonantal nasals, we can be sure that the cause is not merely some peculiarity in one language, such as an atypical spelling of a frequent word or an unusual pronunciation in one dialect. More generally, we could study the effect of a language's sound system, that is, the inventory of speech sounds and their distribution, which varies with the language. English has three nasals, /m/, /n/, and /ŋ/;

it lacks the palatal nasal that is heard in Spanish *señor*, for instance. There are also differences in the relative frequency of speech sounds: /n/ occurs more often than /m/ in English, for instance, but the reverse may be true in another language.

The distribution of these speech sounds also varies. Within an English syllable, the only consonants that follow the nasals are those that are articulated in the same position; /m/ may precede only /p/ or /b/; /n/ may precede only /t/ or /d/, and /ŋ/ may precede only /k/ or /g/. This fact might very well increase the tendency to omit nasals in this position. Moreover, the distribution of /ŋ/ is limited by comparison to /m/ and /n/; it does not occur at the beginning of syllables, though it does so in other languages. We cannot estimate the effect of different inventories, frequencies, and distributions until we have studied children's spelling outside English. It might be that children's spelling has as much to do with phonology (sound systems) as with phonetics (the speech sounds themselves).

There are other differences among languages that may affect children's approaches to literacy, though they are of less immediate relevance to this chapter. The letter names themselves are one such factor: Children's beginning spelling in English is highly oriented toward the letter names; the vowel of *raid* is often spelled *a*, and even the sound at the beginning of *chip* (/č/) is sometimes spelled *h*, because /č/ occurs in the name of the letter *h* (and only that letter).

More basically, the very nature of the writing system, whether alphabetic, syllabic, or logographic, undoubtedly has a profound influence on children's approaches to literacy. A lively body of continuing research has shown that different kinds of orthographies yield different cognitive processes in reading; Tzeng (1983) provides a useful review of this research. Most of it, however, has dealt with mature readers rather than learners, and little research has studied the effect of orthography on children's approaches to writing. Characteristic instructional patterns, attitudes toward spelling, and roles of orthography in the culture may also influence children's beginning literacy in fundamental ways.

Studies in other languages

The significance of studying the development of children's spelling in languages other than English has not gone unnoticed. Since the late 1970s we have seen studies of children's spelling in Dutch (van Rijnsoever, 1979; Niski, 1978), French (Gill, 1981), Spanish (Temple, 1978), and German (Temple, Schlicht, & Henderson, 1981). Al-

though these languages are all still relatively close to English phonologically, they differ enough to help us answer some of the
questions raised above. All the studies included a dictation task in
first grade, with the classroom teacher dictating words in sentence
context. The stimuli were selected for their phonological and morphological structure, including various vowels and consonants and
various kinds of sequences. All in all, these investigations show that
children create spellings in other languages that differ from the
English spellings in ways that can usually be traced to the phonological
structure of the language. The studies certainly confirm that in order
to understand children's development, even in English, we must look
to other languages as well.

The studies of Dutch, French, and Spanish have dealt with the
spelling of nasals. Of these, Niski's was the first, the one with the
largest sample, and the only one focused solely on nasals. Niski
elicited spellings of Dutch words with preconsonantal nasals from
255 children altogether: 143 in 10 first-grade classes and 112 in 4
second grades. The children came from 10 different schools in the
area of Zutphen, in the eastern part of the Netherlands. A Dutch
dialect study (Weijnen, 1966) gives no indication that the Zutphen
pronunciation of nasals differs from that of other regions. Niski also
conducted an experiment like the "pointer" study in Read (1975, pp.
108–112), designed to determine where children locate the difference
between the Dutch phonological counterparts of *bet* and *bent*.

Van Rijnsoever elicited spellings from 54 Dutch first graders in
Overasselt, a village in the southeastern part of the country. He also
studied the spontaneous spellings of 33 preschoolers.

Gill studied the spelling of children in grades 1 through 4 of a
private French-speaking school in Montreal, with an average of 27
children per grade. The 19 words that each teacher dictated included
nine nasalized vowels.

Studies in Dutch

Niski and van Rijnsoever show that the omission of preconsonantal
nasals is approximately as frequent in Dutch as it is in English. First
graders in Niski's study omitted from 25% to 30% of preconsonantal
nasals, and in van Rijnsoever's, from 15% to 27%. Niski also observed
that approximately 75% of all self-corrections by first graders involved
the nasal segment in a vowel–nasal–stop sequence(!), and about 85%
of those consisted of inserting nasal spellings where they had previously been omitted. Van Rijnsoever reports additional evidence from

preschoolers: They omitted from 33% to 50% of preconsonantal nasals, depending on phonological context, or about double the frequency among first graders.

The Dutch studies also confirm the phonological environments in which nasals are most likely to be omitted. Both studies found that the length of the preceding vowel is not by itself a significant factor. Van Rijnsoever found that a voiceless following consonant makes it less likely that the nasal will be represented ($p < .05$), but the difference is entirely among words with short vowels. Thus nasals are most often omitted after a short vowel and before a voiceless consonant, precisely as in English.

This detailed agreement between the English and the Dutch observations in both frequency and context disconfirms explanations that depend on some circumstance in just one language or country. Dutch standard spelling and letter names differ from those in English; instruction in reading and writing is different from that in America or England. Pronunciation also differs, of course, but not in the length of preconsonantal nasals. In this way, cross-linguistic evidence sharply limits the area within which the correct explanation must lie.

Most interesting is the effect of having the nasal and the following consonant articulated at the same place ("homorganic"). This property cannot be studied in English, since, as explained above, all syllable-final sequences of nasal + consonant must be homorganic. Even within Dutch, one would expect that any effect must be attenuated, since a nasal followed by a nonhomorganic stop may actually be produced or perceived with an epenthetic homorganic stop. For example, Dutch *hemd* may be pronounced either [hɛmt] or [hɛmpt], *lengte* may be either [lɛŋtə] or [lɛŋktə], and so on. Despite this variation, homorganicity led to significantly more nasal omissions in van Rijnsoever's study ($p < .02$), although it made no difference in Niski's. Evidently, articulation (kinesthetics) plays a role in these spellings, along with judgments based on acoustics.

Nasals versus clusters of other consonants. Another issue on which the Dutch studies are enlightening is the relation between the omission of preconsonantal nasals and that of other consonants within clusters. Read (1971, 1975) viewed the nasal sequences as different from syllable-final -*st* or -*ld* clusters, for example, and he found a large difference in the frequency of omissions. In his sample of young children's spelling, 30% of preconsonantal nasals were omitted, whereas only 3% of -*st* clusters and 4% of -*ld* clusters were similarly reduced. Marcel (1980), on the other hand, groups all such cluster reductions together and finds that they all characterize the spelling of adults and children with spelling difficulty. Is the omission of nasals just one instance of a general difficulty in segmenting clusters, or is it conditioned by properties, such as brief duration, that are unique to the nasals? Fricatives and laterals in consonant clusters are not particularly brief, and they are not encoded upon the preceding vowel in the manner or to the extent that nasals are, via nasalization. These two accounts are not incompatible, however; it may be that the omission of preconsonantal nasals in beginning spelling is one instance of a general difficulty in segmentation, but a particularly frequent and persistent one because of the phonetic character of those nasals.

The two Dutch studies provide some support for this mixed view. Both Niski and van Rijnsoever find that in syllable-final clusters, nasals are omitted about twice as frequently as other consonants. Niski goes a step further by examining whether it is the same children who reduce initial consonant clusters and omit preconsonantal nasals. He finds that children who omitted the nasal in spelling words like *klomp* were likely to reduce the initial cluster in the same word. Children who omitted nasals in such words also reduced the initial cluster 49% of the time, while other children did so only 21% of the time. Niski makes a similar observation (pp. 82–83) in comparing children's ability to locate the difference between /buk/ and /bruk/ and between /ent/ and/et/; for the most part, it is the same children who locate each difference on neither the stop nor the vowel, but between the two. As Niski points out (p. 12), the initial clusters may be easier to segment both because they are in a more accessible position within the word and because their segments are phonetically more distinct (i.e., longer, not encoded upon the vowel, and not homorganic).

Individual differences. Niski also conducted a partial replication of the "pointer" experiment in Read (1975), with some interesting variations in procedure. In Niski's version, children who had omitted nasals in the dictation were later asked to spell the same words on a playing board using cardboard letters. If asked to spell *klomp*, for example, these children usually selected *klop*. Then the experimenter introduced the word *klop*, that is, the other member of a minimal pair, without the nasal. After checking the child's ability to read back the word which he or she had spelled and to pronounce both words, the experimenter gave the child a pointer to be placed on the spelling *klop* to show where the difference is between the two words.

With a similar task, Read (1975) had found that children who placed the pointer in a consistent position fell into just two groups: those who generally represented the nasal and placed the pointer at that location and those who did not represent the nasal and placed the pointer on the vowel. Read took this as evidence that children who do not yet represent these nasals, but who are able to perform consistently on this explicit segmentation task, generally perceive the vowel as the main difference in such pairs of words. This perception is phonetically accurate.

In addition to these two kinds of responses, however, Niski found two others: children who did not represent the nasal in their spelling but nonetheless consistently pointed to the space between the vowel and the consonant as the location of the difference in sound, and children who pointed to the consonant. Perhaps these latter children regarded the difference between *klop* and *klomp* as /p/ versus /mp/; that is, they regarded the nasal + stop sequence as a single perceptual unit. In terms of articulatory gestures that we can feel, this sequence does form a unit; it is a single movement of the lips, and we cannot feel the intervening movement (of the velum).

Niski's results suggest that children vary in the way they segment speech at the beginning of literacy. When children begin to sense, perhaps vaguely, that nasal + stop sequences (and other clusters) have an internal structure, they may have differing conceptions of this structure, rather like the perception of an ambiguous picture. In fact, segmentation of speech, which is actually a continuous phonetic form, *is* ambiguous: The nasalization that distinguishes *klop* from *klomp* is superimposed upon the vowel and the /p/; only in spelling (and in the percepts of literate speakers) is it a discrete unit. Acoustically, the nasalization goes with the vowel; kinesthetically, it goes with the consonant.

This account of children's beginning spelling raises important questions for further research:

Is this individual variation truly in segmentation, rather than in a response bias? Is there evidence from other tasks that children differ in their segmentation of such sequences?

What might account for the fact that Niski found children who located the difference at all three possible places, while Read found only two?

Do children differ individually in their segmentation of other consonant clusters as well, and is there any relation between their segmentation of the vowel–nasal–consonant sequences and that of other clusters? For instance, does a child who locates the difference between *bet* and *bent* at the vowel do the same for *pet* and *pest*?

Is there any developmental or predictive significance to the differences in segmentation? For example, does segmentation on an acoustic basis develop later than that on an articulatory basis? Does one segmentation lead more readily toward the adult judgment and standard spelling?

In general, as we examine children's literacy development in detail, we need to be alert to this kind of individual variation. Most previous research, emphasizing treatment variables over subject variables, has probably underestimated and overlooked variation in strategies at this level of detail, even when revealing differences in overall literacy development.

Studies in Spanish

Temple (1978) dictated no words containing preconsonantal nasals to first graders in Spanish (Dominican Republic). There were three such words in the dictation to second and third graders: two with /mb/ (*bombon* and *invierno*) and one with /nč/ (*hinchado*). Second graders omitted these two nasals 16% and 5% of the time, respectively, while third graders did so 9% and 6% of the time. A much larger number of errors had to do with whether assimilation is represented in spelling: both *bombon* and *invierno* are pronounced with /mb/, but only the former is spelled with *mb*. These nasal omissions were the second-largest category of nonstandard spellings.

Studies in French

Gill (1981) provides another perspective on children's representation of nasals in her study of children's spelling of Montreal French. The words that teachers in the monolingual French-speaking school dictated included all four of the nasalized vowels of French, two of them occurring in both preconsonantal and word-final position, as in *enfants* ([ɑ̃fɑ̃]).

Gill does not provide phonetic transcriptions of the stimuli as pronounced in the classroom; indeed, the pronunciation probably varied somewhat from one teacher to another. Thus we cannot know whether in a word such as *nombre* the actual pronunciations included a consonantal nasal after the nasalized vowel.

In only about 6% of the spellings did the first graders (*n* = 28) fail to represent the nasalization of the vowel with the letter *m* or *n*.

Second graders omitted even fewer (2%) of these markers, and the third and fourth graders omitted none. There was no difference between the preconsonantal and the word-final environments. In short, there is little indication in this study of French of the nasal omission that is such a salient and robust phenomenon in children's spelling of English and Dutch.

Phonetically, words with preconsonantal nasalized vowels in French are similar to words with preconsonantal "nasals" in English and Dutch:

French:	nombre	[nõbʁ]
English:	number	[nʌ(m)bɚ]
Dutch:	panter	[pɑ̃(n)tɚ]

English *met* [mɛt] contrasts with *meant* [mɛ̃(n)t] in the same way that French *messe* [mɛs] contrasts with *mince* [mɛ̃s], namely in the presence or absence of nasalization on the vowel. In fact, any difference is toward brief nasal consonants in English and Dutch but not in French. Why, then, are the French-speaking children the ones who more frequently represent the nasalization?

It might seem that the phonemic status of nasalized vowels in French accounts directly for this difference. If children tend to represent just the functional contrasts in their language, then since nasalized vowels contrast with oral vowels in French, children should represent them. This explanation is not sufficient, however, for the simple reason that in all three languages, preconsonantal vowel nasalization is the manifestation of *some* phonemic contrast. Moreover, in all three languages, the standard spelling of a nasalized vowel is essentially the same: a vowel spelling followed by *n* or *m*.

If the phonemic status of vowel nasalization cannot account for the difference in spelling, then perhaps the distribution of nasalization can do so. Nasalized vowels are found in more phonological environments in French, after all. It turns out, however, that the only real difference in distribution is that French has syllable-final nasalized vowels, as in *bon* [bõ], whereas Dutch and English do not. Otherwise, all three languages have syllable-initial nasal consonants, nasalized vowels followed by nasal consonants, and the preconsonantal nasalized vowels discussed here. (There are other differences, such as the occurrence of a palatal nasal in French, but these have no direct relevance to the spelling of preconsonantal nasals.) In all three languages, children would produce essentially standard spellings of nasals if they simply inferred that nasals at the beginning of syllables are spelled *n* or *m* and that all the rest are spelled as a vowel followed by *n* or *m*, regardless of whether the nasalization is primarily vocalic or consonantal. (This rule would have to be slightly more complicated to encompass palatal and velar nasals, but the core process would be unaffected.) Although young children do generally try to represent just what is phonemically significant in their language, and nasalized vowels differ in phonemic status and distribution between French and English or Dutch, those facts are not sufficient to explain the difference in first graders' spelling of nasals. In seeking other explanations, we may learn more about the role of segmentation and categorization in beginning spelling.

The difference in the phonemic status of nasalization may, however, help to account for the difference in beginning spelling via adults' awareness of language and its effect on instruction. French-speaking teachers are of course aware that nasalized vowels exist in their language and that there are spelling conventions for representing them. English- and Dutch-speaking teachers do not know that the same is true of their languages. American teachers may know that their students produce spellings such as *dot* for *don't*, but they do not realize how frequently such spellings occur or that they have to do specifically with nasals that precede consonants. Still less, of course, do most American teachers realize that such nasals are really nasalized vowels and that that is the reason for the spelling pattern. Teachers of French-speaking children (and their textbooks and curricula) undoubtedly give more explicit attention to the spelling of nasalized vowels. The teachers' awareness, communicated to the children, may lead to more consistent spelling of nasalized vowels. Thus learning to spell requires more than knowing sound–spelling correspondences; that knowledge itself depends on segmenting speech into discrete sounds and then classifying them. Those classifications may differ from one language to another, even when the sounds themselves are the same.

Possible effect of syllable structure

A structural difference among these languages that may help to explain children's (non)representation of nasals is one of syllable structure. In French, the canonical syllable is an open one, that is, a syllable ending in a vowel. Léon (1966, p. 15–16) estimates that about 80% of French syllables are open, although he does not say whether this refers to types or tokens. Hyphenation in written French reflects this preference; *saucisson* is hyphenated *sau-cisson* rather than *sauc-isson*, for instance. In normal speech, there are probably no phonetic signals of syllable structure where the division might be made in more than one way. That is, there are no cues that divide French *ici* as [i-si] rather than [is-i]. However, both children and adults can produce such divisions in overly slow (unnatural) pronunciation, and in doing so French speakers favor open syllables wherever possible. Ozello (1970) has recordings of French children aged 3 and 8 who consistently produce *saucisson*, for instance, as [so-si-sõ].

It turns out that all the nasalized vowels in Gill's stimuli were in open syllables, both medially as in *pinceaux* [pẽ-so] and finally as in *magazins* [magəzẽ]. On the other hand, the preconsonantal nasals that children so frequently omit in spelling English and Dutch are primarily in closed syllables. All the monosyllables (e.g., *bent*) are closed, and for morphological reasons one might argue that some of the polysyllables are, too (e.g., *bumpy* and *stinker*). There is a plausible relation between syllable structure and spelling in that if the nasal is homorganic with a following consonant in the same syllable, it may be more likely to be omitted in favor of the oral consonant, which is a stop or fricative and therefore relatively salient. Recall that van Rijnsoever found significantly more omissions before homorganic consonants. This effect cannot be tested in English, where consonants must be homorganic with a preceding nasal within a syllable, but it would explain the more frequent omissions in English than in French, assuming primarily closed syllables in the former and primarily open ones in the latter. There are nasalized vowels in closed syllables in French, as in *hampe* /ɑ̃:p/ and *pompe* /põ:p/, which might be used to test this effect.

Conclusions

We can draw some conclusions from the studies of this one spelling pattern across three languages. The Dutch observations confirm the generality of the pattern. They strongly reinforce the hypothesis that the omission of nasals in this position is attributable to the phonetic form, rather than to the orthographic or dialectal peculiarities of English or the instructional peculiarities of the United States. The Dutch studies also help to clarify the roles of vowel length and consonant voicing in conditioning these omissions, and they show that homorganicity may be a conditioning factor, one that could not have been investigated in English. Also in Niski's and van Rijnsoever's work is a strong suggestion that the omission of preconsonantal nasals may be simply one aspect of the general segmentation difficulty that gives rise to the reduction of other consonant clusters in beginning spelling, but that it is a special case because of the phonetic structure of these vowel–nasal–consonant sequences, namely the nasalization of the vowel, the extremely brief duration of the nasal (if any), and the articulation of the nasal and consonant at the same place.

Niski's "pointer" experiment gives us a glimpse of individual variation in the way children segment such sequences. Such variation is important to any detailed understanding of the beginning of literacy. We need to know, for example, whether a child's use of one spelling pattern is predictable from his or her use of any other, and whether patterns such as the omission of preconsonantal nasals occur in an all-or-nothing manner that suggests the learning of a generalization (Read, 1975, p. 106). In general, if we think of spelling as a problem that children solve in different ways, it is both scientifically and educationally important to find out what knowledge and cognitive abilities account for the different approaches.

Gill's study of French, on the other hand, shows that this spelling pattern differs across languages in response to differences in phonological structure; that is, what matters is not only speech sounds, but also their role within a phonological system. Beginning spelling depends on segmenting and categorizing speech sounds, not merely perceiving and representing them. Sapir, writing in the first issue of *Language* (1925, p. 40), similarly observed that speech sounds are not discrete units in a list, but occupy positions in relation to one another: "This is the inner configuration of the sound system of a language, the intuitive 'placing' of the sounds with reference to one another." Compared with the basic interpretation of vocal behavior as speech (e.g., the interpretation of a hissing action as the speech sound /s/), this relational pattern "is more elusive and of correspondingly greater significance for the linguist." In young children's spelling, this elusive configuration becomes observable.

Finally, this study of one spelling pattern shows that cross-linguistic evidence is essential to a real understanding of beginning spelling. What we can observe in one language depends on its phonetics, phonology, and orthography, including even such seemingly minor details as its letter names. Each language poses certain puzzles for the beginning speller while making other choices easy. Only by studying a range of languages can we have much confidence in our hypotheses about why children make the choices they do.

ACKNOWLEDGMENTS

Research reported herein was funded by the Wisconsin Center for Education Research, which is supported in part by a grant from the National Institute of Education (Grant No. NIE-G-81-0009). The opinions expressed in this chapter do not necessarily reflect the position, policy, or endorsement of the National Institute of Education.

This chapter is based on a portion of the author's forthcoming book, *Children's Creative Spelling*, to be published by Routledge & Kegan Paul. Used with the permission of Routledge & Kegan Paul.

REFERENCES

Gill, C. E. An analysis of spelling errors in French (Ph.D dissertation, University of Virginia, 1980). *Dissertation Abstracts International*, 1981, *9*, 3924A. (University Microfilms No. 80-26641).

Léon, P. R. *Prononciation du français standard*. Paris: Librarie Marcel Didier, 1966.

McLuhan, M. *Understanding media: The extensions of man* (2nd ed). New York: Mentor, 1964.

Malécot, A. Vowel nasality as a distinctive feature in American English. *Language*, 1960, *36*, 222–229.

Marcel, T. Phonological awareness and phonological representation: Investigation of a specific spelling problem. In U. Frith (Ed.), *Cognitive processes in spelling*. London: Academic Press, 1980.

Mayhew, D. C. An investigation to determine factors affecting selected kindergarten children's invented spelling (Ph.D. dissertation, University of Georgia, 1977). *Dissertation Abstracts International*, 1978, *38*, 3998A. (University Microfilms No. 77-29788)

Niski, J. A. Nasal omissions in children's spellings. Typescript Instituut voor Algemene Taalwetenschap, Katholieke Universiteit, Nijmegen, Netherlands, 1978.

Ozello, Y. Recording No. FR3.008.07, Laboratories for Recorded Instruction, University of Wisconsin, Madison, 1970.

Read, C. Preschool children's knowledge of English phonology. *Harvard Educational Review*, 1971, *41*, 1–34.
   Children's categorizations of speech sounds in English. Urbana, Ill.: National Council of Teachers of English, 1975.
   Creative spelling by young children. In T. Shopen & J. M. Williams (Eds.), *Standards and dialects in English*. Cambridge, Mass.: Winthrop, 1980.

Sapir, E. Sound patterns in language. *Language*, 1925, *1*, 37–51.

Temple, C. A. An analysis of spelling errors in Spanish (Ph. D. dissertation, University of Virginia, 1978). *Dissertation Abstracts International*, 1979, 2, 721A. (University Microfilms No. 79-16258)

Temple, C. A., Schlicht, R., & Henderson, E. Invented spelling of German-speaking children. Paper presented to the McGuffey Reading Center Conference on the Virginia Spelling Studies, Charlottesville, Va., October 2, 1981.

Tzeng, O. J. L. Cognitive processing of various orthographies. In M. Chu-chang (Ed.), *Asian- and Pacific-American perspectives in bilingual education.* New York: Teachers College Press, 1983.

van Rijnsoever, R. Spellingen van voorschoolse kinderen en eersteklassers. *Gramma: Nijmeegs Tijdschrift voor Taalkunde,* 1979, *3*, 169–196.

Weijnen, A. *Nederlandse Dialectkunde.* Assen, Netherlands: van Gorcum, 1966.

19

Phonology in reading

PAUL A. KOLERS

The preceding chapters in this section are concerned with the relation between print and speech. Roderick Barron approaches the topic from a traditional perspective, that of the relation of sound to reading. Linnea Ehri speculates on the conservative role that print plays in forming speech and proposes a mechanism for the process. Charles Read puts forward some concrete proposals to account for the oddities in children's spontaneous spelling. The chapters make contact at various points and at others go their own ways; my comments will have the same structure.

One of the compelling questions that all three chapters address is the status of print: Is it special or derivative? The standard view from linguistics is that the written language is derivative: Speech is taken as primary and the written language is taken to be a concretization of speech (Bloomfield, 1933). In a more recent form, the proposal has been that the written language is not only derived from but is "parasitic on" speech, and with no interesting characteristics of its own (Cooper, 1972; Liberman et al., 1980). Learning to read is taken to be a matter of first learning the sounds that letters symbolize and then concatenating them – an updated version of the sort of phoneme–grapheme theory of learning put forward by Gibson (1965), among many others. Each of the three preceding chapters in this section affirm the implausibility of the proposal, although for different reasons. Read rejects the proposal because the same letter is often used to represent different sounds; *n* represents both the nonnasalized "en" of *not* and the nasalized en of *don't* or *think*, for example. (This is not even to consider the inconsistent usages of *ough*, as in *through, enough, dough, plough*, etc., or of the vowels, as the *a* in *fat, fate, father, fall*, etc.) Barron, arguing against the strict form of the proposal, suggests that the written language has both a phonological component and a spatial component, and that skilled readers may make use of information derived from both components. Ehri's view is that print does represent sound but not at the analytical alphabetic level of single letters and single sounds; rather, whole printed words symbolize spoken words. Thus the three authors agree that print is something other than the mere transcription of speech sounds, although they do not concern themselves with the characteristics that set it apart from speech or with what its special properties might be.

A second issue is the role of skill or expertise in recognizing print. Barron actually seems to confuse issues when he insists that the skilled reader may use both phonological and "visual" information in reading, whereas the poor reader uses visual information in reading and phonological information in spelling. Read, in contrast, implies that it is the child reaching out to the world of written language who misspells it in a phonology-preserving way. Ehri, in turn, argues that learning how to read teaches children how to speak, for the printed word identifies phonemic constituents that are otherwise hard to discriminate. But let me turn to particulars.

I hold up two issues for Barron to consider. One is the appropriateness to an understanding of reading of experiments on single words, such as lexical decision tasks, word superiority tasks, and the like. Most of those experiments that I am familiar with tend to require the person tested to focus on a single issue, such as whether a word is in the reader's vocabulary, or whether a sequence could be an English word, or which letter was in the nth position, and the like. These are largely tests of discrimination or memory, whereas reading would seem to place many more options before the person. Working with geometrically transformed texts I have often found that people can concern themselves with the typography or with the syntactic or semantic aspects of the text; they can either see through or look at the print, much as we can listen to a person's accent or ignore it as we analyze the message of his or her speech. Moreover, in reading we involve our own associations, conjectures, inferences, and the like, as we try to understand what is written. We may, in addition, examine the typography, layout design, or sentence structure; and we may be sensitive to errors of spelling or to themes – in fact, to all the variety of possibilities for which we have time and competence and of which the work is suggestive. Reading seems to be much more intellectual and much more a composite task than Barron's illustrations induce one to suppose.

A second point has to do with the difference between good and poor readers. Barron strains to conclude that the good reader may use both phonological and visual information in reading, being led to suppose, I suppose, that the poor reader would ordinarily use only visual information. In contrast to the view Barron seems to hold, I would think that a skilled person carries out a task in many different ways and is sensitive to many more features of an object than is a novice or poor performer. I have found, for instance, that better readers are more sensitive to both the message being read and to the features of print that instantiate it, whereas poorer readers grasp only for the message (Kolers, 1975). Expertise consists in part in differentiating or segmenting a whole into analytically or discriminatively useful components; the more skilled one is, the greater the degree of differentiation of the whole. I believe that the skilled reader reads a text with all of the skills that time and purpose allow; hence, the more skilled the reader, the more forces or skills he or she can bring to bear on a text, and the more he or she takes away from an encounter with it. Not only do they use the visual and the phonological features of words in reading them, readers use all the other features that they can exploit as well (Kolers, 1979). The reader applies skill in analyzing a text, not just seeks information *about* it. It is a mistake to think that reading is a matter of only wringing the gist out of a text.

Two strong points are made in Linnea Ehri's chapter. One is her claim (and in truth the claim of many before her) that widespread literacy has a conserving effect on speech, slowing down its rate of change. Here she argues against the linguists whom she understands to claim that the influence of speech on writing is one-way: from speech to writing and the latter is derivative. Her claim, in contrast, is that the influence is, not two-way, but one-way in the other direction, from writing to speech, the written form instructing people in the proper pronunciation (and thus preservation) of the spoken form. I find this somewhat forced. If writing influences speech positively, as it surely does in aiding pronunciation, it may also influence it negatively – in leaving one unsure of what *meander* means, for example, until one learns that it has not two but three syllables, or *chaos*, another word frequently misread. Similarly, speech may influence writing. Although, in light of the multiple ancestry of the English language, we do not (perhaps cannot) do much to regularize its spelling, other nations frequently revise the spelling of their language to make it conform more closely to speech: Russia and the Netherlands are two principal examples of countries that revise their spelling from time to time. Hence Ehri's case seems to be polarized toward a particular aspect of writing, its mapping relation to speech, but at the price of excluding other functions. Moreover, to argue, as she does, from the observation that a feature is found in memory to the notion that that feature is essential to performance, is surely wrong. Many features of a text are found in memory, such as the length of a word, imagined gestures, feelings or rhythms accompanying its reading, its location on a page, and so on (Brown, 1970; Kolers, 1979). Surely these cannot be construed as the basis of literacy. Moreover, memory of distinctive syllables may be stored in mind but not used productively, for children especially may locate distinctive syllables in a word and yet not change its customary pronunciation. Ehri uses the same faulty logic when she argues, from the preservation of sound in memory, that sound is the basis of reading. Both Ehri and Barron seem to short-change the reader by looking for single causes of what is a richly articulated and many-featured skill.

The second point is compound, for it has to do with the mechanisms of reading. Ehri interprets Liberman et al. (1980) as proposing that, in reading, we engage in a continuous constructive operation of translating the graphemes into phonemes that we interpret. She argues against this view because of the severe limitations in English on phoneme–grapheme correspondence: that a single letter can be sounded in many different ways and that a single sound can be represented by many different letter sequences (as *high, eye, lie, buy,* etc.). She finesses the problem of assembly of a word from phonemes or graphemes and proposes instead that, regardless of the way written words are acquired, once they are composed into wholes they stand for or symbolize a sound sequence. These wholes, in her proposal, are stored in mind as visual images representing sounds – templates from which a phonological form can be generated or sounded out.

Her claim strikes me as having all the defects inherent in three different views of mind, templates, images, and ideation. One would like to know in what typeface the templates or visual images exist – Times Roman, Garamond; in bold or italic; serifed or sans serif? Ehri seems to suppose that objects are recognized by matching an imaginal construction to their physical occurrence. The special deficiency of template theories of knowledge is just that we can recognize objects that have been transformed. How objects are recognized that have not been seen before and how an object is acquired by mind the first time are also unsolved problems for such views. Finally, if the printed word symbolizes a sound in mind, how then are the sounds understood? Are they realized as subvocal speech? If so, reading would not go faster than about 200 words per minute. Are they interpreted without transformation into subvocal speech? If so, why claim that they are anything more than symbols?

The main point Ehri insists on seems to me worth keeping in mind – that is, that the written language can influence our understanding and production of the spoken language. Her effort to integrate that point into a theory of performance does not strike me as successful.

Perhaps because it is the most direct and pointed, Charles Read's chapter takes the least commentary. Read has been studying children's misspellings for some time and a few years ago demonstrated some regularity to them. He summarizes some of his arguments here. They are that children are more sensitive to phonetic realizations than adults are and that they try to assign sound classes to marks in as nearly a one-to-one way as possible. Some sounds in a language are not contrastive, however, and thus are not represented in its writing system. This fact is not always known to children beginning to write. When confronted with a word for some of whose sounds they lack a character, they approximate. In Read's example, preconsonantal nasals such as the en in *bent* and *sink* are heard as different from the en in *nap* or *pan*, so the same character *n* is rejected as representing both of them; the child tends to omit the en in the former (perhaps because it is shorter in duration) and produces such irregular spellings as *bet* for *bent* and *sik* for *sink*. Rather than as cute or charming or just like a child, the irregularity is seen as reasoned, plausible, and just like an adult: a judgment resolving an ambiguity.

Presumably children come closer to spelling correctly in languages whose correspondence rules are closer to realizations of phonology than are those of English. Presumably too the misspellings might be interesting to observe in adults acquiring literacy for the first time. Does their greater knowledge of vocabulary deafen them to sounds known to be noncontrastive, or do they also try to approximate the sounds of language in a writing system imperfect for the job? Perhaps Read's underlying theme is that spelling, for all people, is at best an approximation in a language as rich as English; it provides clues to a word's identity, but not absolute identification. It is not the sounds themselves that are most important, he claims, but their roles within a phonological system. Reading seems to require an exercise of intelligence at every level of its execution.

Overview

One issue that seems to be struggling for recognition has to do with representational media. The linguist's arrogance had long held that the written is merely a version of the spoken language. The authors of the three preceding chapters agree that written and spoken are not perfectly equivalent. I propose to go somewhat further and argue that the written and spoken forms are different media, different ways of symbolizing, each with its own conventions. It has been shown many times that the form of written communications is different from the form of spoken communication: Verb forms differ, syntax differs, word choice differs, and even the order of argument has been shown to differ depending on whether one is speaking spontaneously or writing. Important differences characterize composition: We can retrospect accurately and precisely on what we have written, but only imprecisely on what we have spoken; this difference is surely important to the development of more orderly syntax and more orderly argument in writing.

The conventions differ also. In speech we use inflection – sounded variation in pitch, amplitude, and contour – to aid in conveying our meanings, and indeed contour or inflection can often take precedence over the literal interpretation of the words used, as in that famous "This is a fine country" with the contour of "fine" either ascending or descending. (It has even been said that children often listen more to the tone of voice than to the words said.) Print lacks these melodic features. Only the most intransigent and radical proponent of the view that we read by translating print to sound would hold that comma, semicolon, question mark, quotation marks, and the like receive phonological instantiation in being read, for example. Is the first letter of a sentence or the capital letter of a name in the middle of a sentence given a phonological realization? It seems to me rather that these are aspects of the conventions that characterize the use of print; they are for the reader instructions designed to aid interpretation, not pronunciation; techniques to aid understanding, not cues to direct the production of speech. If only to that minimal extent, reading text requires a form of processing not relevant to speech. In addition, Doblin (1980) shows how type style can influence interpretation of the message in a manner perhaps analogous to words of condolence uttered amid laughter or an invitation to a party spoken in tones of mourning. One would not want to say, I believe, that we interpret the visual joke by first translating it to a spoken form and then enjoy that. Other typographic transformations – change of style or orientation of type, shading, weight, or arrangement – can strongly influence reading of a passage, and in a way that is even sometimes difficult to put into words.

The linguist's view of reading as requiring phonological mediation might be said to imply that vision is dumb but hearing is smart; that is, that the visual system has the capability only of recognizing printed marks as surrogates of sound and summoning those surrogates to mind for interpretation. This claim cannot be taken seriously any longer, and the wonder is that it was taken seriously for so long during the 1960s and 1970s. Are faces, scents, and music recognized by finding their surrogates in speech? In fact, these are three instances in which recognition often takes place in the absence of accurate linguistic description. Try to describe the appearance of a face so that another person will pick it out in a crowd; it is often very difficult to do, compared to showing a person a picture of the face. Our vocabulary for smells is so poor that we often name smells in terms of an object we use as a prototype, as "This smells like . . ." And who can convey in words the sounds of an intricate piece of chamber music? The point here is that each of our various representational systems seems to have its unique characteristics, and our understanding of their function is likely to proceed the more quickly the more we appreciate their individuality. Print is print and speech is speech. They are correlated, but not perfectly. We have spent many years studying how they are alike and perhaps have learned a good deal from the study. We surely cannot learn less by studying how they differ and the significance of those differences for a theory of communication.

ACKNOWLEDGMENT

Preparation of this chapter was aided by Grant A7655 from the Natural Sciences and Engineering Research Council Canada.

REFERENCES

Bloomfield, L. *Language*. New York: Holt, Rinehart & Winston, 1933.
Brown, R. Psychology and reading. In H. Levin & J. P. Williams (Eds.), *Basic studies on reading*. New York: Basic Books, 1970.

Cooper, F. S. How is language conveyed by speech? In J. F. Kavanagh & I. G. Mattingly (Eds.), *Language by ear and by eye*. Cambridge: MIT Press, 1972.

Doblin, J. A structure for nontextual communication. In P. A. Kolers, M. E. Wrolstad, & H. Bouma (Eds.), *Processing of visible language 2*. New York: Plenum, 1980.

Gibson, E. J. Learning to read. *Science*, 1965, *148*, 1066–1072.

Kolers, P. A. Pattern analyzing disability in poor readers. *Developmental Psychology*, 1975, *11*, 282–290.

Kolers, P. A. A pattern analyzing basis of recognition. In L. S. Cermak & F. I. M. Craik (Eds.), *Levels of processing in human memory*. Hillsdale, N.J.: Erlbaum, 1979.

Liberman, I., Liberman, A. M., Mattingly, I., & Shankweiler, D. Orthography and the beginning reader. In J. F. Kavanagh & R. L. Venezky (Eds.), *Orthography, reading, and dyslexia*. Baltimore: University Park Press, 1980.

20

Language, literacy, and learning: an annotated bibliography

RON SCOLLON

This is a bibliography of readings on language, literacy, and learning. It is intended to give the reader an idea of some of the main points of discussion in this area during the past decade or so. The bibliography is not complete nor even extensive. It consists of books and articles that have strongly influenced my thinking in the past few years. Other bibliographers would have prepared a somewhat different list. I have made no attempt to separate primary and secondary sources. The bibliographies found in these writings are the best sources of further references by which the student can move more deeply into the field.

Each entry contains a short comment. These comments are not strictly abstracts of the contents. I have written them to indicate my interest in each item and my reason for including it in this list. Many of these sources have a much broader scope than my comment indicates. (Items that have been added by David Olson are identified by his initials at the end.)

Alpers. S. *The art of describing: Dutch art in the seventeenth century.* Chicago: University of Chicago Press, 1983. Alper's beautiful book documents the strikingly parallel developments in Dutch art and in the scientific prose of the seventeenth century. This is the first book to show that new forms of literacy were intricately linked to new forms of art. (D.O.)

Applebee, A. *Writing in the secondary school.* Urbana, Ill.: National Council for Teachers of English, 1981. A survey of the uses of writing and the teaching of writing in American high schools with some suggestions for improving the writing curriculum. (D.O.)

Baker, S., Barzun, J., & Richards, I. A. *The written word.* Rowley, Mass.: Newbury House, 1971. Three essays by distinguished literary theorists on the literary imagination, the literacy "problem," and reading. In one paper, Richards describes his important but largely ignored approach to language and reading. (D.O.)

Barfield, Owen. *History, guilt, and habit.* Middletown, Conn.: Wesleyan University Press, 1979. A lucid discussion of the change of concepts over time and of the centrality of translation and paraphrase even within the same language. Barfield argues that we cannot assume that because the same words and syntax are used by an eighteenth-century author and a twentieth-century author they mean the same things. The mind and language of the ancient Greeks must be nearly opaque to us, according to Barfield. An argument much like Steiner's (1975).

Basso, Keith. The ethnography of writing. In Richard Bauman & Joel Sherzer (Eds.), *Explorations in the ethnography of speaking.* Cambridge: Cambridge University Press, 1974. Basso suggests that we need to study written forms as intently as we have studied spoken ones. How much do we really know about the practice of letter writing? How does one decide whether to sign "Sincerely," "Yours truly," "Best," and so forth? This article suggests ways of asking these questions and others within the framework of the ethnography of communication (see also Hymes, 1974).

Basso, Keith, & Anderson, N. A Western Apache writing system: The symbols of Silas John. *Science*, 1973, *180*, 1013–1022. A description of a unique Native American writing system achieved by revelation to Silas John and associated with intense religious experience.

Bateson, Gregory. *Mind and nature: A necessary unity.* New York: Dutton, 1979. This is probably Bateson's last writing. It presents what he feels "every schoolboy" should know: fundamental concepts of epistemology, cybernetics, biology, evolution, and communication. While some have taken exception to a few of Bateson's ideas, there are none who would say he is speaking of irrelevant things. Any schoolperson should understand these ideas and why they are central.

Bettelheim, B., & Zelan, K. *On learning to read: The child's fascination with meaning.* New York: Knopf, 1982. Bettelheim discusses the current educational methodology utilized in reading instruction, focusing his attention on the use of basal readers and the teacher's response to the child's decoding errors. Bettelheim interprets reading miscues from a psychoanalytical perspective and proposes that reading instruction acknowledge these miscues in order to preserve the integrity of the child. (D.O.)

Cazden, Courtney, B. Language in education: Variation in the teacher-talk register. In James E. Alatis & C. Richard Tucker (Eds.), *Georgetown University Round Table on Languages and Linguistics, 1979.* Washington, D.C.: Georgetown University Press, 1979. A survey article that builds on the idea developed by Penelope Brown and Stephen Levinson ("Universals in Language Usage: Politeness Phenomena," in Esther N. Goody, Ed., *Questions and politeness*, Cambridge, Cambridge University Press, 1979) that different ways of speaking can only be adequately

understood by looking at the relationships among participants. Cazden
suggests that the talk of classroom teachers can be best understood when
we consider the relationship of the teacher to the student.

Cazden, Courtney, & Hymes, Dell. Narrative thinking and story-telling
rights: A folklorist's clue to a critique of education. *Keystone Folklore,*
1978, 22(102), 21–35. Patched together from two separate pieces of the
two authors, this article considers the role of narrative in education.
Cazden and Hymes point out that narratives are normally restricted to
in-group communication in Western education. They argue that education in cross-cultural modes could be facilitated by renewed interest
in narrative.

Cole, Michael, & Bruner, Jerome S. Cultural differences and inferences
about psychological processes. *American Psychologist,* 1971, 26, 867–876.
A thoughtful discussion of theories of cultural difference, the difference–
deficit argument. This includes an analysis of Labov's critique of cultural
deprivation theories for accounting for language differences. Cole and
Bruner introduce the idea of a "cultural amplifier," a tool such as
literacy that can "amplify" human cognitive functions.

Cole, Michael, & Griffin, P. Cultural amplifiers reconsidered. In D. R. Olson
(Ed.), *Social foundations of language and thought: Essays in honor of J. S.
Bruner.* New York: Norton, 1980. A more recent view of Cole and
Bruner's (1971) idea of the "cultural amplifier." Cole and Griffin, as of
1980, doubt that writing systems can "amplify mind" as strongly as Cole
and Bruner (or Goody, 1977) once believed. They nevertheless feel that
understanding literacy is a central issue in understanding human cognition.

Cook-Gumperz, Jenny. Interactive styles in instructional talk. Paper presented at the 77th Annual Meeting of the American Anthropological
Association, Los Angeles, November 14–18, 1978. A study of discourse
and contextual considerations in the giving of instructions – everything
from cake recipes to kindergarten instructions. Cook-Gumperz argues
that the way teachers typically talk to children is not the best way to get
particular tasks done and that present efficiency is being sacrificed to
achieve the long-term goal of literate discourse. An important paper in
seeing in talk to kindergartners the roots of adult literate discourse.

Cook-Gumperz, Jenny, & Gumperz, John. From oral to written culture: The
transition to literacy. In M. F. Whiteman (Ed.), *Writing* (Vol. 1). Hillsdale,
N.J.: Erlbaum, 1978. This essay reviews the literature on the "spoken –
written" issue and then looks at the social implications of literacy. The
authors argue that literacy is essential to successful functioning in the
modern world. They then look at the transition the child undergoes
from preschool to school as an entrance into literacy.

Copperman, Paul. *The literacy hoax: The decline of reading, writing, and learning
in the public schools and what we can do about it.* New York: Morrow Quill
Paperbacks, 1980. Copperman is horrified at the decline of literacy in

the United States in recent years and holds the educational system responsible. He is a strong proponent of the "back to basics" movement as the cure for many of our social ills. Not a scholarly work, this book provides an interesting contrast to some of the views held in some of the scholarly writings on literacy.

Derrida, J. *Of grammatology*. Trans. G. C. Spivak. Baltimore: Johns Hopkins Press, 1976. This is a spectacular, if not completely satisfactory, analysis of the nature and effects of writing. Derrida argues that writing and books are absolutely central to our modern conceptions of language, human beings, and society. Gadamer (1975) covers some of the same ground in a less epigrammatic way. (D.O.)

Donaldson, M. *Children's minds*. London: Fontana, 1978. A good developmental–psychological treatment of the cognitive process involved in children's handling of the "decontextualized" language of the classroom. (D.O.)

The dynamics of writing. *Visible Language*, 1980, *14*, 341–429. A series of articles, edited by Peter Wason, that examine personal aspects of writing. Writing researchers such as Young, Wason, Galbraith, Stack, Lowenthal, Hayes, Flower, and Bracewell contribute to the collection. (D.O.)

Eisenstein, Elizabeth. *The printing press as an agent of change* (2 vols.). Cambridge: Cambridge University Press, 1979. A splendid, thorough, and readable account of the historical effects of the advent of printing on the Renaissance, on the Reformation, and on the rise of modern science. (D.O.)

Erickson, Frederick. Timing and context in everyday discourse: Implications for the study of referential and social meaning (Sociolinguistic Working Paper 67). Austin, Texas: Southwest Educational Development Laboratory, 1980. A fascinating discussion of the timing of talk, especially in interactions between teachers and students. Erickson argues that if the rhythm is broken, things will be heard in the wrong places and probably be misinterpreted.

Erickson, Frederick, & Shultz, Jeffrey. When is a context? *Institute for Comparative Human Development Newsletter*, 1977, *1*(2), 5–10. This paper argues that we cannot simply use the idea of "context" as a way of explicating what happens within a situation. The "context" itself is jointly negotiated by participants.

Faas, Ekbert. *Towards a new American poetics: Essays and interviews. Charles Olson, Robert Duncan, Gary Snyder, Robert Creeley, Robert Bly, Allen Ginsberg*. Santa Barbara, Calif.: Black Sparrow Press, 1978. Essays and interviews of some important modern poets, some in the "ethnopoetics" tradition. One theme that recurs is the relationship between oral language, speech, breath and timing, and the written form. The same subject as Goody (1977) and Ong (1977) but more from the perspective of poets.

Ferguson, Charles A. Patterns of literacy in multilingual situations. In James E. Alatis (Ed.), *Georgetown University Round Table on Languages and Lin-*

guistics. Washington, D.C.: Georgetown University Press, 1978. In this brief article Ferguson identifies four issues for research: functions of literacy, the nature of writing systems, language variation and literacy, and the acquisition of literacy in non-Roman-alphabet systems. He points out how little we really know about literacy outside the Western, Roman-alphabet-based tradition.

Ferreiro, E., & Teberosky, A. *Literacy before schooling*. New York: Heinemann, 1979. A series of impressive experimental studies with a Piagetian orientation that explore the hypotheses children construct and test in the process of achieving alphabetic literacy independently of the directive efforts of teachers. (D.O.)

Flavell, John H. *The developmental psychology of Jean Piaget: An adaptation, assimilation, and accommodation*. New York: Van Nostrand Reinhold, 1963. The best and most comprehensive review of the work of Piaget up to the 1960s. Flavell's treatment is broad and sympathetic, but he never fails to exercise critical caution, especially in making inferential leaps away from Piaget's central concern with "genetic epistemology." It is much easier to read Flavell than Piaget himself, and Flavell is much more reliable than most of the "ed–psych" popularizers.

Foucault, Michel. *The order of things*. New York: Random House, 1973. Difficult to read but with high rewards for the persistent. Foucault argues that in Europe about 200 years ago the field of knowledge was reconstituted into its present form. He argues, as does Barfield (1979), that our attempts to look outside this current world view may be very misleading. Foucault sees the ordering of things – the botanical garden, the military review, the modern hospital, the school, natural history, biology, Newtonian physics – as reflections of this world view (as is this bibliography).

Foucault, Michel. What is an author? In Donald F. Bouchard (Ed.), *Language, counter-memory, practice*. Ithaca, N.Y.: Cornell University Press, 1977. Foucault argues that an "author" is a construction of the social and political world in which a text appears. In other words, the author is a fiction, not a person. This view corresponds with Ong's (1977) view that the audience is always a fiction.

Frederiksen, C. H., & Dominic, J. (Eds.). *Writing* (Vol. 2). Hillsdale, N.J.: Erlbaum, 1982. This volume, together with Whiteman (1981), contains a rich collection of papers on writing and literacy for a major National Institute of Education-sponsored conference by a distinguished group of psychologists, ethnographers, linguists, anthropologists, writers, and educators. (D.O.)

Freedle, Roy; Naus, Mary; & Schwartz, Laraine. Prose processing from a psychosocial perspective. In Roy O. Freedle (Ed.), *Discourse production and comprehension*. Norwood, N.J.: Ablex, 1977. An experimental study showing that social characteristics of a person's audience affect the form in which one creates a text. This is the experimental version of the

Foucault–Ong–Chatman argument that text, author, and audience mutually create each other.

Gadamer, H.-G. *Truth and method*. London: Sheed and Ward, 1975. This book is a major expression of hermeneutics – the theory of understanding or interpretation. The treatment of interpretation of written texts is especially relevant (pp. 351 ff.): "Writing is central to the hermeneutical phenomenon, insofar as its detachment both from the writer or author and from a specifically addressed recipient or reader has given it a life of its own. . . . All writing claims . . . to autonomy of meaning." (D.O.)

Gelb, I. J. *A study of writing*. Chicago: University of Chicago Press, 1952. A venerable study of the history of writing systems. There is precious little of interest here on the social or cognitive consequences or context of writing, but much careful detail about the actual writing systems.

Goody, Jack. *Literacy in traditional societies*. Cambridge: Cambridge University Press, 1968. A collection of articles of varying quality and interest. The main virtue of this collection is that it is still the only work in print that brings together in one place articles concerned with literacy in traditions other than the "great" Western and Eastern ones.

Goody, Jack. *The domestication of the savage mind*. Cambridge: Cambridge University Press, 1977. This book has spurred much interest and research into the issue of the relationship between literacy and cognition. Goody's position is strong: We think as we do because modern society is literate (Copperman and Kozol would question how literate we are!). While many have wanted to make Goody's argument go away, it has not been easy to do. An important book to know and be able to deal with. The first few chapters are slow getting off the ground.

Goody, Jack, & Watt, Ian. The consequences of literacy. *Comparative Studies in Society and History*, 1963, 5, 304–345. Perhaps the first groundbreaking paper on the cognitive importance of literacy. Goody and Watt argue that the Western world has developed as it has as a direct result of the ancient Greek discovery of the alphabet.

Gumperz, John J. The sociolinguistic significance of conversational code-switching. In *Papers on Language and Context* (Berkeley Working Paper 46). Berkeley: Language Behavior Research Laboratory, University of California, 1976. A very important survey of the study of code switching. Gumperz argues that linguistic signs serve both to communicate meanings directly and to communicate in context. In other words, linguistic signs include metacommunication in Bateson's sense. This study of code switching is the basis for Gumperz's work on conversational inference.

Havelock, E. *Preface to Plato*. Cambridge: Harvard University Press, 1963. An early version of the argument extended by Goody (1977) that ancient Greek thought was shaped by the development of the alphabet.

Havelock, E. *Origins of Western literacy*. Toronto: Ontario Institute for Studies in Education Press, 1976. This monograph arose from a series of lectures delivered at the Ontario Institute for Studies in Education, in which

Professor Havelock dramatically demonstrated that some forms of competence highly valued in Western society developed in large part as a consequence of the Greek alphabetic writing system.

Heath, S. B. What no bedtime story means: Narrative skills at home and school. *Language in Society*, 1982, *11*, 49–76. A revealing ethnographic analysis of the variety of uses of literacy in the United States, the variety of ways that children are introduced to literacy, and their consequences for later literacy skills and practices.

Hedden, Mark. Dispositions on the American neolithic: An introduction. *Alcheringa*, 1975, *1*(2), 55–59. This article discusses contrasts between "oral" and "literate" societies. It is a careful consideration of this issue from someone whose primary concern is with art and aesthetics.

Hundeide, Karsten. The origin of the child's replies in experimental situations. *Laboratory of Comparative Human Cognition Newsletter*, 1980, 2(1), 15–18. This article concisely details the role of the environment, the context, in at least partially determining children's answers on Piagetian tasks. An interesting critique of Piagetian research from the point of view of contextualizing frames.

Hunter, C. St.-J., & Harman, D. *Adult illiteracy in the United States: A report to the Ford Foundation*. New York: McGraw-Hill, 1979. This book is a good compilation of the standard view of literacy as a problem. It documents the extent of literacy (50 million illiterate in America), describes social and self-help procedures directed at educating illiterates, admits their failure (only 2% of the target population enroll in and complete them), and advocates a concept of functional literacy – the ability to read and write well enough to achieve one's goals and participate in a literate society. The book fails to recognize that "literacy" is not the problem as much as it is the symptom of the disadvantaged poor. (D.O.)

Hymes, Dell. *Foundations in sociolinguistics*. Philadelphia: University of Pennsylvania Press, 1974. A collection of papers by Hymes covering most of his areas of interest (which are many). The book, which Hymes regards as central to his work, is rarely used or referenced. Neither he nor I see why.

Hymes, Dell. Discovering oral performance and measured verse in American Indian narrative. *New Literary History*, 1977, *8*, 431–457. American Indian narratives have sometimes been characterized as laconic, and many scholars have treated them as a kind of dull, uninteresting prose. Hymes shows how lines, verses, and stanzas are measured out in the narratives of one tradition bearer and begins to form a basis on which a genuine poetics of American Indian oral tradition may be constituted.

Innis, H. A. *The bias of communication*. Toronto: University of Toronto Press, 1951. Innis invented the theory that particular forms of writing have had social consequences, writing permitting the bureaucratic structure of empires, and printing in the vernacular the rise of nationalism. He developed the theory that changing forms of communication alter both

individual forms of thought and forms of social organization. This theme
was taken up and greatly expanded by Marshall McLuhan. (D.O.)

Jacobs, Melville. *The content and style of an oral literature.* Chicago: University
of Chicago Press, 1959. An early and widely influential book in the
study of oral "literature." Jacobs argues that we would do better to think
of American Indian narrative as dramatic poetry rather than as prose.
This book was the first introduction to many of the issues that now
comprise the spoken–written (or oral–literate) issue.

Jordan, Cathie; Tharp, Roland G.; Hu-pei Au, Kathryn; Weisner, Thomas
S.; & Gallimore, Ronald. *A multidisciplinary approach to research in education:
The Kamehameha Early Education Program* (Technical Report 81). Honolulu: Kamehameha Early Education Program, 1977. A collection of
papers by the staff of the Kamehameha Early Education Program
(KEEP). This is one of the very few programs in the United States in
the past decade that has been able to show clear, significant improvement
in standardized reading test scores. No one concerned with literacy in
education should fail to know about this KEEP work.

Kintsch, W. On comprehending stories. In M. A. Just & P. A. Carpenter
(Eds.), *Cognitive processes in comprehension.* Hillsdale, N.J.: Erlbaum, 1977.
This essay reports experiments in which readers used schemata of three
main parts in organizing memory and recall of stories. When Kutchin
stories organized in four parts were used, the subjects, University of
Colorado students, forgot one part in order to restore the expected
three parts. The study provides experimental evidence for the strong
role of expectations in reading and memory as well as evidence that
those expectations are culturally based.

Kintsch, W., & Greene, E. The role of culture-specific schemata in the
comprehension and recall of stories. *Discourse Processes*, 1978, *1*(1), 1–13.
Another Kintsch article extending the idea that the patterns of memory
and comprehension we use in reading are culturally determined to a
considerable extent. An important experimental contribution to the
discussion of the relationship between culture and cognition.

Kozol, Jonathan. *Prisoners of silence: Breaking the bonds of adult illiteracy in the
United States.* New York: Continuum, 1980. A tirade on the state of
literacy in the United States today; part of the "back to basics" literature.
Like Copperman (1980), Kozol believes that illiteracy constitutes a waste
of precious human resources. Kozol's program calls for 5 million (yes,
5 million) volunteers to teach literacy in return for a small government
stipend. Any volunteers?

Kroll, B., & Vann, R. J. *Exploring speaking–writing relationships: Connections
and contrasts.* Urbana, Ill.: National Council for Teachers of English,
1981, An anthology of essays on the relations between speaking and
writing written by literary critics, psychologists, anthropologists, and
educators and addressed primarily to educators and educational researchers.

Labov, William. The transformation of experience in narrative syntax. In *Language in the inner city*. Philadelphia: University of Pennsylvania Press, 1972. Part of a major book on language – specifically, inner-city dialects – this chapter of narrative studies outlines narrative structure much along the lines of Jacobs's (1959) work and is often referred to by those who study oral narratives, especially children's narratives.

Literacy and competency. *Visible Language*, 1982, *14*, 109–176. This special issue is based on the proceedings of the Harvard Reading Conference and edited by Helen Popp. It contains papers by Venezky, St. John Hunter, and Olson. (D.O.)

Literacy and the future of print. *Journal of Communication*, 1980, *30*, 89–210. This special issue on literacy includes articles by Havelock, Eisenstein, Ong, Heath, and Olson. (D.O.)

Lloyd, G. E. R. *Magic, reason, and experience*. Cambridge: Cambridge University Press, 1979. What provoked the conceptual changes that permitted science to replace magic as the primary means of understanding nature? Lloyd traces with exemplary thoroughness and clarity the development of what we would recognize as science in Greek society, an achievement that was more or less complete by the beginning of the fourth century B.C. Lloyd concludes that this achievement was produced by the evolution of the forms of logical, rational argument fostered by free and public debate. He discusses the role that literacy may have played in this development. (D.O.)

McLuhan, Marshall. *The Gutenberg galaxy: The making of typographic man*. Toronto: University of Toronto Press, 1962. By far the most energetic and insightful treatment of the nature of print literacy ever written. Based on literary texts, it attempts to capture the shifts in use of language, forms of thought, and social organization that were encouraged by the printing press. A sample: "But if print discourages minute verbal play, it strongly works for uniformity of spelling and uniformity of meaning" (p. 156). McLuhan amazed many readers by announcing that the Gutenberg era of print literacy is over. (D.O.)

McNeill, David. Speaking of space. *Science*, 1966, *152*, 875–880. McNeill argues that nominal compounds (such as "escape propulsion system" instead of "system that will propel an escape") are used in the space industry to gain a literary effect of technical expertise. Space journals even outdo the technical literature, using 200–300% more nominal compounds. The record McNeill reports is "liquid oxygen liquid hydrogen rocket powered single state to orbit reversible boost system." Aren't you impressed?

Ochs, Elinor. Planned and unplanned discourse. In Talmy Givon (Ed.), *Syntax and semantics*, Vol. 12, *Discourse and syntax*. New York: Academic Press, 1979. A contribution to the spoken–written discussion. Ochs points out features that differ in written and spoken versions of stories and relates these to the amount of planning the speaker/writer is allowed.

Ochs, Elinor. Transcription as theory. In Elinor Ochs (Ed.), *Studies in developmental pragmatics.* New York: Academic Press, 1979. While this essay deals primarily with studies of children's language, Ochs argues the general point that any manipulation of any body of data implies a theory about that data. Not dealing directly with this issue is a way of sneaking into one's data unexamined, pretheoretical concepts.

O'Harrow, Stephen. On the origins of the chu'-nom: The Vietnamese demotic writing system. Paper presented to the Mekong River Festival, Linguistic Society of Hawaii, Honolulu May 1978. One of the very few studies in English of literacy in Asia. O'Harrow's thesis is that differences between Buddhist and Confucianist values were reflected in a differential distribution in Southeast Asia of scripts – specifically, that the inclusiveness of Buddhism fostered the development of a new writing system.

Oliver, Curtis F. Some aspects of literacy in ancient India. *Quarterly Newsletter of the Laboratory of Comparative Human Cognition,* 1979, *1*(4), 57–62. This is a strong critique of the argument of Havelock (1963), Goody (1977), and Olson (1977) that Western thinking is the outcome of the invention by the ancient Greeks of the alphabet. Oliver bases his argument on ancient Indian traditions of memorization and oral transmission of religious texts.

Olson, David R. Review of *Toward a Literate Society* edited by J. Carroll and J. Chall. *Proceedings of the National Academy of Education,* 1975, 2, 109–178. In this review Olson states his conviction that the original objectives of the Right to Read program are unattainable. He discusses the "literacy myth" – that is, a mistaken faith in the power of literacy to eliminate the social and personal consequences of a myriad of unrelated deprivations – and addresses the consequences of literacy from a historical and cultural perspective, pointing out the effects on mental skills of the primacy of written texts in Western cultures. Olson concludes by calling the original Right to Read program "a promise to do the impossible" and advocates settling for some basic research and pilot literacy programs.

Olson, David R. From utterance to text: The bias of language in speech and writing. *Harvard Educational Review,* 1977, *47*(3), 257–281. Olson argues that *utterance* (spoken language) and *text* (written language) are fundamentally different and that a good bit of recent linguistic, psychological, and educational folly has been perpetrated through failure to understand these differences.

Olson, David R. The language of instruction: On the literate bias of schooling. In R. C. Anderson, R. J. Spiro, & W. E. Montague (Eds.), *Schooling and the acquisition of knowledge.* Hillsdale, N.J.: 1977. Olson argues that in the Western world we have equated schooling, knowledge, and literacy. He says that what we call knowledge is not knowledge in general; it is that picture of reality that is constructed to sustain the specialized literate activities of science and philosophy; "standard English" is not a mother tongue but a specialized instrument of this particular brand of knowledge.

Olson, David R. Some social aspects of meaning in oral and written language. In D. R. Olson (Ed.), *Social foundations of language and thought: Essays in honor of J. S. Bruner*. New York: Norton, 1980. This essay examines the social relation between speaker/hearer and reader/writer and argues that in writing, just as meaning becomes "text meaning," so too the authority changes from the authority of the author to the authority of the text. (D.O.)

Ong, Walter. *Ramus, method, and the decay of dialogue*. Cambridge: Harvard University Press, 1958. Ong introduces us to Pierre Ramee (1515–1572: alias Peter Ramus, Petrus Ramus), who first broke down the ideas of Aristotle and other "greats" into a systematic pedagogical curriculum. In Ong's terminology, Ramus "methodized" Western knowledge. People today only remember his followers' methodization of a set of religious views in the modern "Methodist" faith, but his views on curriculum are part and parcel of how we conduct schooling.

Ong, Walter. *The presence of the word*. New Haven: Yale University Press, 1967. A far-ranging collection of essays on issues of literacy, the history of our present way of thinking, and aesthetics. Ong is concerned with two major discontinuities in this history, the one begun by Ramus when knowledge was methodized (see Ong, 1958) and the one we are now undergoing as knowledge is becoming electrified.

Ong, Walter. *Rhetoric, romance, and technology: Studies in the interaction of expression and culture*. Ithaca, N.Y.: Cornell University Press, 1971. Father Ong shows how the shift in communication media from the rhetorical tradition to the romantic literate-tradition accounts for how knowledge was and is stored and retrieved. (D.O.)

Ong, Walter. *Interfaces of the word*. Ithaca, N.Y.: Cornell University Press, 1977. A collection of essays examining the history of literacy and knowledge in the Western world. Father Ong is always interesting and provocative. In one essay he claims that the writer's audience is always a fiction.

Otto, W., & White, S. (Eds.). *Reading expository texts*. New York: Academic Press, 1982. This collection of essays provides an up-to-date account of the psychology of reading and comprehending written, schoollike text. Essays focus on the reader, the text, and reader–text interactions. (D.O.)

Pattison, R. *On literacy: The politics of the word from Homer to the Age of Reason*. Oxford: Oxford University Press, 1982. An impressive treatment of literacy in which the author goes beyond the simple demographic notion of literacy as the ability to read and write to the hypothesis that literacy "involves consciousness by individuals and cultures of the structures and uses of language" and goes beyond the simple-minded notion that the introduction of a writing system causes specific cognitive and social effects to the notion that "the effects of literacy depend upon the nature of the society, the type of writing system and the particular functions of which that technology is part." (D.O.)

Reddy, Michael J. The conduit metaphor – a case of frame conflict in our language about language. In Andrew Ortony (Ed.), *Metaphor and thought.* Cambridge: Cambridge University Press, 1979. This essay claims (and provides a long appendix to demonstrate) that English speakers think of communication as moving ideas from one place to another by means of conduits. An important new contribution to both the discussion of frames and the discussion of language and thought (linguistic relativity).

Sapir, Edward. *Language: An introduction to the study of speech.* New York: Harcourt, Brace, 1921. The best and most readable single book on what linguists know about the nature of language. In 60 years it has not been bettered.

Schank, Roger C., & Abelson, Robert P. *Scripts, plans, goals, and understanding.* Hillsdale, N.J.: Erlbaum, 1977. A most interesting discussion of artificial intelligence, this book sketches the outline of a theory for what must underlie simple comprehension of a newspaper story, whether the comprehender works on blood or electricity.

Scollon, Ron, & Scollon, Suzanne B. K. *Literacy as interethnic communication: An Athabaskan case* (Working Papers in Sociolinguistics 59). Austin, Texas: Southwest Educational Development Laboratory, 1979. An argument that differences in contextualization cues between written and spoken forms constitute as serious a barrier to communication as those between people from different social groups. Where both barriers are present, communication is difficult.

Scollon, Ron, & Scollon, Suzanne B. K. Literacy as focused interaction. *Quarterly Newsletter of the Laboratory of Comparative Human Cognition,* 1980, 2(2), 26–29. An argument that the "spoken–written" problem might be better phrased another way: The central point is whether or not participants can read feedback from each other. Where feedback is limited, the interaction is focused, whether it is written or spoken.

Scollon, Ron, & Scollon, Suzanne B. K. *Narrative, literacy, and face in interethnic communication.* Norwood, N.J.: Ablex, 1981. The focus of this book is on tracing differences between "literate" or Western modes of thinking and Athabaskan modes of thinking. The authors argue that ways of thinking are, at their foundation, outcomes of ways of speaking, ways of speaking are outcomes of values on interpersonal distance, and those values are the outcomes of ways of teaching and learning, which are in turn the outcomes of ways of thinking. A circular argument, to be sure.

Scribner, Sylvia. Modes of thinking and ways of speaking: Culture and logic reconsidered. In Roy O. Freedle (Ed.), *New directions in discourse processing.* Norwood, N.J.: Ablex, 1979. A review of the work of Scribner, Cole, and others on the cross-cultural study of thinking, literacy, and schooling. The author notices, for example, that across a wide sample from very different cultures and culture areas, schooled literates are a more homogeneous group than are nonschooled nonliterates. Furthermore, in many ways two schooled literates in very different societies are more alike cognitively than either is like other members of the same society.

Scribner, S., & Cole, M. *The psychology of literacy.* Cambridge: Harvard University Press, 1981. This major work examines a range of theories on the cognitive consequences of literacy in the natural "laboratory" of the Vai, a small West African group with their own system of writing. In contrast to the substantial effects of schooling, the cognitive consequences of literacy in the native language are small and restricted to the particular functions and activities involved in reading and writing.

Shuy, Roger W. Learning to talk like teachers. Paper presented to the American Educational Research Association, April 1978. A very readable discussion of language functioning and the contexts in which various functions are likely to be displayed.

Smith, F. *Writing and the writer.* New York: Holt, Rinehart and Winston, 1982. A coherent, thoughtful, and sophisticated account of writing, including the nature of composition and transcription, learning to write through reading and through writing, and the development of the perception that one is a writer. (D.O.)

Spiro, R.; Bruce, B.; & Brewer W., (Eds.). *Theoretical issues in reading comprehension.* Hillsdale, N.J.: Erlbaum, 1980. An extensive, sophisticated, and up-to-date treatment of the psychological and linguistic aspects of reading comprehension. One of the book's central concerns is with the ways linguistic structures activate "schemata" in the minds of the reader (D.O.)

Steiner, George. *After Babel.* New York: Oxford University Press, 1975. A textbook on translation, language, linguistic relativity, and the problems of representation and interpretation that I couldn't require anyone to read. It is so richly steeped in the literature and philosophy of the Western European tradition that most nonspecialist readers do not seem to be able to follow the argument. If literature and philosophy are to your taste, I know of no better discussion of the issues that tie this bibliography together. It is the best book listed here.

Sticht, T. G. (Ed.). *Reading for working: A functional literacy anthology.* Alexandria, Va.: Human Resources Research Organization, 1975. A series of studies on the relation between jobs and literacy, this book emphasizes the importance of comprehension: If adults cannot successfully read a text, they probably cannot understand it if it is read to them either.

Stock, B. *The implications of literacy.* Princeton: Princeton University Press, 1983. Stock illustrates how legal and theological thought and practice changed in late medieval times to reflect a growing reliance on written records. From the tenth to the thirteenth centuries, producing, preserving, and interpreting written records came increasingly to be central to judgments of sainthood, the development of religious heresies, and the development of laws and judges as an alternative to dueling and trial-by-ordeal. Stock shows that this increasing reliance upon literacy provided the social and intellectual foundations for modernity. (D.O.)

Stubbs, M. *Language and literacy: The sociolinguistics of reading and writing.* London: Routledge & Kegan Paul, 1980. An excellent treatment by a linguist of the relations between oral and written languages and the communicative functions that they serve in our society. Stubbs pays great attention to the relations between pronunciation and spelling, particularly to the educational problems that result when the indigenous language differs substantially from the national standard.

Tannen, D. (Ed.). *Advances in discourse processes* (Ed. R. O. Freedle), Vol. 9, *Spoken and written language: Exploring orality and literacy.* Norwood, N.J.: Ablex, 1982. A rich collection of essays by linguists, psychologists, and anthropologists on the differences as well as the relations between speaking and writing. Several pieces build on Chafe's argument that speaking enhances involvement between interlocutors while writing enhances the integration of ideas (D.O.)

Tedlock, Dennis. *Finding the center: Narrative poetry of the Zuni Indians.* New York: Dial Press, 1972. The first big publication in the ethnopoetic domain. Tedlock has presented Zuni poetry as scripts for oral performance.

Tedlock, Dennis. On the translation of style in oral narrative. In Americo Paredes & Richard Bauman (Eds.), *Toward new perspectives in folklore.* Austin: University of Texas Press. 1972. This is the analytical essay that corresponds to Tedlock's scripts for oral performance (above). Following Jacobs (1959), Tedlock argues that Zuni narratives translated into prose lose their poetic life in the process.

Tedlock, Dennis. Learning to listen: Oral history as poetry. In Ronald J. Grele (Ed.), *Envelopes of sound.* Chicago: Precedent, 1975.

> Tedlock says
> Poetry is oral history
> and oral history
> is poetry.

He questions whether hundreds of reels of oral history tapes ought to be converted into thousands of pages of prose typescripts.

Tedlock, Dennis. The spoken word and the work of interpretation in American Indian religion. An address at the Myth, Symbol, Reality Symposium of the Boston University Institute for Philosophy and Religion, March 29, 1978. Here Tedlock shows that in a Zuni oral performance the criticism is included as an integral part of the performance. This leads him to question Hymes's (1975, 1977) distinction between performance and talking about performance. He is concerned that this distinction, too easily made, might transform itself into heavy-handed editing by nontraditional analysts who reserve for themselves the right of criticism.

Tedlock, Dennis. The analogical tradition and the emergence of a dialogical anthropology. Harvey Lecture delivered at the University of New Mexico, March 20, 1979. Tedlock's point here is that anthropologists (and lots of others) have based their understanding of others on dialogue with them, but then when it comes time to write and publish the original voices become lost or drowned out by the solo voice of the researcher. The author argues for what Erickson and others have called collaborative research.

Tulviste, Peter. On the origins of theoretical syllogistic reasoning in culture and the child (annotated bibliographic edition by Sondra Buffett). *Quarterly Newsletter of the Laboratory of Comparative Human Cognition*, 1979, *1*(4), 73–80. This Estonian psychologist argues that there is no "natural" human thinking and no one direction in which it should inevitably develop in the course of its ontogenesis and cultural historical development. People who do different kinds of cognitive tasks learn to think in different ways. This very strong anti-Piagetian position is well argued.

Uspensky, Boris. *A poetics of composition*. Berkeley: University of California Press, 1973. Some of Erving Goffman's inspiration (in *Frame Analysis*, New York, Harper & Row, 1974) comes from this study of frames in writing and painting. For those with a taste for art and literature this may be more interesting than Goffman himself.

Vellutino, F. R. *Dyslexia: Theory and research*. Cambridge,: MIT Press, 1979. The best single treatment of the view that reading disorders are by and large caused by deficiencies in one or more aspects of linguistic functioning.

Vygotsky, L. S. *Mind in society: The development of higher psychological processes*. Edited by M. Cole, V. John-Steiner, S. Scribner, and E. Souberman. Cambridge: Harvard University Press, 1978. This important psychologist, ignored until recently by the Western world, advances the idea of a "zone of proximal development," the stage *before* a child can accomplish a task unaided. Vygotskian psychology turns Piagetian psychology back into the prestructural period to look for the most effective arena for pedagogical interaction. Unlike Piagetian thinking, Vygotsky's work is directly applicable to literacy, writing, and education.

Whiteman, M. F. (Ed.). *Writing* (Vol. 1). Hillsdale, N.J.: Erlbaum, 1981. (See Frederiksen and Dominic, 1982, for a description of both volumes.) (D.O.)

Whorf, Benjamin L. *Language, thought, and reality: Selected writings of Benjamin Lee Whorf*. Cambridge: MIT Press, 1956. A collection of most of Whorf's writings. This volume has been read very widely and is a source book in many fields, including linguistics and psychology. It is interesting to me that Whorf's far-ranging views never became institutionalized within an academic discipline. He was never a university professor. More power to him! Whorf's linguistic analysis should be reread as a commentary not only on language but on literacy.

Subject index

abstract subjects, 117–118
accusativity, 152
acknowledgments, 271, 275
action, 217–218
adjectives, 163; attributive (preposed), 109; postposed, 116
adverbial phrases, 110
aesthetic reading, 201, 210
affective component of story theory, 168
affricative sounds, 348, 349
agreement, 115
Alexandria, library at, 41, 42
alphabetic identity of (of a word), 338
Altman, R., see *Nashville* (Altman)
alveolar flap, 348, 349–351, 361
American Indian languages, 355
analgon, 60–61, 63–64
antitopic, 115
appositives, 112
Aretino, 28
"arousal boost," 168
Ashanti, 189
assertions, 271
Atlantis and Atlantans, 36–38, 39
Auditory Discrimination Program, 335
Australian languages, 158
authority register, 89, 91
autonomous language, 129

BE (black English), 354, 355
behavior, 218
Bible printing, 27–28, 29–31
"Bibles for illiterate," 20
Boccaccio, 28
Brahmin speech, 355
brain, 196, 200, 201–204, 208, 209; as an artist, 197, 211–212
Bréal, 149
Bushman language, 158

Calvin, J., 20

Canadian Eskimo language, 162
case alteration disruption, 383
Cattani-Brett, C., 312–313
CDO model, 316–320
central omission, 299
chants, 155
characters, 181, 185, 188
Chinese orthography, 374
citation, 122
Clackamas Indians, 179, 181, 183
classification problems, 219
"clause chaining," 153
clause-final preposition, 115
clause links, 275
cline of person, 125
closed syllable, 400
closing, 183, 186, 188
codes, 61–65; archetypal, 62; cultural, 62–63; elaborated, 132; media and genre, 63; psychophysical, 62; restricted, 132; theoretical, 63
cognitive consequences of literacy, 73–74
cognitive development, 217–218, 222
"cognitive-tuning," 81–82
cohesion hypothesis, 127, 130–132, 143, 286, 290
combinatoria, 226
comments, 259, 271, 272
commitment, 89–90, 96–97
Commonwealth of Learning, 21–22, 32
communication, 56, 74, 84–92, 195; verbal, 74–75, 75–76
"communication game," 75–84
competence, literate and oral, 229–253, 256–282, 285–304
complement clauses, 110
composed texts, 154, 155
conferencing, 314
Confucius, 148
conjunctions, 131, 269, 276, 281, 286, 294–296, 313; trailing, 115

427

conservatism, 114, 116, 122
constituents, 109–110
constructive process of cognitive development, 218
content, 126, 289, 311
contextualization hypothesis, 127–130, 233, 234, 257
contraction, 115
conversation, 128, 129, 132–137, 139, 201–202, 232, 250, 273–280, 309
cooperative overlap, 126–127, 133–134
Copernicus, 30, 43
Cranach, L., 21
critical expository information, 169
curiosity discourse structure, 170, 172, 174
Curle, A., 46
CVC sounds, 359–360
Czech orthography, 368

Darwin, C., 148, 149
decoding–encoding conventions, 237
decoding view of word recognition, 337
decontextualization, 153, 154, 155, 232
deduction, 119–120, 122
De Fabrica, 30
deference, 125
De Motu, 30
dépassements, 218
dependent clauses, 112
De Revolutionibus, 30
descriptions, 200
detachment, 116, 117–118, 122
dialectical process of cognitive development, 218, 307–329
dialogue, 321; internal, 309–310
directives, 259, 271, 272, 273, 275, 277
discourse, 168, 169–170, 172, 174, 182, 189, 258, 259, 287–297; higher-order structures, 257, 270–280; *see also* conversation, episodes, expository prose, story, topics
disembedded thinking, 251
disfluencies, 113
display questions, 230, 232, 234, 240, 246–247, 250, 251, 253
double bind, 125
dreams, 202
Dürer, A., 21
Durkheim, E., 151
Durrell Analysis of Reading Difficulty, 261, 263
Dutch orthography, 392–397, 398, 400, 406–407

Ebbinghaus, 203
editing, 289, 297, 303
efferent reading, 201
"effort justification," 90
elementary literacy, 34–35, 45–58
elite phase of literacy, 34
enjoyment component of story theory, 170–172
Enlightenment, 29
epenthesis, 345
epilogue, 183, 186
episodes, 258–259, 260, 277–281
"equipment for living," 68, 69
Erasmus, 27–28, 30
ergativity, 152
"essayist literacy," 124
Estienne, Henry II, 29
Estienne, Robert, 29
"evaluation" in narrative, 130
events, 64, 167–169, 172–173, 182, 185–186, 187
evidentiality, 118–121
evolution, 150, 151, 152; linguistic, 148–149, 153
"evolved languages," 157
exclamative conversational devices, 273
experience, 203
expository prose, 128, 129, 137, 140, 287

fabula, 168
facts, 198, 199, 218
Fali, 183
fantasy, 200, 202
film, 66–68; and literacy, 51, 57, 61–65
Finnish orthography, 368
flashback, 168, 182, 190
flashforward, 182, 190
flow-monitoring devices, 113
Formalists, Russian, 168
formal operations, 303
fragmentation of spoken language, 105, 154, 286
French orthography, 392–393, 397–400, 401

"galaxies," 66
Galen, 31
Galilei, Galileo, 43
Galois, 228nl
Gauss, 228nl
Geist, 149
genre specialization, 189
German orthography, 392–393
goals of communication, 87–88

grapheme, 220
grapheme-phoneme correspondence, 368–372, 383
Greenlandic language, 162
Gregory, Pope, 20

Hanga, 181, 183
hearsay evidence, 120, 121
"hedges," 120–121, 122
high–grade literacy, 43–45, 48
homorganicity, 394, 400

idea unit, 106–121, 293, 294, 298, 299
Iliad, 67
illocutionary force of speech acts, 258, 259, 260, 273, 280, 282
image in film, 61–62
"image to word" formula, 20–21
imagination, 200
incantations, 155
Index of Prohibited Books, 28
individual literacy, 43–45
Indo-European languages, 148
induction, 119, 122
industrialization and literacy, 34–35, 46–47, 48
inflection, 409
information: shunting, 196, 197, 201, 205; theory, 112–113, 121, 195–196, 197–199, 200–205, 210
initiating event, 169
innovation, 114–115, 116, 122
integration of written language, 105, 127, 139, 154, 155, 157, 249–250, 286
intended meaning, 257–258
intent, 304
internal variation, principle of, 225
interpretation, 198–199, 200, 205, 237–238
intonation, 205
intrusion, 298–302
Inuit, 155
Inuit and the Law, 161
Inuit Today, 161
Inuktitut language, 158–164
involvement, 116–117, 118, 122, 124–125, 126, 127, 129, 142

Jerome, St., 30
juxtaposition, 313
juzet, 168

Kamba, 183
Kepler, J., 43
Khaling, 181, 183–184
Kham, 181

kinesthetics, 394
knowledge, 54–56; *see also* reliability of knowledge
knowledge telling strategy, 313–314
Kuhn, T., 44
Kwakiutl language, 150

labeling, 88–89
language, 63, 195–196, 204–209; differences between spoken and written, 105–122, 249–250, 282–303, 333, 337, 409–410; *see also individual languages*
langue, 154, 157
"Law of Demise," 37
learning, 197, 202–204
letters, 334, 339
lexicalization, 131–132, 133, 137, 143
lexical symbols, 334
Library (Atlantan city), 37
Limba, 181, 182–183, 184
"Literacy and the future of print," 420
literate strategies, 124, 125
"locus of meaning," 250
logic, 224
Longuda, 181

Macedonian, 155
Machiavelli, 28
Madvig, 149
Mann-Whitney U test, 238, 246, 247, 248
Manutius, A., 25
Marx, K., 32
matrices, 260, 314
meaning, 74, 88, 205, 257–258
mediated human activity, 50–51, 54–56
memory, 88–89, 209; *see also* recall
message, 137, 195; focused, 129–130, 131–132, 141–142; modification, 77–79, 96; *see also* metamessage
meta-affect hypothesis, 172
metalinguistic skills, 360–361
metamessage, 128–129, 130, 137
metaphor, 195, 209
migration and literacy, 47
"mind," 198
minimum quantity, hypothesis of, 219, 220, 221, 225
modality, 286, 287, 289, 292, 297, 301–302, 303–304
model, 195
monologue, assisted, 321
"mother tongue," 256, 257
motif, 182
motivation, 89–90

narrative, 63–66, 183–184, 186–188, 290–304; component of story theory, 167–168, 173–174
nasals: palatal, 392, 398; preconsonantal, 345, 347–349, 361, 389–391, 393–395, 397, 400–401, 408; sequences, 396; vowels, 345, 347
Nashville (Altman), 51–52, 59–60, 62–63, 65, 70
natural languages, 205
natural selection, 149
Navaho, 181
Newman-Keuls test, 326
Newton, I., 43
Nez Percé, 181
no (as adjective), 116
"noise," 198
nominalization, 108–109, 153, 154
nonsense syllable, 203
nonspontaneous narrative texts, 156, 157
North American Indians, 181

object, 217, 218
"observables," 217
Odyssey, 67
Ojibway, 158
omission, 298
opening, 179, 184, 188
open syllable, 399–400
oral: culture, 22, 44, 48–49; fluency, 137; language, 124, 132–137, 143; strategies, 124, 125; tradition, 126, 178–184, 188–190; *see also* competence, literate and oral
orthographic neighbors, 375
orthography, 56, 368; *see also individual languages*

palatal nasals, *see* nasals, palatal
Paleo-Siberian languages, 158
paradigm, 195
parallel constructions, 138
paraphrase, 298
parole, 154, 157
participles, 161–163; clauses, 112; past, 109; present, 109
passives, 117
past perfect, 116
peer response, 314
permanent texts, 154, 155
phoneme-grapheme correspondence, 404, 407
phonemic awareness, 344
phonetics, 392; segmentation in, 334, 339, 340–351, 363; symbols in, 334

phonological identity of a word, 338
phonology, 368, 392
plans, 200
play, 202
politeness markers, 273
Port Royal grammarians, 149
pragmatic mode, 152
preconsonantal nasals, *see* nasals, preconsonantal
prepositional phrases, 109
present participles: postposed, 109; preposed, 109
prewriting activities, 314–315
"primitive languages," 148, 150, 157
Principia, 30
print, 26–27, 56–57, 66–68, 334, 335, 337, 404, 405
printing, 21, 22, 25–27, 29–31
printing press, 24
printshop, 24–25, 28–29
problem space, 310–312
procedural facilitation, 315
production of communication, 84–86
pronouns, 115, 116, 163
propositional content of speech acts, 258, 259, 260
proto-Indo-European language, 159
pseudohomophones, 378–379
Ptolemy, 30, 31

question: indirect, 110; sequences, 314
quotations, indirect, 110

Rabelais, 28
readers, good and poor contrasted, 266–269, 354, 374, 379–384, 405, 406
reality, 195, 200, 202
recall, 286–287, 297–302, 303, 360; *see also* memory
recognition, 301–303
recontextualization, 140
referents, 334
reflectivity, 327
reflexive pronoun, postposed, 116
Reformation, 27
regular-exception word effects, 375–383, 385nl
relationship between the whole and its parts, 219, 220, 222, 223
reliability of knowledge, 118–119, 121, 122
Renaissance, 26–27, 42–43
Republic (Plato), 67
resolution, 182–183, 186
"response cries," 133

responsives, 271
restricted relative clauses, 110
revision, 308–309, 315–320
Rhetoric (Aristotle), 67
rhetorical space, 310–312
rhythm, 139
"ritual naming," 232, 240
rituals, 154
Romeo and Juliet: Shakespeare's, 51, 57–58; Zeffirelli's, 51–52, 58–59, 65
Ruffini, 228nl
Russian orthography, 406–407

Samoyed, 158
scenarios, 200
schemata, 176–187, 199–200, 287
schwa vowels, 345, 348, 349
SE (Standard English), 354, 391
segmentation, 395, 396–397, 399, 401, 406
"self-contextualizing" stories, 237–238
self-perception, 90–92
semantic (propositional) cohesion, 271–273
semantic identity of a word, 338
Seneca, 155, 158
sensory evidence, 120, 122
sentence, 111, 334; meaning, 257–258
Serbo-Croatian orthography, 368, 374
setting, 179–181, 184–185
Shakespeare, W., *Romeo and Juliet,* 51, 57–58
Sherpa, 181, 183
Shoshone, 182, 183
shot (cinematic), 63–64
sight word strategy, 337
signals, 198, 199
significant event, 170
silent letters, 342–344, 362
situation, 169
social context of communication, 86–87
"societies of intimates," 152–153
"societies of strangers," 152–153
Somali, 155
songs, 155
Spanish orthography, 368, 392–393, 397
speaker's meaning, 257–258
"spectator role," 252
speech acts: assertions, 271; directives, 259, 271, 272, 273, 275, 277; illocutionary force of, 258, 259, 260, 273, 280, 282; propositional content of, 258, 259, 260; requests, 271–272, 276, 279, 280; theory, 257–261; verb, 258

spelling, 210, 219–222, 224–227, 249, 290, 333–363, 368–385, 389–401, 405, 406–407, 408
spells, 155
spoken language, 196, 205–209, 250, 253; *see also* oral: language
spontaneous texts, 154, 155
statistical probability, 119, 122
stop sequences, 396
story, 134–136, 237–238, 246, 251–253, 290–304, 312–313; conventions, 179–191; intuitions, 174–176; schemata, 176–187; theory of, 167–176
"storying," 252
structural-affect component of story theory, 169–170, 172
subject, 217, 218
subjunctive, 116
subordination, 153, 157–164, 260, 264, 266, 282
substantive space, 310–312
surprise discourse structure, 169, 172, 174
suspense discourse structure, 169–170, 172, 174, 182
syllabic hypothesis, 224, 226, 227
symbols, 334; and literacy, 50
syntactic identity of a word, 338
syntacticization, 152, 157
Syuwa, 184

text organicity, 307
text permanence, 157
"thematization," 222
theme, 258–259
"this," indefinite, 115
thought, 53, 197; sustained, 308
topics, 115, 258–259, 260, 276–277, 278, 279, 280–281
topic shift, 313
totality, 219, 223, 227
Toura, 182
tradition, literate, 126
tree diagrams, 314
turnabouts, 259, 260, 269, 271, 272, 275
turns, 259, 260, 273, 275

"unacknowledged revolution," 22–23
understanding, 64
UNESCO, 46–47
unitization, 338
universal grammar, 158
universal literacy, 34–35
universal politeness phenomena, 125
universal properties of story schema, 187–188

Uralic languages, 158
utterance meaning, 257–258

Vai speech, 356
verbs, 159–163, 164n3; cognitive, 264–270, 282; psychological, 263, 266, 268, 276, 277, 280, 281–282; speech act, 268
verbatim, 298
Visible Language, 307
visual–spatial representational system, 333
vocabulary, 114
vowel–nasal–consonant sequences, 396–397, 401
vowels, short, 352

Western governments and literacy, 34–35

Whitney, 149
whole word strategy, 337
WISC Block Design and Vocabulary subtest, 261, 263
Wolof, 233
words, 334, 335
world, theory of, 199
"World 3," 198
WPPSI subtest, 261
writing, 66–68, 307–308
written language, 107–108, 124, 137–140, 143, 196, 205–209, 235, 240, 246, 251; stories; 184–187; tradition, 188–190

Zeffirelli, F., *Romeo and Juliet*, 51–52, 58–59, 65
Zulu, 182
Zuni, 179, 181

Author index

Abelson, R. P., 167, 200, 423
Alegria, J., 335, 344
Alpers, S., 412
Altenbernd, L., 186
Amiran, M., 314
Anderson, J. R., 209
Applebee, A., 412
Aristotle, 29, 67
Arnheim, R., 61, 67
Arsleff, H., 149
Asch, S. E., 81
Atkinson, G., 27
Austin, J. O., 258

Baird, W., 299
Baker, S., 412
Bakhtin, M. M., 69
Barfield, O., 413
Barnes, M. A., 377
Barnes, S. B., 229
Baron, J., 370, 376
Barritt, L. S., 316
Barron, R. W., 377, 378, 380, 381–382, 404–406, 407
Barthes, R., 52, 60, 63, 169
Bartlett, E., 313, 316
Bartlett, F. C., 89, 200
Barton, D., 342, 348, 361
Barzun, J., 412
Bascom, W., 179, 188
Basso, K., 413
Bates, E., 87
Bateson, G., 74, 125, 128, 130, 131, 198, 413
Bauer, D., 377
Bauer, R. A., 78
Bearth, I., 182
Becker, A. L., 125, 314
Beers, J. W., 344
Bell, B. J., 260, 270, 272
Bellefroid, B., 222
Bem, D. J., 91
Ben-Amos, D., 179

Benson, J. D., 260
Benveniste, E., 159
Bereiter, C., 285, 286, 289, 308, 309, 313, 315, 316–320, 321, 322, 327
Berkowitz, A., 86
Berlyne, D. E., 168, 170
Bernstein, B., 132, 229, 233, 256
Bertelson, P., 335, 344
Besner, D., 376, 377, 378, 379
Bettelheim, B., 125, 413
Bias, R. G., 377
Bierwisch, M., 258
Blank, M., 250
Bloch, M., 24
Block, K. K., 362n2
Bloom, L., 75
Bloomfield, L., 335, 404
Blumberg, P., 363n2
Boas, R., 150, 188
Bobrow, D. G., 200
Bolinger, D. L., 368–369, 370, 371–373
Booth, W. C., 178, 187
Boring, E. G., 203
Botkin, P. T., 75, 77
Bourne, L. E., 89
Bower, G. H., 209
Bracewell, R. J., 289, 316
Bradley, L., 380, 382
Brehm, J. W., 90
Brewer, W. F., 167, 168, 169, 172, 173, 174, 179, 189, 190, 424
Bright, W., 355
Brilhart, B. L., 75
Britton, J., 252, 313
Brooks, C., 185, 186
Brown, P., 144
Brown, R., 277–278, 281, 407
Bruce, B., 424
Bruner, J. S., 52, 53, 232, 233, 240, 414
Brunvand, J. H., 179
Bryant, P. E., 380, 382
Buck, C., 355
Burgess, T., 313

Burke, K., 52, 68
Burling, R., 354
Burroughs, E. R., 373

Cary, L., 335, 344
Cattani, C., 308, 313, 316–320
Cawelti, J. G., 186
Cazden, C. B., 413–414
Chafe, W. L., 84, 85, 88, 105, 106, 111,
    118, 127, 130, 131, 139, 153, 154,
    158, 190, 237, 249, 267, 285, 286,
    293, 294, 296
Chaiken, S., 80, 87
Chatman, S., 168, 169
Chomsky, C., 344
Chomsky, N., 352, 363n4, 371–372
Cohen, A. R., 81, 90
Cohen, M., 158
Cole, M., 52, 54, 56, 176, 414, 424
Cole, R. A., 353, 358, 360
Colker, L., 177
Collins, J., 136, 141–142
Coltheart, M., 376, 377, 378, 379, 384
Conrad, R., 374
Cook-Gumperz, J., 126, 130, 132, 136,
    140–141, 414
Cooper, F. S., 335, 404
Cooperman, P., 414–415, 419
Cornell, S. D., 77, 78
Cosky, M., 376
Creider, C., 162
Cronnell, B. A., 354
Culler, J., 169
Czerlinsky, T., 78, 80

Davelaar, E., 376, 377, 378, 379
Davenport, W. H., 189
Davis, K. E., 80
DeForest, M., 176
Dégh, L., 179, 181, 182, 183, 188
Deutsch, M., 229
Derrida, J., 415
Desberg, P., 354
Doblin, J., 409–410
Doman, G., 208
Dominic, J., 416
Dominowski, R. L., 89
Donaldson, M., 251, 415
Dore, J., 258, 260
Drake, S., 29
Duncan, H. D., 139
Dupree, D. A., 168

Eagly, A. H., 74, 80, 87
Ehri, L. C., 285, 336, 338, 339, 343,
    344, 357, 359, 363n2, 404, 406–408

Eisenstein, E., 19–33, 415
Eisenstein, S., 70
Ekstrand, B. R., 89
Elbow, P., 314
Elliott, D., 354
Ellsworth, P. C., 91
Ennulat, J. H., 183
Erickson, F., 86, 139, 415
Ervin-Tripp, S., 287, 296
Estes, W. K., 200

Faas, E., 415
Febvre, L., 23
Feldman, L. B., 368–369, 374
Ferguson, C. A., 415–416
Ferreiro, E., 219, 222, 223, 235, 416
Festinger, L., 80
Fillmore, C. J., 128, 137
Finnegan, R., 179, 181, 182, 183, 184,
    188, 189, 190
Fischer, F. W., 337, 380
Fischer, J. L., 182, 188, 189
Flavell, J. H., 75, 77, 416
Flower, L., 288, 289, 310, 324, 327
Fondacaro, R., 74, 75, 76, 79, 81, 82,
    83, 88, 93, 94
Foucault, M., 416
Fowler, C. A., 337, 380
Francis, H., 361
Francis, W. M., 378
Frederiksen, C. H., 416
Freedle, R., 416–417
Friedman, N., 187
Friedrich, P., 138
Frith, U., 382
Fry, C. L., 75, 77

Gadamer, H.-G., 415, 417
Galanter, E., 200
Gallimore, R., 419
García, R., 228n2
Gelb, I. J., 335, 355, 417
Geva, E., 293, 313
Gibson, E. J., 198, 404
Gill, C. E., 392, 393, 397–399, 401
Gilmore, M., 24–25
Givón, T., 152–153, 157
Gleason, H. A., 335–336
Glenn, C. G., 290
Glucksberg, S., 74, 75, 77
Glushko, R. J., 56, 375–378
Goelman, H., 286, 309
Goffman, E., 125, 133
Goldstein, E., 313
Golinkoff, R. M., 344
Gombrich, E. H., 67

Goodman, K. S., 286, 355
Goodman, Y. M., 286
Goodson, J. L., 167–168
Goodwin, W. W., 159
Goody, E. N., 413
Goody, J., 52, 53, 54, 126, 285, 414, 415, 417
Gough, P., 376
Gould, J. P., 149, 286
Graves, D. H., 314, 316
Gray, B., 309
Greaves, W., 260
Greenbaum, S., 262
Greenberg, J., 150, 152, 156
Greene, E., 176, 419
Greenfield, P., 53
Gregory, M., 260
Gregory, R. L., 252
Grice, H. P., 287
Griffin, P., 414
Griffiths, M., 233
Groff, P., 354
Gross, H. S., 75
Gumperz, J. J., 126, 130, 132, 136, 140, 414, 417
Gutfreund, M. D., 229
Guttentag, R. E., 383

Haas. W., 370, 371–372
Haber, L. R., 360, 382
Haber, R. N., 382
Halle, M., 198, 352, 363n4, 371–372
Halliday, M. A. K., 258, 259, 272–273, 290, 293
Hamilton, M. E., 342, 361
Harmon, D., 418
Harper, K., 162
Hasan, R., 258, 259, 272–273, 290, 293
Hastorf, A. H., 91
Hatano, G., 56
Havelock, E. A., 53, 56–57, 67, 69, 126, 417–418
Hawkins, H. L., 379
Hayes, J. R., 288, 289, 310, 324, 327
Heath, S. B., 232, 251, 418
Hedden, M., 418
Hegel, G. W. F., 32, 148, 149, 151
Heider, E. R., 75
Heider, F., 80
Henderson, E. H. A., 344, 392
Henderson, L., 373, 383
Hidi, S., 285, 299
Higgins, E. T., 74, 75, 76, 77–78, 81, 82, 83, 84–85, 88, 93, 94
Hildyard, A., 74, 75, 87, 258, 285, 286–287, 293, 299, 313

Hill, C., 132
Hillinger, M. L., 377
Himmelfarb, S., 74
Hirsch, 23
Hogaboam, T., 380
Höhlig, M., 184
Holden, M. H., 357
Holmes, D. L., 198
Holquist, M., 55, 69
Horowitz, M. W., 84, 86, 286
Householder, F. W., 336, 370–371
Houston, S., 47
Humboldt, W. V., 148–149
Hundeide, K., 418
Hung, D., 374
Hunt, G. F., 181, 183
Hunter, C. St.-J., 418
Hu-pei Au, K., 419
Huttenlocher, J., 75
Hymes, D., 128, 413, 414, 418, 425

Inhelder, B., 224
Innis, H. A., 418–419
Ivanov, V. V., 62

Jacobs, M., 179, 181, 182, 183, 184, 188, 189, 190, 419, 420
Jacobson, R., 198
Jaeger, J. J., 352, 363n4
Jaffe, A. H., 185
Jakimik, J., 353, 358
Jarvis, P. E., 75, 77
Jellison, J. M., 80
Johnson, N. S., 168, 173, 290
Johnson, R. L., 75
Johnston, J. C., 380
Jonasson, J. T., 376, 377, 378, 379
Jones, B. F., 314
Jones, E. E., 80
Jordan, C., 419
Jose, P. E., 169
Jung, U. O. H., 359

Kalmár, I., 158, 164n2, 267
Kaltman, H., 130
Katz, L., 368–369, 374
Kay, P., 126, 128, 132
Kaye, K., 260
Keenan, J. J., 287
Kelley, H. H., 80, 91
Kellogg, R., 186
Kerek, A., 336, 343, 370, 371
Keyssar, H., 67, 70
Kiesler, C. A., 90
Kintsch, W., 176, 200, 287, 288, 289, 419

Kirshenblatt-Gimblett, B., 136
Kleinschmidt, S., 162, 164n2
Kligman, D. S., 354
Kolers, P. A., 406, 407
Kozminsky, E., 287
Kozol, J., 419
Krauss, R. M., 74, 75, 77
Kroeber, A., 151
Kroll, B. M., 131, 316, 419
Kücera, H., 378
Kuno, S., 159

La Berge, D., 338
Labov, W., 130, 134, 178, 229, 420
Lakoff, B., 120, 125, 287
Leich, G., 262
Lenneberg, E. H., 151
Leon, P. R., 399
Leventhal, H., 81
Levinson, S., 144
Lewis, L. L., 186
Lewkowicz, N. K., 344
Li, C. N., 159
Liberman, A. M., 335, 337, 352, 380,
    404, 407
Liberman, I. Y., 337, 344, 352, 380,
    404, 407
Lichtenstein, E. H., 167, 168, 169, 172,
    173, 174, 179, 190
Lindamood, C. H., 335
Lindamood, P. C., 335
Lloyd, G. E. R., 420
Locke, J., 285
Longacre, R., 153
Lord, A. B., 67
Lowry, M., 25
Lukatela, G., 368–369

McCann, C. D., 74, 75, 76, 79, 81, 82,
    83, 88, 93, 94
McClelland, J. L., 375, 380
McCusker, L. X., 377
McDermott, R., 258
MacGinitie, W. H., 357
McGuire, W. J., 74, 81
Macken, M. A., 348
McKoon, G., 287
McLeod, A., 313
McLuhan, M., 19, 27, 44, 52, 53, 54, 59,
    66, 389, 420
McNeill, D., 420
Malcolm, K., 260
Malécot, A., 390
Mandler, J. M., 64, 168, 173, 176, 290
Manis, M., 77, 78
Mann, V. A., 380

Mannheim, K., 25
Marcel, T., 394–395
Marsh, G., 354
Mark, L. S., 380
Martin, J. H., 23
Martin, N., 313
Mason, M., 380
Massaro, D. W., 373
Mattingly, I. G., 336, 352, 404, 407
Mayhew, D. C., 389
Mayzner, M. S., 380, 385n1
Mehan, H., 232
Mehrabian, A., 74, 77
Meillet, A., 158
Metz, C., 63, 70
Michaels, S., 136, 140–142
Miller, G. A., 70, 198, 200
Miller, R., 348
Mills, J., 80
Mitchell-Kernan, C., 287
Mitterer, J. O., 383
Monaco, J., 70
Moon, B. C., 247–248
Moore, J. C., 77, 78
Morais, J., 335, 344
Moscovici, S., 85, 86
Moskowitz, B. A., 352–353

National Assessment of Educational
    Progress, 308, 309, 316, 319
Neale, M. D., 248
Neisser, U., 89
Newman, J. B., 84, 86
Newman, J. F., 181
Newtson, D., 78, 80
Nezworski, t., 173
Nicely, P. E., 198
Nicholls, J. C., 118, 232
Ninio, A. Z., 232, 240
Niski, J. A., 392, 393, 394, 395, 396,
    400, 401
Njovana, C. A., 47
Nold, E. W., 289, 309, 316
Norman, D. A., 200
Nystrand, M., 128

Ochs, E., 127, 130, 131, 420, 421
O'Connor, M. C., 130
O'Faolain, S., 185, 186
O'Harrow, S., 421
Oka, I. G. N., 125
Oliver, C. F., 421
Olrik, A., 181, 182, 188, 189
Olson, D. R., 52, 54, 55, 57, 74, 75, 87,
    89, 124, 126, 132, 140, 200, 206, 250,
    258, 260, 268, 285–287, 360, 421–422

Olver, R., 53
Ong, W. J., 52, 126, 415, 416, 422
Onions, C. T., 370
Otto, W., 422
Ozello, Y., 400

Paris, G., 149
Paris, P., 313
Parkin, A. J., 377
Pattison, R., 422–423
Pawley, A., 106
Percy, W., 55
Perfetti, C. A., 313, 380
Perrine, L., 185, 186
Peterson, L., 379
Piaget, J., 217, 223, 224, 228n2
Pike, K. E., 314
Pitman, J., 370
Plato, 67, 148
Popp, H., 420
Popper, K., 36, 40, 44, 198, 203, 204
Portnoy, S. A., 84
Powell, F. A., 81
Pribram, K. H., 200
Propp, V., 290
Pudovkin, V. I., 61

Quirk, R., 262

Raban, E. B., 247
Rader, M., 128, 137
Ramanujan, A. K., 355
Rasmussen, K., 155, 162
Rattray, R. S., 189
Read, C., 344, 389, 391, 393, 394, 395–
    396, 401, 404, 408
Reddy, M. J., 423
Reddy, R., 353
Reder, S., 356
Reed, H., 74, 77
Reicher, G., 379
Renault, M., 67
Rholes, W. S., 77–78, 93, 94
Richards, I. A., 412
Robinson, F., 314
Rogers, M., 379
Rommetveit, R., 74
Rosen, H., 313
Rosenblatt, L. M., 201
Ross, J., 314
Rudnicky, A. I., 358
Ruesch, J., 74
Rumelhart, D. E., 173, 209, 375

Sachs, H., 138
Sachs, J., 285
Saenger, P., 23

St. John, J., 370
Sales, B. D., 360
Salomon, G., 52, 62, 70
Samuels, M. L., 370
Samuels, S. J., 338
Sapir, E., 150, 151, 401, 423
Satterly, D., 229
Saville-Troike, M., 139
Scardamalia, M., 285, 289, 309, 313,
    315, 316–320, 321, 322, 327
Schallert, D. L., 287
Schank, R. C., 167, 200, 313, 423
Schleicher, A., 148–149, 151
Schlicht, R., 392
Schmandt-Besserat, D., 52, 53
Schmidt, C. F., 167–168
Schneider, D. J., 91
Scholes, R., 186
Schöttelndreyer, B., 181, 183
Scollon, R., 125, 139, 232, 252, 423
Scollon, S. B. K., 232, 252, 423
Scott, V., 185
Scragg, D. G., 369, 370
Scribner, S., 52, 54, 56, 176, 423–424
Searle, J., 258, 268
Seidenberg, M. S., 358, 377
Seldes, G., 57
Shankweiler, D., 335, 337, 344, 352,
    380, 404, 407
Shannon, C. E., 198
Shatz, M., 87
Shimkin, D. B., 181, 182, 183
Shultz, J., 139, 415
Shuy, R. W., 424
Simon, H. A., 310
Skorik, P. J., 158
Skousen, R., 360
Smith, E. W., 179, 182
Smith, F., 197, 198, 199, 204, 210, 296–
    297, 337, 424
Smith, P. T., 371, 372
Snyman, J. W., 158
Spencer, M., 252
Spiro, R., 424
Spoehr, K. T., 379
Sprat, T., 285
Sridharan, N. S., 167–168
Stanovich, K. E., 377
Steffensen, M. S., 177
Stein, N. L., 173, 290
Steiner, G., 413, 424
Sternberg, M., 169, 185
Steward, J. H., 151
Sticht, T. G., 424
Stock, B., 424–425
Stone, L., 20

Strawson, C., 370, 376
Streby, W. J., 287
Strickler, R. D., 75
Stross, B., 181, 182
Stubbs, M., 425
Studdert-Kennedy, M., 335
Sutton-Smith, B., 202
Svartvic, J., 262
Syder, F., 106

Tanenhaus, M. K., 358, 377
Tannen, D., 124, 126, 127, 133, 138,
  178, 285, 286, 293, 425
Teberosky, A., 219, 223, 416
Tedlock, D., 179, 181, 184, 188, 425–
  426
Temple, C. A., 392, 397
Templeton, S., 352–353
Thompson, S. A., 159, 179, 181, 182,
  183
Thomson, D. M., 203
Thorndyke, P. W., 173
Thorp, R. G., 419
Thurman, R., 153
Toba, S., 181, 183–184
Toelken, B., 181, 184, 189
Torrance, N. G., 260, 285, 360
Tresselt, M. E., 380, 385n1
Tulving, E., 203
Tulviste, P., 426
Turvey, M. T., 368–369
Tzeng, O. J. L., 374, 392

Uspensky, B., 426

Vachek, J., 285, 368–369, 371–372
Valtin, R., 359
van Dijk, T. A., 168
Vann, R. J., 419

van Rijnsoever, R., 392, 393–395, 400
Vansina, J., 22
Varenne, H., 132
Vellutino, F. R., 426
Vendler, Z., 268
Venezky, R. L., 371–372, 373
Verna, G. B., 354
Vygotsky, L. S., 84, 86, 236, 307, 426

Walstea, E., 80
Warren, R. P., 185, 186
Wason, D., 415
Waters, G. S., 377
Watt, I., 126, 285, 417
Watters, D., 181
Weaver, W., 198
Weijnen, A., 393
Weisner, T. S., 419
Wells, C. G., 229, 230, 232, 233, 234,
  245, 247, 248, 254n1, 256, 262, 285
White, F., 314
White, S., 422
Whitehead, A. N., 38–39
Whiteman, M. F., 426
Whorf, B. L., 426
Wicklund, R. A., 90
Widdowson, H. G., 287, 290, 309
Wijk, A., 373
Wilce, L. S., 339, 343, 357, 359
Wood, W., 80
Woodbury, A. C., 160, 162
Wright, J. W., 75, 77

Yates, F., 20–21
Young, R. E., 314

Zajonc, R. B., 81
Zelan, K., 413
Zimmerman, C., 78